DCU LIBRARY

020046758

RL.

Clare

SCHOOLS AND SOCIETY IN IRELAND

SHORT LOAN	**3 HOUR LOAN**	DCU LIBRARY

Fines are charged **PER HOUR** if this item is overdue.
Check at www.dcu.ie/~library or telephone (01) 700 5183 for fine rates and renewal regulations for this item type.
Item is subject to recall.
Remember to use the Book Bin when the library is closed.
The item is due for return on or before the latest date shown below.

1 4 MAY 2012

@18£4b.

D1380799

Schools and Society in Ireland

SHEELAGH DRUDY *and* KATHLEEN LYNCH

Gill & Macmillan

Published in Ireland by
Gill & Macmillan Ltd
Goldenbridge
Dublin 8
with associated companies throughout the world

© Sheelagh Drudy and Kathleen Lynch 1993
0 7171 2049 X
Index compiled by Helen Litton
Print origination by Seton Music Graphics Ltd, Bantry, Co. Cork
Printed by ColourBooks Ltd, Dublin

All rights reserved. No part of this publication may be copied, reproduced or transmitted in
any form or by any means, without permission of the publishers.

A catalogue record for this book is available from the British Library.

370.1909417 DRU

020046758

We would like to dedicate this book to our children,
Aisling, Conor, Aoife, David, Nora, and John, with love.

Contents

Preface   ix

Acknowledgments   xiii

I: The Structure and Ideology of Formal Education   1

1. Schooling in the Republic of Ireland: an Overview   3
2. Education and Society: Sociological Interpretations   26
3. Paradigms and Perspectives in Irish Education   48

II: Control of Education   71

4. The Churches and the State   73
5. The Teachers   90
6. The Dynamics of Control and Resistance   113

III: The Reproduction of Inequality   135

7. Social Class and Education   137
8. Gender Differentials and Education   167
9. The Co-Education Debate   189

IV: Curriculum Issues and the Organisation of Learning   207

10. Education and the Economy   209
11. Intelligence, the Curriculum, and Education   228
12. Ability Grouping in Schools: Patterns and Implications   244

V: A Second Chance?   259

13. Adult Education: a Second Chance?   261

Index   276

Preface

If the mythical Martian were to arrive in the Republic of Ireland to investigate the dominant activity of its citizens, she or he might be forgiven for assuming that its principal industry is education. Figures show that nearly one-third of the population, or 968,457 people, are engaged in full-time education (Department of Education, 1992b, 3). In addition to these, a considerable body of workers provides a service to these students as teachers and lecturers and in the administration of the education system. When one takes into consideration that for each of these students there are also parents and other family members supporting or monitoring their progress through the system, one can reasonably conclude that education is a central institution in Irish society. But it is not just because of the large numbers of people involved in it that education occupies such a crucial social position. Education has a number of important and complex roles in Irish society. In this book we examine these roles in detail.

We are writing this book because we feel it needs to be written. Education is central to all of us living in Ireland, yet the wealth of insight and research into education provided by Irish sociologists has never been drawn together into one volume. This book is for anyone who is interested in education, be they teachers, parents, students, administrators, or simply people who wish to examine education analytically.

Irish education is currently facing into a period of enormous change. This will happen not only because of the OECD report on Irish education (1991) or the Green Paper (Department of Education, 1992a) but also because of the responses of the various interest groups to the debate. Indeed, educational change occurs, irrespective of policy, as the result of complex social processes examined later in this volume. These changes will affect every part of the education system, from junior infants to postgraduate and adult education.

Change can be threatening and upsetting; it can also be challenging and invigorating. However, if change is to represent personal and collective growth rather than retrenchment, action must be taken by teachers and schools working in collaboration with other groups and agencies. It has been argued that what is needed for educational change to be meaningful is the development of 'collaborative cultures' in our schools (Fullan and Hargreaves, 1992). By this is meant patterns of beliefs, expectations and actions in schools that involve teachers working together as a team, but also relating to other schools and agencies within the school environment (ibid., 51–83).

Fullan (1992) suggests that the most productive collaborative school cultures are those that critically assess state-level policies and use the policies as catalysts for making improvements. He also suggests that understanding the orientations and working conditions of the main actors in schools and school systems is a prerequisite for planning and coping with educational change effectively (Fullan, 1991, 113). We would argue that the sociology of education in Ireland and internationally can provide important conceptual tools of critique for teachers and others interested in education to assess policy, to identify the pitfalls and constraints to action, and to creatively plan and manage change in their schools.

There is now a substantial amount of evidence on the education system resulting from sociological research. This research has examined Irish education both north and south of the border (Drudy, 1991). However, because the two systems are so different in important respects, not least their administrative structures, we confine our discussions mainly to the system in the Republic. Thus, with our apologies to our northern colleagues and friends, when we refer to 'Irish education' we are referring, for the most part, to education in the Republic.

The purpose of this book is to present a sociological perspective on a range of central issues in contemporary Irish education. We provide data on the school system and also outline key concepts of social analysis. We draw together the main findings of sociological research on these issues and attempt to analyse and explain the structure and role of education in Irish society. We deal with the educational policy changes, controversies and reforms of the past twenty-five years. We analyse the attitudes and vested interests that lie behind policy initiatives and changes. We locate Irish sociological debates, as far as possible, within the context of international debates on education.

The book is divided into five parts. In part I, 'The Structure and Ideology of Formal Education', we outline the structure of the Irish education system and document its principal ideological features. Chapter 1 focuses on the structure of schooling in Ireland and on its system of management, as well as participation rates and school and class size. Chapter 2 gives an outline of the role of education in society and of the main concepts and principal theoretical approaches to education in sociology. In chapter 3 we examine the perspectives that have been brought to bear on education by contemporary Irish educationalists, as well as the ideological orientations evident in official publications on education.

Part II focuses on the control of education. In chapter 4 we explore the role of the churches in the formation and development of Irish education, and we examine the relationship between church and state in education. We look at the main body in the provision of education—the teaching profession—in chapter 5, and analyse the social characteristics, background and roles of its members, and the role of teachers in educational change. Chapter 6 presents an analysis of the dynamics of control and resistance, and examines the parts played by the main interest groups—state and local administrators, the churches, teachers, and parents—in relation to change.

Part III, 'The Reproduction of Inequality', is devoted to the issue of inequality and its reproduction through the education system. In chapter 7 we examine the concept of social class and explore its relationship to educational success and failure, and present data on Irish patterns. The relationship between gender and education is explored in chapter 8, and is analysed within the context of wider social relationships. The nature of the current debate on co-education is explored in chapter 9, and the results of Irish research are compared with international findings.

Part IV, 'Curriculum Issues and the Organisation of Learning', explores a range of issues relating to the curriculum and school organisation. In chapter 10, questions are raised concerning the appropriateness of the technicalisation of the second-level curriculum and the argument that education should be more closely related to the needs of the economy. Chapter 11 discusses the concept of 'intelligence' and the way in which it is defined and measured, and suggests that a much wider concept of intelligence is necessary. This has implications for assessment. The composition and effects of different forms of ability grouping in schools are explored in chapter 12.

Finally, in part V, 'A Second Chance?', we explore some of the aspects of 'second chance' education. In particular we look at the possibilities offered by adult education for those whose education has been adversely affected by their social class background, their sex, or other disadvantages.

References and Further Reading

Department of Education (1992a), *Education for a Changing World: Green Paper on Education*, Dublin: Stationery Office 1992.

Department of Education (1992b), *Statistical Report, 1990/91*, Dublin: Stationery Office.

Drudy, S. (1991), 'Developments in the sociology of education in Ireland, 1966–1991', *Irish Journal of Sociology*, vol. 1, 107–27.

Fullan, M. (1991), *The New Meaning of Educational Change*, London: Cassell.

Fullan, M. (1992), 'We do not have the choice of avoiding change just because it is messy', *Times Educational Supplement*, 9 October.

Fullan, M., and Hargreaves, A. (1992), *What's Worth Fighting For In Your School?*, Buckingham: Open University Press.

Organisation for Economic Co-operation and Development (1991), *Reviews of National Policies for Education—Ireland*, Paris: OECD.

Acknowledgments

Although our names appear on the cover of this book, we are only part of the team that produced it. There are many people to whom we owe thanks and without whose help it would never have been published.

Our first word of thanks must go to our colleagues in the Sociological Association of Ireland and in the Educational Studies Association of Ireland who encouraged us to persist with the project and convinced us of its importance when spirits were low. Many thanks too to our colleagues in the Departments of Education in Maynooth and UCD for their great help and support.

There were numerous people who helped by making us aware of sources, or by making their own materials available to us. We want to begin by expressing our thanks to staff in the Department of Education. We obtained consistent and generous help from a number of sections, particularly the Statistics Section. The courtesy and professionalism of people in the Statistics Section made our task much easier, and we are deeply grateful to them. Indeed, there is probably nobody involved in education to whom we do not owe some gratitude. Our special thanks to members of the Secretariat of the Higher Education Authority, the Secretariat of Secondary Schools, the Education Commission of the Conference of Major Religious Superiors, Frank Murray of the Association of Community and Comprehensive Schools, Joe Rooney of the Irish Vocational Education Association, Gráinne O'Flynn and Mairín Ganly of the Teachers' Union of Ireland, Leonie Warren and Moira Leydon of the Association of Secondary Teachers, Ireland, Anne McElduff and John Carr of the Irish National Teachers' Organisation, and to staff of the National Council for Curriculum and Assessment and of Aontas for their help and support.

We are also grateful to the four anonymous reviewers for their encouragement and helpful comments, and to Hubert Mahony of Gill & Macmillan for his advice, courtesy, and considerable patience! The actual physical production of a book like this is a major task. We want to express our thanks to all those involved and in particular to those who helped us type the completed manuscript: Aisling Drudy, Anne Coogan, and Niamh Flanagan. Many thanks too to Jo Redmond of the Equality Studies Centre, UCD, who was always helpful and kind. Special thanks to Noël Barber, Anne Lodge, Sheila Briody, and Deirdre Haslett.

We would also like to express our appreciation to our families and many friends for their constant encouragement and support. They were always there in the background, with love and help. Finally we want to thank our two greatest supporters, P. J. Drudy and John Lynch, for their constructive critical comments on the text; they gave us the space, the time and the encouragement to write.

I

The Structure and Ideology of Formal Education

Schooling in the Republic of Ireland: an Overview

In this chapter we look at the structure of the Irish education system and its principal characteristics. We give an outline of the different types of school and the patterns of ownership and management at the various levels. We examine participation rates at the different levels of the system, and some of their implications. We also look at issues such as school and class size.

PARTICIPATION IN SCHOOLING

One of the more striking features of Irish education in the 1990s is its very high participation rates. The high value placed on education and educational credentials that characterises Irish society can only be fully understood within the context of Ireland's position as a postcolonial state.

In common with postcolonial states in other parts of the world, Ireland has never developed a large, indigenous industrial base, and indeed Irish indigenous industry has continued to perform badly from the foundation of the state until the present day (Drudy, 1991). There are also serious questions surrounding the impact of foreign industry in Ireland. Foreign industry has not performed well in terms of local industrial linkages (i.e. the spin-off effects on local industry). Also, although foreign industry is characterised by advanced technological processes of production, it is backward in that a high proportion of its workers are employed at a semi-skilled level. In any case, the poor performance both of indigenous and foreign industry has resulted in fewer people being employed in manufacturing in 1989 than in 1973 (Drudy, 1991). Consequently, educational qualifications are a far more important determinant of status and power than is the case in core capitalist states with considerable indigenous industrial wealth. In the absence of industrial opportunities, educational credentials have become the major determinants of wealth, status, and power (Lynch, 1989).

Schooling is compulsory in Ireland from ages 6 to 15. In the 6–15 age cohort, participation is virtually universal. State provision for pre-school education is extremely limited and is provided only to children with special educational needs, such as the children of the travelling community. However, participation of four-year-olds in primary school is relatively high at 55 per cent (Department of Education, 1992a, 3). The Department of Education defines the first two years of primary schooling as the kindergarten stage (ibid., 9), although neither parents nor teachers would tend to define it this way.

A total of 72.6 per cent of the 4–24 age cohort is in full-time education (ibid., 3). Although the minimum school leaving age at fifteen is low by international standards, participation rates in the postcompulsory phase, i.e. the senior cycle of second-level schools, is comparatively high. Some 73 per cent of those who enter second-level education complete the senior cycle (Department of Education, 1992b, 37). The high participation rate from age four to eighteen is reflected in the high proportion of school leavers who leave school having sat for their Leaving Certificate. In 1990 the proportion was 77.5 per cent (Department of Labour, 1991).

An examination of school leaver surveys conducted by the Department of Labour from the late 1970s onwards reveals the rise in participation at senior cycle that took place during the 1980s. Over the decade 1979–89 the proportion of school leavers who had sat for the Leaving Certificate rose from 61.0 per cent (Breen and Whelan, 1986) to 70.1 per cent (Department of Labour, 1989). This proportion jumped sharply at the end of the 1980s and into the beginning of the 1990s, as we can see from the most recent figure of 77.5 per cent (Department of Labour, 1991). The actual numbers taking the Leaving Certificate increased from 38,800 in 1979 (Breen and Whelan, 1986) to 60,074 in 1990 and 59,507 in 1992 (statistics from the Department of Education). 1992 was the first year in which the results of just one sitting of the Leaving Certificate were reckonable for entry to third-level colleges, and this may account in large measure for the drop in Leaving Certificate candidates in that year. Overall, though, the substantial increases at senior cycle reflect both increasing demand for certification and the deepening economic crisis in Ireland and in the traditional destinations for Irish emigrants, particularly Britain. Indeed, the results of the annual school leaver survey show that in 1991 there was a drop in emigration for school leavers for the first time in eight years (Department of Labour, 1991, 4).

The pattern of increasing participation at the senior cycle of second-level schooling has resulted in increasing demands and expectations of the school system. It has also meant that the principal curricular option at senior cycle— the Leaving Certificate—has been evaluated as unsuitable for a substantial proportion of senior-cycle pupils, about one in four in the case of voluntary private secondary schools (Curriculum Awareness Action Group, 1991). These observations arise from the experiences of educators (Coolahan, 1990) and from findings on the performance levels of candidates taking the Leaving Certificate (Curriculum Awareness Action Group, 1990; Martin and Hickey, 1992).

Study of the Leaving Certificate results shows that almost a quarter of first-time school candidates who sat for the Leaving Certificate took all their subjects at ordinary (i.e. 'pass') level (Martin and Hickey, 1992). This group are among those who are least satisfied with the education they received when they give their views after some years of labour market experience (Hannan and Shorthall, 1991). At ordinary level, 20 per cent or more were awarded a grade of E or lower in thirteen out of the thirty-two subjects. Among all school candidates, 14 per cent achieved fewer than five D grades at either level in the examination (Martin and Hickey, 1992, 33–4), i.e. were deemed to have achieved a pass at that level. Concern about the programmes offered at senior cycle has led to calls for the expansion of alternatives to the academically oriented Leaving Certificate (McNamara and Williams, 1990) and for restructuring of the senior cycle (Department of Education, 1992b, 97–109). (We discuss issues related to the curriculum at senior cycle in greater detail in chapter 10.)

At the junior cycle of second-level education, and at primary level, participation in full-time education is virtually universal. In the 5–14 age group (which includes primary level and some junior-cycle second level) the participation rate is 99.9 per cent. However, it is worth noting that after the minimum school leaving age there is a drop-out from the junior cycle. This is evident from the participation of sixteen-year-olds, many of whom would be at junior cycle, whose rates fall to 92.5 per cent (Department of Education, 1992a, 3).

The labour market position of these young people is particularly problematic. Pupils who drop out of the junior cycle are among those who leave school with no qualifications. Leavers who have taken no examination currently form 5.4 per cent of all leavers (Department of Labour, 1991, 5). When combined with those who have failed junior cycle examinations, the figure is between 10 and 12 per cent of the total school-leaving cohort (Hannan and Shorthall, 1991, 4). This figure is not high by European levels (ibid.), but leaves no room for complacency. Unqualified school leavers are far more likely than any other group to be unemployed or still seeking their first job a year after leaving school, with 53.4 per cent of them in this position, compared with 31.2 per cent of those who had reached the level of the Group or Intermediate Certificate and 11.8 per cent of those who had reached Leaving Certificate level (Department of Labour, 1991, table 2; see also Sexton, Whelan, and Williams, 1988; Breen, 1984).

Early labour market experience is crucial for this very disadvantaged group. Results from a study of young people in the labour market show that labour market differentials based on educational qualifications increased over a five-year period after leaving school (Breen, 1991). This suggests that employers use two criteria when deciding whether or not to hire a young person. The higher the level of educational qualifications the more likely someone is to be hired; the better his or her labour market record, the more likely he or she is to get a job. The longer a job seeker has been unemployed, the smaller the chances of employment (ibid.).

The unqualified school leaver is also, not too surprisingly, the least satisfied with the experience of schooling. Hannan and Shorthall suggest that unqualified leavers were dissatisfied with all the dimensions of their education, even their basic education. These leavers were actually the group most likely to recognise the importance of educational or training qualifications. However, such was the level of their alienation and hurt that this did not lead to any intention to go back to school, even if the opportunity existed (Hannan and Shorthall, 1991). (There is further discussion of the labour market position of school leavers in chapters 6 and 10.)

PATTERNS OF OWNERSHIP AND MANAGEMENT IN THE SCHOOL SYSTEM

Let us now turn to the issue of the control of the education system. Perhaps one of the most remarkable features of Irish education is its unique pattern of ownership and management. The dominant pattern is one of church ownership and management but with the state responsible for the bulk of both capital and current costs and with the state also having central control of curriculum and assessment. This apparently contradictory situation of private ownership and control combined with substantial public funding arises primarily for historical reasons (Coolahan, 1981).

Church ownership and control is found at both primary and second level. At primary level, church ownership is practically universal. (Chapter 4 discusses church control of primary education in some detail.) At second level the situation is more complex. There are four distinct school types to be found in the second-level sector. These are (1) secondary schools, (2) vocational schools and community colleges, (3) comprehensive schools, and (4) community schools. Secondary schools are in the 'voluntary' sector and are privately owned and managed; ownership is mainly in the hands of the churches and religious orders. The remaining four types are in the 'public' sector, but each has a somewhat different management structure. In figure 1.1 (page 8–10) we summarise the pattern of ownership, management and funding at second level. We will now examine each sector in detail.

Secondary schools form by far the greatest proportion of postprimary schools. In 1990/91 there were 792 second-level schools in the system aided by the Department of Education[1]; some 60 per cent (476) of these were secondary schools (Department of Education, 1992a). These schools were originally established, many in the nineteenth and early twentieth century, by the voluntary efforts of the bodies concerned (Coolahan, 1981). As with all second-level schools, secondary schools must have full recognition from the Department of Education. They have a strong 'academic' tradition (i.e. a concentration on academic subjects). Pupils are prepared for major public examinations—the Junior Certificate at junior cycle and the Leaving Certificate at senior cycle. Other programmes are also offered at senior cycle, for example vocational preparation and training (VPT) and transition year. There is a higher transfer rate to third-level education, especially university, among secondary school pupils than among pupils in other school types (Clancy, 1988), though this is related to the slightly higher socio-economic status of their intake compared with other schools. (See chapter 7 for further discussion of this issue.)

Most of these schools are owned and managed by religious bodies affiliated to the Catholic Church. Of the 476 secondary schools, 253 are owned by female religious orders and 136 by male religious orders, with 7 amalgamated schools run by more than one religious order. A further 28 are owned by the diocesan authorities. Protestant denominations own 22 secondary schools. There is one Jewish secondary school, a German school, and 28 schools owned by lay Catholics (Secretariat of Secondary Schools, 1992).

Until recently a minority of these schools had boards of management, the running of the schools being entirely in the hands of the religious bodies concerned, although discussions between managements and the Association of Secondary Teachers, Ireland, concerning the establishment of boards of management had been going on since the early 1970s (O'Flaherty, 1992, 93–111; see chapter 4 for further discussion). Since 1985 there has been a movement towards management structures more akin to those in community schools, including representation from trustees, teaching staff, and parents. (See chapter 4.) In 1991/92 some 238 secondary schools had such boards of management (Secretariat of Secondary Schools, 1992). In the case of the teaching staff of these schools, the school trustees (for the most part the bishop or the religious order) are the employers and pay the teachers' 'basic salaries' (£400 per annum). 'Incremental' salary (the remainder) is paid by the Department of Education. This reflects the importance attached by the managers of secondary schools to the power to hire and fire staff (O'Flaherty, 1992, 116). The fact that secondary teachers' 'basic' salaries are paid by trustees is symbolic of this power.

Although all these schools are privately owned, all receive state funds. Since 1986 non-fee-paying ('free scheme') secondary schools receive 90 per cent of approved capital expenditure from the state (it was 80 per cent at the beginning of the 1980s and rose first to 85 per cent and then to the current figure). These schools are thus expected to raise the remaining 10 per cent themselves. In the case of a new school they must also provide a fully serviced site. Fee-paying schools have not, in general, an entitlement to grants for capital expenditure. However, the Minister for Education has discretion to make funds available in certain circumstances (information from Department of Education).

Figure 1.1

Ownership and control of second-level schools

Type	Secondary schools	Vocational schools, community colleges
Number of schools (1990/91)	476	248
Percentage of total	60.1%	31.3%
Ownership	Denominational—churches and religious orders (447), lay Catholics (28), other (1)	Non-denominational—VECs
Management	Trustees/owners (238) Boards of management, most having representatives of trustees, parents, and teachers (238)	Majority have boards of management, which are subcommittees of VEC. Some managed by school principal, directly answerable to chief executive officer of VEC
Teachers employed by	School trustees/owners	VEC
Teachers' salaries paid by	'Basic' salary (£400) by trustees/owners, 'incremental' salary (remainder) by Dept of Education	VEC (but funded by Dept of Education); small proportion (less than 5 %) from local sources
Percentage of approved capital expenditure paid by Dept of Education	Trustees/owners provide site. Non-fee-paying: 90 % of initial and subsequent costs. Fee-paying; in general no entitlement, but minister has discretion to make funds available	100 % of initial and subsequent costs paid by department, channelled through VEC
Basis on which recurrent costs are paid	Non-fee-paying: capitation grant based on number of pupils (1990–93: £150 per pupil). Fee-paying: not eligible for grant	Each VEC receives budget for pay & non-pay expenses, based on programmes & circumstances. Small proportion of VEC funding comes from local sources

Figure 1.1 (cont.): Ownership and control of second-level schools

Type	Comprehensive schools	Community schools
Number of schools (1990/91)	16	52
Percentage of total	2.0%	6.6%
Ownership	Denominational—named trustees, nominated & approved by Minister	Denominational (in that Catholic religious orders are among trustees)—named trustees nominated & approved by minister
Management	Boards of management: Catholic (10): 1 bishop's nominee, 1 minister's nominee (invariably an inspector), 1 VEC nominee (chief exec. officer or representative); Protestant (5) & 1 Catholic: 3 bishop's nominees, 1 minister's nominee, 1 VEC nominee (CEO)	Boards of management. General model: 3 nominated by religious orders, 3 nominated by VEC, 2 elected parents' representatives, 2 elected teachers' representatives, school principal as non-voting member
Teachers employed by	Board of management	Board of management
Teachers' salaries paid by	Dept of Education	Dept of Education
Percentage of approved capital expenditure paid by Dept of Education	100 % of initial & subsequent costs paid by Dept of Education	Local contribution towards initial costs (usually 5 %) paid by trustees; 100 % of subsequent costs paid by Dept of Education
Basis on which recurrent costs are paid	Each school receives budget to cover pay & non-pay expenses (excluding teachers' salaries) based on size & age of school & number of pupils	

Figure 1.1 (cont.): Ownership and control of second-level schools

	Green Paper proposals*
Type	All schools to be 'secondary schools'
Ownership	No changes in ownership proposed
Management	Board of management: 5 nominated by owners/trustees, 2 elected parents' representatives, 2 elected teachers' representatives, 1 co-opted from local business community, school principal as voting member
Teachers employed by:	Board of management
Teachers' salaries paid by:	Dept of Education (not specific on whether basic/incremental distinction will continue in voluntary schools)
Percentage of approved capital expenditure paid by Dept of Education	Not specific on capital costs.
Basis on which recurrent costs are paid	New funding mechanism based on cost per pupil. Additional budget allocation for schools serving disadvantaged areas, special needs, & non-mainstream programmes. Conditions for funding: admissions policy that does not discriminate on grounds of means, educational level, or social background; provision by school of comprehensive education for all abilities; provision by school for community education.

*Department of Education (1992b), 144–55

Non-fee-paying ('free scheme') schools receive a capitation grant of £150 per pupil for recurrent costs; this is to cover teachers' 'basic salaries', secretarial, part-time teaching and maintenance staff, and general maintenance costs. Most of these schools find it necessary, however, to ask for a voluntary contribution from parents to meet the running costs of the schools. The capitation grant has been discontinued for fee-paying schools since 1985 (details from the Department of Education). Teachers' incremental salaries are paid by the state in all 'free scheme' secondary schools. In fee-paying schools (58 in number, 36 Catholic and 22 other, mostly Protestant) the incremental salaries of teachers within the 'quota' for the school size are paid by the state.

Although Protestant secondary schools do not differ in their management structure, there are some differences in the administration of funding arrangements. While there is no difference in capital funding, from the beginning of the 'free scheme' in 1967 the capitation grant was not considered appropriate in the 'special circumstances' of Protestant schools. The Secondary Education Committee, representing the four main Protestant churches, receives a block grant in lieu of capitation grants, to administer as it sees fit (Ó Buachalla, 1988, 161). In addition, Protestant schools are permitted to charge fees without prejudice to state funding.

As we illustrate in chapter 5, there has been a consistent decline in the proportion of clerical and religious teachers in Catholic secondary schools. Since the 1970s, in response to this and other circumstances, the religious managers have devised strategies to perpetuate their role in secondary education (O'Flaherty, 1992, 93). These have included the devolution of management in their schools. The result has been that the denominational character of secondary schools has been guaranteed, even though many of them will be, in effect, lay schools in the future (ibid.).

Ownership and management of *vocational schools and community colleges* are vested in local education authorities, the vocational education committees. These were established under the Vocational Education Act, 1930, to provide vocational and technical education, and their schools have a strong practical tradition. There are 38 of these authorities, organised mainly on a county basis, though a number of urban areas have their own VECs. Members of these committees are nominated by the local authority and are re-nominated after each local election. They are not, however, answerable to the local authority but to the Minister for Education. Each VEC consists of 14 people: between 5 and 8 from political parties, and the remainder from representatives of industry, trade unions, and people with experience in education. These schools are non-denominational under the Act. In 1990/91 there were 248 postprimary schools under VEC control, 31.3 per cent of the total (Department of Education, 1992a). Of these, approximately 218 were vocational schools and 30 community colleges (figures from the Irish Vocational Education Association).

In the past, most vocational schools did not have boards of management; the school principal was directly answerable to the VEC and its chief executive officer. VECs functioned in some ways like boards in administering the schools in their areas (O'Flaherty, 1992, 28). Since 1974, however, the majority have boards of management (Coolahan, 1981). The composition varies somewhat according to the size and needs of the school. The norm is for each to have a VEC representative, two parents, and at least one staff representative (details from the IVEA). A few also have a pupil representative. Teaching staff, however, are employed by the relevant VEC rather than by the board of management.

The curriculum of vocational schools typically has a strong practical and technological bias, although academic subjects are also offered. Pupils are entered for the major public examinations—the Junior Certificate and the Leaving Certificate. However, other programmes are also offered at both junior and senior cycle. The vocational sector is more likely than others to offer VPT courses. Some 19 per cent (16,383) of vocational pupils are on 'vocational training and other' courses, compared with 1.3 per cent (2,751) of secondary and 6 per cent (1,197) of community and comprehensive school pupils (Department of Education, 1992a, 36). Also included in the VEC figures are pupils on courses developed by bodies other than the National Council for Curriculum and Assessment (for example the Curriculum Development Units at Shannon Comprehensive School and the City of Dublin VEC). Relatively fewer vocational school pupils are on the Leaving Certificate programme—26 per cent (22,487) of their total, compared with 36.4 per cent (77,452) of senior-cycle secondary school pupils and 33.3 per cent (14,307) of senior-cycle pupils in community and comprehensive schools in 1990/91 (ibid.).

The transfer rate to third-level education is lower from the vocational sector than from other schools (Clancy, 1988). In addition, those going on to third-level education are more likely than other groups to transfer to regional technical colleges (RTCs) or to the Dublin Institute of Technology (DIT), colleges that have been until recently also under the control of the VECs (Clancy, 1988). As noted earlier, however, vocational schools tend to have a higher proportion of pupils from lower socio-economic groups than all other types of school (Breen, 1986). The lower rates of retention at senior cycle and the lower transfer rates to universities and other third-level colleges must be interpreted in the light of this.

Community colleges are also under the control of the VECs. The community college is modelled on the community school, described below. They evolved as the VEC response to the development of community schools, and were established under section 21 of the Vocational Education Act, 1930 (O'Flaherty, 1992, 76). They have a wider curriculum than either secondary or vocational schools, with a range of academic and practical subjects. They aim to have a comprehensive intake of pupils of varying levels of ability. The structure of the boards of management of community colleges is broadly similar to those of community schools, but they are, in effect, subcommittees of the VEC (ibid., 75). However, there are variations in representation to suit local needs and circumstances. In the case of community colleges that have arisen as the result of mergers between secondary and VEC schools, there is representation on the board of management from the religious order. In such schools the boards of management—using the 'partnership model'—are identical in structure to those of the community school, although they are under the control of the VEC (details from the IVEA).

At present there are approximately 30 community colleges, some 22 having arisen as the result of mergers between existing secondary and vocational schools (figures from the IVEA). It is difficult to be more specific concerning the numbers of community colleges as here defined. This is because, as all schools in this sector are under the management of VECs, some schools that might more accurately be called vocational schools from the curricular and organisational point of view have simply adopted the title 'community college'. Other schools that do correspond to the community college model have titles such as 'St —'s Postprimary School'. However, teachers in community colleges, like those in vocational schools, are employees of the VEC.

Funding in vocational schools and colleges (for teachers' salaries and capital and recurrent costs) is provided mainly by the Department of Education. A small proportion (less than 5 per cent) comes from local sources, mainly rates (information from the Department of Education and the IVEA). All funds, however, are channelled through the VECs.

The third school type to be found at postprimary level is that of the *comprehensive schools*. These are very similar in organisational and curricular matters to community schools and colleges. There are just 16 comprehensive schools. The building of these began in the 1960s as a result of Department of Education initiatives. They were introduced as co-educational schools open to all classes and levels of ability, offering a wide curriculum to match the aptitudes of their pupils (Coolahan, 1981). These are denominational schools: at present 11 of the 16 are under Catholic management and 5 under Protestant management (details from the Association for Comprehensive and Community Schools). The standard model of management for comprehensive schools under Catholic management is a board of management composed of one religious (i.e. the bishop's) representative, one VEC representative, and one representative of the Minister for Education (in all cases a school inspector).

The management arrangements for the Protestant schools differ in the greater number of denominational representatives (three) appointed, which allows greater denominational control. One of the Catholic schools also has this model. None of these schools have representation from parents or teaching staff. Teaching staff in the comprehensive school, as in the community school, are employees of the board of management of the school.

The community school concept was a development of the comprehensive school, with its emphasis on reciprocal relations between the school and the surrounding community. Since 1970, therefore, no further comprehensive schools have been built, with the exception of one Protestant comprehensive opened in 1987. The management structure of the comprehensive school has proved to be a more acceptable model to the Protestant community than the community school one, as it allows greater control over the running of the school.

The fourth category of school in the second-level system is the *community school*. There were 52 community schools in the 1990/91 school year, an increase of five over the previous year. The first of these was opened in 1972. In common with the comprehensive schools, community schools are part of the Department's attempt to create a unified rather than a bipartite postprimary system (Coolahan, 1981).

The community school is, on average, larger than secondary or vocational schools: 70.6 per cent of community schools have over 500 pupils, compared with 40.1 per cent of secondary and 22.2 per cent of vocational schools (Department of Education, 1992a, 38). These schools are comprehensive in philosophy, offer a range of academic and practical subjects, and prepare pupils for the major public examinations as well as other work experience and certificate programmes. Community schools also provide adult education and make their facilities available to community groups.

After a great deal of controversy in the 1970s, deeds of trust were finally agreed between the interested parties, and provide the model for the management structures of these schools. There are three different types of deed of trust. There is one for community schools resulting from amalgamations, one for completely new community schools, and one that is unique to a community school in the Dublin area (information from the Association for Comprehensive and Community Schools; see also O'Flaherty, 1992). The standard board of management model consists of three representatives of the religious trustees, three VEC representatives, two elected parent representatives, and two teaching staff representatives. All boards of management have the principal as a nonvoting member. In addition, in the community school model there is provision for the religious order to nominate members to the teaching staff, provided that the nominee is duly qualified.

Although they are in the 'public sector' of education, therefore, these schools allow for substantial church influence, and are in effect partly denominational, as a result of the involvement of Catholic religious orders in their management. All community schools currently have representatives of one or more religious orders, as well as VEC representatives, as named trustees, nominated and appointed by the Minister for Education. They also have representatives of the religious orders on their management boards. There is evidence that a good number of religious see their future in the community school, believing that they can best preserve and transmit their ethos through their participation in the management of such schools (Barber, 1989). The development and growth of the community school has thus enabled the Catholic Church to greatly extend its influence in the public sector of postprimary education, particularly through its influence on the selection of teachers for the community schools and for those community colleges in which it has agreed to participate (O'Flaherty, 1992, 119; see also chapter 4 for further discussion).

Teaching staff in community schools are recommended for appointment to the Minister for Education by a selection board appointed by the board of management, which must include a departmental inspector. Staff are, in effect, employed by the board of management, unlike secondary school teachers, who are employees of the voluntary bodies concerned, and vocational teachers, who are employees of VECs.

Funding for both comprehensive and community schools is almost entirely from central sources. In both school types, teachers' salaries are paid in full by the Department of Education. In comprehensive schools all initial and subsequent approved capital costs are paid by the department. In community schools there is a small local contribution to initial costs, usually 5 per cent (information from the Department of Education). All subsequent approved capital costs are paid by the Department. Both comprehensive and community schools receive a budget for recurrent costs to cover pay (excluding teachers' salaries) and non-pay expenses. This budget is based on the size and age of the school and the number of pupils (information from the Association for Comprehensive and Community Schools).

There are, as we have seen, a variety of administrative and ownership structures in second-level education (summarised in figure 1.1). These diverse arrangements have arisen as the result of historical factors in the growth of the system. However, in the future there are likely to be changes in the administrative structures at second level. The proposals in the Green Paper (Department of Education, 1992b) envisage changes in the management of schools, though not in the patterns of ownership.

It is suggested that in the future all second-level schools will be classified as 'secondary' schools, in line with international practice. They are to have a common form of management, representative of concerned interests. Boards of management at second level are to consist of five members nominated by the trustees or owners, two elected by parents, two elected by teachers, one to be co-opted from the local business community, and the principal as a voting member. The chairperson is to be elected from within the board, and it is envisaged that there would be minimal intervention from the owners or trustees and the Department of Education (Department of Education, 1992b, 139–46). These proposals would clearly reduce the influence of the owners or trustees in most cases, as boards of management would be potentially more independent, since trustees would not have a majority on the board.

It is also suggested that in future all teachers would be employees of the board of management. This might be seen to imply that all teachers would be paid directly by the Department of Education, although the Green Paper is not specific on this. Nor is it specific on whether 'basic' salaries would continue to be paid by owners or trustees to teachers in secondary schools or to be channelled through the VECs to teachers in VEC-owned schools. The Green Paper does not refer specifically to the funding of capital expenditure.

With regard to recurrent costs, a new funding mechanism based on cost per pupil is proposed. There would be a standard budget based on school size and school level, subject to a minimum provision for very small schools. There would be additional budget allocation for schools serving disadvantaged areas and for those providing for children with special needs, as well as for those offering non-mainstream programmes. The Green Paper proposes three conditions for funding for state-aided secondary schools: (*a*) an admissions policy that would not discriminate on the basis of means, educational level, or social background; (*b*) a comprehensive system of education suitable for a wide ability range; and (*c*) an obligation to provide for the educational needs of the local community (Department of Education, 1992b, 153–4).

At the time of writing, these matters are the subject of debate and discussion by interested parties and have yet to be implemented by legislation. A strong response by the churches is emerging in relation to their desire to preserve denominational education (Daly, 1992; Meredith, 1992). It remains to be seen what the effect will be on the exisiting balance of power and ownership within the education system when the processes of negotiation and resistance that we analyse in chapter 6 are taken into account.

SCHOOL SIZE AND CLASS SIZE
The Irish school system has traditionally been characterised by the predominance of small schools at primary and postprimary level. These have been particularly valued by local communities, especially in rural areas; they are thought to give a focus to the villages and localities in which they are situated. This is graphically illustrated by the degree of local resistance that is common when there are proposals to 'rationalise' or to close schools, very apparent in the 1960s, when an active policy was adopted of closing small schools wherever possible. In spite of the 1960s and subsequent closures, the proportion of small schools (i.e. one-teacher to three-teacher schools) in the primary sector remains quite large, at 43.1 per cent of the total (Department of Education, 1992a, 24). Just over one-fifth of the total of 3,235 primary schools (21.1 per cent) are big enough to have a 'walking' principal—i.e. one who does not have full responsibility for a class—with a staff of nine or more teachers (ibid.).

At second level, schools are also small by international standards, except for those in the comprehensive sector. A total of 28 per cent of secondary schools have fewer than 300 pupils, while only 4.2 per cent have more than 800 pupils (OECD, 1991, 58). In the vocational sector 54.8 per cent of schools have fewer than 300 pupils. Small schools are generally preferred by teaching staffs, because of their more intimate ethos and because teachers believe it is easier to give more personal attention to each pupil in a small school (ibid.). Whether this happens in practice is a matter for research.

The impact of the dramatic decline in births in Ireland throughout the 1980s, combined with high levels of emigration, has already been felt in schools at both primary and postprimary levels. This has led to closures, amalgamation and 'rationalisation' at postprimary level. For example, in the school year 1988/89 there were 808 second-level schools (Department of Education, 1990, 34); by 1990/91 this had fallen to 792. It has been estimated by official sources that this number could decline further to between 500 and 600 schools over the next decade as a result of closures or amalgamations (Department of Education, 1992b, 106). Although schools in different localities have evolved a number of arrangements in the process of amalgamation or rationalisation, the typical pattern has been for one or two secondary schools to amalgamate with each other and/or with a vocational school and to arrive at a community school model of management structure. This process inevitably means that average school size will become somewhat bigger over the coming years. (The implications of amalgamations for the education of girls and boys in co-educational settings are discussed in chapter 9.)

The issue of pupil-teacher ratio (PTR) and class size is possibly the most contentious and deeply felt educational issue among Irish teachers at all levels of the system. Large class sizes have been held responsible for difficulties in implementing the group and individual aspects of the primary school curriculum (INTO, 1987, 19) and for teacher stress. Ireland has the least favourable PTR among EC countries for both primary and second-level education (OECD, 1991, 81). In the school year 1991/92 the ratio stood at 25.8 : 1 in primary schools and 19.5 : 1 at second level (figures from the Minister for Education's response to a Dáil question, 19 February 1992, quoted in *Irish Education Decision Maker,* no. 6, autumn 1992, 80). However, the overall primary school ratio results in 68 per cent of primary school children being taught in classes of over 30 and 3.6 per cent in classes of 40 or more (Department of Education, 1992a, 14).

While it has been argued that there is no exact correlation between PTR and the performance of pupils (OECD, 1991, 81), research suggests that reducing class size provides an opportunity for improvements in classroom processes. While class size has no magical, unmediated effect on student achievement, it influences what goes on in the classroom, what the teacher does with pupils, and what the pupils themselves do or are allowed to do. These differences in classroom processes in turn influence outcome measures such as pupil achievement, pupil attitudes, and teacher morale (Glass et al., 1982, 67).

It has been argued that only when numbers of around fifteen pupils or fewer are attained do decisive gains in pupil achievement occur (Fullan and Hargreaves, 1992). It is unlikely that such class sizes could be achieved in Irish schools in the current economic climate. A guideline suggested by the recent OECD inquiry is that a class is too big when the teacher can no longer give individual attention to each pupil (OECD, 1991, 81). The report suggests that a steady reduction in the PTR is desirable, but in the short term recommends a discriminatory lowering of the PTR by employing more teachers in disadvantaged schools (ibid., 82). Within larger classes it has been suggested that work with small groups can be achieved through the use of active learning methods, creative arrangements for team teaching, teachers covering colleagues' classes, and the like (Fullan and Hargreaves, 1992, 47).

STRUCTURES AT THIRD LEVEL

As is the case at second level, there is a diversity of educational provision in third-level education. In state-aided third-level education there are three broad types of provision: the universities, the technological colleges, and the colleges of education. In addition, particularly in recent times, there has been a growth in the private, non-state-aided provision of third-level education. Here we confine our discussion to the state-aided sector, as it caters for the great majority of students.

There are four universities in the Republic. These are the National University of Ireland, the University of Dublin (Trinity College), Dublin City University (formerly the National Institute for Higher Education, Dublin), and the University of Limerick (formerly the National Institute for Higher Education, Limerick). The National University of Ireland comprises three constituent colleges—University College, Cork, University College, Dublin, and University College, Galway—and one recognised college, St Patrick's College, Maynooth (Department of Education, 1992a). There were three other recognised colleges in that year: two primary education colleges and the Royal College of Surgeons in Ireland. These, however, are not classified as universities.

The NUI constituent colleges lay down their own programme and carry out their own examinations, subject to the overall authority of the NUI. The recognised colleges plan their programmes and examinations with the advice of academic personnel in the constituent college to which they are linked (Coolahan, 1981, 257). St Patrick's College, Maynooth, is somewhat different from other state-aided colleges, as it also includes on its campus a pontifical university and a seminary.

The four universities and their constituent colleges in the HEA sector (see below) are funded through a combination of state grants, student fees, and other income. While exact proportions vary slightly from college to college, in the universities in 1993 state grants accounted for approximately 62 per cent of income and student fees for 34 per cent, with the remaining 4 per cent coming from other sources (information from the Higher Education Authority).

Trinity College was established under royal charter in 1592 and was Ireland's only university until the middle of the nineteenth century (Coolahan, 1981, 111). The NUI is governed by the Irish Universities Act, 1908 (ibid., 258). However, it is likely that this Act will be amended to create four constituent universities within a federal NUI structure (Department of Education, 1992b, 203). The Government set up the National Institutes for Higher Education in Limerick and Dublin in 1972 and 1975, respectively (Coolahan, 1981, 260). In 1989 legislation established the two NIHEs as universities.

The government and administration within all the universities is under a statutory governing body, on which representation is either ex officio (for college officers), by election, or by nomination. There is both staff and student representation on these bodies. If new legislation is passed to create new structures within the NUI, it is likely that there would be changes at governing body level.

In the third-level technological sector there were nine regional technical colleges and eleven technological and other colleges under the management of VECs in 1990/91 (Department of Education, 1992a). Since then a further RTC has been opened in Tallaght, Co. Dublin. The first five RTCs were opened in 1969 in Carlow, Waterford, Athlone, Dundalk, and Sligo; these were followed later by others in Cork, Galway, Letterkenny, and Tralee. They were established to provide technological education to certificate, diploma and, later, degree level. In Dublin the six higher-level colleges under the VEC were reorganised in 1978 as the Dublin Institute of Technology. Since their foundation, state funding has been channelled to these colleges through the VECs. Student fees are another source of income.

In 1972 the Government set up the National Council for Educational Awards to act as the academic authority for RTC and DIT courses and awards as well as courses in other non-university colleges (Coolahan, 1981, 249–51). In 1992 legislation was passed to establish independent governing bodies for the RTCs and DIT. Henceforth RTC governing bodies will consist of 19 members, of whom just 6 will be nominees of the relevant VEC (Regional Technical Colleges Act, 1992). The DIT governing body will consist of 20 members, of whom 6 will be VEC nominees (Dublin Institute of Technology Act, 1992). There will be staff, student, trade union, professional and industrial representation on these bodies. This legislation represents, in effect, the removal of these colleges from the control of the VECs and a very substantial loss of VEC influence, although VEC approval will be required for budget proposals by governing bodies before submission for ministerial approval.

In the academic year 1990/91 there were five colleges of education for the preparation of primary school teachers. These were St Patrick's College of

Education, Drumcondra, Dublin; Mary Immaculate College of Education, Limerick; the Church of Ireland College of Education, Rathmines, Dublin; St Mary's College of Education, Marino, Dublin; and Froebel College of Education, Blackrock, Co. Dublin. These five colleges are denominational and co-educational and under the private management of the religious bodies concerned. All receive state funds, and charge fees. For some time the five colleges of education have been recognised by the universities for the purpose of the bachelor of education (BEd) degree—St Patrick's College and Mary Immaculate College by the NUI, and St Mary's College, Church of Ireland College and Froebel College by Trinity College.

Teacher education has been affected by reduced employment opportunities resulting from high pupil-teacher ratios and declining pupil numbers. (See chapter 5 for further details.) Consequently, the 1980s saw the closure of one college of education (Our Lady of Mercy, Blackrock, Co. Dublin) and declining enrolment in the others (Primary Education Review Body, 1991, 19). Currently, further changes are taking place, and 'strong institutional links' are being established between Mary Immaculate College and the University of Limerick and between St Patrick's College and Dublin City University (Department of Education, 1992b, 198).

Specialist teachers for the postprimary system are educated in a number of colleges. Thomond College in Limerick was established to offer a four-year BA degree to physical education students. Since 1979 trainee craft and rural science teachers have also attended Thomond College (Coolahan, 1981, 228). Since 1991 Thomond College has been integrated with the University of Limerick. Teachers of home economics are educated in St Angela's College, Sligo, and St Catherine's College, Blackrock, Co. Dublin, whose awards are validated by the NUI and Trinity College, respectively. Mater Dei Institute of Education, Dublin, specialises in the preparation of teachers of religious education; it is affiliated to St Patrick's College, Maynooth. All these teacher education colleges are under religious management. Most teachers of art are trained in the National College of Art and Design, Dublin. This college was designated as an institution of higher education under the Higher Education Authority Act, 1971 (Coolahan, 1981, 263).

In addition to the NCEA, which has a remit for awards for technological education, there is another body placed between the Government and the third-level institutions. From its establishment, the Higher Education Authority had powers and responsibilities ranging over the whole of third-level education. Under the 1971 Act it is the funding agency for universities and other designated third-level institutions from funds provided by the state. It has advisory functions for all third-level education. It also has functions such as the promotion of the value of higher education and research, the promotion of equality of opportunity in higher education, and the democratisation of the structure of higher education (Higher Education Authority Act, 1971). Under new proposals its responsibilities may be extended to include others such as the monitoring of cost-effectiveness and quality assurance, and the promotion of links between colleges and industry (Department of Education, 1992b, 199). This represents a shift in emphasis from its original functions.

PARTICIPATION AT THIRD LEVEL

We saw earlier that participation in full-time education is high at second level. This is also true at third level. Almost 40 per cent of the age group who complete second-level education proceed to third-level education, and a further 20 per cent follow a post-second-level vocational training programme within the school system (Department of Education, 1992b, 36). Participation rates have not yet reached saturation levels, and the Green Paper envisages that 45 per cent would transfer to higher education and a further 25 per cent to post-second-level vocational training by the end of the century (ibid., 37). Present trends suggest that this is likely to be achieved and even exceeded.

While there are difficulties in international comparisons because of differing definitions and data-bases, it appears that even now enrolment rates compare well with rates in many other countries, particularly if one takes into account Ireland's much less favourable economic circumstances. As we saw earlier, Ireland has a participation rate of 72.6 per cent in full-time education for the 4–24 age group. This compares with a rate of 72 per cent of the 5–24 age group in the EC as a whole and 73 per cent in Denmark, and with one of 61 per cent for the 5–24 age group in the United Kingdom (Eurostat, 1991, 114–15).

If we focus on the twenty-year-old group, the enrolment rate in Ireland in full-time education is 14.2 per cent (Department of Education, 1992a, 3). In Germany the figure is higher, at 17 per cent, but in Sweden it is 9.5 per cent, in Switzerland 15.1 per cent, and in the United Kingdom 13.9 per cent (OECD, 1989). Sweden and Switzerland, however, have high rates of enrolment in part-time education, perhaps indicating their more favourable employment and on-the-job training opportunities. Countries such as Canada, the United States and Denmark have significantly higher full-time enrolment rates for twenty-year-olds, at 35 per cent, 32.2 per cent, and 22.4 per cent, respectively (OECD, 1989).

The numbers in full-time education aged eighteen and over clearly reflect high participation in third-level education. The distribution of students currently in full-time third-level education in Ireland is shown in table 1.1.

In 1990/91 over half of full-time third-level students were in universities, and close to 40 per cent were in technological colleges. It should be added that the proportion in technological colleges is not an indicator of the total number of students taking technological, business or science courses (in which these colleges tend to specialise): substantial proportions of students in the university sector also take these subjects, which now account for 41.5 per cent of primary degrees in the Higher Education Authority sector (Sheehan, 1992). This indicates a very substantial shift in the universities away from the traditional professional and liberal arts courses (ibid.). There has, consequently, been a very substantial growth in the technical, scientific and business areas in higher education over the last two decades. By contrast, a very small proportion of the total higher education students were in colleges of education. Even if we add the students registered for higher diploma in education (HDE) courses—601 in 1990/91 (information from HEA)—the proportion is still very small, with 2.9 per cent of total third-level students in teacher education.

Table 1.1

Distribution of students in full-time third-level education, 1990/91

Type of institution	Percentage
Universities	54.2
Other HEA institutions	2.2
Colleges of education[1]	2.1
Regional technical colleges and vocational technological institutions	38.9
Other (mainly non-state-aided) institutions	2.6
Total	100.0
n	69,988

Source: Department of Education (1992a), 2.

1. Includes 391 students following teacher training courses in Thomond College.

ADULT AND PART-TIME EDUCATION

We saw above that transfer rates to third-level and further education courses are quite high and that a large proportion of the total population is enrolled in full-time education. These figures do not take into account the numbers of people who follow part-time educational programmes. In the HEA sector in 1989/90, for example, 5,946 students took part-time degrees and diplomas (Central Statistics Office, 1991, 232). In third-level RTCs and technology colleges the number following part-time courses in that year was 29,048 (Department of Education, 1991, 146). If we add to these the further 111,712 who were regis-tered on part-time courses in vocational, community and comprehensive schools (ibid.) we can see that part-time education is a very significant part of the Irish education system. The number of people on part-time courses classified as availing of 'adult education' in the RTCs and schools came to 114,194, the majority (70.2 per cent) of them women (ibid., 148).

Many of the courses under this heading are not accredited and might be described as 'general interest' courses. These courses, nonetheless, can be very enriching. (We discuss adult education at greater length in chapter 13.)

CONCLUSIONS

We have seen that the Irish education system is characterised by high participation rates. The system is, to a great extent, a denominational one at both primary and second level. Even at third level there is an important denominational element in the area of teacher training. Education is, however, mainly state-funded. Although there is a diversity of ownership in the school system, it is combined with a rather centralised system of curriculum development and assessment. There has been a marked rise in credentialism in education over the 1980s, i.e. an increase in the importance of qualifications, in the level of qualification required for occupational entry and in the use of such qualifications to restrict access to the more prestigious occupations. This is combined with grave labour market difficulties for the unqualified. This is a period of profound change for the structure and administration of the system, as is evidenced by recent Government proposals.

The features of the education system described above did not grow Topsy-like in a haphazard way. Rather, they are the outcome of processes connected with the distribution of economic, social and political power and domination, the processes of decision-making and negotiation, and the influence of diverse interest groups during the evolution of the education system. These issues are discussed in greater detail in the following chapters.

Note
1. There are two 'secondary tops' and three 'other' schools listed under the heading of second-level schools 'aided by Department of Education' in the 1990/91 statistical report (Department of Education, 1992a). These are excluded from our analysis.

References and Further Reading
Barber, N. (1989), *Comprehensive Schooling in Ireland*, Dublin: Economic and Social Research Institute.
Breen, R. (1984), *Education and the Labour Market: Work and Unemployment Among Recent Cohorts of Irish School Leavers*, Dublin: Economic and Social Research Institute.
Breen, R. (1986), *Subject Availability and Student Performance in the Senior Cycle of Irish Post-Primary Schools*, Dublin: Economic and Social Research Institute.
Breen, R. (1991), *Education, Employment and Training in the Youth Labour Market*, Dublin: Economic and Social Research Institute.
Breen, R., and Whelan, B. (1986), *School Leavers, 1980–1985*, Dublin: Department of Labour.
Central Statistics Office (1991), *Statistical Abstract*, Dublin: Stationery Office.
Clancy, P. (1988), *Who Goes to College?: a Second National Survey of Participation in Higher Education*, Dublin: Higher Education Authority.

Coolahan, J. (1981), *Irish Education: History and Structure*, Dublin: Institute of Public Administration.

Coolahan, J. (1990), Foreword to G. McNamara, K. Williams, and D. Herron (eds.), *Achievement and Aspiration: Curricular Initiatives in Irish Post-Primary Education in the 1980s*, Dublin: Drumcondra Teachers' Centre.

Curriculum Awareness Action Group (1990), *Low Achievement at Senior Cycle*, Dublin: Marino Institute of Education.

Daly, C. (1992), 'Cardinal Daly on Education: in Interview with Larry McCluskey', *Irish Education Decision Maker*, no. 6, 10–11.

Department of Education (1990), *Statistical Report, 1988/1989*, Dublin: Stationery Office.

Department of Education (1991), *Statistical Report, 1989/1990*, Dublin: Stationery Office.

Department of Education (1992a), *Statistical Report, 1990/1991*, Dublin: Stationery Office.

Department of Education (1992b), *Education for a Changing World: Green Paper on Education*, Dublin: Stationery Office.

Department of Labour (1989), *Economic Status of School Leavers, 1988*, Dublin: Department of Labour.

Department of Labour (1991), *Economic Status of School Leavers, 1990*, Dublin: Department of Labour.

Drudy, P. (1991), 'The regional impact of foreign industry in Ireland' in T. Foley and D. McAleese (eds.), *Overseas Industry in Ireland*, Dublin: Gill and Macmillan.

Dublin Institute of Technology Act, 1992.

Eurostat (1991), *Basic Statistics of the Community*, Luxembourg: European Communities.

Fullan, M., and Hargreaves, A. (1992), *What's Worth Fighting For in Your School?*, Buckingham: Open University Press.

Glass, G., et al. (1982), *School Class Size: Research and Policy*, California: Sage.

Hannan, D., and Shorthall, S. (1991), *The Quality of Their Education: School Leavers' Views of Educational Objectives and Outcomes*, Dublin: Economic and Social Research Institute.

Higher Education Authority Act, 1971.

Irish National Teachers' Organisation (1987), *Primary School Curriculum: Report of a Consultative Conference*, Dublin: INTO.

Lynch, K. (1989), *The Hidden Curriculum*, Lewes: Falmer.

McNamara, G., and Williams, K. (1990), 'An agenda for the 1990s' in G. McNamara, K. Williams, and D. Herron (eds.), *Achievement and Aspiration: Curricular Initiatives in Irish Post-Primary Education in the 1980s*, Dublin: Drumcondra Teachers' Centre.

Martin, M., and Hickey, B. (1992), *The 1991 Leaving Certificate Examination: a Review of the Results*, Dublin: National Council for Curriculum and Assessment.

Meredith, D. (1992), 'The Green Paper: a challenge for pluralism', *Irish Education Decision Maker*, no. 6, 44–5.

O Buachalla, S. (1988), *Education Policy in Twentieth-Century Ireland*, Dublin: Wolfhound.

O'Flaherty, L. (1992), *Management and Control in Irish Education: the Post-Primary Experience*, Dublin: Drumcondra Teachers' Centre.

Organisation for Economic Co-operation and Development (1989), *Education in OECD Countries, 1986/87: a Compendium of Statistical Information*, Paris: OECD.

Organisation for Economic Co-operation and Development (1991), *Reviews of National Policies for Education—Ireland*, Paris: OECD.

Primary Education Review Body (1991), *Report*, Dublin: Stationery Office.

Regional Technical Colleges Act, 1992.

Secretariat of Secondary Schools (1992), 'End of Year School Statistics', Dublin: Secretariat of Secondary Schools.

Sexton, J., Whelan, B., and Williams, J. (1988), *Transition from School to Work and Early Labour Market Experience*, Dublin: Economic and Social Research Institute.

Sheehan, J. (1992), *Education, Training and the Culliton Report* (Policy Paper Series), Dublin: University College (Centre for Economic Research).

2

Education and Society: Sociological Interpretations

In this chapter we explore the role education plays in Irish society. We then outline the main theoretical approaches to schooling in the sociology of education. We concentrate mainly on the theoretical dimensions that have had some impact on Irish educational research. Examples of the use of sociological theory in the study of Irish education are presented.

THE ROLE OF EDUCATION IN IRISH SOCIETY

Education plays a critical role in the socialisation of the young and in the transmission of culture. The term 'socialisation' refers to all the learning we do in order to become competent and functioning members of our social group, community, or society. It is a process that starts the moment we are born, and continues until we die. It is achieved through interaction with others, and involves a variety of processes, including observation and imitation of others, identification with and internalisation of behaviour patterns and values, social control of the behaviour of individuals by group members, the manipulation of symbols and language, and formal learning. By the term 'culture' we mean the attitudes, values, tradition, language, knowledge and way of life of a social group.

Education, therefore, involves forming young people as humans and citizens with a specifically Irish identity—largely according to the way in which that is interpreted by the dominant social groupings in education and in society. This formation is achieved by means of the formal curriculum at primary and second level—and indeed at pre-school level, where such exists. It is also achieved at all levels of the system, and sometimes more effectively, through the hidden curriculum. (For a fuller discussion of the hidden curriculum see chapter 8.)

In addition to socialisation and the transmission of culture, the education system selects individuals, even from the earliest stages, for different types of occupation through its assessment and certification. In this way it not only allocates people to different positions within the economic system but also controls the level of social mobility in society. Social mobility refers to the degree of movement from one social class to another in each generation, and to an individual's chance of moving from one class to another during his or her lifetime. Examination of the relationship between social class and education in Ireland has shown that Ireland has a quite rigid class structure and that it is more difficult for the child of an unskilled manual worker to reach university than it is in a number of other European countries (Whelan and Whelan, 1984).

The education system also plays a significant part in the reproduction of the social relations of production. This refers to the way in which social structures are passed on and endure from one generation to another. It also refers to the manner in which this occurs in western capitalist societies, in spite of rapid industrial, technological and occupational change.

In any society, social relationships are established during the course of producing the everyday necessities of life, such as food, shelter, consumer goods, and all the services necessary for the functioning of that society. If we want to assess these relationships we must examine the nature of ownership and control of resources, such as land, factories, financial institutions, technology, and even knowledge. We must also examine how widely ownership of these is distributed among the population. We must establish what type of technology is used in production (for example craft, assembly line, or automated processes; information and administrative systems) and what the dominant form is in that economy. We must also examine the distribution of income throughout the population, i.e. whether the bulk of it is highly concentrated among a relatively small group of people or whether it is more equitably distributed. We must examine the degree of poverty in a society and how this is defined.

Finally, we need to explore and define the existence of social classes and assess the degree of rigidity or openness of the class structure and the nature of the relationship between the dominant and subordinate classes. Because social class relations are compounded by factors such as gender, race, and disability, we must also assess the impact of these variables on the social relations of production as well. (For a discussion of many of these issues see Clancy et al., 1986, and Breen et al., 1990). It is only when all these factors are taken into account that a full picture of the social relations of production can emerge.

In most societies, except perhaps during periods of revolution, the social relations of production remain relatively stable from one generation to the next. Indeed, it can be argued that it is the social relations of production that give a society its characteristic form and that shape its major institutions and dominant culture and people's awareness of themselves. The education system plays an important role in ensuring that these social relationships remain relatively enduring from one generation to another. It also plays a role in ensuring that in a society such as Ireland, in which the economy is subject to periodic expansion and contraction and in which there is fairly rapid technological change, resulting in the creation of new occupational positions and the disappearance of others, there are individuals who are sufficiently educated and adaptable and have the appropriate attitudes to change.

However, because the social relations of production are often inequitable, schools play a part in reproducing social outcomes that are far from positive at times (Bowles and Gintis, 1976). Reproduction can occur in a number of ways. It operates both through the formal and the hidden curriculum. We can learn a lot about the aims and aspirations of Irish society, and especially about those of its most powerful interest groups, by examining the formal curriculum of the school. When we do this we should consider the degree of emphasis given to the academic, the practical, the scientific, the personal, the technological, the aesthetic, and other qualities. (This is done in some detail in part IV of this book.) Reproduction also occurs through the various elements of the hidden curriculum, notably through the authority structure, the degree of competitiveness of the system, and the operation of examination and certification.

Education is a central social institution in Ireland and in other societies, because of its crucial ideological role. It is a central arena where the ideologies of powerful interest groups are articulated. This has been particularly obvious in Irish education when we look at the way the churches have seen the control of the education system as crucial to their interests (see for example Whyte, 1980). However, the churches are not alone in seeing education as a key social institution in which their ideology and world view should be represented. Other groups, for example employers, have in recent years sought to bring about educational changes conducive to their interests. In the public arena this has been evidenced by the numerous public statements by representatives of the Confederation of Irish Industry on educational and curricular matters (e.g. Sweeny, 1992). Indeed, recognition was given to such interest groups when the Curriculum and Examinations Board (later the National Council for Curriculum and Assessment) was established in the early 1980s.

Boards of studies were set up to devise frameworks for various elements of the curriculum. These included representatives from the churches, the employers, and the trade unions, as well as from the teaching profession, subject associations, and higher education. This is still reflected in the composition of the NCCA, on which the CII (now the Irish Business and Employers' Confederation) and the ICTU are still represented, along with a range of church and educational representative bodies.

The OECD report on Irish education recommended the inclusion of representatives of the employment sector in curriculum planning, as well as representatives of parents and 'community groups' (OECD, 1991, 75). The Green Paper on education reinforces this through its proposal that representatives of the 'business community' be included on the boards of schools and that 'industrial interests' be represented on the boards of universities and colleges (Department of Education, 1992, 142, 200).

If all the above elements imply that the role of the education system has much to do with social control, the reason is that historically that is how education systems have developed in most societies. Few people enter teaching or other branches of education with this consciously in mind, however. Indeed, many take up education as a career with quite altruistic motives. In addition, there is a significant movement among educators (among whom we would count ourselves) whose concept of the role of education is emancipatory or liberating. While the views of a number of such educators have their origins in a liberal philosophical tradition such as that to be found in the work of Dewey (1963), others take their inspiration from the work of the Latin American educator Freire, as represented in books such as *The Pedagogy of the Oppressed* (1972) and *Cultural Action for Freedom* (1972), or, more recently, from feminist theory. In an Irish context an emancipatory approach to education has been expressed by Ó Súilleabháin when he suggests that 'the essence of education is *becoming,* the gradual discovery of what it means to be human, the search for a personal identity, an identity which brings individual autonomy within a community structure' (Ó Súilleabháin, 1986, 91).

However, even the most fervent advocates of emancipatory education admit that the institutional constraints on its achievement are considerable. It has been one of the tasks of the sociology of education to document those constraints and to attempt to analyse and explain their persistence. There have also been attempts to identify possible modes of resistance to these constraints and the locations and means of potential change and emancipation (e.g. Giroux, 1983; Willis, 1977).

DIFFERING PERSPECTIVES IN THE SOCIOLOGY OF EDUCATION

Given the centrality of education as a social institution in society, then, it is not surprising that it has been an important area of sociological interest since the emergence of sociology as a distinct area of scientific and philosophical inquiry towards the end of the nineteenth century. Indeed, one of the 'founding fathers' of sociology, Émile Durkheim, was professor of education rather than of sociology for much of his career. For Durkheim, the role of education in socialisation and the transmission of culture was central. He suggested that the school was the key place where modern societies achieved social consensus and order, through the inculcation of central moral values (Lukes, 1973, 109–36). This tradition has also been evident in American sociology.

However, it would be misleading to suggest that the sociology of education, any more than any of the other branches of sociological inquiry, offers a single interpretation of the role of the education system. We will therefore now outline the principal approaches to the interpretation of education systems and the role of education in the social structures of modern societies.

THE FUNCTIONALIST PERSPECTIVE

Until the 1970s the dominant theoretical approach in sociology was one that is variously called 'functionalism', 'structural functionalism', or sometimes 'consensus theory' (Clancy et al., 1986). This form of analysis has its origins in the work of European sociologists around the beginning of the twentieth century, such as Durkheim and, to some extent, Weber, with whom we deal below.

However, the form in which functionalism influenced Irish sociology and educational analysis did not come directly from these Europeans for the most part but was mediated by North American interpretations and reformulations of this work (see, for example, Parsons, 1952) and by the manner in which it was adopted in Britain (Halsey, Floud, and Anderson, 1961). This occurred for two principal reasons: the late development of Irish sociology of education as a form of inquiry (Drudy, 1991a), and the fact that a high proportion of Irish academics and researchers until recent times took their postgraduate training either in the United States or in Britain.

Functionalist analysis has to a very large extent been concerned with social structures and with processes at a macro level, i.e. at the level of whole societies or of major social structures, such as the education system or the economy. The model of society proposed by functionalist analysis is that of a social 'system', analogous in many ways to a biological organism. The component parts of this system are thought to be interrelated. They can be divided into 'subsystems', such as the education system, the family, the economic system, the religious system, the political system, and so on. Change in one part or subsystem, it is argued, will lead to changes in other parts—or, indeed, in the whole.

For functionalist analysts, the great engine of change and development in modern societies is industrialisation. The degree of industrialisation is thought to be the key to our understanding of the structure and functioning of a given society. Industrialisation and economic change are thought to bring in their wake changes in all other areas of the social structure. One can expect modernisation to follow industrialisation. This involves such phenomena as increased urbanisation, secularisation, the development of democratic political structures, and the growth of mass education, along lines similar to those in 'advanced' western economies (Wickham, 1986).

While industrialisation is seen as the key to social change, there is also a strong strand of thought that argues it to be perfectly possible to reverse the order of some of these relationships. Functionalist thought suggests that a society could facilitate and encourage economic growth and industrialisation by altering other institutions, for example the education system.

Although functionalists address the problem of conflict and social disintegration, there is an assumption that modern societies are based more on 'consensus' and co-operation, and are normally in a state of equilibrium. Indeed, a major preoccupation of functionalists is with the question of order—that is, how do societies remain cohesive and maintain themselves from one generation to another? The answer tends to be couched in terms of shared values, or the central value system. Although many institutions are thought to play essential roles in the maintenance and transmission of these shared values, not surprisingly the education system is seen as playing a central part in the process (Parsons, 1961).

This approach is not exclusive to sociology. It is shared to some extent by other social sciences, particularly history and political science. Indeed, one could say it is part of our intellectual culture. Assumptions of this kind appear to underlie many political decisions. The reason for this, perhaps, is that the discourses, spoken and written, of the processes of ruling help to organise and shape the world they describe. Sociological frameworks not only use the concepts of that sphere but also provide conceptualisations of the way the world works, for managers and administrators, politicians, reformers, and political movements (Acker, 1989).

We can certainly find strong overtones of functionalism in that famous precursor of the opening up of the postprimary education system, *Investment in Education* (1966), and in many subsequent official publications, up to the most recent. *Investment in Education* and the majority of Government policy documents on education reflect a variant of functionalist theory known as 'human capital' theory. This implies that increasing investment in education brings automatic economic benefits both at a personal and societal level. It also implies that the increasing trend towards more technically oriented education is both natural and inevitable (Lynch, 1992a). (These issues are discussed in more detail in chapters 3 and 10.)

One of the most enduring debates in sociology and educational policy in Ireland and elsewhere has been that surrounding the concept of equality of educational opportunity. This concept is firmly embedded within the functionalist frame of reference. Functionalists have tended to discuss the problem of education and social class, in particular, in the liberal language of 'equality of educational opportunity' (Floud, Halsey, and Martin, 1956; Craft, 1970; Silver, 1973). This approach examines the influence of 'educationally irrelevant' variables, such as social class background, gender, and place of residence (Greaney and Kellaghan, 1984), on educational outcomes.

The 'equality of opportunity' argument rests on the idea that modern industrial societies are, or should be, meritocratic, that is, that achievement and success should be based on a combination of ability and effort and not on one's social position, family connections, race, religion, or gender. The education system is seen as playing a crucial role in identifying ability and talent, nurturing it, accrediting it, and eventually assisting in slotting it into appropriate positions in the social and economic hierarchy. However, this approach does not assume that inequalities can, or should be, eliminated. Indeed, functionalism sees a certain amount of social and economic inequality as both inevitable and necessary ('positively' functional) to the proper functioning of industrial societies (Davis and Moore, 1945; Marshall, 1971).

According to functionalists, therefore, one of the principal functions of education is to encourage and facilitate social mobility. Mobility can be horizontal (i.e. from one occupation to another at the same social class level) or vertical (from one social class to another, either upwards or downwards). It is assumed by functionalists that occupations and social classes are ranked in hierarchical fashion according to the degree of prestige, rewards and skills attached to them (Lipset and Bendix, 1959). Thus it is the task of education to make sure that every member of a society has, as it were, an equal chance to be unequal and can move according to skill and effort into the social position most appropriate to their talents.

In the introduction to their study of equality of opportunity in Irish schools, Greaney and Kellaghan (1984) divide conceptual thinking on this idea into three phases: access, participation rates, and rates of achievement. (See below for further discussion of Greaney and Kellaghan's research.) In the early part of the twentieth century and up to the period after the Second World War, the concept of educational equality was couched in terms of access by children from different social groups to different levels of the education system (Silver, 1973, xi). This approach assumed that in order to remove inequalities in education it was necessary only to remove legal or, more often, financial barriers (in the form of fees, for example) so as to equalise access and facilitate social mobility. In Ireland this underlay the thinking of *Investment in Education* and many subsequent ministerial decisions. In Britain, more than twenty years earlier, it lay behind the reforms in the 'Butler' Education Act of 1944.

It quickly became apparent in Britain that the removal of fees, transport costs etc. was insufficient to bring about parity among the different social classes in relation to education. Nor did it eliminate the 'wastage of talent'. As early as the mid-1950s British sociologists were describing major differences in the representation of working-class and middle-class children at the different levels of education and in different types of schools (Floud, Halsey, and Martin, 1956). Likewise in Ireland, though at a later period, it became evident that the opening up of the postprimary education system in 1967 and the consequent increase in participation rates had not benefited all equally (Tussing, 1978 and 1981).

More recently the question of equality of educational opportunity, in Ireland and elsewhere, has been examined by considering the participation rates of different social groups at the various levels of the education system (Rottman et al., 1982; Clancy, 1982 and 1988). This approach assumes that one should measure educational equality by comparing the representation of different social groups or classes at the various levels of the education system with the representation of the appropriate age group in each social category in the population at large. Using this comparison, each social group may be proportionately represented, underrepresented, or overrepresented. Thus any marked degree of underrepresentation or overrepresentation among social categories would indicate educational inequalities.

The third phase of assessing educational equality is to examine the level of achievement of different social classes or groups at successive stages of the education system. Only where there is a proportionate distribution of different types of qualification among categories (for example if the achievement of a minimum of five D grades at Leaving Certificate were distributed in proportional fashion among all social classes) could equality of educational opportunity be said to have been achieved. Assessment of differential levels of achievement is a useful yardstick by which to measure the degree of educational inequality. Participation rates and achievement are the two indicators most commonly used in contemporary educational research.

Although there had been some debate on equality of opportunity in Ireland before the mid-1960s, *Investment in Education* was the first major report to give public expression to the principle of 'equality of opportunity'. One of the more recent contributions to the debate has been Greaney and Kellaghan's work *Equality of Opportunity in Irish Schools* (1984). This was a longitudinal study of a cohort (group of the same age) of 500 children selected from a sample of primary schools throughout the Republic. Information was first collected on these children in primary school, and their progress through school and college was monitored until entry to their first job.

Greaney and Kellaghan do not explicitly adopt any theoretical position in their study. However, the international literature on which they draw, the concepts they use and the parameters of their discussion of the data indicate an acceptance of the functionalist approach. The question of equality of educational opportunity is couched therefore in terms of how closely the educational progress of these children through the system approaches the 'meritocratic ideal' (Greaney and Kellaghan, 1984). While the findings of this report are presented later (in chapter 7), let us now turn to some of the arguments raised relating to conceptual issues.

In Ireland, where research funds are limited, studies of this magnitude are very important in shaping our understanding of the education system and in influencing public policy. It is not surprising, therefore, that this study came under very close scrutiny. In fact, such was the level of concern that this most important issue be fully discussed that an issue of the *Economic and Social Review* (vol. 16, 1985) was given over to a critique of the study. A number of scholars working in the field of equality studies contributed.

The principal unease was with the concepts and assumptions used in the study (Lynch, 1985) and the methodology used (Lynch, 1985; Raftery and Hout, 1985; Whelan and Whelan, 1985). In particular, the notion that meritocracy is, or should be, an ideal for Irish education was challenged. The concept of meritocracy, to which we have referred above, is usually signified by the equation 'IQ + effort = merit.' It was first popularised by Young (1961). This concept, it can be argued, presupposes the existence of a hierarchical social order (Lynch, 1985), as we have argued that functionalism in general does. It assumes that ability can be measured accurately—usually by means of IQ tests. (This contention is problematic, and is explored in chapter 11.) It was contended that it is a logical and social fallacy to suggest that anyone who has talent and makes the effort can attain merit when the meritorious occupations or positions are simply not available in large enough numbers even for those who are technically eligible to occupy them. The large number of qualified school and college leavers who currently cannot get access to the jobs for which they are qualified is clear proof of this (ibid.). In their response to their critics, Greaney and Kellaghan point out that they were aware of the problematic nature of the meritocratic model but used it because they believed it underlay attempts at educational reform since the 1960s (Greaney and Kellaghan, 1985).

More recently an equality debate has arisen as a result of the publication of the Green Paper on education (Department of Education, 1992). This is a debate on which we ourselves have somewhat divergent views. The issue relates to the implication of the concept of 'equity' in the Green Paper.

One view suggests that the use of the language of equity has replaced the language of equality, representing a major conceptual shift. From this standpoint, 'equity' is a loose term that can be interpreted in widely different ways depending on the authority defining it. Baker (1987) suggests that it generally connotes 'fairness' in philosophical terms, but that it can also mean something as vague as reasonableness. Although there are major weaknesses in the traditional liberal demand for equality of opportunity, the claim in the Green Paper that 'equity' is to be the guiding principle in education represents, in this view, a backward step. Rather than advancing from prior notions of equality of access and participation to a focus on equality of outcome and achievement, the Green Paper has focused thinking on the rather ambiguous concept of equity. If equality issues are defined in terms of equity, then the language of equality will be removed from the debate (Lynch, 1992b).

An alternative view is that, in practice, equity is interpreted in the Green Paper as 'equality of opportunity', and in particular as equality of participation. For example, in the preamble to chapter 2 there is a clear indication that concern for equality of participation is a central theme. This represents an advance on public policy in previous periods, when the primary emphasis was on access: 'In translating equality of access into full equality of participation, the priority must be to tackle barriers to participation which militate against those from disadvantaged backgrounds, or those suffering from particular difficulties or handicaps.' There is also a recognition that 'tackling the problem requires integrated action and collaboration between education, health, social welfare, labour and training and, equally, co-operation between schools, parents and the wider community.'

The Green Paper proposes giving priority to schools in disadvantaged areas in the matter of resources, when extra resources become available, and positive intervention in favour of students from disadvantaged areas in access to third-level education (ibid., 52). The paper also proposes, for the first time in Irish educational policy, that there be an obligation on all educational institutions to develop and publish an active policy to promote gender equity, and to aim at gender balance in all boards of management and selection committees (ibid., 70–1).

In a context in which, again for the first time, equity is spelt out as the first aim of education, some would argue that equality is not removed from the discourse of the paper; indeed the terms 'equity' and 'equality' are sometimes used interchangeably. However, this is part of the problem. While the dominant rhetoric of the Green Paper is that of 'equity', a number of the policy proposals are defined in terms of equality of opportunity, and in particular equality of participation. Two analytically distinct ideas are used interchangeably, and this has led to ambiguity and differences in interpretation. One thing is clear in the Green Paper, and that is that the underlying assumptions that are evident are those that most easily fit within a human capital approach to education. Human capital theory, functionalism and liberal philosophy all share one thing in common: they do not deal adequately with the problems of equality in the context of class-based societies characterised by major differences of power and resources between social groups. We will now turn to two perspectives that address these problems. The first of these is neo-Marxism, the second neo-Weberian sociology.

NEO-MARXISM AND EDUCATION

While, as we have seen, the concept of 'equality of educational opportunity' arose out of the functionalist frame of reference, examination of participation rates and achievement is also carried out by researchers with other theoretical approaches. One of the principal challenges to the functionalist analysis of the relationship between education and social class has come from researchers with a neo-Marxist perspective on the workings of capitalist societies. Neo-Marxism as a theoretical approach in sociology arises out of a western European and American tradition of social and academic analysis; it should not be confused with the political philosophy of former Eastern Bloc states, and indeed it was often very critical of them. In fact the focus of neo-Marxist scholars has been on the analysis of contemporary western capitalist societies.

Since the early 1970s, and continuing into the 1980s and 1990s, Marxist perspectives have made a significant contribution to educational debate. Educational sociologists operating within this frame of reference apply concepts that originate in the socio-economic analysis that Marx made of the capitalist system. These concepts have been modified to take account of the social, economic and technological changes that have taken place since then, and are applied to contemporary societies. In contrast to the functionalist approach, neo-Marxists suggest that the social relations of capitalist societies are characterised by class-based conflict rather than consensus. It is the nature of capitalist production, with its attendant social implications, that is thought to be crucial, rather than industrialisation *per se*.

It is suggested that every kind of production system entails a definite set of social relationships existing between individuals involved in the production process. It is the relationships that people enter into during the process of producing the ordinary material things of life that bring about the characteristic shape and form of any society. This is theoretically defined as the theory of base and superstructure. This theory contends that in any society, at any given historical epoch, the nature of and relationships in the economic 'base' determine the nature and form of the social and cultural 'superstructure'.

By 'base' is meant the dominant type of technology in use in production, the level of industrial production, the nature of ownership and control of the means of production (i.e. whether production is privately owned and whether ownership or management is highly concentrated or more widely distributed), the type of class structure, and the distribution of income and wealth. The term 'superstructure' refers to structures such as the political system, the judiciary, the family, the media, and, not least, the education system (see, for example, Miliband, 1973).

It is suggested by a number of analysts that over time some of these institutions develop a dynamism of their own—'relative autonomy'. This is the argument that while economic forces condition the nature of superstructural institutions, there is a reciprocal interaction in which these institutions have an impact on the economic base.

The notion of relative autonomy has been thought to be particularly applicable to the education system. The French sociologist Bourdieu has contended that the education system, unlike other systems, has a strong relative autonomy with respect to the economy. A capitalist system may thus have an education system containing mediaeval elements, such as a focus on the classics (Bourdieu and Passeron, 1977). Bourdieu also states that under certain conditions of capitalism, the education system becomes the main agency for the 'production of producers', i.e. for training for industrial work (Bourdieu and Boltanski, 1977). However, it is also argued that in the final analysis it is the economic forces that are dominant (Althusser, 1972).

Thus, it is suggested, the education system mirrors and reflects the characteristic relationships to be found in the system of industrial production. Where, for instance, the structure of industrial relations is hierarchical, authoritarian, and bureaucratic, one can expect the education system to be organised in a similar fashion. The relationships within and the discipline of the school prepare and inure the pupil for the relationships and discipline of the work-place. In their book *Schooling in Capitalist America,* Bowles and Gintis (1976) argue along these lines. It is also suggested by these and many other neo-Marxist researchers, such as Bourdieu, that one of the principal (though by no means overt) functions of modern education systems is the reproduction and legitimation of the social relationships of the capitalist economic order (Bourdieu and Passeron, 1977). This is achieved in particular by the role played by education systems in the reproduction of class inequalities. It is from this perspective that Marxist researchers examine and interpret such data as participation rates and achievement.

Within a neo-Marxist framework the parameters of the debate shift from the concept of 'equality of educational opportunity' to the concept of 'the reproduction of inequalities'. Unlike many functionalists, Marxists do not accept that the existence of socio-economic inequalities are necessary to the orderly and harmonious functioning of societies. They do accept, however, that such inequalities are characteristic and inevitable under the capitalist system of production. This is especially because the nature of this system stems from the relationship between the two fundamental groups involved in the production process: the bourgeoisie (owners and controllers) and the working class. This relationship, it is suggested, is one of inequality, domination, exploitation, and conflict. Although in contemporary societies there are intervening classes that may be more numerous, the relationship between these two fundamental groups is the crucial one. Education is seen as playing a vital role in the maintenance of these relations.

For functionalists, as we stated above, the acceptance of a degree of social inequality led to the idealisation of the concept of meritocracy. For them, an industrial society, in order to flourish, expand, and develop, needs to be able to change rapidly. Too great a degree of rigidity in the system of social stratification would be an impediment to innovation, change, and expansion. It is thus necessary, functionalists argue, that positions of power, influence and decision-making be filled by the most able and most skilled. It is the task of the education system to identify ability, provide it with the requisite skills according to the needs of society, and slot it into appropriate social positions. For the functionalist perspective, the education system is malfunctioning, not to the extent to which it fails to remove inequalities but to the extent to which it fails to identify talent or to slot it into appropriate positions. This led to a focus on the problem of 'social mobility'.

We referred earlier in this chapter to the issue of social mobility and the relationship of the education system to it. Some neo-Marxists have suggested that the intense focus on this issue in the analysis of the relationship between education and the economy is a mistaken one—'an absurd problematic' (Poulantzas, 1978). The reasoning is that, even were there to be perfect mobility from one generation to the next, with all middle-class positions, for example, filled by people from working-class origins, the structural inequalities would still be there. While many Marxists would agree on the persistence of structural inequalities, not all dismiss the problem of social mobility as lightly as Poulantzas. Rather it tends to be rephrased and interpreted in terms of the 'reproduction' of inequality from one generation to another.

Neo-Marxist scholars, then, diverge from functionalist analyses of educational inequality in three principal areas: the acceptance of socio-economic inequality, the idealisation of meritocracy, and the preoccupation with social mobility. The Marxist challenge thus focuses on the underlying acceptance, and reproduction, of inequality on which the concept of meritocracy fundamentally rests. (In part III we examine the role of education in the reproduction of inequality in Ireland.)

It must be pointed out here, however, that while there are important differences between functionalism and Marxism in their assumptions and interpretations, there are also quite a number of similarities. Both can be described as 'structuralist' approaches to the social order, as they conduct most of their analyses at the level of social systems (such as the education system) and focus primarily on social structures, such as class and occupational structures. Both use very similar methodologies and rely heavily on aggregate statistical data—such as censuses and official figures—and the results of social surveys.

Consequently, their findings regarding, for example, the links between the education system and the economy tend to be broadly similar. It is in the conclusions drawn from these that the chief differences are to be found.

Likewise, just as there are some similarities in methodology and focus, these two approaches also share some weaknesses. For example, there has been a comparative neglect in both approaches, until fairly recently at least, of the internal processes of the school and the dynamics of classroom interaction. This has been even more marked in Irish sociology of education than in the study of education internationally, and is evidenced by the paucity of research based on educational ethnography, i.e. systematic observation in schools and classrooms (Drudy, 1991a). Both traditions have also failed traditionally to analyse the interrelationship between class, gender, racial and disability-related inequalities.

THE NEO-WEBERIAN PERSPECTIVE

There is a third major perspective on the role of education in society. In Ireland and internationally, much valuable research has been done by sociologists who are best described as 'neo-Weberians'. Their work is influenced by the theories of the German sociologist Max Weber. Like Durkheim and Marx, Weber is commonly regarded as one of the founders of modern sociology. Weber's work, like that of Marx, represents an attempt to come to an understanding of the workings of capitalist society. However, Weberian sociology is much less inclined to see human behaviour as determined by the social structures in which people participate.

Weber liked to think of sociology as a science of understanding ('verstehende sociology'). He was concerned to explore the meanings people attach to their actions, and regarded 'meaningful social action' as the basic unit of analysis. Action, for Weber, is social to the extent that its subjective meaning takes account of the behaviour of others and is influenced by that behaviour (Weber, 1968, 4). What Weber advocated was that sociologists should try to get an inter-pretative grasp of the meanings present in three types of context: (1) in the case of individuals, the actually intended meaning for concrete individual action; (2) in the case of sociological mass phenomena, the average of, or approximation to, the actually intended meaning; (3) pure types ('ideal types') of common phenomena, which the sociologist should try to formulate, as is done for example by economics in the formulation of concepts and 'laws' (ibid., 9). It is clear, then, from Weber's work that social actors may be either individuals or groups. Interest groups, for example—such as teachers, the churches, and politicians—may be regarded as actors.

Weber's work is more voluntaristic, less deterministic, than that of either Durkheim or Marx, because, although he acknowledges the necessity to treat collectivities such as states, associations and business corporations as if they were individual people, for the interpretation of action, he says, we must focus on the results and modes of organisation of the particular acts of individuals, since these alone can be treated as agents in the course of subjectively understandable action (ibid., 13).

Weber's emphasis on the centrality of intention for all sociological investigation makes the purposes and goals of actors (whether individuals or collectivities) essential to social analysis (Lewis, 1975, 66). In education this has led to the development of a political sociology of education. This approach is typified in Archer's comparative analysis of the development of four modern education systems. Archer stresses that education is about the purposeful action of human beings. She argues that education has the characteristics it has because of the goals pursued by those who control it. When change occurs, it does so because new goals are pursued by those who have the power to modify education's previous structural form, definition of instruction, and relationship to society (Archer, 1984, 1). Weber's influence is also evident in Collins's analysis of the way in which education is used by various groups as one of the means of attaining their ends in the struggle in society for economic advantage, status, and domination (Collins, 1977). (We return to the work of Archer and Collins in chapter 10.)

In Ireland, neo-Weberian analysis of the education system is most obvious in the work of researchers at the Economic and Social Research Institute. Some of the analysis is specifically based on Weberian theory as articulated by Giddens (1973). Their theoretical model attributes inequalities in income to the distribution of resources—property, skills, and educational credentials. These, they suggest, are associated with the main social class categories (Rottman et al., 1982, 17).

This group's theory of the state, within which their analyses of the education system are located, suggests that the state, as the main administrative institution in society, is continually engaged in the regulation of conflict between the other structures of society. Their interest lies in the extent to which the state can determine societal outcomes, such as the distribution of life chances (Breen et al., 1990, 12–13). In their examination of educational reforms since the 1960s their main objective is to assess the goals the state hoped to achieve through reform and to look at the degree of success in attaining goals and the unexpected consequences that resulted. The state's lack of control over the system that it funds, they argue, has been crucial in determining these consequences (ibid., 123–42).

Thus we can see that a Weberian perspective focuses on individual and collective action, and on intention, purposes, and goals. It examines the way action and interaction are influenced by, and influence, the existing social and economic system. Weber also draws our attention to concepts such as power, domination, and authority; to the conflict over economic resources and rewards; to the competition for status and prestige; to the struggle for political control; and to the role of bargaining, negotiation, and compromise (Blackledge and Hunt, 1985, 336). (The goals, relative power and actions of key interest groups in Irish education are examined in chapter 6.)

Although Weber's work represented a challenge to the Marxist analysis of the capitalist society of his time (late nineteenth and early twentieth century), nevertheless there are areas of analysis where there is a substantial amount of agreement—for example in relation to many aspects of the class structure (Westergaard and Resler, 1976; Drudy, 1991b). In recent times it is possible to see an element of synthesis of concepts originating in Marxist and Weberian theory in the study of education systems in Ireland (Lynch, 1988; 1989b) and elsewhere—for example in the analysis of the French education system offered by Bourdieu (Bourdieu and Passeron, 1977).

SYMBOLIC INTERACTIONISM
Although the three perspectives outlined above have been the dominant ones in the sociology of education over the last twenty years, they are by no means the only ones. Furthermore, not all studies fall neatly into one category or another. Many studies combine insights derived from two or more approaches.

An important, if minority, form of educational research into Irish schools is that known as 'symbolic interactionism'. This takes as a fundamental concern the relationship between individual conduct and forms of organisation, of which the most important are social groups. This perspective explores the way in which selves emerge out of the social structure and social situations. The perspective of the *acting* person is given primary importance. It suggests that there is a link between the person and the social structure that rests on the role of symbols and common meanings. Interactionists rely on methods of analysis such as experiments and surveys (Denzin, 1971) but also, increasingly, on participant observation and ethnography.

The name of this particular line of sociological research was coined in the United States in the 1930s. Its focus is on processes of interaction. It lays particular stress on the symbolic character of social action. In contrast to the more structuralist theories examined above, symbolic interactionism sees social relations not as stabilised once and for all but as open and tied to continuing common acknowledgment (Joas, 1987).

All interactionists take everyday life as the fundamental human and sociological reality. As a result, many of these studies pay less attention to structural constraints on behaviour than do functionalists, neo-Marxists, or neo-Weberians, and have been criticised for this neglect. The focus of this form of sociology is on the 'situational' aspects of everyday life.

Although interactionism is an approach that has not been used extensively in Irish sociology, it has been used in a number of key studies in the United States and Britain. One of the classic examples in American education is Cicourel and Kitsuse's study of high-school students, which shows how student and parental orientations to higher education and future employment are defined, redefined and processed by the everyday activities of the school bureaucracy (Cicourel and Kitsuse, 1963). In Britain the work of Woods (1983), Delamont (1983) and Denscombe (1985) in the study of the internal dynamics of schools and classrooms has provided useful insights into the way pupils and teachers interact and negotiate order and discipline. There have also been attempts to combine the insights and focus provided by ethnography, now the characteristic methodology of the interactionists, and neo-Marxism in studies of primary schools (Sharp and Green, 1975) and second-level schools (Willis, 1977).

The interactionist approach in Ireland is illustrated in a study of two primary schools—one Catholic, one Protestant—carried out in Northern Ireland by Murray (1985). The role of symbols in the creation of very different identities for the children in the two types of school is very clearly documented. Unfortunately we have no comparable published research on the ethnography of schools in the Republic. Some examples of the use of the interactionist perspective are to be found in the Republic, however, although they do not necessarily make use of ethnography. O'Sullivan's work in special schools, which is a rich source of information on adolescent boys in industrial schools, is one example (O'Sullivan, 1974; 1979). Ryan's approach to the study of early school leavers is another (Ryan, 1967).

Feminist Theory and Education

Since the beginning of the 1980s there has been a remarkable growth in research and publications on the issue of the relationship between gender and education. Before this period the differential educational experiences of girls and boys were rarely problematised. Thus it was not unusual for there to be, for example, studies of the relationship between education and social mobility, such as *Origins and Destinations* (Halsey, Heath, and Ridge, 1980) or *Social Mobility in the Republic of Ireland: a Comparative Perspective* (Whelan and Whelan, 1984), that appeared on the basis of their titles to be studies of total educational cohorts but were in reality studies of males only.

There are many other examples of this from different areas of sociology and education. The relationship of gender to education was totally absent from published work in Ireland, both north and south of the border, in the 1960s and 1970s (Drudy, 1991a). The position both in Ireland and in other countries has changed since then. One of the main reasons for the change has been the development of feminist thought.

Feminist theory in sociology has developed as a critique of male theories of society and social relations, and has been directed at all sociological perspectives (see, for example, Sydie, 1987). A theory may be defined as feminist if it can be used to challenge, counteract or change a status quo that disadvantages or devalues women (Wallace, 1989; Chafetz, 1989). The creation of knowledge is a central concern to feminism, because knowledge creation means power. Thus, one of the tasks of feminist scholarship is to assert the validity of women's experience of the world and to find ways of incorporating that experience into the 'naming', or the definition, of the nature of reality (Sydie, 1987, 211).

This is not to imply that feminist theory is a unitary body of knowledge. Feminism, like most broadly based philosophical perspectives, is composed of a variety of interpretations of the social order, some closely related to the older social theories out of which they developed (Tong, 1989). Nevertheless, it has been suggested that feminist theory represents a 'paradigm shift' in social thought (Acker, 1989).

The use of the term 'paradigm' originates in the work of Kuhn (1970). For Kuhn a paradigm refers to the framework of theories and concepts within which 'normal science' is carried out. Certain works serve for a time implicitly to define the legitimate problems and methods of a research field for succeeding practitioners. While these works represent a level of achievement that is sufficiently unprecedented to attract an enduring group of adherents, they are sufficiently open-ended to leave all sorts of problems for the group of practitioners to solve. A paradigm is thus an object for further articulation and specification (ibid., 141–50).

While there are many strands within feminist theory (including radical feminism, socialist feminism, liberal feminism, and postmodernist feminism), Acker suggests that a new feminist paradigm would place women and their lives, and the question of gender roles, in a central place in understanding social relations as a whole. Such a paradigm would not only pose new questions about women and gender roles but also help to create a more complex and adequate account of industrial, capitalist society. Feminist thinking, which is about transformation and liberation, she argues, must start in ways of thinking that pose change and the elimination of oppression as central questions (Acker, 1989).

The development of this frame of reference internationally and within an Irish context has given rise to an enormous amount of research that emphasises gender as a fundamental differentiating variable in the study of education. The first major study in the Republic to focus in detail on the relationship between gender and education was *Sex Roles and Schooling* (Hannan et al., 1983). Since then there has been a considerable growth in research and publications on this issue. These studies have included those that focus on gender differences in subject choice, participation rates and achievement in Ireland (see, for example, Clancy, 1988; Clancy and Brannick, 1990; Lynch, 1991; Mahon, 1986). Studies have also focussed on the ethos of schools (Lynch, 1989a; 1989b) and on the quality of women's education, past and present (Cullen, 1987) as well as on a variety of other issues. There has also been some cross-cultural comparison of girls' education in Ireland and Switzerland (Murray, 1985; 1987). (The findings of Irish research on gender and education are presented in chapters 8 and 9.)

CONCLUSIONS

In this chapter we have examined the role of education in society, and have outlined five major sociological perspectives that have been used to interpret educational phenomena. We have argued that education plays a number of crucial roles in Irish society. It plays a significant part in socialisation and the transmission of culture. Through its assessment and certification it plays a significant part in the selection of individuals for the occupational structure and in the control of social mobility. Through a variety of structures and practices it is involved in the reproduction of the social relations of production. It is a central arena in which the ideologies of interest groups are articulated. Finally, the manner in which education systems have developed has resulted in social control becoming a key element of their role. These social roles of education place constraints on its emancipatory potential.

We outlined five principal frameworks within which education has been analysed in the sociology of education. Functionalism, for long the dominant educational paradigm in sociology and in political discourse, places the emphasis on industrialisation as the key to social and economic change. From this viewpoint it is argued that changes in the education system can be used to facilitate industrialisation and modernisation. It is also within this framework that the notion of equality of opportunity arises.

Equality is also a major concern for scholars working within a neo-Marxist framework. However, from this viewpoint capitalist society is one that is seen as fundamentally class-based and revolving around conflict over resources. In this approach it is argued that education plays a significant part in the legitimation and reproduction of class inequalities. In recent years, neo-Marxists have also examined the relationship between the reproduction of class, gender and race inequalities. Reproduction occurs through the myriad practices and organisational structures of the school and the wider education system.

The third major framework we present is the neo-Weberian one. Here too class is seen as a crucial organising feature of capitalist society, and power and domination as important explanatory concepts. However, Weber developed a theory of social action in which great emphasis is placed on intentionality and on the goals and purposes of social actors. In education this perspective leads to an evaluation of the goals and actions of interest groups in educational change.

Symbolic interactionism is a sociological perspective that leads to a focus on micro-processes within the school. It lays particular stress on the symbolic character of social action. Although not widely used in Irish sociology of education, it has nevertheless produced some valuable insights into the dynamics of schools.

Feminist theory is of recent origin but is one with great explanatory potential. A theory is feminist if it can be used to challenge or to change a situation that disadvantages or devalues women. As an emergent sociological paradigm, feminism perhaps offers a more adequate account of industrial capitalist society than theories that are male-centred. The last decade has seen a remarkable increase in the number of studies, in Ireland and throughout the world, that have focused on women's education and on sex as a differentiating educational variable.

Finally, it is only reasonable to indicate our own perspectives on education. Naturally, we have some differences of interpretation on specific issues.

However, in general our viewpoints on education and society are very close. In this book we draw on the insights provided by research from all the perspectives we have described. However, the social theories that we feel have greatest explanatory value are those that emphasise the stratified nature of society (be that by class, gender, race, or disability) and that draw attention to the goals and actions of power groups in the analysis of educational change. Nevertheless we are also acutely aware of the need to link such analysis with the study of micro-processes within the school and the classroom—an aspect of sociological research that is as yet underdeveloped in Ireland.

References and Further Reading

Acker, J. (1989), 'Making gender visible' in R. Wallace (ed.), *Feminism and Sociological Theory*, California: Sage.

Althusser, L. (1972), 'Ideology and ideological state apparatuses' in B. Cosin (ed.), *Education, Structure and Society*, Harmondsworth (Middlesex): Penguin.

Archer, M. (1984), *Social Origins of Educational Systems*, London: Sage.

Baker, J. (1987), *Arguing for Equality*, New York: Verso.

Blackledge, D., and Hunt, B. (1985), *Sociological Interpretations of Education*, London: Croom Helm.

Bourdieu, P., and Boltanski, L. (1977), 'Qualifications and jobs' in *Two Bourdieu Texts* (Occasional Papers), Birmingham: University of Birmingham (Centre for Contemporary Cultural Studies).

Bourdieu, P., and Passeron, J.-C. (1977), *Reproduction in Education, Society and Culture*, London: Sage.

Bowles, S., and Gintis, H. (1976), *Schooling in Capitalist America*, London: Routledge and Kegan Paul.

Breen, R., et al. (1990), *Understanding Contemporary Ireland*, Dublin: Gill and Macmillan.

Chafetz, J. (1989), 'Gender equality: towards a theory of change' in R. Wallace (ed.), *Feminism and Sociological Theory*, California: Sage.

Cicourel, A., and Kitsuse, J. (1963), *The Educational Decision-Makers*, New York: Bobbs-Merrill.

Clancy, P. (1982), *Participation in Higher Education: a National Survey*, Dublin: Higher Education Authority.

Clancy, P. (1985), 'Symposium on "Equality of Opportunity in Irish Schools": editorial introduction', *Economic and Social Review*, vol. 16, no. 2, 77–82.

Clancy, P. (1988), *Who Goes to College?: a Second National Survey of Participation in Higher Education*, Dublin: Higher Education Authority.

Clancy, P., and Brannick, T. (1990), 'Subject specialisation at second level and third level field of study: some gender differences', *Irish Educational Studies*, vol. 9, 158–73.

Clancy, P., et al (eds.) (1986), *Ireland: a Sociological Profile*, Dublin: Institute of Public Administration.

Collins, R. (1977), 'Some comparative principles of educational stratification', *Harvard Educational Review*, vol. 47, no. 1.

Craft, M. (ed.) (1970), *Family, Class and Education*, London: Longman.

Cullen, M. (ed.) (1987), *Girls Don't Do Honours: Irish Women in Education in the 19th and 20th Centuries*, Dublin: Women's Education Bureau.

Davis, K., and Moore, W. (1945), 'Some principles of stratification', *American Sociological Review*, vol. 10, 242–9.

Delamont, S. (1983), *Interaction in the Classroom*, London: Methuen.

Denscombe, M. (1985), *Classroom Control: a Sociological Perspective*, London: Allen and Unwin.

Denzin, N. (1971), 'Symbolic interactionism and ethnomethodology' in J. Douglas (ed.), *Understanding Everyday Life*, London: Routledge and Kegan Paul.

Department of Education (1966), *Investment in Education*, Dublin: Stationery Office.

Department of Education (1992), *Education for a Changing World: Green Paper on Education*, Dublin: Stationery Office.

Dewey, J. (1963), *Experience and Education*, London: Collier-Macmillan.

Drudy, S. (1991a), 'Developments in the sociology of education in Ireland, 1966–1991', *Irish Journal of Sociology*, vol.1, 107–27.

Drudy, S. (1991b), 'The Classification of Social Class in Sociological Research', *British Journal of Sociology*, vol. 4, no. 2, 24–41.

Floud, J., Halsey, A., and Martin, F. (1956), *Social Class and Educational Opportunity*, London: Heinemann.

Freire, P. (1972), *Cultural Action for Freedom*, Harmondsworth (Middlesex): Penguin.

Freire, P. (1972), *The Pedagogy of the Oppressed*, Harmondsworth (Middlesex): Penguin.

Giddens, A. (1973), *The Class Structure of the Advanced Societies*, London: Hutchinson.

Giroux, H. (1983), *Theory and Resistance in Education: a Pedagogy of Opposition*, London: Heinemann.

Greaney, V., and Kellaghan, T. (1984), *Equality of Opportunity in Irish Schools*, Dublin: Educational Company.

Greaney, V., and Kellaghan, T. (1985), 'Factors related to level of educational attainment in Ireland', *Economic and Social Review*, vol. 16, no. 2, 141–56.

Halsey, A., Floud, J., and Anderson, C. (eds.) (1961), *Education, Economy and Society*, New York: Free Press of Glencoe.

Halsey, A., Heath, A., and Ridge, J. (1980), *Origins and Destinations*, Oxford: Clarendon Press.

Hannan, D., et al. (1983), *Schooling and Sex Roles: Sex Differences in Subject Provision and Student Choice in Irish Post-Primary Schools*, Dublin: Economic and Social Research Institute.

Joas, H. (1987), 'Symbolic interactionism' in A. Giddens and J. Turner (eds.), *Social Theory Today*, Cambridge: Polity.

Kuhn, T. (1970), *The Structure of Scientific Revolutions*, Chicago: University of Chicago Press.

Lewis, J. (1975), *Max Weber and Value-Free Sociology: a Marxist Critique*, London: Lawrence and Wishart.

Lipset, S., and Bendix, R. (1959), *Social Mobility in Industrial Societies*, Berkeley: University of California Press.

Lukes, S. (1973), *Émile Durkheim: His Life and Work*, London: Allen Lane.

Lynch, K. (1985), 'An analysis of some presuppositions underlying the concepts of meritocracy and ability as presented in Greaney and Kellaghan's study', *Economic and Social Review*, vol. 16, no. 2, 83–102.

Lynch, K. (1988b), 'Reproduction in education: an elaboration of current neo-Marxist models of analysis', *British Journal of Sociology of Education*, vol. 9, no. 2, 151–68.

Lynch, K. (1989a), *The Hidden Curriculum*, Lewes: Falmer.

Lynch, K. (1988b), 'The ethos of girls' schools: an analysis of differences between male and female schools', *Social Studies*, vol.10, 11–31.

Lynch, K. (1991), 'Women and education in the Republic of Ireland' in M. Wilson (ed.), *Girls and Education: a European Perspective*, Oxford: Pergamon.

Lynch, K. (1992a), 'Education and the paid labour market', *Irish Educational Studies*, vol. 11, 13–33.

Lynch, K. (1992b), 'Equality of educational opportunity: what does it mean?' (proceedings of the annual conference of the Physical Education Association of Ireland, 2–4 October 1992).

Mahon, E. (1986), 'Gender and education', *Social Studies*, vol. 9, 69–77.

Marshall, T. (1971), 'Social selection in the welfare state' in E. Hopper (ed.), *Readings in the Theory of Educational Systems*, London: Hutchinson.

Miliband, R. (1973), *The State in Capitalist Society*, London: Quartet.

Murray, B. (1985), *Sex Differences in Education: a Comparative Study of Ireland and Switzerland*, Bern and New York: Peterlang.

Murray, B. (1987), 'Education of girls in two European societies: a comparison' (paper presented at the Third International Interdisciplinary Congress on Women, Dublin, 1987).

Murray, D. (1985), *Worlds Apart: Segregated Education in Northern Ireland*, Belfast: Appletree.

Ó Súilleabháin, S. (1986), 'Towards our professional identity' in P. Hogan (ed.), *Willingly to School?: Perspectives on Teaching as a Profession in Ireland in the Eighties*, Dublin: Educational Studies Association of Ireland.

O'Sullivan, D. (1974), 'Pre-existing acquaintance and friendship among industrial school boys', *Social Studies*, vol. 3, no. 1, 14–24.

O'Sullivan, D. (1979), 'Case study in an Irish industrial school', *Social Studies*, vol. 6, no. 3, 265–313.

Organisation for Economic Co-operation and Development, (1991), *Reviews of National Policies for Education—Ireland*, Paris: OECD.

Parsons, T. (1952), *The Social System*, London: Tavistock.

Parsons, T. (1961), 'The school class as a social system: some of its functions in American society' in A. Halsey, J. Floud, and C. Anderson (eds.), *Education, Economy and Society*, New York: Free Press of Glencoe.

Poulantzas, N. (1978), *Classes in Contemporary Capitalism*, London: Verso.

Raftery, A., and Hout, M. (1985), 'Does Irish education approach the meritocratic ideal?: a logistic analysis', *Economic and Social Review*, vol. 16, no. 2, 115–40.

Rottman, D., et al. (1982), *The Distribution of Income in Ireland: a Study in Social Class and Family Cycle Inequalities*, Dublin: Economic and Social Research Institute.

Ryan, L. (1967), 'Social dynamite: a study of early school leavers', *Christus Rex*, vol. 21, no. 1, 7–44.

Sharp, R., and Green, A. (1975), *Education and Social Control*, London: Routledge and Kegan Paul.

Silver, H. (1973), *Equal Opportunity in Education*, London: Methuen.

Sweeny, S. (1992), 'In search of total quality: leadership in Irish post-primary schools, *Irish Education Decision Maker*, no. 5.

Sydie, R. (1987), *Natural Women, Cultured Men: a Feminist Perspective on Sociological Theory*, Milton Keynes: Open University Press.

Tong, R. (1989), *Feminist Thought: a Comprehensive Introduction*, London: Unwin Hyman.

Tussing, A. (1978), *Irish Educational Expenditure: Past, Present and Future*, Dublin: Economic and Social Research Institute.

Tussing, A. (1981), 'Accountability, rationalisation and the White Paper on educational development', *Journal of the Statistical and Social Inquiry Society of Ireland*, vol. 24, no. 3, 71–83.

Wallace, R. (1989), 'Introduction' in R. Wallace (ed.), *Feminism and Sociological Theory*, California: Sage.

Weber, M. (1968), *Economy and Society—vol. 1*, New York: Bedminster.

Westergaard, J., and Resler, H. (1976), *Class in a Capitalist Society*, Harmondsworth (Middlesex): Pelican.

Whelan, C., and Whelan, B. (1984), *Social Mobility in Ireland: a Comparative Perspective*, Dublin: Economic and Social Research Institute.

Whelan, C., and Whelan, B. (1985), '"Equality of Opportunity in Irish Schools": a reassessment', *Economic and Social Review,* vol. 16, no. 2, 103–14.

Whyte, J. (1980), *Church and State in Modern Ireland*, Dublin: Gill and Macmillan.

Wickham, J. (1986), 'Industrialisation, work and unemployment' in P. Clancy et al. (eds.), *Ireland: a Sociological Profile*, Dublin: Institute of Public Administration.

Willis, P. (1977), *Learning to Labour*, London: Saxon House.

Woods, P. (1983), *Sociology and the School: an Interactionist Viewpoint*, London: Routledge and Kegan Paul.

Young, M. (1961), *The Rise of the Meritocracy, 1870–2033*, London: Pelican.

3

Paradigms and Perspectives in Irish Education

In his review of the ideational basis of Irish educational policy, O'Sullivan (1989) claims that there has never been an open debate in Ireland about the merits and demerits of different paradigmatic perspectives on education. (See chapter 2 for a definition of 'paradigms'.) Irish educational thinking, he says, is fundamentally atheoretical (ibid., 265). In the arena of public political debate on education, 'slogans replace principles in that slogans provide a moral loading but they differ from principles because they are not derived from a social theory or vision . . .' Slogans are grounded in appeals of a high moral loading 'which are considered self evident, beyond dispute and not demanding justification to anyone educationally, economically or socially alert' (ibid.). Examples of slogans abound, including such well-worn phrases as 'the development of pupils' full potential,' 'equality of educational opportunity,' 'cherishing all the children of the nation equally,' and 'child-centred primary education.' Such slogans are regularly used by policy-makers and politicians when they are called on to rationalise the working or effectiveness of the system. The theoretical premises on which they are based are never articulated in the policy arena, and indeed often not even in academia itself.

The purpose of this chapter is to present an analysis of some of the major paradigmatic assumptions of academic educationalists in the Republic of Ireland from the late 1950s to the present day and to update and extend an earlier analysis on this subject (Lynch, 1987). During the last thirty years, educationalists have been both more numerous and more prolific than hitherto (Coolahan, 1984). A review of their background assumptions is therefore timely.

An analysis of the writings of sociologists in education in Ireland has already been undertaken (Drudy, 1991). This has shown how, from 1966 to 1991, the dominant theoretical approach, both North and South, more often unarticulated than acknowledged, has been a consensual one, based on structural-functional presuppositions and problematics (ibid., 110–11). Most sociological research on education has adopted an empirical (in the statistical sense) approach to the analysis of issues and problems, with theoretical debates being of secondary importance. The atheoretical approach is not confined to sociology (where it is the type of research to which most funding is given) but also characterises the work of historians and economists. And it is the latter who have had most influence in the analysis of many areas of public policy (ibid., 109).

The absence of paradigmatic debates does not mean that Irish educationalists do not work within definite paradigmatic assumptions (Lynch, 1989a). However, these assumptions often exist at the level of deep structure; they remain intellectually 'underground'. Also implicit in the dominant, albeit unarticulated, assumptions of educational intellectuals are a number of value assumptions and beliefs about the nature of the social order and the relationship of the individual to that order.

Before we outline the major themes to be addressed in this chapter, it is necessary to make some comment on the methodology adopted. The analysis of theoretical assumptions presented here is based on documentary analysis of a variety of texts and papers. This involved the content analysis of a selection of Irish educational journals, books and articles published by Irish authors, and major Government-funded reports and documents on education. As it is not possible to comment on every single book or article in detail, we will focus on research and discourse pertaining to second-level education.

Analysing the paradigmatic assumptions of educationalists through their published works has its limitations. Because of heavy teaching commitments, many academic educationalists do not publish widely. Furthermore, as Nettl observes, only ideas that have gained a certain social acceptability get published (1969, 59). Hence, intellectual assumptions and ideologies may be far wider than those that find their way into print. The fact that certain ideas do find their way into print, however, does inform us about which paradigms dominate educational discourses in the public spheres of the written word.

Dominant Ideologies in Educational Discourse

Through the analysis of the works of Irish educationalists we have identified three of the most prominent ideological standpoints in the literature. The first of these involves a particular conception of society itself (consensualism), the second a particular conception of the individual (essentialism), and the third a particular conception of the relationship of the individual to society (meritocratic individualism). As we shall see later, both essentialism and meritocratic individualism are common assumptions among educationalists internationally. Consensualism is, however, a much more distinctively Irish phenomenon. These are, however, by no means the only ideological assumptions underpinning education (Lynch, 1992).

CONSENSUALISM IN EDUCATIONAL THOUGHT

Liam O'Dowd has observed that 'most Irish intellectuals, until recently at least, seem to take a communal/national rather than an explicitly class view of social order' (1985, 6). Indeed, he suggests that they have not traditionally existed as 'an "independent" group adopting a critical or dissenting role in periods of rapid social change.' Rather, they have generally been 'identified with particular interests, usually those of the upper classes to which they often belong' (1985, 6). O'Dowd's comments here refer of course to the entire intelligentsia, not specifically to educationalists. However, there is evidence to suggest that educationalists also adopt what we would call a 'consensual understanding of the social order' in their work. As for the class position of educational intellectuals, we shall reserve comment on this issue until the later part of the chapter.

When we suggest that educationalists have adopted a consensual view of the social order, what does this mean? It means that society is represented as an undifferentiated whole. It is assumed that there is agreement within all sectors of that whole on what is the 'public interest' or 'collective interest' in education. This does not suggest that educationalists do not use concepts such as social class or gender, at least occasionally, in their analysis, although it must be said that there is very little reference to gender divisions in society in most of the literature until recent times, and virtually none to race or disability. When issues of class (especially) or gender are raised they are not analysed as generative forces of action. Conflicting class, gender or other interests are not represented as potent forces determining the direction of the education system. Rather, social class, gender or religion, for example, are defined as attributes of individuals. This is the practice that Bourdieu termed 'substantialist atomism'. It treats social class, gender, race etc. as attributes of individuals but without due regard for 'the structure of relations whence these elements derive all their sociologically relevant determinations.' It fails to address the

> mechanisms which tend to ensure the reproduction of the structure of relations between classes [and, one might add, between the sexes, racial groups, etc.]. It is unaware that the controlled mobility of a limited category of individuals, carefully selected and modified by and for individual ascent, is not incompatible with the permanence of structures, and that it is even capable of contributing to social stability in the only way conceivable in societies based upon democratic ideals and thereby may help to perpetuate the structure of this [and other unequal] relations. (Bourdieu, 1977, 487)

CONSENSUS VIEWS IN OFFICIAL DOCUMENTS AND GOVERNMENT-FUNDED REPORTS

There are two types of published work in which one finds the consensualist ideology in evidence: in Government reports and discussion documents, and in the published writings of academics. We will begin by commenting on the former. We will address the analysis to three different types of Government document, as each represents a different form of consensualism.

Firstly, one finds the consensualist ideology to be implicit in prescriptive documents such as the *Teacher's Handbook,* part 1, for the new primary school curriculum. In its outline of the aims of primary education, for example, it states:

> The scale of values in a society inevitably determines its educational aims and priorities. We in Ireland have our own scale of values.
> Each human being is created in God's image. He has a life to lead and a soul to be saved. Education is therefore concerned, not only with life but with the purpose of life. (p. 12)

What this statement presupposes is that there is universal agreement in Ireland about the 'scale of values' that should direct the educational process. There is no recognition of the fact that several groups do not share the religious assumptions expressed in this statement.

The consensus view evident in the essentially prescriptive *Teacher's Handbook* is distinctive from the form of consensualism evident in analytical documents such as *Investment in Education* (1965). It is in the authors' use of concepts that their consensualism becomes evident in the latter. In their analysis of participation rates, the authors of *Investment in Education* certainly recognise that Ireland is far from being an equal place. However, they do not interpret regional or social differences in rates of participation as either injustices or inequalities. Indeed, they do not even use the term 'social class' in their analysis at all. Thus regional conflicts and class conflicts become subsumed under the neutral terminology of 'social groups' and 'social differences' (ibid., 148–76). Such neutral terminology has the effect of desensitising us to inequalities, as it fails to link the phenomena in question to the structural relationships of power and wealth that generate their development in the first place.

Partners in Education: Serving Community Needs (1985) represents another type of official document that employs consensus language, namely, a Government discussion document. The title, for example, refers to 'community'. This word is also used within the text (p. 9), but there is no attempt to define what is meant by the term. From the context in which it is used it could be surmised that 'community' refers to a territorial or geographical entity. Such an assumption ignores the growing body of social science research that shows that 'community' is an increasingly redundant concept when used to signify locality-based neighbourliness. This is especially the case in urban areas, including urban Ireland (McKeown, 1985). The term 'community' seems to be used therefore for rhetorical purposes: to help create a climate of consent rather than to represent what is actually the case.

Both reports on the primary education system published in 1990 (the report of the Review Body on the Primary Curriculum and the report of the Primary Education Review Body) are also written in a consensus mode. This is no doubt related to the fact that these documents are 'compromise' publications: they reflect the accommodation reached among the various corporate interests in education (churches, parents, teachers, Department of Education) on the issues involved. While neither the OECD report (1991) nor the Green Paper (Department of Education, 1992) display the same type of consensus as the previous two documents, they are nonetheless broadly consensual in many of their suppositions. For example, both of them, in different ways, extol the virtues of technological education (OECD, 1991, 69); and the Green Paper uses the present tense to suggest that education for an 'enterprise culture' is essential because we live in one (Department of Education, 1992, 11, 85). What is evident here is what we noted above about *Partners in Education*: there is an attempt to create a climate of consensus through the use of consensus language. A further example of this practice in the Green Paper is the claim that

> in the business world there is wide recognition that many Irish young
>   people lack:
> The range of technical skills needed in today's industry;
> The communication and other interpersonal skills sought by employers;
> The critical thinking, problem solving ability and individual initiative
>   that an enterprise culture requires;
> The language skills to work and win markets across the EC, and to
>   take part in tourism-related activities. (Department of Education,
>   1992, 11)

However, there is no empirical evidence cited in support of this view (although empirical evidence is cited selectively in the text to substantiate other arguments). Part of the problem is undoubtedly the fact that there is no empirical evidence that there is a skills shortage in Irish industry (FÁS, 1991). At least one leading industrialist has claimed that there is not 'wide recognition' in the business world that school leavers lack all the skills listed above. Furthermore, he observes that the schools cannot teach enterprise, as their fundamental remit is education and not enterprise (Teeling, 1992). So the language of consensus appears to be used at times to create a climate of consent.

In all the reports of the 1990s cited above there is one other example of consensus language, and that is the use of the structurally detached term 'disadvantage' to denote social class inequalities in education. This is a very interesting phenomenon, if only because the practice is so widespread in education generally. The teachers' unions have also tended to use the term 'disadvantage' as a synonym for social class inequality (Dowling, 1992). The language of disadvantage has its origins in the cultural deprivation theory of the 1960s (Flude and Ahier, 1974). In this framework, working-class underachievement in education is attributed to inadequacies in working-class culture itself: the victim is blamed for his or her own failure. (See chapter 7 for a further discussion.) By using a phrase such as 'disadvantage' one is, as noted above, abstracting the discussion about social class from the structural forces that generated it in the first place. The problem is defined, at best, as one of unequal opportunity in a meritocratic society; the language of disadvantage creates a semantic context in which it is impossible to analyse social class inequality in terms of structurally determined disadvantage, which no liberal equal opportunities policies will resolve.

CONSENSUALISM AMONG 'INDEPENDENT ACADEMICS'

Consensus ideology is not confined, however, to Government reports, discussion documents, or policy guidelines. It is also evident, though in a more latent form, within the writings of academics in various research and teaching positions. One finds it in all types of analysis, including those in the curriculum, historical and empirical fields. A brief review of some of the major works in these areas will demonstrate the point.

Mulcahy's work *Curriculum and Policy in Irish Post-Primary Education* (1981) is a case in point. This book provides a valuable analysis of second-level curriculum policy, combined with a series of proposals for change. The author is critical of the lack of attention given to aims and objectives in education, and proceeds from this to identify four major 'demands of living' that he suggests should provide the focus for the second-level curriculum (chapters 3 and 6). Mulcahy does not address the fact, however, that the 'demands of living' (vocational, recreational, philosophical, and practical) in a highly stratified society such as Ireland are by no means identical for all classes and both sexes. His consensual understanding of society is epitomised in the following paragraph, introducing us to a discussion on the 'demands of living':

> One way of viewing the demands of living is to see them as being social . . . in origin. Thus one can say that society demands of us that we abide by its customs and mores and that we play our parts in promoting and sustaining its well being. To meet these demands normally calls on one to engage in some socially productive activities and to adopt certain attitudes and skills in interpersonal behaviour. For, in important respects man [*sic*] is a social being, and the adoption of a socially acceptable life-style is necessary for his own survival and for the survival and continuity of society. (Mulcahy, 1981, 82)

Neither here nor elsewhere does Mulcahy refer to the fact that schools are agencies of social selection and allocation as well as agencies of socialisation.

Consequently his work does not address the ways in which educational 'aims' in a stratified society are closely interwoven with the social class, gender and other hierarchies of the given system.

Crooks and McKernan (1984) do not employ the concepts of class and gender in their analysis of curriculum either. Undoubtedly one could argue that class and gender differences in curriculum change were not the central focus of their analysis—any more than they were in Mulcahy's work. Therefore, the authors should not be expected to use these concepts in their discourses. While this argument has legitimacy with respect to the overall theme of *The Challenge of Change,* it is less tenable when one examines particular discussions within it. In chapter 5, for example, participation rates and class group allocation are both discussed without reference to gender or social class. Yet at the time, work by Clancy (1982), Rottman et al. (1982) and Hannan et al. (1983) all showed that class and gender are major determinants of both.

An important empirical work published in the 1980s was Greaney and Kellaghan's *Equality of Opportunity in Irish Schools* (1984). In so far as the study identifies gender, class and 'ability' as major independent variables in their analysis, one cannot say that it ignores the stratified nature of society. However, recognising differences does not amount to identifying conflicts of interest as central dynamics of society. Greaney and Kellaghan's work is very much within the tradition of abstracted empiricism—what Karabel and Halsey (1977, 1–85) term 'methodological empiricism'. It presents statistical evidence as 'fact', without identifying the conceptual frameworks of analysis that inevitably inform the interpretation.

The absence of a theoretical perspective, no matter what its orientation, has two consequences. Firstly, explanation of the interrelationships between the phenomena in question is confined to what is immediately observable. Secondly, in the absence of theory, statistical (or indeed any) evidence assumes an unwarranted objectivity: the implicit assumptions of the authors, incorporated in their statistical interpretations, remain unarticulated.

A number of works have been published subsequently that challenge the validity of Greaney and Kellaghan's methodology, conceptual frameworks, and findings—notably the work of Whelan and Whelan (1984) and the analyses of Lynch (1985) and Raftery and Hout (1985). Greaney and Kellaghan (1985) in turn have replied to these. The critiques mentioned above and the work of Wickham (1980), Clancy (1982; 1988), Lynch (1989a) and Breen et al. (1990) all represent a departure from the consensus model in education to various degrees (Drudy, 1991, 112). The work of Hannan, Breen and Whelan challenged the consensus mode through use of a Weberian framework, for example, while Wickham and Lynch rely more heavily on neo-Marxist theory. These authors signify an emerging shift, therefore, towards a conflict model of analysis in the area of empirical research—especially in sociological research on education. Emergent, however, is what the conflict perspective remains in education (O'Sullivan, 1989).

In summary, therefore, what we are suggesting is that Irish educationalists have tended to adopt a consensual view of the social order in their analyses of educational events. By representing society in this symbolically consensus form they have forestalled the development of a critical structural analysis of the education system.

IMPLICATIONS OF CONSENSUALISM

The consensus mode of analysis also has implications for our understanding of the individual in education. The predominance of the consensualist tradition has meant that neither indigenous nor imported conceptions of the individual have been subjected to much critical scrutiny. In particular, it is suggested here that consensualist thinking has predisposed educationalists towards an essentialist view of the individual—that is to say, it has predisposed them to define the individual as having a given and fixed nature, which in turn predetermined his or her educational needs. By defining society in consensual terms, educational-ists had to look to the individual to explain social variability. Differences in the educational context (differences in attainment especially) could not be explained by reference to structural conflict or forces, as structural conflicts were not assumed to exist in the consensual view. Consequently, differences have had to be accounted for in terms of the essential or given nature of the individual.

We are not suggesting that the essentialist view is unique to Ireland—unlike consensualism, essentialism is an international phenomenon. Educationalists as diverse as Jackson (1968), Bourdieu (1974) and Bidwell (1980) have all noted the tendency in educational research generally to explain differences in school attainment in terms of individual rather than structural attributes. White has observed also that individual development in education has been popularly defined in terms of allowing 'the pupils' inner capacities to develop to their fullest extent' (1980, 177). What makes Ireland unique is that consensualism has forestalled any critique of essentialism or indeed of meritocracy. While a vast array of literature has been published internationally challenging the essentialist view of the individual—especially as expressed in IQ theory—no such tradition exists in Ireland.

THE ESSENTIALIST VIEW OF THE INDIVIDUAL IN EDUCATION

The most pervasive understanding of the individual that one finds in Irish education is one that defines the person in terms of fixed or given (sometimes innate) talents, abilities, or intelligence. Indeed, talent or intelligence are fre-quently defined in purely intellectual terms. One of the first writers in recent history who clearly subscribed to the primacy of intellectual ability was

Ó Catháin. We see evidence of his essentialism and intellectualism in the series of articles he published in *Studies* from 1951 to 1956. In these he proclaimed the view that the development of what he termed God-given gifts—especially intellectual ones—was the primary aim of secondary education. Writing in 1955, for example, he stated that the aim of secondary education was to prepare the pupil 'to lead the full life, to make the most complete use possible, in the way meant by God, of the gifts he has received from God' (p. 393). While he regarded the development of the intellect, the will and the emotions as all within the educational ambit, he attached primary importance to the intellect. In his 1956 article he set out 'the formal aim of the classroom work' as being 'to inculcate intellectual excellence because the use a man makes of his intellect determines, in the natural order, how he will act, how he chooses and decides between alternatives that may present themselves' (p. 50).

ESSENTIALISM IN GOVERNMENT-FUNDED REPORTS AND OFFICIAL DOCUMENTS

Ó Catháin's essentialist view of ability was by no means confined to himself in the late 1950s and early 1960s. The Council of Education report (1960) was a collective publication, and it also reflected this tradition. In the context of a discussion on the organisation of the pass and honours syllabuses for the Inter-mediate Certificate, the authors identify three types of student: 'the slow, the average and the really bright' (p. 108). Later, in their dismissal of the ideal of 'free secondary education for all' as 'untenable', the writers also appeal to the notion of limited talents to justify their claim. They suggest that the notion of 'secondary education for all' should only apply to those 'able and willing to profit by it.' They claim that 'only a minority of pupils would be capable of profiting by secondary (grammar school) education' (p. 252).

The opening pages of the *Teacher's Handbook* (1971) for the new primary curriculum show that official thinking on 'ability' was still fairly essentialist ten years after the Council of Education report. The handbook opens by recog-nising the importance of environment in determining the pupil's development. It also asserts, however, that the child is born with 'the stamp of his heredity', and that the curriculum must be designed to take account of the fact that children vary widely in their 'natural endowment' (p. 12, 14). Later on in the introduction to the handbook the influence of Piagetan essentialism is what comes directly to the fore. The authors endorse the claim that there are definite 'stages' in the child's development, suggesting, of course, that the sequence and not the rate of progress is what is fixed. Factors such as social and cultural background as well as natural endowment are then identified as the major factors affecting 'the individual's rate of progress' (p. 18, 19).

In the 1970s two major reports pertaining to second-level education were published: the report by Madaus and Macnamara on *Public Examinations* in

1970, and the *Intermediate Certificate Examination Report,* published in 1975. As their titles imply, these reports were primarily concerned with the pragmatics of school assessment. There is therefore little reference to the theory of education. Despite this, there are indications that the authors of both subscribe to the notions of individual ability that are the by-products of essentialism, if not its pure representation (cf. Kleinig, 1982, for a discussion of this distinction). For example, the authors of *Public Examinations* imply that students who enter the teacher training colleges must be 'bright', as they have obtained high grades in the Leaving Certificate examination (Madaus and Macnamara, 1970, 109). In the report on the Intermediate Certificate it is suggested that many pupils are not suitable candidates for the Intermediate Certificate (now Junior Certificate) examination. Responsibility for their difficulties, however, is not located in the school or in social structures but in the character of individual pupils: pupils' differing interests, aspirations *and* abilities are documented as the major cause of their difficulties (Department of Education, 1975, 31).

The year 1980 saw the publication of another publicly funded report on second-level public examinations, *The Public Examinations Evaluation Project.* The authors here (Heywood, McGuinness, and Murphy) are explicit in their expression of the view that the individual's 'intelligence' (IQ) is a major determinant of his or her educational success and that individuals can be ranked in terms of the amount of intelligence they possess. In the context of a discussion on the content validity of tests and subtests they claim that 'among fifteen year olds it might be expected that the level of general intelligence would make a substantial contribution to performance in school work and examinations in which case those with high intelligence quotients would do well across the range of subtests while those with low intelligence quotients would do badly' (Heywood, McGuinness, and Murphy, 1980, 29).

From the evidence both of official Government documents and Government-funded reports, therefore, we can see that a highly essentialist understanding of individual ability has underpinned public thinking in the last twenty-five to thirty years. It is assumed that individuals are characterised by the possession of a quantifiable entity called 'intelligence'. 'Intelligence' or ability is generally interpreted as a 'given' entity, something that remains fixed through time. Indeed, some official documents clearly state that differences are due to innate factors.

ESSENTIALISM AND ACADEMICS

Much of the work of the Educational Research Centre has been concerned with the development of standardised tests and the assessment of their impact on teachers and pupils in recent years. Given the nature of such tests, it is not surprising to find that the 'educational' individual is defined in terms of measurable linguistic and logical-mathematical capabilities. The equation of 'ability' with verbal reasoning ability is also evident in an article by Kellaghan and Newman in 1971. 'Giftedness' is in fact equated with scoring within the top 10 per cent on the Drumcondra Verbal Reasoning Test. The authors suggest that while some investigators 'might not regard all such children as 'gifted' . . . since they are well above average in verbal ability, they may be regarded as academically talented and they obviously contain valuable intellectual resources for their society' (Kellaghan and Newman, 1971, 5). There is no reference to the multiple forms intelligence can take. (See chapter 11 of the present book.)

Greaney and Kellaghan also equate 'high ability' with intellectual-type ability. A score of 108 or more on the Drumcondra Verbal Reasoning Test was taken as a cut-off point for distinguishing the 'more able' students from the 'less able' in that study (Greaney and Kellaghan, 1984, chapter 9).

It is not, however, the equation of 'ability' or 'intelligence' with intellectual capacities that proves that one adheres to the essentialist position. It is rather an allegiance to the view that ability is fixed and measurable. One sees such allegiance in *Equality of Opportunity in Irish Schools* (1984). Although the authors of this work do not comment on the stability of verbal reasoning ability (VRA)— their measure of ability in this study—over time certain features of the work indicate that they regard VRA as a relatively fixed entity (Lynch, 1985, 92).

In reply to criticisms of their study, Greaney and Kellaghan did not deny that they held an essentialist-type view of mental 'ability'. They merely stated that they had 'epistemological problems' with terms such as 'essentialism' (Greaney and Kellaghan, 1985, 144). However, O'Sullivan (1989, 247) points out that other work undertaken by Kellaghan et al. has adopted an environmentalist approach to ability; the most obvious example is the Rutland Street Project for 'disadvantaged' children (Kellaghan, 1977). This project was based on the assumption that 'measured intelligence could be augmented using well planned educational and social strategies' (ibid.). While O'Sullivan is correct on this point, the fact remains that intelligence was defined according to narrow cognitive criteria.

A variety of other educationalists also subscribe to essentialist views of human ability. Swan (1978) has attributed considerable importance to the 'individual's genetic endowment' in determining his or her ability to read. Indeed he suggested that 'general intelligence' is perhaps more important than 'any other single factor' in determining 'reading standards' (Swan, 1978, 67). Thus it is implied— in the context of this discussion on the determinants of reading standards—that intelligence is itself a product of genetic endowment. Swan also uses evaluative and essentialist terms such as 'bright' and 'dull' to categorise pupils in his analysis (ibid., 6, 15). As in Kellaghan's work, it is assumed that abilities of the abstract-reasoning type constitute the essence of intelligence (ibid., 14–16).

So far most of the authors whose works we have reviewed are educational psychologists. The essentialist perspective, however, is by no means confined to them. With the exception of some work by Bell (1978)—in which he questions the essentialism of child-centred pedagogy—sociologists do not seem to regard the prevailing definitions of intelligence or ability as problematic either. In their re-analysis of Kellaghan and Greaney's work, for example, neither Whelan and Whelan (1985) nor Raftery and Hout (1985) make any reference to the narrow essentialist definition of ability contained in the study.

Finally, two articles published in the *Irish Journal of Education* show—albeit in very different ways—the extent to which essentialist views of human ability are pervasive in Ireland. In one article Cyril Burt proclaims his hered-itarian views of intelligence with full force (Burt, 1969, 75–94). Not only was Burt given a platform to popularise his views but (as far as we can discern from Irish educational literature) these views went unchallenged. Certainly they were never subsequently challenged in the *Irish Journal of Education* itself. Secondly, in an article published in 1983, Fontes et al. show that Irish primary teachers are more likely than their American colleagues to believe that innate factors have an important role to play in determining one's intelligence. Furthermore, comparing the attitudes of American and Irish adults in general they found the Americans (including teachers) to be 'more environmentalist, interventionist and egalitarian' (Fontes et al., 1983, 56, 65).

In summary, therefore, what we suggest is that the conception of the individual that predominates among Irish educationalists is basically an essen-tialist one. The individual is defined primarily in terms of the 'amount' of 'intellectual ability' or 'intelligence' he or she is deemed to possess. This has a number of implications. Firstly, because 'intelligence' is equated with logical-mathematical and linguistic ability, schools in effect either demean or dis-qualify other forms of human intelligence (Gardner, 1983). That is to say, schools are the principal institutions in our society for transmitting, credential-ising and thereby publicly legitimating cultural forms. The cultural practices that schools certify become part of the public sociocultural agenda; those that they do not certify become marginal. Because schools (and by schools we mean here all educational institutions) only partly credentialise the intelligence required in manual and related forms of labour (i.e. bodily kinesthetic intel-ligence), and because they do not credentialise the personal intelligence required in love labour (i.e. the labour required to reproduce caring relation-ships *per se*), these latter cultural forms become devalued and marginalised. (See chapter 11 for further discussion of this, and see Lynch (1989b) on love labour.)

Secondly, by defining the individual in terms of 'given' talents, educational-ists (including teachers) are predisposed to regard educational development as having definite limits with certain kinds of people. After all, if the individual's ability is judged fixed by a given age, then it is very likely that teachers will set limits to what they will subsequently expect him or her to attain educationally.

Related to this is the issue of social class. On most, if not all, standardised tests purporting to measure mental ability, working-class pupils tend to score lower than middle-class pupils (the Drumcondra Verbal Reasoning Test is a case in point). Thus, there is a particular danger that the failure of working-class children in school will be attributed to their lack of so-called 'intelligence' or 'ability' and thereby be seen as inevitable and/or justified. As Lawler (1978), Gould (1981) and others have shown, however, tests of mental ability are themselves biased in social class terms. They are not valid measures, therefore, of pupils' abilities. The relatively low scores of working-class pupils on standardised tests and their higher rates of educational failure are the products of a variety of cultural, political and social forces that, we suggest, have little or nothing to do with individual differences in 'fixed mental abilities'. Essentialism as expressed in the fixed ability thesis, therefore, merely provides an ideological façade behind which policy-makers and even practitioners can hide when they wish to avoid public accountability.

MERITOCRATIC INDIVIDUALISM

The third ideology we comment on—albeit more briefly than on the others—is that of meritocratic individualism. The meritocratic ideology is a way of conceiving the individual's relationship to society. (It is of course by no means exclusive to Irish educationalists, although, as with essentialism, it has not been subjected to analytical critique here, unlike elsewhere. See Bowles and Gintis, 1976, for an elaborate critique.) It suggests that those individuals who have talent and who make the effort deserve to be rewarded in society, in other words that IQ + effort = merit (Young, 1961). It is based on the premise that social rewards are and should be given on the basis of achieved rather than ascribed criteria. In many respects the meritocratic ideology represents an extended form of essentialism. Not only do its adherents suppose that talent can be measured accurately but they go on from there to claim that those with measured talents should be rewarded highly.

We referred above to the ideology emanating from the meritocratic perspective as individualist, and this is something that it is also necessary to comment on. It means that the individual is defined within the meritocratic perspective in asocial terms—that the individual is defined as relating to society *qua* individual. He or she is not seen as a structurally located relational being whose educational choices, therefore, are highly contingent on their structural location. Rather, the equation 'IQ + effort = merit' supposes that any individual can succeed as well as the next provided that he or she makes the effort and has the talent. Success is, as it were, entirely a function of individual attributes and effort. As we well know from educational research, however, this is far from being the case. Social class, gender, disability and race are major determinants of the level and/or kind of educational credentials any given individual is likely to attain.

MERITOCRACY AND GOVERNMENT-FUNDED REPORTS AND DOCUMENTS
Because allegiance to the meritocratic ideal is so pervasive in educational discourse, it is rather arbitrary to identify it with any group or individual. The works identified here, therefore, are the representatives of a tradition, not its sole bearers. Secondly, espousal of meritocratic principles does not often come in Ireland in simple meritocratic language. Rather it is represented frequently as the underlying procedure for equalising educational opportunities. Greaney and Kellaghan show this to be the case, for example, in their review of Government policies on education in the 1960s. They point out that at least some ministerial statements indicated 'that ability or aptitude . . . was a consideration in determining equality of opportunity' (Greaney and Kellaghan, 1984, 26). The poor child was to be given the chance to reach the top of the educational ladder provided he or she had sufficient ability (ibid., 27).

The Department of Education obviously endorsed this policy too, as *Ár nDaltaí Uile: All Our Children* expressed similar views in 1969. The document suggests that the aim of equalising educational opportunities was to ensure that 'every child, without exception . . . will receive the best possible education suited to his or her individual talents' (ibid., 4). More importantly, perhaps, the *Investment in Education* report also espoused the cause of equality of opportunity, although it too remained meritocratic in spirit. Its basic message was that the talent needed by the economy was being wasted because of the low educational participation of particular social groups. Equality of opportunity was necessary, therefore, primarily as a means for securing and selecting talent. (See chapters 7 and 10 for examples from *Investment in Education*.)

That the Government's preoccupation with meritocratic goals persisted into the 1970s and 1980s is evident from the nature of the Government-funded reports published during this period. Many of the major reports published on second-level education particularly were concerned with the assessment of ability—Madaus and Macnamara's report on *Public Examinations* (1970), the *Intermediate Certificate Examination Report* (1975), and the *Public Examinations Evaluation Project* (1980). While these do not discuss either equality of educational opportunity or meritocratic issues *per se,* they are nonetheless premised on the assumption that effective selection of the 'talented' is very important in society.

MERITOCRACY AND ACADEMIC WORK
Many other Irish educationalists subscribe to the meritocratic view in an implicit if not an explicit way. It could be argued therefore that because they do not treat it as problematic, Irish educationalists implicitly place a value on meritocratic individualism.

Whelan and Whelan's study on *Social Mobility in the Republic of Ireland* (1984) and Breen et al.'s work *Understanding Contemporary Ireland* (1990) are, in many ways, similar to Greaney and Kellaghan's research in their treatment of meritocracy. They assume that the 'able' working class should move up the social ladder, and that if they do not, society is unequal. The fact that a meritocratic system is also an unequal one—albeit according to different criteria—does not seem to be called into question.

Other studies, such as those on educational participation by Mac Gréil (1974), McCluskey (1977), Clancy and Benson (1979), and Clancy (1982; 1988), do not discuss the issue of meritocracy *per se,* although meritocracy is the yardstick by which the success of the education system tends to be measured. In effect, equality by social class or gender is judged in terms of proportionality. It is assumed that if there is a one-to-one relationship between the representation of a given social group in the population as a whole and its representation in higher education (for example), then equality has been achieved. This is the classic liberal interpretation of equality, and it does not challenge in any way the inequalities of power, wealth and privilege that perpetuate inequalities in one generation and reproduce them in the next (Hall, 1986; O'Neill, 1977).

IMPLICATIONS OF MERITOCRATIC INDIVIDUALISM AND ESSENTIALISM
To conclude, we will examine some of the educational and social implications of meritocratic individualism. First of all, the meritocratic ideal helps perpetuate the existence of a hierarchical social order. The idea that 'ability and effort should lead to reward' implicitly suggests that those who have not got ability or who do not make the effort should be given lesser rewards. The hierarchy remains, only the criteria for distributing privilege change (Baker, 1987).

Secondly, the work of Clancy (1982; 1988), Rottman et al. (1982), Hannan et al. (1983) and Whelan and Whelan (1984) raises serious questions about the legitimacy of using meritocratic mechanisms such as educational credentials to select people for occupations. They have found that there is a high probability that children from the upper socio-economic groups will get a disproportionate number of the more valuable (third-level) credentials in the first place. Thus the meritocratic ideology may merely provide a smokescreen behind which privilege is perpetuated—albeit through cultural rather than economic practices.

Thirdly, the notion of meritocracy also perpetuates the belief that 'talent' is limited in society. Even if one does accept the debatable assumption that there is a scarcity of talent for certain jobs, this scarcity is a function, in many ways, of the hierarchical ordering of society itself. In an economically unequal society, such as ours, many groups lack the opportunity to develop their talents in the first place. Scarcity of talent is thus a by-product of social inequality, not an intrinsic characteristic of individuals (Tumin, 1953).

Finally, the realisation of the meritocratic ideal is a logical impossibility, given the present structure of the labour market; there are, for example, only a small proportion of jobs available that are prestigious, high-paying, and

Can a talent be learned?
with the talent comes the ability to
develop on it.

obtainable by educational credentials. It is nonsense to suggest, therefore, that anyone who has 'talent' and 'makes the effort' can attain one of these jobs; they simply do not exist in large enough numbers to accommodate all those who would be technically eligible for them.

Both essentialism and meritocratic individualism have one other serious implication for education. They imply that failure or success in school is a function of what the individual *qua* individual is or does. By representing the individual in abstract terms, rather than as a structurally located relational being, they encourage us to look for educational solutions through changing individuals rather than by changing social structures. Very often individuals cannot change until the structures within which they are located change first to accommodate them. Furthermore, when responsibility for success or failure is attributed to the individual *per se,* those who fail are likely to feel that they lack some vital human ability (such as IQ) required in society (and therefore that they are lesser human beings than others) and/or that it is their own fault for not trying hard enough.

THE SOCIAL CONTEXT OF CONSENSUALISM

There are at least four factors that help explain the predominance of the consensus model of society among Irish educationalists. Firstly, Ireland is a country that experienced a national revolution in the relatively recent past. As a postcolonial state trying to establish its own identity internationally, it placed, almost inevitably, a strong emphasis on developing a unitary nationalist consciousness. Education was indeed a major instrument of this purpose. Schools were used deliberately to propagate nationalist views and values (Coolahan, 1981). What we are saying, therefore, is that consensus theory is a by-product of the nationalist perspective arising in the new state.

Secondly, the Republic of Ireland has been a predominantly rural society for the greater part of the twentieth century. Conflicts have consequently centred more on proprietorial rights over land rather than on class divisions between workers and employers. As late as 1951, for example, 46.2 per cent of all male employed persons were self-employed (mostly farmers). It was only from the late 1960s to the 1980s that the balance shifted and Ireland became a more urban employee society, with 76 per cent of the paid labour force being employees in 1989 (Department of Labour 1990, table 16).

A society dominated by a proprietorial peasantry and their offspring was not a very fertile soil for the generation of left-right dichotomies in either political or intellectual life. Indeed, in that educationalists have tended to come traditionally from western counties and farm families, they were especially likely to be influenced by the consensus tradition of their origins.

Perhaps the most important reason for the perpetuation of the consensualist view has been that identified already by O'Dowd, namely the influence of the

Catholic Church on Irish intellectual life (O'Dowd, n.d.). Catholic religious personnel have exercised administrative control over the socialisation of most educationalists at primary and second level for the greater part of this century. That control still exists today, although it has recently declined somewhat. For example, in 1986 there were 937 entrants to the colleges of education; all but 207 of these (22 per cent) were in colleges under Catholic management (Clancy, 1988, 13). Furthermore, while most staff in the colleges of education and the university education departments are not now religious, it is reasonable to suggest that they are still predominantly people who have been trained professionally in Catholic colleges of education or in education departments controlled by Catholic religious personnel.

One must ask then, what is the significance of all this for consensualism? Because the Catholic Church has dominated so many educational institutions, it exercises a powerful role in setting the intellectual agenda for other educationalists. One of the most pervasive themes in Catholic social commentary has been the view that rural society most closely approximates the ideal Catholic social order. Rural society is idealised as a place devoid of class conflict and dissension; it is represented as a repository of Catholic virtue, neighbourly solidarity, and good will. There is no reference to the socio-economic and sexual inequalities that exist within it in the real world as opposed to the ideal one.

What we are suggesting, therefore, is that the consensual view of society—which, O'Dowd (1975: 1985) claims, has dominated Irish intellectual thought in the twentieth century—is itself a product of Catholic influences on intellectual discourse. Peillon (1982, 65–6) also adverts to this phenomenon. The Catholic view of the good—in terms of the social order—has been transformed from being a religious ideal into a conceptual model of the world that purports to represent empirical reality. In other words, educationalists (among other intellectuals) have uncritically borrowed an ideal from the religious site and translated it into an analytical construct in the educational one.

A further factor propagating the consensus view in recent years has been the nature of the postgraduate socialisation of educationalists. The trend throughout the 1970s and 1980s has been for Irish educationalists to pursue postgraduate studies in the United States. The dominant educational paradigm in the United States, however, is still the positivist one. Indeed, until very recent times there was little discussion among American educationalists of the powerful role that scientific paradigms and perspectives play in the interpretation of evidence. If one is never trained to realise that there is a variety of perspectives for interpreting data and therefore for explaining educational phenomena, then the question of perspective never arises. Consensus models of society are not called into question, as there is no framework for contesting them. The influence of the atheoretical approach of the American positivist tradition has therefore, we suggest, helped to guarantee the perpetuation of consensualism in Irish educational discourse.

UNDERSTANDING THE PERSISTENCE OF ESSENTIALISM AND THE MERITOCRATIC VIEW

The strong belief in the essentialist view of the individual and in the related meritocratic ideal is also largely accounted for by the factors outlined above. As stated already, it is only since the 1970s that Ireland could be classified as an urban society. The Irish intelligentsia has been drawn therefore from a rural (predominantly peasant) society in which one's livelihood was (and indeed still is) often dependent on the whims of nature. In such a society it was almost inevitable that naturalistic explanations would hold sway. It predisposed people to accept essentialist explanations for differences. Rural society has also tended to be strongly hierarchical (and patriarchal), both within the family (Hannan and Katsiaouni, 1977) and in the general social order (Arensberg and Kimball, 1940). Again we would suggest that this predisposed the intelligentsia emanating from it to accept a meritocratic ideology, as both are premised on a similar hierarchical view of the social system.

What is being suggested here is that the domain assumptions (those arising from biographical and cultural experience) of educationalists influence their theoretical views. As Gouldner (1970) pointed out, the paradigmatic presuppositions of intellectuals are not just explicable in terms of the theoretical approaches within the disciplines; they are also influenced by the life experience of the researchers themselves.

Catholic teaching and church organisation must also have played a role, however, in facilitating acceptance of essentialism and the meritocratic view. There is a strong appeal in Catholic teaching, for example, to the 'natural law' as an explanatory paradigm. Thus educational models that attribute the cause of success or failure to an individual's 'given nature' can readily be absorbed by an intelligentsia reared in a 'natural law' tradition. Secondly, in its internal social organisation the Catholic Church tends to be both hierarchical and patriarchal. Again it would seem likely that people educated within such an organisation are likely to be predisposed towards seeing the hierarchical order as 'natural'. They fail, therefore, to see the hierarchical assumptions of the meritocratic view as problematic.

Another major reason why meritocratic and essentialist ideologies persist is that these paradigms have widespread acceptance among educationalists internationally, especially in the United States. In fact it would be safe to say that the United States is the home of the essentialist-psychometric model of the individual (Gould, 1981). Given the long-standing associations between Irish and American educationalists, it is not surprising to find that neither the essentialist nor the meritocratic views are called into question.

It should be noted too that Irish universities, colleges of education and research institutes are themselves strongly hierarchical and patriarchal. Control in many such institutions and departments is exercised almost exclusively by the heads or directors, who are, with few exceptions, male. Thus, working conditions are likely to predispose educationalists to view the hierarchical order as natural and/or inevitable. This accords well, in turn, with a meritocratic view of the social system.

Finally, the absence of a strong critical tradition in Irish sociology, psychology or philosophy must also help explain the persistence of all three ideologies identified here. Sociological thought, emanating from the philosophical traditions of critical theory and neo-Marxism, has been the main source of critique for meritocratic, consensual and essentialist ideologies elsewhere. Critical perspectives, however, are still marginal in Irish educational discourse. Indeed they are still far from being central to Irish sociological thought as well (Clancy et al., 1986, 1–17).

CONCLUSION

The paradigms and perspectives of Irish intellectuals both reflect and reinforce their own class position as members of the intelligentsia: that is, as members of that class whose claim to power is based on their educational credentials; to that extent they are ideological. (See Barrett, 1991, for a detailed discussion of current debates on ideology.) In what way do the ideologies reflect and reinforce the intelligentsia's position? Firstly, the meritocratic and essentialist ideologies provide an ideal rationale for intelligentsia rule. They imply that only a small number of people are gifted in society and that these must be selected and rewarded if society is to survive. In other words, they glorify the intelligentsia as indispensable to society's existence. The meritocratic and essentialist ideologies therefore both reflect and reinforce the myth of intelligentsia superiority.

Secondly, it was noted above that educationalists tend to adopt a consensual model of the social order in their analysis and that this consensualism is partly a by-product of theoretical blindness. The fact that intellectuals do not present their views within their perspectival limits implies that they are locating themselves (be it inadvertently or intentionally) beyond paradigmatic allegiance. This claim to perspectival neutrality must be seen for what it is, however: a legitimating mechanism for gaining access to power. It is similar in character to the general legitimating mechanism used by intellectuals in claiming the right to rule—namely claims to 'objectivity' and 'expertise'. The consensualism and related perspectival indifference of Irish educationalists, therefore, could be interpreted as an attempt by an intelligentsia class to legitimate their claim to power. (See Konrad and Szelenyi (1979) for a discussion of this point regarding Hungarian intellectuals.) By purporting to be perspectivally neutral and objective they (unconsciously) conceal the interest of their own position.

References and Further Reading

Arensberg, C., and Kimball, T. (1940), *Family and Community in Ireland*, Cambridge: Cambridge University Press.

Baker, J. (1987), *Arguing For Equality*, New York: Verso.

Barrett, M. (1991), *The Politics of Truth: From Marx to Foucault*, Stanford: Stanford University Press.

Bell, D. L. (1978), 'Child-centred pedagogy, ideology and educational theory', *Proceedings of the Educational Studies Association of Ireland*, New University of Ulster, 1978, 145–52.

Bidwell, C. E. (1980), 'The sociology of the school and classroom' in H. Blalock (ed.), *Sociological Theory and Research*, London: Collier Macmillan.

Bourdieu, P. (1974), 'The school as a conservative force' in J. Eggleston (ed.), *Contemporary Research in the Sociology of Education*, London: Methuen.

Bourdieu, P. (1977), 'Cultural reproduction and social reproduction' in J. Karabel and A. Halsey (eds.), *Power and Ideology in Education*, New York: Oxford University Press.

Bowles, S., and Gintis, H. (1976), *Schooling in Capitalist America*, London: Routledge and Kegan Paul.

Breen, R. (1984), *Education and the Labour Market* (ESRI paper no. 119), Dublin: Economic and Social Research Institute.

Breen, R., et al. (1990), *Understanding Contemporary Ireland*, Dublin: Gill and Macmillan.

Burt, C. (1969), 'Intelligence and heredity: some common misconceptions', *Irish Journal of Education*, vol. 3, no. 2.

Clancy, P. (1982), *Participation in Higher Education*, Dublin: Higher Education Authority.

Clancy, P. (1988), *Who Goes to College?: a Second National Survey of Participation in Higher Education*, Dublin: Institute of Public Administration.

Clancy, P., and Benson, C. (1979), *Higher Education in Dublin*, Dublin: Higher Education Authority.

Clancy, P., et al. (1986), 'Introducing sociology' in P. Clancy et al. (eds.), *Ireland: a Sociological Profile*, Dublin: Institute of Public Administration.

Coolahan, J. (1981), *Irish Education: History and Structure*, Dublin: Institute of Public Administration.

Coolahan, J. (1984), 'The fortunes of education as a subject of study and of research in Ireland', *Irish Educational Studies*, vol. 4, no. 1, 1–34.

Crooks, T., and McKernan, J. (1984), *The Challenge of Change*, Dublin: Institute of Public Administration.

Department of Education (1960), *Report of the Council of Education*, Dublin: Stationery Office.

Department of Education (1966), *Investment in Education*, Dublin: Stationery Office.

Department of Education (1969), *Ár nDaltaí Uile: All Our Children*, Dublin: Stationery Office (cited by Greaney and Kellaghan in *Equality of Opportunity in Irish Schools* (1984), 4).

Department of Education (1971), *Primary School Curriculum: Teacher's Handbook, part 1*, Dublin: Stationery Office.

Department of Education (1975), *Intermediate Certificate Examination Report*, Dublin: Stationery Office.

Department of Education (1985), *Partners in Education: Serving Community Needs*, Dublin: Stationery Office.

Department of Education (1990a), *Report of the Review Body on the Primary Curriculum*, Dublin: Stationery Office.

Department of Education (1990b), *Report of the Primary Education Review Body*, Dublin: Stationery Office.

Department of Education (1992), *Education for a Changing World: Green Paper on Education*, Dublin: Stationery Office.

Department of Labour (1990), *Labour Force Survey, 1989*, Dublin: Stationery Office.

Dowling, T. (1992), 'The teacher unions, class inequality in Irish education and the compensatory approach' (master of equality studies thesis, University College, Dublin).

Drudy, S. (1991), 'Developments in the sociology of education in Ireland, 1966–1991', *Irish Journal of Sociology*, vol. 1, 107–27.

Flude, M., and Ahier, J. (1974), *Educability: Schools and Ideology*, London: Methuen, chap. 2.

Fontes, P. J., et al. (1983), 'Opinions of the Irish public on intelligence', *Irish Journal of Education*, vol. 17, no. 2, 55–67.

Foras Áiseanna Saothair (1991), *Skills Survey*, Dublin: FÁS.

Gardner, H. (1983), *Frames of Mind: the Theory of Multiple Intelligences*, London: Paladin.

Gould, S. J. (1981), *The Mismeasure of Man*, Harmondsworth (Middlesex): Penguin.

Gouldner, A. V. (1970), *The Coming Crisis of Western Sociology*, London: Heinemann.

Gramsci, A. (1971), 'The intellectuals', *Selections from Prison Notebooks*, London: Lawrence and Wishart.

Greaney, V., and Kellaghan, T. (1984), *Equality of Opportunity in Irish Schools*, Dublin: Educational Company.

Greaney, V., and Kellaghan, T. (1985), 'Factors related to level of educational attainment in Ireland', *Economic and Social Review*, vol. 16, no. 2, 141–56.

Hall, S. (1986), 'Variants of liberalism' in J. Donald and S. Hall (eds.), *Politics and Ideology*, Milton Keynes: Open University Press.

Hannan, D., and Katsiaouni, L. (1977), *Traditional Families* (ESRI report no. 87), Dublin: Economic and Social Research Institute.

Hannan, D., et al. (1983), *Schooling and Sex Roles: Sex Differences in Subject Provision and Student Choice in Irish Post-Primary Schools*, Dublin: Economic and Social Research Institute.

Heywood, J., McGuinness, S., and Murphy, D. (1980), *The Public Examinations Evaluation Project*, Dublin: School of Education, University of Dublin.

Jackson, P. (1968), *Life in Classrooms*, New York: Holt, Rinehart and Winston.

Karabel, J., and Halsey, A. (1977), 'Educational research' in J. Karabel and A. Halsey (eds.), *Power and Ideology in Education*, New York: Oxford University Press, 1–85.

Kellaghan, T. (1973), 'Intelligence and achievement in a disadvantaged population: a cross-lagged panel analysis,' *Irish Journal of Education*, vol. 7, no. 1, 23–8.

Kellaghan, T. (1977) *The Evaluation of an Intervention Programme for Disadvantaged Children*, Windsor: National Foundation for Education Research.

Kellaghan, T., and Newman, E. (1971), 'Background characteristics of children of high verbal ability', *Irish Journal of Education*, vol. 5, no. 1, 5–14.

Kleinig, J. (1982), *Philosophical Issues in Education*, London: Croom Helm.

Konrad, G., and Szelenyi, I. (1979), *Intellectuals on the Road to Class Power*, Brighton: Harvester.

Lawler, J. (1978), *IQ, Heritability and Racism*, New York: International Publishers.

Lynch, K. (1985), 'An analysis of some presuppositions underlying the concepts of meritocracy and ability as presented in Greaney and Kellaghan's study', *Economic and Social Review*, vol. 16, no. 2.

Lynch, K. (1987), 'Dominant ideologies in Irish educational thought,' *Economic and Social Review*, vol. 18, no. 2, 110–22.

Lynch, K. (1989a), *The Hidden Curriculum*, London: Falmer.

Lynch, K. (1989b), 'Solidary labour: its nature and marginalisation', *Sociological Review*, vol. 37, no. 1, 1–13.

Lynch, K. (1992), 'Ideology and the legitimation of inequality in education' in P. Clancy, M. Kelly, et al. (eds.), *Ireland and Poland: Comparative Perspectives*, Dublin: University College (Department of Sociology).

McCluskey, D. (1977), *Access to Secondary Education*, Dublin: Secretariat of Secondary Schools.

Mac Gréil, M. (1974), *Educational Opportunity in Dublin*, Maynooth: Research and Development Unit.

McKeown, K. (1985), 'The individual and the city: the changing role of locality', paper presented at An Foras Forbartha colloquy 'Ireland in the Year 2000: Urbanisation', 22–23 October 1985, Kilkea Castle, Castledermot, Co. Kildare.

Madaus, G., and Macnamara, J. (1970), *Public Examinations: a Study of the Irish Leaving Certificate*, Dublin: Educational Research Centre.

Mulcahy, D. (1981), *Curriculum and Policy in Irish Post-Primary Education*, Dublin: Institute of Public Administration.

Mulcahy, D., and O'Sullivan, D. (1989), *Educational Policy: Process and Substance*, Dublin: Institute of Public Administration.

Nettl, J. P. (1969), 'Ideas, intellectuals, and the structures of dissent' in P. Rieff (ed.), *On Intellectuals: Theoretical Studies, Case Studies*, New York: Doubleday.

Ó Catháin, S. (1955), 'Secondary education in Ireland (part 1),' *Studies*, vol. 44, 385–400.

Ó Catháin, S. (1956), 'Secondary education in Ireland (part 2): choosing the curriculum', *Studies*, vol. 45, 50–66.

O'Dowd, L. (1975), 'The construction of Irish social reality: some implications for social knowledge', *Proceedings of the Sociological Association of Ireland*, Belfast: Queen's University.

O'Dowd, L. (1985), 'Intellectuals in 20th century Ireland, and the case of George Russell (AE),' *Crane Bag*, vol. 9, no. 1, 6–25.

O'Dowd, L. (n.d.), 'Intellectuals on the Road to Modernity: Aspects of Social Ideology in the 1950s', Belfast: Queen's University (Department of Social Studies).

O'Neill, O. (1977), 'How do we know when opportunities are equal?' in M. Vetlerling-Braggin et al. (eds.)., *Feminism and Philosophy*, Totowa (New Jersey): Littlefield, Adam.

Organisation for Economic Co-operation and Development (1991), Reviews of *National Policies For Education—Ireland*, Paris: OECD.

O'Sullivan, D. (1989), 'The ideational base of Irish educational policy' in D. Mulcahy and D. O'Sullivan, *Irish Educational Policy: Process and Substance*, Dublin: Institute of Public Administration.

Peillon, M. (1982), *Contemporary Irish Society: an Introduction*, Dublin: Gill and Macmillan.

Raftery, A., and Hout, M. (1985), 'Does Irish education approach the meritocratic ideal?: a logistic analysis,' *Economic and Social Review*, vol. 16, no. 2, 115–40.

Rottman, D., et al. (1982), *The Distribution of Income in the Republic of Ireland: a Study of Social Class and Family Life Cycle Inequalities*, Dublin: Economic and Social Research Institute.

Swan, T. D. (1978), *Reading Standards in Irish Schools*, Dublin: Educational Company.

Teeling, J. (1992), 'What Does Business Want from the Education System?' (paper presented to Association of Principals and Vice-Principals of Community and Comprehensive Schools, 19 May 1992).

Tumin, M. (1953), 'Some principles of stratification: a critical analysis,' *American Sociological Review*, vol. 18, no. 4.

Whelan, C., and Whelan, B. (1984), *Social Mobility in Ireland: a Comparative Perspective* (ESRI paper no. 116), Dublin: Economic and Social Research Institute.

Whelan, C., and Whelan, B. (1985), 'Equality of opportunity in Irish schools: a reassessment', *Economic and Social Review*, vol. 14, no. 2, 103–14.

White, J. (1980), 'Conceptions of individuality', *British Journal of Educational Studies*, vol. 28, no. 3, 173–85.

Wickham, A. (1980), 'National education systems and the international context: the case of Ireland', *Comparative Education Review*, vol. 6, no. 4, 323–37.

Young, M. (1961), *The Rise of the Meritocracy, 1870–2033*, London: Pelican.

II

Control of Education

4

The Churches and the State

Although the churches (in particular the Catholic Church) have occupied a central role in the formation and development of Irish education, they have received remarkably little sociological attention. While historians such as Akenson (1970), Coolahan (1981) and Ó Buachalla (1988) have devoted considerable attention to the analysis of the churches' role, and while others, such as McKernan (1988; 1990), have taken issue with traditional Catholic perspectives on curriculum matters, sociologists have generally only addressed the role of the churches in education as a secondary consideration (Peillon, 1982; Inglis, 1987; Lynch, 1989). Unlike the analysis of social class issues in education, therefore, the issue of the churches' control has received scant sociological attention.

There are a number of reasons why the churches have received so little attention as a social force in Irish education. Firstly, as noted elsewhere in this book, Irish sociologists have been strongly influenced by the theoretical frameworks developed in other countries, especially those of Britain and North America. Because the sociology of education in those countries has not been centrally concerned with the role of powerful educational mediators such as the churches, and has focused on power issues in class, gender and racial terms, this has meant that Irish sociologists have not had sociological models at their disposal that were sensitive to the issue of church control.

A second, and very powerful, factor that makes the analysis of church influence on education rather difficult is the private nature of church organisations. This means that researchers do not have ready access to the kind of research material that would explain the procedures and processes by which the churches maintain power. This privacy is further protected by the unavailability of information on church-state negotiations.

In addition, the problem of analysis is complicated by the 'pluralism' that exists within the churches themselves. While official church teaching on educational matters has several universalistic features, it is by no means interpreted in an identical fashion by different sectors of the church. One very obvious area where there is a considerable tension within the Catholic

Church, for example, is on the question of religious support for private education in the form of fee-paying schools.

Finally, because the churches are seen as the arbiters of moral goodness in society, there has been a strong tendency to regard them as being 'above and beyond analysis'. The institution of the church was accorded the sacred status of its dogmas; it was almost a profanity to subject it to the critical analysis of social-scientific research.

With these limitations borne in mind, what is clear from the limited research available is that the churches, especially the Catholic Church, exercise great power over first and second-level education and over primary teacher education in Ireland (Peillon, 1982, 146–54; Inglis, 1987, 156–65). The questions that need to be addressed, therefore, are how and why the church maintains such influence, and what, if any, its implications are for Irish education.

THE SYMBIOTIC RELATIONSHIP BETWEEN THE CHURCHES AND THE STATE

As noted by several researchers (Whyte, 1981; Coolahan, 1981; Ó Buachalla, 1988), the churches' foothold in Irish education was well established by the time the state was founded. The new state was confronted with problems of political legitimacy and economic impoverishment. In this climate it had neither the political will nor the financial resources to challenge the power of the churches in education. Reflecting the organic limits within which state education operates (Dale, 1982), a symbiotic relationship (i.e. a mutually beneficial one) developed between the churches and the state.

For the state, the gain from strong church involvement is both financial and ideological. The financial benefits are evident in primary and second-level education and involve both capital and current savings. Because almost all primary schools are either parish schools or owned by religious orders (over 90 per cent being Catholic), a considerable proportion of the day-to-day running expenses must be borne by the parish or the religious community involved. Estimates by the National Parents' Council (1990) indicate that only 65 per cent of the cost of running schools is borne by the state (59 per cent from capitation grants and 6 per cent from other Department of Education grants), and the shortfall has to be met by the parish, parents, or religious community.

One can see immediately how the state benefits from underwriting the churches' administrative control in the primary sector. The churches organise the collection of money from their members to subvent the state's contribution. Add to this the fact that school managers are (with the exception of the ten multidenominational schools) almost all clergymen, mostly parish priests, and that these are unpaid posts, and one can see again the high level of savings arising from church involvement. In capital terms, the state also benefits from the liaison, as it is saved up to 15 per cent of the cost of building new primary schools when the school is a parish school; in addition, the site is also provided for the school without charge to the state. Although these latter conditions also apply to all multidenominational schools, the precedent of paying 15 per cent of capital costs was set in the context of denominational education, and it is questionable whether it would continue in its absence.

At second level the state also benefits considerably from church involvement. Education is provided for the state either in buildings owned by the churches and that involve no direct expense to the state or (in the case of newer schools) in buildings to which the state contributed just 90 per cent of the costs. (See chapter 1.) If the state were to be fully responsible for the cost of such buildings for educational purposes, these costs would be prohibitive. Finally, in the past—although less so at present, because of the decline in religious vocations—the state has also benefited from the unpaid labour that religious communities and bodies invested in their schools.

The state's gain from the churches' involvement in education cannot be assessed solely in financial terms, however. The state also gains ideologically from their involvement in at least two distinct ways.

As Offe (1984) has noted, one of the features of parliamentary democracies is that political groups can only maintain power if they have legitimacy. While legitimacy is undoubtedly maintained by balancing the interests of capital with those of civil society, it is also maintained by developing a society in which the ideological state apparatus, including education, develops a commitment in civil society to the other apparatus of the state (Althusser, 1971). In Ireland the churches have played a central role in developing such an ideological commitment. As Inglis (1987, 156–65) points out, the Catholic Church has been the principal 'civilising' force in Irish society.[1] It has developed, through the schools, many qualities that are vital for establishing and maintaining political legitimacy, including self-control, orderliness, obedience, and discipline (ibid.).

In conjunction with this, the churches' involvement in education actually adds legitimacy to the educational process *per se* and, by implication, to the social selection and labour allocation processes that follow from it. As noted by Clancy (1983, 15–17), the status of members of religious communities is high in Irish society. By virtue of their high moral status, the churches bring an aura of legitimacy to bear on the education system, immunising it from attack. The involvement of the churches in education therefore adds to the political legitimacy of the system, since the churches' legitimating armoury (as the moral arbiters in society) is transferred to the educational scene; this forestalls criticism and debate (Lynch, 1989, 130–2).

The gains from the church-state partnership are not one-way: the churches are also beneficiaries. In return for their current and capital investment in schools, the churches are granted considerable autonomy in the management of their schools, and complete autonomy in religious matters.

With regard to religious education, the state lays down no regulations save that religion must be taught. The content of programmes therefore is determined by the church body running the school. The net effect of this has been that a comprehensive programme of religious education does not take place in most schools. Catechetics rather than religious education forms the basis of the religious programme.

In the management sphere, the churches exercise considerable control, especially over the appointment of teachers. The control the churches exercise over appointments helps to ensure that the values and beliefs that they espouse are upheld in the schools. In return for their financial investment in education, therefore, and their contribution to political legitimacy within the state, the churches are given vast scope to influence the moral and religious perspectives of almost all the country's children.

It would seem that the benefit of the church-state partnership is essentially ideological for the church while it is primarily financial for the state. However, the state also makes some ideological gains in the form of an electorate socialised into a culture of order and respect for authority.

One of the factors that undoubtedly facilitates harmony in this church-state liaison is the shared cultural experience and social networks between the élites of church and state. Although there is no empirical evidence available on this question, what is true is that Ireland is a small country. Those who hold positions of power in church and state (mostly men) are very likely to have attended the same types of school (in this case fee-paying, male secondary schools) and college, and to be involved in the same social, familial and recreational networks. Such social interchange oils the wheels of communication and paves the way for negotiation and collaboration when it is required.

Although the relationship between the churches and the state is basically symbiotic, it is by no means an equally balanced power relationship at all times. The balance of power between the churches and the state varies with each level of education, and within each level it varies depending on whether one is talking about ownership, administrative control, or the curriculum.

Ownership and Control at Primary Level

All but ten of the 3,235 ordinary national schools are denominational schools—93 per cent of which are under the patronage of the Catholic Church. (In fact one-sixth of national schools are convent or monastery schools, and these cater for about one-third of all pupils.) The remainder of the denominational schools are mainly controlled by various Protestant denominations. Although there are very few multidenominational schools, there are some indications that the demand for this type of school is much greater than the provision (Hyland, 1989, 105). However, the likelihood that multidenominational education will become the norm seems very remote. While obstacles posed by the state to the development of multidenominational schools have lessened in recent years, 'even to-day, the sheer effort in terms of time, commitment and money which must be shouldered by the parents makes the establishment of a multi-denominational school a very onerous undertaking' (Alvey, 1991, 90).

While the state controls the curriculum of primary schools and sets basic standards, the ownership and day-to-day administration of these schools is very much under church control. This becomes evident when one examines the constitution and procedures for boards of management in national schools.

National schools have a patron (who is, in most cases, the local bishop). He appoints three members to the six-person board of management;[2] the three remaining members comprise two elected representatives of parents with children in the school, and the school principal (Department of Education, 'Boards of Management of National Schools', 70). It is the patron, however, who appoints the chairperson of the board of management (usually the local parish priest), and in the event of a tied vote in the board, the chairperson has a casting vote (ibid., 72).

The selection board for the appointment of new teachers is also under the control of the patron (ibid., 81). It comprises the chairperson of the board of management and two other appointees of the patron. The teachers appointed must, however, be suitably qualified for the post in accordance with Department of Education regulations. Given the administrative control that the churches (notably the Catholic Church and the Church of Ireland) exercise over boards of management and selection boards for the appointment of teachers in their schools, one can see that they have considerable scope to influence the social climate of primary schools.

The proposals for boards of management for primary schools in the Green Paper (Department of Education, 1992, 114) allow for less influence by the nominees of the trustees or owners than at present; if these are agreed, the nominees of trustees or owners would be in a minority (of one) on boards. However, this is merely a proposal for discussion and is not yet agreed as public policy. Public debate, however, indicates that there is considerable disquiet among representatives of various church bodies about reducing their level of influence on boards of management.

Church influence is not confined, however, to the administrative sphere. Rule 68 of the regulations governing the running of national schools states that 'Religious Instruction is . . . a fundamental part of the school course, and a religious spirit should inform and vivify the whole work of the school' (Department of Education, 'Rules for National Schools', 38). This principle is reiterated in the *Teacher's Handbook* for the primary school curriculum (Department of Education, 1971, 23). Indeed the handbook strongly endorses the view that the integration of religious and secular instruction is desirable (ibid., 19). Not only are national schools explicitly recognised as being denominational, therefore ('Rules for National Schools', preface, 8) but their whole curriculum is meant to convey religious values.

Table 4.1

Proposed constitution of boards of management for primary schools with five or more teachers

Nominees of the trustees or owners	5
Representatives of parents	2
Representatives of teachers	2
Representative of the local community (preferably a representative of the local business community)	1
Principal (as voting member)	1
Total membership	11

Source: Department of Education (1992), 144.

There is a certain contradiction here, however, between the Constitution of the state and the regulations for schools (Hyland, 1989, 91–6). Under article 44.2.4 the Constitution states that '*legislation providing State aid for schools* shall not discriminate between schools under the management of different religious denominations, *nor be such as to affect prejudicially the right of any child to attend a school receiving public money without attending religious instruction at that school.*' [Emphasis added.]

If all subjects are to be imbued with religious values, it would seem impossible to protect the pupil's constitutional right not to receive religious instruction should he or she not want it. This is a dilemma for a growing number of Irish parents, and it has been recognised both in the Green Paper (Department of Education, 1992, 90) and in the report of the Review Body on the Primary Curriculum (1990, 18). In most areas (outside Dublin and a few other large towns) one has no choice but to send one's child to the local denominationally controlled national school. This means in effect that one's child will be exposed to a religious climate in the school (even if they do not attend religion classes *per se*), whether one wants it or not.

Although the state recognises the dilemma posed by the conflict between the Constitution and the guidelines for primary schools, there is no indication either in the Green Paper or in the review of the primary curriculum of how the state intends to resolve it.

CONSULTATIVE ROLE OF THE CHURCHES

It is clear from the above that the state has operated according to the Catholic principle of subsidiarity (see the Papal encyclical *Divinis Illius Magistri*, 1929) in relation to denominational schooling in Ireland. It underwrites the churches' controlling interests in schooling by its annual multi-million-pound investment in labour and capital. While the Department of Education drafts the curriculum and is ultimately responsible for the sanctioning of the appointments of teachers and the choice of textbooks, it does not exercise these powers independently of the church. There are at least thirty-three designated educational associations[3] that have formal consultative rights with the Department of Education.[4] What is interesting about these designated bodies is that sixteen of the thirty-three are specifically church-related, nine being Catholic and seven representing other denominations. The churches therefore represent by far the largest formally recognised lobby group in the Department of Education. They are strongly represented on all decision-making and consultative bodies set up by the Minister, including the Review Body on the Primary School Curriculum, the Primary Education Review Body, and the National Council for Curriculum and Assessment (IPA, 1991).

In summary, therefore, while the churches' ownership powers are immediately evident (through their control of school sites and buildings), their consultative and administrative powers, though less evident, are equally significant. In administrative terms, the churches, and in particular the bishops, through their patrons and nominees on the boards of management of primary schools, exercise considerable control over the teaching staff appointed to primary schools. This is a contested issue, however (especially in the Irish National Teachers' Organisation in recent years). When one combines the degree of influence that the churches can exercise in the appointment of teachers with the education of teachers in denominationally controlled colleges of education, it is clear that primary teachers are unlikely to be appointed if they do not support the educational ethos to which the given denomination subscribes.

While there is no direct evidence of church intervention in curriculum issues at primary level in recent years, the Catholic Church's consultative powers have been clearly in evidence in the intervention in curriculum matters at second level; the opposition of certain branches of that church to the life skills programme and the AIDS education programme are two well-known cases in point. In the former case the church was successful in undermining the programme, while in the case of AIDS education it succeeded in having its own views accorded equal, though not superior, status to those of the state. It should be noted, however, that not all members of the Catholic Church supported these interventions. As noted by Ó Buachalla (1988, 162–8), there is often division within the church itself on educational policy issues. Certain religious orders and individual members dissent strongly from the official view of the hierarchy on education. However, 'since the middle sixties it seems certain that the important and decisive consultative process in relation to major policy issues occurs at the senior levels i.e. between the bishops and church leaders and the minister and his department . . .' (ibid., 168).

It is clear from this that although the churches, especially the Catholic Church, may not directly intervene very often on general curricular matters at primary level, they can and would do so if they deemed their own interests to be in jeopardy. The churches exercise influence, therefore, over primary education in three areas: they exercise wide-ranging ownership and administrative rights while also having considerable scope to influence the curriculum.

Ownership and Control at Second Level
The balance of power between the churches and the state at second level varies among the different types of school, with vocational schools the only fully non-denominational schools at second level. (See chapter 1.)

It would be a mistake, however, to assume that the governing authorities for vocational schools, the vocational education committees, are devoid of church influence. In 1989/90, while ten of the thirty-eight VECs had no clergy or religious persons among their members, twenty-eight had (all but one of the religious on VECs being men). Of these twenty-eight, four were chaired by clergymen and sixteen had two or more clergy on the committee; County Cork had no less than seven clergy on the committee, including the chairperson and vice-chairperson (IPA, 1989, 109–15). In numerical terms there has been a slight decline in clerical representation on VECs from 1982/83, when all but six VECs had clergy on them and ten were chaired by clergy (Ó Buachalla, 1988, 205–6). However, both Catholic and Protestant clergy are still well represented at the management level of the only fully public education system at second level.

Since the 1970s, the VECs have established approximately thirty community colleges. (See chapter 1.) These—unlike community schools—are entirely under VEC control. However, it is interesting to note that although the VECs have the autonomy to determine the composition of boards of management in community colleges, in the case of the twenty-two community colleges that have resulted from mergers between VEC and secondary schools they have in practice tended to adopt a similar board structure to that of community schools, thereby giving the churches, especially the Catholic Church, a say in the management of a significant proportion of community colleges. A formal agreement has been reached between the relevant VECs and dioceses where the colleges have been established, although this agreement was only signed in Counties Dublin and Cork at the time of writing.

As noted in chapter 1, the churches also exercise considerable control in the administrative systems of both community and comprehensive schools. The formal involvement of religious orders in community schools, and the more informal involvement of the churches in community colleges, has given Catholic Church interests a degree of influence in what is theoretically public second-level education that they did not have before the 1970s. The religious orders involved in a community school have a number of teaching posts reserved for them, according to the deeds of trust. This concession, combined with the guaranteed position for religious on boards of management, means that the Catholic Church has acquired a new zone of educational influence in what has been the most rapidly expanding sector of second-level education over the last twenty years.

Because the Catholic Church controls a clear majority of secondary schools and exercises significant administrative controls over both community and comprehensive schools, it can have a major impact on the appointment of teachers at second level (as we have seen in chapter 1). In this way it can exercise control over the ethos of schools. In addition, the agreed articles of management for secondary schools give further evidence of continued church influence in the secondary sector.

Up to 1985 secondary schools could, subject to basic academic and administrative regulations laid down by the Department of Education, appoint whoever they wished as teachers. No outside consultation was required. In 1985 an agreement was reached between the managers of Catholic secondary schools and the Association of Secondary Teachers, Ireland, regarding the establishment of boards of management in Catholic secondary schools. The articles of management agreed in June 1985 are outlined in appendix 1 of 'A Manual for Boards of Management of Catholic Secondary Schools, 1985' (private circulation only). Under these articles each secondary school was to have a board of management consisting of eight persons: four nominees of the trustees (i.e. the religious order or Catholic authority involved), two elected representatives of parents, and two elected representatives of teachers (article 3a). The principal of the school is the non-voting secretary to the board (article 10). The trustees appoint the chairperson of the board (article 10), and in the event of a tied vote the chairperson has a casting vote (article 12). As is the case in the primary sector, the controlling religious authority in the school (via its nominated chairperson) has an effective veto on any decision made by the board of management should it wish to exercise it (including decisions on the appointment of teachers, article 23).

Thus, even though Catholic secondary schools are increasingly lay institutions, both in their management and teaching staff, and even though almost all their current and recurring capital expenditure is supplied by the state, they are ultimately subject to the control of the religious owning body involved. The Green Paper's proposals for boards of management for all state-aided second-level schools (the proposal is to call all second-level schools 'secondary schools'), if agreed, would result in a diminution of the power of the trustees or owners in what are currently called secondary schools. The proposals for representation of different interest groups on secondary school boards are identical to those outlined above for primary schools with five teachers or more, with one difference: the proposal to co-opt a representative of the local business community is a recommendation at primary level but is a stated requirement at second level (Department of Education, 1992, 143–4). Whether these policy proposals are implemented or not depends on negotiations and consultations currently under way, and there are plenty of indications that the churches will resist any proposal that threatens their control over the 'ethos' of their schools.

In matters of curriculum, denominational influence at second level is considerably less evident than in the primary sector; there is no formal regulation (such as rule 68 at primary level) specifying that the teaching of all subjects be imbued with a religious spirit. Religion is a subject at second level, however; as in primary schools, it comprises largely catechetical instruction in the doctrines of the church involved. Furthermore, it is the only non-examination subject that is allocated a significant amount of time on the school timetable (Lynch, 1989, 61–2). Not surprisingly, secondary schools in particular give a considerable amount of time to religion; and girls' secondary schools give the highest proportion of time to religion of all school types (ibid., 63–5).

Various denominational bodies also exercise control over the curriculum indirectly through their educational associations, which, as noted above, are consulted by the state on major policy matters. Given its consultative role in curriculum matters, the Catholic Church is not an insignificant force in designing curriculums for second-level schools. In general, however, the churches' effectiveness in shaping students' attitudes should not be overestimated. An ever-increasing proportion of pupils' time in second-level schools is spent studying subjects that are far removed from religious values. More and more students are studying scientific, commercial and technological subjects, which teach students to seek empirical proof for the existence of phenomena, to maximise profit, and to rely on technological solutions for human problems. Such principles are very much at variance with a faith based on dogma or belief in the efficacy of divine intervention for the resolution of human difficulties. In addition, most schools have a highly competitive, individualistic ethos (Lynch, 1989, 139–53). This is in sharp contradistinction to the collectivistic values that are idealised in much of the Judaeo-Christian tradition.

Ownership and Control in Adult and Higher Education
The only sector of higher education that is under the churches' control is the training of primary teachers, all the colleges of education being denominational

institutions, mostly Catholic. While one of the colleges of the National University of Ireland—St Patrick's College, Maynooth—is under Catholic management, all the other universities and higher education colleges are secular institutions. Although the universities have not been directly under Catholic Church control, the church has exercised considerable influence within them— in particular the colleges of the National University of Ireland—in such areas as education, sociology, and philosophy. Until very recent times senior posts in these fields were dominated by religious personnel. Indeed, one of the major intellectual traditions that influenced the development of Irish sociology up to the late 1950s was 'Catholic sociology' (Clancy et al., 1986, 6–7).

Not only is there a dearth of statistical data on adult education in Ireland (Commission on Adult Education, 1983) but there is also a dearth of research in the area. What is clear from the limited research available, however, is that the major providers of adult education courses are the vocational education committees (Commission on Adult Education, 1983; Aontas, 1986).[5] While the Catholic Church does play a role in this field through some of its postprimary schools, community groups, and colleges such as the Institute of Adult Education and the National College of Industrial Relations, its role is secondary to that of the state-controlled VECs. (Table 4.2 provides the details.)

The Significance of Church Influence in Education

When one examines the balance of power between the churches and the state in Irish education one can identify different patterns in the four sectors. Overall there is clear evidence that as one moves from compulsory to non-compulsory education the churches' power declines. In the primary and entirely compulsory sector of education the churches exercise considerable power over all aspects of schooling, including ownership, administration (and the appointment of teachers), and the curriculum. The curriculum is influenced through rule 68 for national schools and the terms of reference for the national so-called 'New Curriculum' as set out in 1971. In addition, the churches control the education of primary teachers.

At second level the churches' ability to influence the curriculum is not enshrined in any regulation or rule, save the general rule giving each denomination control over the teaching of its own religion in all schools. The churches can and do exercise influence in the general curriculum sphere, however, as Catholic interventions on life skills and AIDS education have shown. Furthermore, because the churches, in particular the Catholic Church, are strongly represented on all policy-making bodies on curriculum matters, they can influence curriculum developments when they so wish. The Catholic Church, however, seems to exercise its consultative powers mostly on curricular issues that pertain to sexual morality. In terms of ownership and administrative control the churches' power at second level goes from a high in the secondary sector to a low in the vocational sector. Community and comprehensive schools represent the medium ground, with a more equitable balance of power between church and state both in matters of ownership and control.

Table 4.2

Knowledge of providers of adult education

(Base: all saying that there were courses or classes in the area)

Mentioning	Unprompted	Prompted
VEC officers, teachers, technical school, etc.	61	4
AnCO	11	35
Regional college	10	22
Community or comprehensive school	10	19
Adult education centre	5	10
ACOT centre, farm centre	5	11
University extramural studies department	4	8
ICA women's clubs	3	17
Community centre or council	3	8
NIHE, Thomond College	3	6
Religious-controlled postprimary schools	3	6
Institute of Adult Education	2	6
Secondary schools or teachers (not religious-controlled)	2	7
Irish-language organisation or group	1	8
Macra na Feirme	1	7
Sports club or centre	1	6
Parish clergy, church committee or council	1	5
Art college or art groups	1	5

No other individual or organisation was mentioned by more than 4 per cent after prompting.

Source: Commission on Adult Education (1983), 105.

In third-level education the churches' main area of influence is in the education of primary teachers, while its zone of influence in fourth-level (adult) education is limited to a small number of specific projects initiated by the church itself.

There can be little doubt that the influence of the Catholic Church on education is an important force in creating legalistic and ritualistic Catholics (Inglis, 1987). Whether adherence to church rules and regulations represents the epitome of the church's ideal in religious behaviour is difficult to determine. There would appear to be strains and tensions within the Catholic Church itself concerning what constitutes the nature of Catholic education. However, because the Catholic Church has not traditionally encouraged the laity to understand the ethical principles on which the rules and regulations pertaining to moral behaviour are founded, one can only conclude that it has not favoured a religious behaviour based on an awareness of principled ethics (Inglis 1987, 11–32). Whether this serves the church's interest in the long term is very doubtful. Having one of the highest retention rates in education in the EC, Ireland is fast becoming a sophisticated, well-educated, industrialised society in which rational rather than traditional authority holds sway. In this social context a faith based on simple rules is unlikely to be adhered to, especially when the rules prescribe behaviour that is undesirable for other social (rational) purposes. Current disregard for Catholic teaching on contraception is a classic example of this. When it is both economically and socially advantageous, therefore, for people to part company with church teaching they will, especially when their religious upbringing has not developed in them the kind of principled ethical code of conduct that is rationally based.

There is therefore a fundamental contradiction between the nature of the religious education traditionally given to Catholics and adherence to Catholic precepts in a well-educated society. The irony in this contradiction is that it is the churches, especially the Catholic Church, that have most assisted in the creation of this educated society.

While the nature of religious education may not facilitate principled religious behaviour, there is an array of other factors that may also undermine the impact of the churches' control of education.

When one examines both the formal and hidden curriculum, of second-level schooling especially, one can see a number of ways in which it implicitly challenges different religious values. Over the last twenty years the take-up rate in the sciences, applied sciences, business and technical subjects has expanded considerably, while the take-up in the arts and humanities has declined. (See chapter 10.) The political, social-scientific and philosophical traditions remain demonstrably absent from second-level education. The net effect of this has been that the knowledge to which students are exposed at second level is increasingly removed from religious-type values. While literature and the arts are suffused with questions of value and ethics that if not religious in themselves nevertheless represent close approximations (in literature, for example, jealousy, love, death, despair and the meaning of life are common themes), the same cannot be said of the subject matter of business organisation, accountancy, economics, engineering, technical drawing, applied mathematics, or chemistry.

The arts and humanities could be, and were, used to propagate religious values, but the same is most unlikely to happen in scientific and technical or business subjects. Indeed, as noted above, these subjects may propose values or develop attitudes that are very much at variance with religious beliefs. The practice in science of seeking empirical proof for the existence of phenomena would appear to be in conflict with a religious tradition that encourages faith without proof. In the business subjects, education to maximise profits is not entirely congruent with the Christian precepts of brotherly and sisterly love, as it is often premised on assumptions of exploitation, be this on a global or individual scale. Within all subjects there is an increasing emphasis on developing the ability to evaluate (often regarded as the highest level of cognitive functioning). This is a mode of thinking that is at variance with the practice of accepting dogma uncritically because it is part of one's faith. Thus, the modes of thinking into which pupils are increasingly socialised in schools may contradict the very message that the churches' control of schools was designed to transmit.

The hidden curriculum of schooling may also contradict that message. All schools are agencies of social selection and allocation. Because of this, schools constantly grade, stratify and evaluate their pupils. This results in a highly competitive social climate, especially at second level (Lynch, 1989). It also leads to the differential and unequal treatment of students based on streams or bands (Hannan and Boyle, 1987). By its very organisation, therefore, schooling can, in several ways, contradict some of the values that the churches preach.

It is not only through the curriculum and organisation of schooling, however, that pupils may be exposed to contradictions between doctrine and practice. The churches themselves are key institutions in the upholding of fee-paying secondary schools, which fits uneasily with their claim that their primary concern is for the poor and underprivileged. In addition, while the Catholic Church is strong in its criticism of materialism (Peillon, 1982), most of its own clerical and religious members live in a state of financial security and have access to privileges and comforts (should they wish to avail of them) that are beyond the reach of many of those they reproach for being materialistic.

The treatment by the Catholic Church of women as subordinate to men within its own organisation belies that church's claimed concern for equality and justice in society. Also, as the churches (along with almost every other public institution in western society) have been dominated by men for centuries, patriarchal assumptions have been enshrined in theory and in the interpretation of dogma and scripture. In the case of the Catholic Church, in particular, the men who theorise and interpret are unmarried; parenthood is not on their agenda, nor is pregnancy and all that goes with it. The remoteness of such people's experience—what Gouldner (1970) called the domain assumptions of intellectuals—from the lives of the men and women (especially) about whom they theorise casts doubts on the validity of their pronouncements.

The contradictions between the church's organisational goals, which are concerned with self-preservation and the maintenance of institutional power and influence, and its spiritual values, which emphasise peace, love, equality, and justice, are growing increasingly evident in a society that is highly educated but in which there are increasing divisions between the rich and the poor, the powerful and the powerless. And indeed certain members of the church itself are furthering this awareness.

It is quite possible, therefore, that the legitimacy of the church's message and its ability to influence thinking and behaviour will, over time, be circumscribed by its own internal contradictions and the character both of its message makers and its bearers. Adding a further challenge to the legitimacy of the church's message are the contradictory values emanating from both the formal and hidden curriculum of schooling.

Notes

1. Not all would agree with the use of the term 'civilising' to describe the impact of the churches in Ireland. Terms such as 'colonising' and 'proselytising' have also been used to describe what the churches have done in the name of 'civilising'.

2. If schools have six or fewer teachers, the board of management has six members. If schools have seven or more teachers there are eight board members: four nominees of the patron, two elected representative of the parents, the principal, and one elected representative of the teaching staff. The same rules on voting etc. apply in both large and small schools.

3. The following were the education associations in August 1988:

   Association of Chief Executive Officers of VECs
   Association of Church of Ireland National School Managers
   Association of Primary Teaching Sisters
   Association of Principals and Vice-Principals of Community and
       Comprehensive Schools
   Association of Principals of Technical Institutes
   Association of Professional Staff in Colleges of Education
   Association of Secondary Teachers, Ireland
   Association of Vocational Education Colleges
   Catholic Headmasters' Association
   Catholic Primary School Managers' Association
   Church of Ireland Board of Education
   Church of Ireland Representative Body
   Committee of the Heads of the Irish Universities
   Conference of Convent Secondary Schools
   Conference of Major Religious Superiors
   Congress of Catholic Secondary School Parent Associations
   Federation of Christian Brothers' Primary Schools' Parent Councils
   Institute of Guidance Counsellors
   Irish Federation of University Teachers
   Irish National Teachers' Organisation
   Irish School Masters' Association

Irish Science Teachers' Association
Irish Vocational Education Association
Jewish Schools Representative Council
Joint Managerial Body
Methodist Board of Education
National Parents' Council
Presbyterian Board of Education
Secondary Education Committee (Protestant Schools)
Secretariat of Secondary Schools
Teachers' Union of Ireland
Teaching Brothers' Association—Primary
Teaching Brothers' Association—Secondary

4. Written communication from the Department of Education, August 1988, in response to a verbal request for information on associations or bodies that are formally consulted by the Department on policy issues.
5. Sample survey of total population over 16 not still in initial education.

References and Further Reading

Akenson, D. (1970), *The Irish Education Experiment*, London: Routledge and Kegan Paul.

Althusser, L. (1971), *Lenin and Philosophy and Other Essays*, New York: Monthly Review Press.

Alvey, D. (1991), *The Case for Secular Reform*, Dublin: Church and State.

Aontas (1986), *Priority Areas in Adult Education: a Report on Provision in Four Areas of Adult Education in Ireland*, Dublin: Aontas.

Clancy, P. (1983), 'Religious vocation as a latent identity for school principals', *Economic and Social Review*, vol. 15, no. 1, 1–23.

Clancy, P., et al. (eds.) (1986), *Ireland: a Sociological Profile*, Dublin: Institute of Public Administration.

Commission on Adult Education (1983), *Lifelong Learning: Report of the Commission on Adult Education*, Dublin: Stationery Office.

Coolahan, J. (1981), *Irish Education: History and Structure*, Dublin: Institute of Public Administration.

Council of Managers of Catholic Secondary Schools (1984), 'A Handbook for Managers of Secondary Schools', Dublin: Council of Managers of Catholic Secondary Schools (private circulation).

Dale, R. (1982), 'Education and the capitalist state: contributions and contradictions' in M. Apple (ed.), *Cultural and Economic Reproduction in Education*, London: Routledge and Kegan Paul.

Department of Education (1971), *Primary School Curriculum: Teacher's Handbook*, Dublin: Stationery Office.

Department of Education (1990), *Report of the Review Body on the Primary Curriculum*, Dublin: Stationery Office.

Department of Education (1992), *Education for a Changing World: Green Paper on Education,* Dublin: Stationery Office.

Department of Education (n.d.), *Boards of Management of National Schools: Constitution of Boards and Rules of Procedure,* Dublin: Stationery Office.

Department of Education (n.d.), *Rules For National Schools,* Dublin: Stationery Office.

Gouldner, A. (1970), *The Coming Crisis in Western Sociology,* London: Heinemann.

Hannan, D., and Boyle, M. (1987), *Schooling Decisions: the Origins and Consequences of Selection and Streaming in Irish Post-Primary Schools* (ESRI paper no. 136), Dublin: Economic and Social Research Institute.

Hyland, A. (1989), 'The multi-denominational experience in the Irish national school system of education', *Irish Educational Studies,* vol. 8, no. 1, 89–114.

Inglis, T. (1987), *Moral Monopoly,* Dublin: Gill and Macmillan.

Institute of Public Administration (1989), *IPA Yearbook and Diary,* Dublin: IPA, 109–15.

Institute of Public Administration (1991), *IPA Yearbook and Diary,* Dublin: IPA.

Lynch, K. (1989), *The Hidden Curriculum: Reproduction in Education: a Reappraisal,* London: Falmer.

McKernan, J. (1988), 'In defence of education for living in post-primary curriculum', *Oideas,* no. 32, 65–83.

McKernan, J. (1990), 'Values clarification: a response to Frank Dorr', *Oideas,* no. 35, 74–85.

National Parents' Council (1990), *The Cost of Free Education,* Dublin: National Parents' Council.

Ó Buachalla, S. (1988), *Education Policy in Twentieth-Century Ireland,* Dublin: Wolfhound.

Offe, C. (1984), *Contradictions of the Welfare State,* London: Hutchinson.

Peillon, M. (1982), *Contemporary Irish Society: an Introduction,* Dublin: Gill and Macmillan.

Whyte, J. (1981), *Church and State in Modern Ireland, 1923–1980,* Dublin: Gill and Macmillan.

5

The Teachers

In this chapter we draw together research on one of the major interest groups in Irish education, the teaching force. We look at the religious and gender composition of the teaching force. We examine the social backgrounds from which teachers are drawn, and suggest possible implications for their interactions with pupils. We also outline current career and management structures in teaching, and draw together observations on the role of teachers and on teachers as organised labour. Finally, we assess the role teachers play in educational change.

As we have argued in chapter 2, the education system plays a crucial role in the maintenance and reproduction of social and cultural relations in Irish society. We also suggest in chapter 6 that the nature of the education system is forged through the interplay of a number of powerful interest groups in Irish society. One of these consists of organisations representing the interests of the teaching force.

Teachers represent the largest 'professional' group in Ireland. However, even the very concept of 'profession' has long been a matter for debate in the international literature on teaching. There has been a tendency either to focus on the union activities of teachers or to adopt 'professionalism' as a defining concept for teacher behaviour (Ozga and Lawn, 1981). While definitions of what constitutes a profession vary, Burke suggests that when a sufficiently developed knowledge base exists to support, inspire and inform the practice of teaching—and he argues that it does—then one is dealing with a professional area and with professional people (Burke, 1992, 216). Burke also points out that professionals in bureaucratic employments are torn between maintaining their professionalism and striving for working conditions that benefit their status and responsibility (ibid., 194).

Sociologists such as Johnson (1972; 1977) have challenged this descriptive use of the concept of professionalism. He argues that professionalism is a peculiar type of occupational control and that it is not an inherent expression of the nature of certain occupations. An occupational group is called a profession when it exercises collegiate control, i.e. when it is the primary authority defining the relationship between the giver and receiver of its services. Professional groups, Johnson claims, are those that exercise considerable control over the services they offer, hence the desire of emerging occupations to label themselves 'professional'.

In Johnson's schema, teachers are not professionals, because they do not exercise sufficient control over their services. Because of the suggestion that developments in teaching have involved a certain amount of de-skilling, for example in the area of curriculum planning and design (Apple, 1982, 146), the position of teachers in the labour process has been somewhat unclear. Some analysts have included teachers among the 'dominant classes' (e.g. Poulantzas, 1978; Bourdieu, 1973). Indeed, Bourdieu lists them alongside top civil servants, engineers, managers, heads of industry, and heads of commerce (Bourdieu, 1973, 71–112). No doubt most teachers would heartily wish that their salaries reflected such a classification. On the other hand, others have definitively classified teachers as 'workers', albeit workers who have used their professionalism strategically (Ozga and Lawn, 1981, 147). In this latter sense they are seen to occupy contradictory class locations.

Because of the lack of research on the class position of teachers in Ireland, it is not possible to locate them clearly in their interrelations with other classes. This said, there is no doubt that teachers are a significant 'interest group' in education (as we will see in chapter 6); they are also middle-class by destination if not by origin. However, we agree with Ozga and Lawn that to place teachers more accurately in the class structure requires much more detailed investigation of teachers' work and teachers' actions. In the following sections, therefore, we draw together Irish and some international research on teachers, their backgrounds, and their roles. While we have not got a great deal of systematic sociological data on teachers as an occupational grouping in Ireland, we can nevertheless obtain a composite picture of the group by assembling statistical data and the results of a number of small-scale studies.

The Composition of the Teaching Profession

At present there are almost 40,000 full-time teachers at primary and second level in the Republic of Ireland. Of these, 20,410 are teaching full time at primary level, 11,550 full time in secondary schools, 2,458 full time in community and comprehensive schools, and 4,836 full time in vocational schools (Department of Education, 1992a, 27, 123, 127, 132).

Figures on the number of part-time teachers are harder to establish. The Department of Education collects and publishes statistics on the number of 'full-time equivalents' in community-comprehensive and vocational schools—86 and 1,993, respectively, in 1990/91 (ibid., 127, 132). That, of course, does not tell us exactly how many *people* are involved part time in these sectors. The department does not publish statistics on part-time staff in the primary or secondary sectors. If we were to include all the people who act as part-time (or substitute) teachers the number of teachers in the system would be considerably higher than the figure for full-time teachers alone. Since we have no details on the characteristics of part-time teachers any more than on their actual numbers, the discussion will focus on full-time teachers.

RELIGIOUS OR LAY

While 61 per cent of second-level schools are 'voluntary' (i.e. private) schools—mostly owned and managed by religious authorities—and the great majority of primary schools are under the management of the churches, in recent years the number of religious personnel in the schools has become quite small. At present 10.2 per cent of secondary school teachers are religious personnel, and just 5.0 per cent of primary teachers. In the community-comprehensive sector the proportion of religious or clerical teachers is 6.2 per cent (Department of Education, 1992a). The deeds of trust of community schools specify that a minimum number of teachers from the religious order represented on the board of management be nominated to the teaching staff. Therefore, although these schools are within the 'public sector' at second level (that is, they are owned by the state), they are not non-denominational.

Figures on the proportion of religious teachers are not published in the department's *Statistical Reports* for the vocational sector. These schools are non-denominational under the Vocational Education Act, 1930, and consequently there are very few religious personnel as teachers on the staffs of vocational schools (Diggins, 1990, 127), although school chaplains are attached to many of these schools.

It is in the secondary schools that the greatest changes have taken place with regard to the religious composition of the teaching force over the last twenty-five years. Just before the introduction of 'free' postprimary education in 1966 the majority of staff in these schools were clergy and members of religious orders (Coolahan, 1984, 186). The entry of most of these schools into the 'free scheme', the expansion of postprimary provision and the consequent dramatic increase in pupil participation occurred at a time when entry to religious orders and the clergy began to fall rapidly, giving rise to the predominantly lay teaching force that we have today. However, religious personnel still play a significant role in the management structures of the school, and we look at their distribution at management level later in this chapter.

GENDER COMPOSITION

Teaching is predominantly a female profession. A total of 63.9 per cent of all teachers are women. However, there are some variations by sector. It is in the primary sector that women are in the largest majority, at 76.5 per cent (figures from the Department of Education). Women predominate in the secondary sector too, but to a much lesser extent. They account for 55.4 per cent of the total number of secondary teachers on incremental scales. In the community-comprehensive schools men are somewhat in the majority, at 53.8 per cent. Men are also in the majority in vocational schools, at 56.6 per cent (Department of Education, 1992a, 123, 127, 132).

The higher proportion of men in the vocational and community-comprehensive schools may be attributable to the gender-biased nature of teaching in the practical subjects, such as woodwork, metalwork, mechanical drawing, and home economics. These subjects are provided to a much greater extent in vocational and community-comprehensive schools than they are in secondary schools. There are virtually no women teachers in the woodwork, metalwork and mechanical drawing areas, while men are not represented among home economics teachers.

The lower proportion of women teachers in 'public sector' schools may also reflect high numbers of women among part-time teachers. As we have already pointed out, the Department of Education does not provide a detailed breakdown of part-time teachers in its *Statistical Reports*. However, statistics on the first destination of higher education graduates produced by the Higher Education Authority show that men who qualify as teachers at both primary and second level are more likely to get full-time posts than women.

Although teaching is a predominantly female profession, there are two qualifying observations to be made relating to this. Firstly, as one moves from the more junior to the more senior levels, the proportion of women declines. This is illustrated above through the figures on the proportion of women in the primary and postprimary levels; it is even observable within the primary system as one moves from the junior to the senior classes. Men are less likely to be allocated to teaching infant classes, while proportionately fewer women are allocated to senior classes among mixed staffs (Kellaghan et al., 1984). If we were to include third-level teachers in our discussions, this tendency would become even more marked. At third level, women are poorly represented among the academic staff in universities, at just 14.5 per cent of lecturing posts (Higher Education Authority, 1987).

The second observation concerns management structures, which will be dealt with in detail later in this chapter. What these observations show is that while teaching is a predominantly female profession, it is largely administered and managed by men. (See table 5.3.)

SOCIAL BACKGROUND
There have been remarkably few studies of the social background of teachers. We therefore have very little systematic information on this. Twenty years ago Kelly did a study of primary teachers in the city of Dublin. At that time two social groups were very strongly represented among the teachers in the study: some 34 per cent were from farming backgrounds, and a further 50 per cent

were from professional or white-collar backgrounds. Just 10 per cent were from manual backgrounds, compared with 40 per cent in the population as a whole. There were male/female differences: more women came from the farming and professional categories, and more men from manual backgrounds (Kelly, 1970). In addition, although these teachers were all teaching in Dublin, and many in inner-city areas, most of them came from outside Dublin. This means that a substantial number of the teachers were very different in social origins and background from the pupils they were teaching.

Work by O'Sullivan among primary teachers in Cork reflects similar patterns, with the majority coming from non-manual or professional backgrounds and the children of farmers overrepresented. The Cork study did, however, indicate a tendency for the relatively small proportion of teachers from manual backgrounds to be more highly represented in predominantly working-class schools than in predominantly middle-class schools (O'Sullivan, 1980a).

These studies confirm the view that teaching recruits very much from the middle-class sector and that the children of farmers also are strongly represented in teaching. In this the Irish teaching profession differs from those in some other European countries. For example, in Britain the teaching profession is a much more diverse group in its social origins. Because of the very small proportion of the population engaged in agriculture in Britain, it is not surprising that the children of farmers form a negligible proportion of the teaching force. While the majority of teachers are from middle-class origins, a more significant proportion is drawn from skilled, semi-skilled and working-class manual backgrounds than in Ireland (Burgess, 1986, 137–8).

A more recent survey (1987) of entrants to teaching can tell us whether the trend for teachers to come from farm and middle-class backgrounds in Ireland has continued. A study of entrants to colleges of education (Greaney, Burke, and McCann, 1987) showed that these trends are indeed continuing: the children of farmers were over-represented, while manual workers' children were very under-represented on entry to colleges of education. As for geographical area, this recent study showed that Dublin entrants were under-represented, accounting for approximately half the numbers one would expect based on population statistics, while western seaboard regions were strongly overrepresented.

We have not got comparable surveys of postprimary teachers or entrants. However, there is no reason to suppose that their general profile would differ greatly from that of primary teachers. In particular, it is unlikely that the under-representation of the children of manual workers differs significantly at postprimary level. Clancy's study of university entrants (from whom postprimary teachers are eventually drawn) shows that those from manual working-class backgrounds continue to be significantly under-represented in comparison with their distribution in the population (Clancy, 1988).

The apparent difference in the social origins of teachers and a sizable proportion of their pupils has implications for the learning process and for teacher-pupil interactions. In particular, it may aggravate cultural differences between teachers and disadvantaged working-class children. There is evidence from O'Sullivan's work (1980b; 1984) that some teachers have a 'deficit model' in their perceptions of working-class children. That is, the working-class child's background is perceived as lacking in 'educational' or 'formative' character. There was evidence also of a 'pathological' model of working-class children: there were more frequent perceptions of them (compared with middle-class children) as abnormal, morally reprehensible, or the product of a social malaise. There were also indications that these pupils were more vigorously socialised to be respectful, submissive, non-inventive and rule-following than middle-class children (O'Sullivan, 1984).

The studies carried out by O'Sullivan, though providing interesting and thought-provoking material, were on a limited scale. Clearly there is a need for further research in this area. As Lynch (1989, 128–30) has argued, teachers are very much part of the propertyless middle classes and may well have a specific class interest in maintaining aspects of the status quo, especially those concerning traditional hierarchical distinctions between mental and manual labour. If intellectual labour were no longer defined as superior to manual labour, then the whole basis of teachers' differentials, which distance them from manual workers, would not be legitimated (ibid.). In a profession that recruits on such a small scale from among working-class young people and that is so important for the articulation and preservation of middle-class values and culture, it would hardly be surprising that this would be so. Indeed, we have argued this in chapter 3, where we suggest that people's 'domain assumptions' (Gouldner, 1970) influence their attitudes. It can also be argued that while individual religious orders and personnel have shown concern for class inequalities, the corporate location of religious personnel in the middle classes has meant that they have more often acted in line with the interests of that class than in promoting the interests of the unemployed or the working class in education (Lynch, 1989, 131). (In chapters 4 and 6 we discuss further the role of the churches in education.)

Teaching as a Career

Lortie argues on the basis of a study of American teachers that compared with most other kinds of middle-class work, teaching is relatively 'careerless', that there is less opportunity for upward movement, which is the essence of a career. He suggests that the typical career line of the classroom teacher is a gentle incline rather than a steep ascent. The status of the young tenured teacher is not appreciably different from that of the highly experienced old-timer. He suggests that as a consequence, teachers are less 'future-oriented' than other professions.

He suggests also that the 'gentle incline' is less attractive to men than to women. Lortie argues that the main opportunity for making major status gains in teaching rests in leaving classroom work for full-time administration. He argues that the incentive system is not organised to respond to variations in effort and talent among classroom teachers (Lortie, 1984). We often hear similar comments made by Irish teachers.

We can begin to consider the career patterns of Irish teachers by examining the patterns of entry to postprimary teaching. This can be done by looking at the first destinations of higher diploma in education (HDE) graduates and graduates of the colleges of education. Great changes took place during the 1980s as a result of financial cut-backs by the Government and consequent changing patterns and conditions in schools. Let us compare 1982 with 1985 and 1990 to get a view of these changes.

Table 5.1

**First destination of HDE graduates, 1982, 1985, 1990,
and of primary degree graduates (BEd), 1985, 1990**

	HDE 1982 %	HDE 1985 %	HDE 1990 %	BEd 1985 %	BEd 1990 %
Permanent teaching in Ireland	25.9	12.2	5.5	36.8	8.2
Part-time, temporary, or substitute	30.8	45.5	54.5	58.5	79.0
Teaching abroad	6.9	10.9	18.7	0.4	3.8
Further study	8.2	8.0	8.3	1.1	4.7
Other	13.0	14.4	10.9	2.3	3.7
Seeking employment	15.2	9.0	2.1	0.9	0.6
Total	100.0	100.0	100.0	100.0	100.0
n	1,121	903	567	762	657

Source: Higher Education Authority (1991), 91, 97.

The figures in the table relate to placements just nine months after graduation, and while they do not tell the full story about entry to teaching by HDE and BEd graduates, they certainly give an indication of shifting patterns. The most obvious shift is away from a substantial proportion of graduates getting permanent employment during the first year to a pattern of temporary or part-time employment for the majority. Many people might suggest that this is in fact a good thing, since it means that most graduates get a couple of years of different experiences before they become permanently appointed. This is much more akin to what happens in other fields of employment. There is also a notable increase in the proportion teaching abroad. There is a marked decrease in the proportion still seeking employment nine months after graduating; this would appear to be explained by the increased willingness of graduates over the period to take part-time or temporary employment, and to go abroad to teach.

There were substantial sex differences in the proportions in permanent and in temporary or part-time employment in all years. For example, in 1991 8.9 per cent of male but only 4.4 per cent of female HDE graduates were in permanent employment, compared with 45.9 and 57.2 per cent, respectively, in temporary or part-time teaching. Similar differences were observable among BEd graduates. In 1991 13.3 of male but only 6.4 per cent of female BEd graduates were in permanent employment a year after graduation, compared with 64.7 and 84.1 per cent, respectively, in temporary or part-time teaching (Higher Education Authority, 1991, 92, 97).

Over this period there was also a significant drop in the number of students taking teacher education courses. The numbers in table 5.1 represent response rates to a survey. The total number of those graduating as teachers, at primary and second level, declined significantly in the period—from 1,967 in 1985 to 1,455 in 1990 (ibid., 90, 96). These changing patterns for graduate teachers certainly indicate a keen responsiveness and adaptability by these young teachers to 'market forces' within the system. What these figures do not show is the subsequent development of graduates' teaching careers and 'survival rates' in teaching. There is a clear need for research in this area.

Irish teachers are well paid in relation to teachers in many other countries. A total of 92 per cent of expenditure on primary schools and more than 70 per cent on second-level schools goes to salaries (OECD, 1991, 47–8). However, there is general agreement that management structures in Irish schools are less than satisfactory. There are a number of reasons for this. Firstly, in primary teaching, for example, posts of responsibility exist only in larger schools. In smaller schools, still in the majority, the only senior posts are those of principal and vice-principal. Secondly, there is a lack of clear definition of the responsibilities attached—especially to middle management posts. Thirdly, promotion procedures have been criticised, especially in the secondary sector, where they are based on seniority. Such recruitment procedures, it can be argued, lead to lack of initiative and poor leadership in schools. Fourthly, the availability of posts has been criticised as inadequate in the light of diverse responsibilities and changing needs in schools.

Let us now examine the situation at second level. In the school year 1990/91, 53.1 per cent of teachers in community or comprehensive schools and 55.5 per cent in secondary schools were in promotional posts—the majority 'B' post holders (figures provided by the Department of Education). The position in the different sectors is shown in table 5.2.

Although there is still a high percentage of principals in the secondary sector who are religious personnel, the number is rapidly declining. Each year a higher proportion of lay teachers is appointed—especially as schools amalgamate. However, clergy and members of religious orders are still trustees of schools and thus ultimately responsible for policy and for staff appointments, although the proposals for boards of management contained in the Green Paper (Department of Education, 1992, 144), if implemented, may change this somewhat, as the nominees of the trustees or owners would be in a minority (of one) on the proposed boards.

Table 5.2

Promotional posts in secondary, community/comprehensive, vocational and primary schools

	Secondary		Comm./comp.		Vocational		Primary	
(Figures in parentheses represent religious as percentage of total)								
		%		%		%		%
Principals	479	(65.6)	72	(9.7)	250	(0.0)	3,789	(9.6)
Vice-principals	480	(2.5)	80	(7.5)	247	(0.0)	2,016	(1.5)
'A' posts	1,800	(2.3)	388	(1.5)	692	(0.0)	354	(2.3)
'B' posts	3,650	(3.8)	766	(1.8)	1,443	(0.0)	1,837	(3.6)
Total	6,409	(7.9)	1,306	(2.5)	2,632	(0.0)	7,996	(5.9)

Source: secondary, community and comprehensive schools: figures provided by the Department of Education (1990/91); vocational schools: TUI (1990, 5); primary schools: figures provided by the Department of Education (1991/92).

While table 5.2 shows that a reasonable number of teachers are at middle management levels in second-level schools, this does not mean that a coherent management structure for schools has evolved. In many schools these posts are ill defined. Again to quote the OECD, 'in a situation where schools should be equipped to cope with new demands, it is regrettable that an effective middle management capability scarcely exists' (OECD, 1991, 108). They therefore suggest incorporating this element into initial training, and providing much more in-service education.

In the primary sector, as indicated above, promotional posts are linked to the number of pupils and, therefore, to the size of school. It is only in the larger schools that 'A' and 'B' grades exist. Very small schools will often qualify only for a principal's post, depending on pupil numbers. As a result, the proportion of teachers in promotional posts is much lower than at second level, at 38.5 per cent overall. Here, as in the second-level schools, the proportion of religious personnel in promotional posts is small.

As indicated earlier, teaching as a career is highly differentiated by gender. Table 5.3 sets out the relationship.

Table 5.3

**Promotional posts in secondary, community/comprehensive,
vocational and primary schools, by gender**

Posts	Secondary		Comm./Comp.		Vocational		Primary	
	Female	Male	Female	Male	Female	Male	Female	Male
	%	%	%	%	%	%	%	%
Principals	50.5*	49.5	8.3	91.7	4.8	95.2	48.1	51.9
Vice-principals	43.1	56.9	22.5	77.5	12.6	87.4	82.6	17.4
'A' posts	46.9	53.1	31.2	68.8	22.8	77.2	67.2	32.8
'B' posts	51.9	48.1	45.4	54.6	36.2	63.8	75.5	24.5

*81 % of these are religious women. In 1988/89 lay women comprised only 6.2 % of the principals of secondary, community and comprehensive schools. The comparable figure for lay men was 27 %. At the vice-principal level lay women fared better, with 40 % of posts. However, 58 % were held by lay men (Lynch, 1991, 131).

Source: secondary, community and comprehensive schools: figures from the Department of Education (1990/91); vocational schools: TUI (1990), 5; primary schools: figures from the Department of Education (1991/92).

While teaching is a predominantly female profession, table 5.3 illustrates that at management level women are significantly underrepresented, especially in the second-level public sector. In the public sector the underrepresentation of women is very marked at principal level. However, it is also significant at other levels of responsibility. As promotion to the position of principal is often dependent on the applicant's previous career profile and responsibilities, the lack of representation at 'middle' management is doubly disadvantageous to women.

In secondary schools the position of women in the management of schools is more favourable. However, this is true only of principals' posts and 'B' posts. It is not true of vice-principalships or 'A' posts, at which levels men are over-represented. The more favourable position of women at principal level is related to the structure of ownership of secondary schools, where religious orders predominate. The majority of female principals are members of religious orders (81 per cent). However, as the number of religious personnel decreases and religious orders increasingly appoint lay principals, there is evidence that in this sector also the position of women in management will be eroded. That this is already happening is apparent if we examine the proportion of women principals in 1989/90 and 1990/91. The proportion of women principals in secondary schools declined from 52.3 per cent to 50.5 per cent in these two years. In addition, the under-representation of women in vice-principalships and 'A' posts may also be a problem, since it is from these positions that future principals are normally appointed.

While at first glance women may seem to be well represented in principals' positions in primary schools, they are also underrepresented here in comparison with their distribution in primary teaching. Women make up over three-quarters of the teaching force in primary schools, yet just 11.5 per cent of female primary teachers are principals, in comparison with 40.3 per cent of male primary teachers. It is interesting to note that there has been little improvement in this regard since the study of gender inequalities in primary teaching carried out in the early 1980s (Kellaghan et al., 1984), in spite of an awareness-raising campaign conducted by the Irish National Teachers' Organisation.

In addition to movement to posts of responsibility and to principalships, another career route for teachers is to the school inspectorate. In 1991 there were 141 inspectors attached to the Department of Education, of whom 11.3 per cent were women (IPA, 1991, 32). Apart from the Chief Inspector and two deputy chief inspectors, 77 inspectors were attached to the Primary Branch and 54 to the Post-Primary Branch, while a further 7 had responsibilities in both. The proportion of women was lower among those who dealt exclusively with primary education (7.8 per cent), although it might have been expected to reflect the high proportion of women teachers in primary schools. Among postprimary inspectors, women were somewhat better represented, at 13 per cent. In the inspectorate there were 50 senior posts: chief inspector, deputy chief inspectors, assistant chief inspectors, divisional inspectors, and senior inspectors. Of these, just 4 per cent were women (ibid.).

Although in 1991 there was a female Minister for Education, the senior administrative posts in the department were mainly held by men. The Secretary and five Assistant Secretaries were men. Of the 19 principal officers just 10.2 per cent were women, while among the assistant principals women formed 16.1 per cent (ibid., 30–2). Therefore, while teaching is a predominantly female profession, especially at primary level, school management, inspection and the administration and management of the system is conducted mainly by men. These structures reflect the wider patriarchal structures in society, which we discuss in chapter 8.

Career structures for women in third-level teaching are even less favourable than for women in primary or second-level teaching. Women are poorly represented in third-level teaching as a whole, as shown by a survey carried out by the Higher Education Authority (see table 5.4).

Women are not well represented on the teaching staffs of the universities or the technological colleges. There is a somewhat better representation in colleges of education. At the senior academic level the disparities between women and men are even more pronounced. The same study shows, for example, that in the universities at professorial level women form just 2.7 per cent of the total. At the level of senior lecturer the proportion is 6.9 per cent, while at lecturer level the proportion is 21.6 per cent.

Women are best represented in the lower echelons of the academic staffs, where they form 31.5 per cent of the total in the 'assistant lecturer and other' category (ibid., 16). Among the reasons suggested for the poor representation of women at all levels in third-level teaching is that female students represent only 36 per cent of postgraduate degree recipients. Postgraduates are the pool from which academic staff are drawn (ibid.). Although our focus in this chapter is mainly on the teaching profession in the school sector, we can see that in the matter of gender differences there are greater disparities in third-level education than in any other sector.

Table 5.4

Women as a percentage of staff in third-level colleges

Type of institution	Women as percentage of total
Universities*	12.9
Dublin Institute of Technology	12.3
Regional technical colleges	12.1
Colleges of education	43.9
Other colleges	23.7
Total	14.9

*'Universities' includes the figure for the then NIHEs. This figure differs slightly from the overall figure for women in the universities given earlier, as it is based on the distribution of respondents to a survey.

Source: Higher Education Authority (1987), 22.

TEACHERS' ROLES

Although there has been little Irish research into the social background of teachers, somewhat more attention has been paid to their role and their perceptions of it. Role is a key concept in social science. Roles prescribe certain ways of behaving, but they also allow for 'creative interpretation', so that, for example, people may develop different teaching styles. Likewise, teachers may obviously have different teaching roles, depending on the type of institution and the level at which they are teaching.

Delamont, referring to the international literature on teachers' roles, identifies two characteristic elements that she calls 'immediacy' and 'autonomy'. Quantitative studies of classrooms show that the teachers may be engaging in up to a thousand interpersonal exchanges every day. This frequency means that many of the teachers' decisions have to be immediate. There is little chance to reflect, and no chance to get a 'second opinion'. This is a radically different working environment from that of other professionals, such as doctors or lawyers. The doctor can send a patient to hospital for tests before diagnosing or prescribing;

the lawyer can ask a colleague for a second opinion. Usually in the classroom the teacher's professional colleagues are out of reach, and many decisions have to be made on the spot (Delamont, 1983, 49–50).

The problem of immediacy is related to the issue of privacy, as is the question of autonomy. The teacher is alone and in control—the 'four-wall syndrome', as some call it. Indeed, the most common state for the teacher is one of professional isolation (Fullan and Hargreaves, 1992, 52). The teacher has power or authority over many aspects of pupils' lives. Knowledge, behaviour, speech, and clothing—all come within the sphere of her or his control. Seeing the teacher in terms of her or his control over pupils brings power to the centre of analysis. Teachers and pupils come to the classroom in very different bargaining positions (Delamont, 1983).

While these aspects of teacher authority are legitimated by the school and by society, the establishment of the teacher's authority does not come about automatically but must be established through the use of classroom management skills, and also through processes such as negotiation (Denscombe, 1985, 129–35). Indeed control and classroom management can cause great difficulties to the neophyte teacher, as Ó Síoráin's study of probationer teachers shows (Ó Síoráin, 1983).

Delamont argues that the teacher's most potent resource is her or his possession of, access to and control over knowledge. The teacher has knowledge and defines what should and should not be learnt (within the educational context of the curriculum and examination system). In the studies of classroom interactions there are many examples of the way teachers impose this control through the way they deal with children's contributions in class.

In fact, teachers seem very vulnerable on this issue. Threats to their control over knowledge disturb teachers at all levels, from infant school to university. Studies of curriculum developments that have tried to change the traditional relationship between teacher and knowledge base (for example Nuffield science in England, which emphasised guided discovery rather than lecturing and demonstrating) illustrate some of the pitfalls for curriculum development. This study showed that while the formal curriculum changed as the exam system incorporated Nuffield ideas, the hidden curriculum of classroom life changed little. The study found through observation of over a hundred teachers in over three hundred lessons that there was little evidence of the new techniques (Delamont, 1983, 54–5).

There are important lessons here for us with regard to the implementation of curriculum development in Ireland. In particular the findings on the Nuffield study are of relevance. At postprimary level the Irish education system is going through a period of curricular reform. At junior cycle the new Junior Certificate has introduced a syllabus that depends much more on experiential than on didactic learning and that demands a variety of approaches, including field and project work, discovery learning, and role playing. While no systematic evaluations of the Junior Certificate based on observations in classrooms are planned at present, the English experience suggests that while the formal curriculum may change, the hidden curriculum of the classroom might not change with it.

Research carried out on the implementation of the new curriculum introduced in primary schools in 1971 suggests similar outcomes at primary level. The 1971 primary school curriculum represented a move away from a teacher-centred, didactic pedagogy to an integrated, child-centred curriculum, emphasising activity and discovery methods and environment-based learning. Although there may have been initial resistance to the new curriculum, by 1986 a survey of its members carried out by the INTO showed a very high level of support among teachers for the principles of the new curriculum.

In spite of this, the same survey also showed that 60 per cent of the teachers surveyed expressed a preference for a didactic approach to teaching, and nearly two-thirds reported spending more than half the time available to them in class teaching (INTO, 1987, 18–19). There was a difference in the responses of older and younger teachers, the younger teachers (who would have been trained in the use of the new methods during pre-service education) reporting greater use of the newer methods. This perhaps indicates the need for substantial in-service education in the implementation of curriculum change. The survey also suggests that while teachers may be well disposed to curriculum reform, appropriate resources must be provided to ensure implementation. Large class sizes and paucity of equipment were identified here as part of the explanation of the apparently contradictory attitudes and practices (ibid., 19).

However, while further research based on classroom observations would be required to build a systematic picture of classroom practices, these studies highlight the importance of the role of the teacher in the implementation (or lack of it) of curriculum change. As we pointed out in the preface, international research indicates that for educational change to be meaningful, collaborative cultures must develop in our schools (Fullan and Hargreaves, 1992). Research on the role of the teacher suggests that one of the greatest obstacles to this is the tradition of professional isolation of teachers and the individualism resulting from this (ibid., 52–9).

HOW IRISH TEACHERS VIEW THEIR ROLES

There has been very little research in Irish sociology of education based on independent observations in classrooms (Drudy, 1991). However, there have been a number of studies that have focused on teachers' perceptions of their roles, of teaching, and of their pupils. Kelly's study, for example, suggested that teachers saw teaching as a wide-ranging activity, involving the attainment of such relatively diffuse goals as the moral, intellectual and social development of their pupils (Kelly, 1970).

O'Sullivan gives us some insight into classroom organisation as reported by primary school teachers. This work indicates relatively high levels of teacher control, compared with pupil control, over curriculum content, and relatively smaller amounts of group as opposed to individual work. As regards teaching styles, there was a high concern among teachers to conform to conventional educational standards, and a fairly moderate use of discovery techniques (O'Sullivan, 1980a). However, teachers in working-class schools were significantly more likely to report the use of discovery techniques compared with teachers in middle-class schools.

Clearly, since this study is based on teachers reporting what they do rather than on systematic independent observations in classrooms, there may be a divergence between perceived and 'objective' reality. Nevertheless, teachers differed in reportage of their classroom practice. This could, as O'Sullivan argues, be the result of a greater concern among these teachers for the education of 'disadvantaged' children, or it could be associated with the fact that in his study, class size in the working-class schools was significantly lower than in the middle-class schools (ibid.). Or it could perhaps be related to the characteristic of many middle-class parents of expecting more traditional education, as they believe it to produce better results.

A study of the role of the primary school principal published in 1980 by Clancy looks at the role of the principal as seen by non-teaching principals themselves. Clancy found a great deal of disagreement among principals concerning appropriate role behaviour. They differed on how much control they should try to exercise over other teachers' behaviour or their teaching methods. While they favoured involvement by teachers in discussion during the decision-making process, they differed about when teachers could make administrative decisions.

While principals in Clancy's study almost universally felt that they should take prime responsibility for the general rules concerning discipline, and felt they should support staff, they disagreed on whether they should back a teacher who they felt had acted unfairly. They also differed on how much background information should be given to teachers about pupils. There was uncertainty also about the exact role of parents.

These studies indicate that the role of teacher and principal is a changing one, and one over which there is still a degree of uncertainty. Not only is there uncertainty but there is evidence that teachers, especially principal teachers, experience little control over the definition of their role. Work carried out by Herron for the INTO on changes in the roles of primary principals over the last decade suggests that

an analysis of the shifts that have occurred . . . leads one to the conclusion that the Irish principal teacher suffered more changes in role and responsibility than they initiated for themselves. Neither as individuals nor collectively did they perceive themselves in a position to influence the matters which were to dramatically change the content, processes or contexts of their jobs. Principal teachers, therefore, found themselves in a *reactive* position to the changes which were initiated. (INTO, 1991, 35)

At second level the role of the principal has traditionally been somewhat different. As Cooney points out, in secondary schools principals have had control in the key areas of staff selection and the formulation of school aims. In addition, a large (although declining) proportion of school principals are members of religious congregations and thus enjoy all the prerogatives of ownership (Cooney, 1981).

Although secondary school principals have had the type of control outlined above, Diggins's study of second-level principals (in all sectors) nevertheless indicates a lack of clarity about role definitions. In particular, he points to the lack of a clearly defined role in teacher evaluation. Second-level principals spend most of their time dealing with students. He argues that principals choose to solve difficulties that could and should be solved by teachers. Therefore teachers cannot engage in creative expansion of their own roles, and there is consequently less job satisfaction and a lessening of educational quality (Diggins, 1982). In the small number of instances where principals act as educational administrators, he suggests that they do so effectively (ibid.).

Changing needs and new curriculums in schools are offering a challenge to the teaching profession. This was recognised in the recent OECD report on Irish education, where the need for in-service education and the in-service development of management and leadership skills was particularly identified. This important report (OECD, 1991, 91) suggests that teachers' roles are variously defined as follows:

Teachers' roles . . . must encompass not only the instructional, the custodial, the inspirational, and the disciplinary but extend into practically all spheres of life with teachers acting as agents of physical, moral and spiritual development, emotional and mental health, and social welfare. Among the qualities called for—in addition to the academic and the pedagogical—are political and negotiating competence, accountancy and fund-raising abilities, a repertoire of skills to assume extracurricular responsibilities and to communicate with widely diverse groups, planning and management skills, and an up-to-date knowledge of developments in technology and working life . . . An urgent requirement is to determine priorities in the teacher's tasks and to examine the possibilities for greater role differentiation within the profession of teaching.

This report sees the teacher's role as a very wide-ranging and diffuse one, even if it does suggest role differentiation and specialisation within schools. It proposes a range of activities and responsibilities for which a large proportion of Irish teachers are not well prepared. Consequently, it also recommends a great expansion in the provision of in-service education.

TEACHERS' UNIONS

As we indicated earlier, much discussion of teachers as a group has focused on their behaviour as part of organised labour. It has been argued that the professional organisation of teachers has been based predominantly on a trade union model (McKeown, 1982; Burke, 1992). Teachers are represented by three very powerful unions, each covering one of the different sectors of education. Teachers in the primary sector are represented by the Irish National Teachers' Organisation (INTO). This is the only one of the teachers' unions that claims to be an all-Ireland union, as it also represents teachers in Catholic primary schools in Northern Ireland. Secondary school teachers are represented by the Association of Secondary Teachers, Ireland (ASTI). This is numerically the larger of the two postprimary unions. The Teachers' Union of Ireland (TUI) represents teachers in the vocational sector; it also represents lecturing staff in the regional technical colleges, which until 1992 were under the management of vocational education committees. Teaching staff in community and comprehensive schools are represented by either the ASTI or TUI, for the most part depending on their former sector, in the case of amalgamated schools. At present inter-union discussions are under way to move towards a form of federation of the three unions in order to increase negotiating power.

Teachers' unions are very powerful, not only because of their numerical strength and increasing willingness to work collectively to influence educational policy and members' conditions but also because of the consultative nature of their roles. While the ASTI has no formal arrangement whereby it can influence state managers directly (through regular meetings with Department of Education staff), meetings are arranged when requested (Lynch, 1989, 128). The TUI has a standing arrangement with the Department of Education to hold monthly meetings on matters of mutual concern; and the INTO has regular meetings also with senior Department of Education staff. Unions are also well represented on committees and review bodies set up to develop policies in particular areas (ibid., 129). Indeed, Burke argues that special interest representation on such bodies as those that recently reviewed primary education and the primary curriculum, and on the NCCA, is so strong that teachers' unions and other special interest groups (such as managerial bodies) enjoy a virtual veto on the formulation of national educational policy (Burke, 1992, 201).

Traditionally, the collective action of teachers' unions has been primarily used in pay bargaining, as is illustrated in Coolahan's history of the ASTI (1984). However, teachers' unions have also engaged in collective bargaining over a wider range of issues, as is illustrated by the Programme for Economic and Social Progress agreed in 1991. The implementation of this programme has subsequently become a matter for further negotiation and industrial action. Teachers' unions have also been active in responding to the proposals in the 1992 Green Paper on education (see, for example, Gilmore, 1992; Riordan, 1992; Ruane, 1992).

We saw earlier that management structures in education reflect patriarchal structures in society. Patriarchal relations are also reflected in the composition of the executive committees of the teachers' unions. Although women form a substantial proportion of the membership of the teachers' unions—a majority in the case of the INTO and the ASTI—they are very poorly represented on the executive committees of these unions. In 1992/93 the Executive Committee of the INTO is composed of twenty-two people, including elected representatives and officers. Of these, two are women. The Standing Committee of the ASTI is composed of fifteen people, of whom one is a woman. The TUI, with a 22-member executive committee, has the largest female representation at this level: there are four women members, although this is the only union where men are somewhat in the majority in the membership.

The reasons for such poor representation are no doubt complex. However, it would seem almost certain that the dual roles of many female teachers who have both professional and family commitments, combined with organisational features within the unions themselves, have much to do with the problem. Our own discussions with teachers during in-service work, as well as more public debate at teachers' congresses, would indicate that this is perceived as a problem by many teachers. The issue is being addressed within the unions also— for example, at the time of writing there are proposals to reform the Standing Committee of the ASTI. These would involve enlarging and regionalising it, and establishing reserved places for women.

TEACHERS AND EDUCATIONAL CHANGE

The potential is thus there for teachers to be a powerful force for change in education. However, historically they have not really fulfilled this role, for a variety of reasons. Many changes have taken place in teaching, however, including the professionalisation of teaching through the extension of degree awards to all sectors, the growth of specialist in-service courses (Coolahan, 1981, 228–30), and the increasing laicisation and feminisation of the profession. Teachers are still drawn primarily from the non-manual, professional and farming classes, and there is, as we have seen, some evidence also of social conservatism on the part of teachers in the form of negative stereotyping of working-class children, although further research would be useful on this.

Although there were major curricular initiatives at primary level in 1971 with the introduction of the new primary school curriculum and at second level in 1989 with the introduction of the Junior Certificate, there is evidence of methodological and pedagogical conservatism in the adherence of teachers to didactic and individualistic approaches in the classroom. However, it would perhaps be unfair to hold teachers entirely responsible for this, since so little in the way of in-service education has accompanied these changes. There is also, at the time of writing, resistance by the ASTI, the largest of the unions at second level, to the introduction of school-based assessment at Junior Certificate level, although there is some support for it in the TUI.

There has been a tendency for the teachers' unions to focus their efforts on negotiations on the pay and conditions of their members. While this has not served to put teachers' salaries on a par with other professions, particularly the older ones, such as law and medicine, it has served to maintain the differentials between teaching and all forms of manual work. It can thus be argued, as we have suggested above, that teachers have a class interest in the maintenance of the existing middle-class domination of the education system, since they themselves are very much part of the propertyless middle classes, whose power and influence is contingent on maintaining traditional hierarchical distinctions between mental and manual labour.

Lest we appear to overstate this, it has to be pointed out that the teaching profession and teachers' unions are not monolithic institutions. There are tensions, divergences of interest and contradictions within them. It has already been suggested that there are resistances to social, pedagogical and curricular change within the teaching profession. Yet, as we have seen, on the review bodies and committees that initiated such changes, teachers and subject associations were well represented and worked very hard to bring about these changes. Teachers' unions have been involved in attempts to initiate research or action to effect change. For example, the INTO, conscious of the underrepresentation of women as principals in primary schools, commissioned a study to collect basic data (Kellaghan et al., 1984), and has followed it up with action within the membership and as a pressure group on the Department of Education. The TUI has participated in action research designed to implement greater equality between girls and boys through the organisation of schooling within the public sector (McMenamin, Fogarty, et al., 1990) and have also carried out research into promotional structures among its membership (TUI, 1990).

Burke points out that with notable exceptions, such as Britain, western countries have come round to a more professional vision of teachers and an expectation that they should be involved in all aspects of education, including the shaping of educational reforms (Burke, 1992, 198). From a somewhat different perspective Apple also argues that, as education enters more and more into the political and economic arena, the work culture of teachers can be used for educative purposes. He suggests that it can be employed in a process of political education by using elements of it as exemplars of the very possibility of regaining at least partial control over the conditions of one's work and for clarifying the structural determinants that set limits on progressive pedagogic activity. This can be done through curricular action (Apple, 1982, 88–9; 1986).

Aronowitz and Giroux also point to the emancipatory possibilities of curricular action by teachers. They suggest that teachers have the potential to be transformative intellectuals, who can emerge from, and work with, any number of groups, other than and including the working class, that advance emancipatory traditions and cultures. This may be done through the use of the language of critique and the development of a critical pedagogy. Central to this is the task of making the pedagogical more political and the political more pedagogical. This involves treating students as critical agents, using dialogue, and making knowledge meaningful, critical, and ultimately emancipatory. Such action has its starting point not just with individual students but also with collective action (Aronowitz and Giroux, 1985, 36–7). Given the representation of teachers and teachers' unions on committees, review bodies, and the NCCA, it can be argued that there is at least some potential for Irish teachers to involve themselves in educational reform and transformation.

CONCLUSION

In this chapter we have examined the changing composition of the Irish teaching force. It is now a predominantly lay, predominantly female (especially at primary level) profession, though its recruits continue to be mainly from middle-class and farming backgrounds. The middle-class origins and orientation of the profession may have implications for teachers' interactions with working-class pupils, and for their actions as a major interest group in education. The career structure of teaching is still best described as a 'gentle incline'. However, recent analyses have pointed to the need for changes in the management structure of teaching. The main changes suggested relate to clearer definitions of roles, and to anxieties concerning the gender inequalities at management level. Among third-level teachers, in the inspectorate and in the administration of the Department of Education gender inequalities are very marked.

Teachers' unions are powerful forces in Irish education, and there are sometimes tensions between their professionalism and their desire to improve working conditions. Because of their strength and because of their representation on key statutory bodies and committees, teachers are in a more favourable position than formerly to influence and shape educational change. In structural terms, they face a dilemma that is not unlike that confronting the churches: they have to decide whether, when and where corporate interests as an occupational group take precedence over their professional interests as educationalists.

References and Further Reading

Apple, M. (1982), *Education and Power*, London: Ark.

Apple, M. (1986), *Teachers and Texts*, New York: Routledge and Kegan Paul.

Aronowitz, S., and Giroux, H. (1985), *Education Under Siege: the Conservative, Liberal and Radical Debate Over Schooling*, London: Routledge and Kegan Paul.

Bourdieu, P. (1973), 'Cultural reproduction and social reproduction' in R. Brown (ed.), *Knowledge, Education and Cultural Change*, London: Tavistock.

Burgess, R. (1986), *Sociology, Education and Schools*, London: Batsford.

Burke, A. (1992), *Teaching: Retrospect and Prospect* (special Edition of *Oideas*, vol. 39).

Clancy, P. (1980–81), 'The role of the primary school principal', *Social Studies*, vol. 6, no. 4, 335–73.

Clancy, P. (1988), *Who Goes to College?: a Second National Survey of Participation in Higher Education*, Dublin: Higher Education Authority.

Coolahan, J. (1981), *Irish Education: History and Structure*, Dublin: Institute of Public Administration.

Coolahan, J. (1984), *The ASTI and Post-Primary Education in Ireland, 1909–1984*, Dublin: Cumann na Meánmhúinteoirí, Éire.

Cooney, M. (1981), 'Teacher union (ASTI) stewards' perceptions of the role of the principal teacher', *Irish Educational Studies*, vol. 1, 360–75.

Delamont, S. (1983), *Interaction in the Classroom*, London: Methuen 1983.

Denscombe, M. (1985), *Classroom Control: a Sociological Perspective*, London: Allen and Unwin.

Department of Education (1991), *Statistical Report, 1989/1990*, Dublin: Stationery Office.

Department of Education (1992a), *Statistical Report, 1990/91*, Dublin: Stationery Office.

Department of Education (1992b), *Education for a Changing World: Green Paper on Education*, Dublin: Stationery Office.

Diggins, P. (1982), 'A study of the task of the principal in second-level schools in the Republic of Ireland', *Irish Educational Studies*, vol. 2, 125–38.

Diggins, P. (1990), 'Development of educational administration in second-level schools in Ireland' in G. McNamara, K. Williams, and D. Herron (eds.), *Achievement and Aspiration: Curricular Initiatives in Irish Post-Primary Education in the 1980s*, Dublin: Drumcondra Teachers' Centre.

Drudy, S. (1991), 'Developments in the sociology of education in Ireland, 1966–1991', *Irish Journal of Sociology*, vol. 1, 107–27.

Fullan, M., and Hargreaves, A. (1992), *What's Worth Fighting For in Your School?*, Buckingham: Open University Press.

Gilmore, B. (1992), 'Green Paper for Education', *Irish Education Decision Maker*, no. 6, 16–18.

Gouldner, A. (1970), *The Coming Crisis of Western Sociology*, London: Heinemann.

Greaney, V., Burke, A., and McCann, J. (1987), 'Entrants to primary teacher education in Ireland', *European Journal of Teacher Education*, vol. 10, no. 2, 127–40.

Higher Education Authority (1979), *Annual Report of First Destination of Award Recipients in Higher Education,* Dublin: HEA.

Higher Education Authority (1987), *Women Academics in Ireland,* Dublin: HEA.

Higher Education Authority (1991), *Annual Report of First Destination of Award Recipients in Higher Education,* Dublin: HEA.

Institute of Public Administration (1991), *Administration Yearbook and Diary, 1992,* Dublin: IPA.

Irish National Teachers' Organisation (1987), *Primary School Curriculum: Report of a Consultative Conference,* Dublin: INTO.

Irish National Teachers' Organisation (1991), *The Role of the Principal Teacher: a Review,* Dublin: INTO.

Johnson, T. (1972), *Professions and Power,* London: Macmillan.

Johnson, T. (1977), 'The professions in the class structure' in R. Scase (ed.), *Industrial Society: Class, Cleavage and Control,* London: Allen and Unwin.

Kellaghan, T., et al. (1984), *Gender Inequalities in Primary School Teaching,* Dublin: Educational Company.

Kelly, S. (1970), *Teaching in the City: a Study of the Role of the Primary School Teacher,* Dublin: Gill and Macmillan.

Lortie, D. (1984), 'Teacher career and work rewards' in A. Hargreaves and P. Woods (eds.), *Classrooms and Staffrooms,* Milton Keynes: Open University Press.

Lynch, K. (1989), *The Hidden Curriculum: Reproduction in Education: a Reappraisal,* Lewes: Falmer.

Lynch, K. (1991), 'Girls and young women in education—Ireland' in M. Wilson (ed.), *Girls and Young Women in Educatioon: a European Perspective,* London: Pergamon.

McKeown, M. (1982), 'Professional status as an operational and aspirational characteristic of the teaching force in the Republic of Ireland', *Irish Educational Studies,* vol. 2, no.2, 109–24.

McMenamin, P., Fogarty, C., et al. (1990), *Pilot Programme of Inservice for Teachers in Public Sector Post-Primary Schools on the Promotion of Equal Opportunities for Boys and Girls in Education: Report Submitted to TENET National Co-ordinator,* Dublin: Department of Education.

Organisation for Economic Co-operation and Development (1991), *Reviews of National Policies for Education—Ireland,* Paris: OECD.

Ó Síoráin, P. (1983), 'An investigation into some factors affecting the reactions of primary teachers in their first year on probation in the primary school', *Irish Educational Studies,* vol. 3, no. 1, 270–86.

O'Sullivan, D. (1980a), 'Teacher profiles, school organisation, and teaching styles in contrasting socio-economic contexts', *Irish Journal of Education,* vol. 14, no. 2, 75–87.

O'Sullivan, D. (1980b), 'Teachers' views on the effects of the home', *Educational Research,* vol. 22, no. 2, 138–42.

O'Sullivan, D. (1984), 'Social class and sexual variations in teachers' perceptions of their pupils', *Oideas,* vol. 28, 15–24.

Ozga, J., and Lawn, M. (1981), *Teachers, Professionalism and Class: a Study of Organized Teachers*, London: Falmer.

Poulantzas, N. (1978), *Classes in Contemporary Capitalism*, London: Verso.

Programme for Economic and Social Progress (1991), Dublin: Stationery Office.

Riordan, E. (1992), 'The Green Paper: back to the future?', *Irish Education Decision Maker*, no. 6, 12–14.

Ruane, W. (1992), 'The Green Paper: an ASTI view', *Irish Education Decision Maker*, no. 6, 21–3.

Teachers' Union of Ireland (1990), *Equality of Opportunity in Teaching*, Dublin: TUI.

6

The Dynamics of Control and Resistance

The purpose of this chapter is to analyse the dynamics of power and control in Irish education with a view to understanding the process of change and resistance to change. The chapter will focus especially on how the interests of particular classes react with the interests of the mediators of educational services (i.e. those who manage and control the service on a day-to-day basis, such as parent bodies, the churches, and teachers). We will argue that it is the conflation of interests between the various power groups, classes and strata in education that makes radical change difficult.

The discussion is set in the context of debates about resistance in education (Willis, 1977; McRobbie, 1978; Giroux, 1983; Aronowitz and Giroux, 1991). It argues that while resistance (on the part of the alienated) can and does occur in education, it is often counter-resisted by the mediators of educational services, whose own power and influence is dependent on recycling resistance into institutionally non-threatening forms. The ability of the mediators to counter-resist is itself related to the fact that they share much of the class project of the propertyless middle classes (the word 'project' is used here in the sense defined by Peillon, 1982). In terms of power and influence, however, the mediators have their own project.

There are, we suggest, two potential forces of counter-resistance in education, the one being those classes that rely on education to perpetuate their class power and the other being the mediators of educational services, whose status and power interests are bound up with the educational status quo. The ability of particular classes and educational mediators to influence national education policies can only be known, however, by taking account of the unique cultural and historical conditions within which a given education system operates. The particular historical and cultural conditions in the Republic of Ireland greatly enhance the ability of the propertyless middle classes and educational mediators to influence state policies on education and to counter-resist changes they may regard as undesirable.

THE UNIQUE HISTORICAL AND CULTURAL CONTEXT OF IRISH EDUCATION

At one level the Republic of Ireland displays many of the features of a so-called advanced capitalist society. 'Average Irish incomes rank 27th among the 126 countries with populations in excess of one million recorded by the World Bank . . . Levels of literacy, nutrition and health are high, as is life expectancy. The incidence of disease and of child and infant mortality is low' (Crotty, 1986, 1). Furthermore (as we have seen in chapter 1), educational retention rates are among the highest in the EC: 93 per cent of 16-year-olds, 75 per cent of 17-year-olds and about 50 per cent of 18-year-olds were in full-time education in 1992 (Department of Education, 1992, 36).

Like most of its western European neighbours, Ireland operates an extensive welfare state machinery, of which education forms a part. In its administrative structure Irish education has much in common with other highly centralised systems, such as that of France: all major policy changes are dependent on central government for approval. In many respects, therefore, Irish education operates within a socio-economic and administrative structure that is not very different from that of other western European countries. However, to understand the dynamics of social reproduction in Irish education one must also examine those cultural and historical features of Irish social life that distinguish it from other capitalist states in Europe and that have a major impact on educational policies.

By far the most distinguishing feature of Irish society, as we have pointed out earlier, is that it is a postcolonial state of relatively recent origin.[1] The economic infrastructure of the country displays a number of the features of postcolonial underdevelopment. Ireland is, for example, a major debtor country. Per head of population, it has a larger foreign debt than a number of the major 'Third World' debtor countries (Crotty, 1986, 7). In addition, high standards of living have only been maintained at the cost of massive emigration: net emigration between 1911 and 1961 was 45 per cent of the number of births registered (ibid., 2).[2]

The significance of colonisation for education today is that Ireland never developed a large indigenous industrial base. A large proportion of the profits from grass farming was transferred to London in the eighteenth and nineteenth centuries, where it was used to finance British industrial growth, which in turn destroyed Irish manufacturing (ibid., 47–8; see also chapter 1). Consequently, cultural capital—particularly credentialised cultural capital—is a far more important determinant of status and power than is the case in core capitalist states with considerable indigenous industrial wealth. This has been especially noticeable in Ireland in the last twenty years as employment opportunities declined rapidly in the agricultural sector, resulting in a massive increase in the employee labour force (and, of course, in unemployment and emigration); in 1989, for example, 76 per cent of those at work were employees, compared with 54 per cent in 1951 (Central Statistics Office, 1990, table 16; Whelan and Whelan, 1984, 21).[3]

In the absence of industrial opportunities, therefore, educational credentials have become a major determinant of wealth, status, and power. As we have argued elsewhere in this book, repeated surveys of school leavers show how important educational credentials are in determining one's employment opportunities. In June 1987, 50 per cent of those who left school one year earlier with no qualifications were still unemployed, compared with 24 per cent of those with the Intermediate and/or Group Certificate and 12 per cent of those with the Leaving Certificate[4] (Department of Labour, 1987, table 2). The findings of a survey by FÁS (1989) are similar. Thus, the higher one's educational credentials the better one's chances of being employed, even though the job one gets may not require the particular skills that the credentials certify.

It is not only the postcolonial context that must be taken into account, however, if one is to understand how social reproduction occurs in Irish education. One must also take cognisance of the power and influence exercised by the churches, particularly the Catholic Church, and the other educational interest groups, such as the teachers' unions and, increasingly, parent bodies.

As we pointed out in chapter 4, the Catholic Church exercises a degree of control in Irish education that is probably unequalled in late twentieth-century industrial Europe. The teachers' unions also represent a very significant power group in education (see chapter 5). By comparison with teachers in Britain and the United States, Irish teachers are extremely well organised and influential; they have not been proletarianised in the way that has happened in other countries.

Having identified some of the culturally specific features of Irish education, and before going on to explain how these and other forces influence state action, we must clarify some central concepts in the chapter, namely, what we mean by the 'state'; how we define the state's role in education; and what we mean by 'educational mediators'.

THE STATE AND STATE MANAGERS

Although the state is often referred to in educational literature as a unitary, almost reified, entity, this, as Skocpol (1979) and others have observed, is to ignore the institutional dynamics of the state itself. At the managerial and executive level the state sector of education comprises two very different groups, whose interests are by no means synonymous: the elected and appointed state managers. Broadly speaking, the elected state managers (ESMs) are politicians and the appointed state managers (ASMs) are civil servants. While ESMs are under regular pressure to take account of democratic demands in decision-making (Chubb, 1982, 118–41, 167–81), ASMs are not pressured in this direct way. Under Irish law, as in many countries, ASMs are subject to ESMs; in the case of education they are subject to the Minister for Education. However, senior ASMs do exercise independent power, as it is they who guide the decisions of ministers. Senior civil servants are, as Chubb observes, among the proximate policy-makers of the state (1982, 171–99).

In this section most of the analysis of the state will be focused on the role of the ESMs. The reason for this is that the ESMs play a much more central role than the ASMs in defining educational policy in a country such as Ireland that has a highly centralised system of control and within which education plays a key role in both creating and distributing privilege. Given the political sensitivity of educational issues, ASMs are not likely to be granted the kind of autonomy and power they might well attain in societies where education plays a less vital role in the creation and distribution of privilege. This is not to say that the consultative influence of senior ASMs is insignificant, especially in that they are very much part of the propertyless middle classes themselves.

Because neither the elected nor appointed state managers decide matters of educational policy without consultation and negotiation with their corporate state partners, especially the churches, parent bodies, and teachers' unions, it is not intended to suggest here that the state comprises only the elected and appointed state managers. Through the use of a corporatist strategy of decision-making (whereby the various partners and power brokers in education are represented and consulted on all major decisions) the state managers liaise closely with the mediators of state services. The mediators are themselves part of the state machinery, albeit as mediators, not as executives or managers.

THE ROLE OF THE STATE IN EDUCATION

In this chapter it is assumed that the state's role in education within a capitalist welfare state society is to ensure that the demands of civil society are accommodated only in so far as they do not threaten the interests of capital (Offe, 1984, 119–29). On the one hand the state must ensure that the conditions necessary for capital accumulation are reproduced through schools: it must ensure that the skills and attitudes required for capital accumulation are transmitted in education. On the other hand the political survival of elected state managers is contingent on ensuring that the democratic demands of civil society are accommodated within the school system. The education system must accommodate democratic demands that are not specifically of value to capital and that may indeed put demands on it, for example the demands for increased spending on the education of travelling people, working class students, and students with disabilities.

To fully comprehend the dynamics of the state's role in education, however, we need to elaborate a little on Offe's model. We would suggest that creating the conditions for capital accumulation does not simply refer to creating the conditions for the accumulation of material (i.e. financial, industrial or commercial) capital. It may also refer to creating the conditions necessary for *cultural capital accumulation*. In a society such as Ireland, for example, in which 'institutionalised cultural capital' (Bourdieu, 1986, 243) constitutes a major form of wealth, much of the resources and energy of the state machinery is deployed in ensuring that the conditions necessary for cultural capital accumulation are reproduced.

Reproducing the conditions necessary for cultural capital accumulation is especially significant for those propertyless white-collar and skilled blue-collar workers whose status and income differentials are largely contingent on their educational credentials. One cannot draw a clear distinction therefore between those who want to promote democratic rights and those who wish to promote accumulation: democratic demands do not always conflict with accumulation demands. The voting preferences of the majority of the electorate may well be in favour of promoting accumulation—in particular of promoting cultural accumulation—if their own class futures depend on it. Thus while the interest of the bourgeoisie[5] in education may differ from that of the middle classes and skilled manual workers, all have a stake in the educational status quo in a society like Ireland: the bourgeoisie want schools to produce workers who will promote financial and industrial accumulation, while the propertyless middle class and skilled working class see schools as a mechanism for reproducing the existing relations of cultural capital accumulation.

The Mediators of Education Services

Roger Dale (1982, 139) has observed that government control over education is subject to two major limitations, one practical and the other organic. Firstly, the scale of the education bureaucracy makes it practically impossible for central government to exercise complete control over all aspects of education. Secondly, each state apparatus, including education, has its own unique history. The balance of powers that exists therefore within education is historically and culturally conditioned; state managers must negotiate with existing power brokers in their exercise of power. One of the significant outcomes of the organic and practical controls identified by Dale is that the actions of state managers are strongly influenced by the established mediators of educational services within a given system.

The mediators of educational services are basically those groups that manage, oversee and administer the services at local level. The principal mediators in Ireland are the teachers, the churches, the vocational education committees, and parents' organisations. The character of state policies in education, therefore, is not only contingent on the ability of particular classes to engage in the political manipulation of elected state managers but is also dependent on the co-operation and compliance of those who administer the services on a day-to-day basis, namely the mediators. By drawing a distinction here between social classes and educational mediators we are not implying that the mediators are somehow outside the class system, which they are not; however, as mediators of the services they can often have power and status interests in education that may not necessarily be related to their structural location in the class system.

Having identified some of the unique cultural and historical contexts within which Irish education operates, and identified the major parties to the struggles within the state apparatus of education, our next task is to examine the inter-relationships between the parties involved in order to explain how resistances in education can lead to counter-resistances and the reproduction of existing power relations.

THE RELATIONSHIP BETWEEN STATE MANAGERS AND SOCIAL CLASSES

There is no doubt that the state managers of Irish education operate within a system of high political accountability, the accountability of the appointed state managers being a direct function of the accountability of the elected state managers. As Joyce (1985, 17) observes, 'the Department of Education is under direct Ministerial control. Under the terms of the Ministers and Secretaries Act 1924 . . . it is the Minister not civil servants, who makes decisions. As a result, the Minister is accountable to the Dáil and to the public for all the decisions of his Department.'

The question that immediately comes to mind is, to which groups are the minister and other state managers in education accountable? Are state managers more accountable to some groups than to others? From a purely administrative or civil service standpoint the answer to the latter question would appear to be no. Joyce's study of middle management in the civil service claims that in both the Department of Education and the office of the Revenue Commissioners 'civil service decision-making is deeply imbued with the idea of serving the public interest . . . Favouritism to any one person or group is not permitted. Rules ensure that there is equity in decision-making.' (1985, 43).

Two qualifying points must be made here. Firstly, Joyce's analysis is of middle managers, not of top managers or senior civil servants. The latter, as Chubb observes, have much more power and autonomy than more junior civil servants. They play a central role both in defining and interpreting public policy decisions (Chubb, 1982, 167–81). They therefore have the power to influence the rules and not merely to interpret them. Secondly, even if the rules are interpreted impartially, this does not mean that they were designed to foster equality in the first place. This is especially the case in education.

The reasons why educational policies may have favoured some social groups more than others have to do with the central role education plays in creating and distributing privilege in a postcolonial state and the power of particular classes within that state. As discussed earlier, Ireland has not got much indigenous industrial wealth. Consequently, cultural capital rather than material capital is what gives access to power and privilege for an increasing proportion of the population. The group that is most reliant on cultural capital to maintain its relatively privileged position in Ireland—and to pass it on to its children—is the expanding propertyless middle class. As a power group the middle classes are well positioned to have their interests defined as the public interest in education. In particular, they are in a position to hold the elected state managers to political account, because they are politically numerous,[6] highly articulate,[7] and strategically located within the state machinery itself.[8]

The bourgeoisie—comprising 4.6 per cent of the non-agricultural paid male labour force in 1985 (Breen et al., 1990, 57)—are also benefactors from education. The massive reorientation of both second-level and third-level education towards technical (i.e. commercial, scientific and technological) knowledge over the last twenty years is indeed proof both of their influence on and interest in education (Peillon, 1982; Clancy, 1988). Their power over state managers does not rest in their numerical strength but rather in their ability to influence the level of material accumulation in the country. Because the exercise of power by state managers is dependent on continued material accumulation in capitalist welfare states, the managers must safeguard the accumulation interests of the bourgeoisie for the sake of their own power at the very least (Offe, 1984, 120). As Peillon has observed, however, both national and international capital in Ireland relies heavily on state subsidisation to engage in accumulation in the first place. This contradiction within the Irish capitalist economy may in time lead to a reordering of relationships between the bourgeoisie and the state (1982, 161).

Should they wish to enact changes in educational policies, therefore, the state managers are fairly strongly constrained. Both democratic legitimacy and accumulation demand that those who are already highly successful consumers of educational services should continue to be so. In other words, the propertyless middle class in particular, and the bourgeoisie to a lesser degree, are potentially powerful agents of counter-resistance in education. Change within education will only be accommodated, therefore, in so far as it does not alter existing patterns of privilege distribution. To seek radical alterations in the latter could be politically and/or economically suicidal for the state managers.

The proof of our assertion that resistances are counter-resisted and give way to accommodations rather than radical change is evident from a brief perusal of some of the changes in second-level education in recent decades. The second-level curriculum (senior cycle in particular) was expanded greatly in the sciences, applied sciences, business and practical spheres throughout the 1970s. In both content and mode of assessment, however, the emphasis has remained on academic learning rather than practical skills. In other words, while attempts were made to recognise practical (and therefore more working-class) forms of knowledge—through the incorporation of construction studies, technical drawing and engineering on the Leaving Certificate programme, for example—there is a strong bias within the practical subjects introduced towards academic learning. Furthermore, in the Leaving Certificate examination less than a quarter of the marks in the higher level paper in construction studies and only a third of those in engineering are given for practical skills. There is no practical test in technical drawing. Almost all the remaining twenty-eight Leaving Certificate subjects are also assessed by written examinations.

Even languages are primarily assessed in this way, although there are proposals in the Green Paper to change the mode of assessment in Irish and in Continental languages. The proposal to give 60 per cent of marks to oral and aural work in modern languages, however, would still favour middle-class children, as it is these children whose parents will be able to send them abroad for exchange trips, etc. Thus, changes in the formal curriculum of second-level schools have remained favourable to the middle classes and the bourgeoisie in that a wide range of technical subjects is now incorporated in the curriculum that were not included before the 1970s, and because the mode of assessment in all subjects still favours those who are most proficient in written language.

Apart from changes in the Leaving Certificate curriculum, there have been other curriculum developments in second-level schools. With the introduction of free second-level education in the late 1960s and the raising of the school leaving age to fifteen in 1972, large numbers of working-class and small farmers' children stayed on longer in school. As the formal curriculum was not altered significantly to accommodate their interests and culture, pressure grew throughout the 1970s to develop alternative courses in schools to counteract increasing working-class resistance. Pre-employment courses (PECs) and vocational preparation and training programmes (VPTs) were gradually developed, especially in schools with significant numbers of working-class pupils who had opted out of the formal Leaving Certificate programmes. Pastoral care, health education and transition year programmes have also been introduced across a range of schools (Crooks and McKernan, 1984; Williams and McNamara, 1985).

A number of these programmes, in particular the PEC and VPT programmes, are, we would suggest, classic attempts at counter-resistance. They represent successful attempts to recycle working-class indifference and resistance to schooling into viable educational products. This is not to say that VPT and PEC programmes were not valuable educational programmes in themselves, as they were. However, they were not equal in status to the Intermediate or Leaving Certificate programmes. In structural terms they were an educational palliative to the alienated; they pre-empted the development of rebellion (especially of working-class rebellion) and thereby reproduced existing relations of educational consumption. By siphoning off resistances they enabled the mainstream system to proceed in its traditional reproductive role.

What is being suggested here, therefore, is that the education system does respond to the democratic demands of civil society, but only in a way that does not threaten the reproduction of skills and attitudes required for capital accumulation. Modifications are made on the 'fringes' of education to accommodate discontent. This accommodation involves the incorporation of resistances into the system and the reformulation of them as educational commodities.

State Managers and the Mediators of Education Services

The state managers' role in determining educational policy is not only influenced by democratic claims or accumulation pressures, however. State actions in education are also closely monitored and assessed by those groups that administer, manage and deliver educational services in school—what we call the educational mediators. The principal mediators of educational services in Ireland are the churches (the Catholic Church being by far the most significant one), the teachers' unions, the vocational education committees, and parents' organisations. Although there is a certain amount of overlap in membership between these groups, they are sufficiently distinct as popular forces or strata to be able to identify their separateness in both interests and legitimating ideologies. We will only analyse the role of some of the more powerful mediators in education here: the teachers' unions, the churches, the VECs, and the parents.

TEACHERS' UNIONS AS MEDIATORS

The teachers' unions are among the most powerful mediators of educational services. The OECD report on education policies (1991, 38) notes, for example, that they are 'very active and well organised' and that they possess 'formidable negotiating skills.' They also note that they 'heard frequent allusions to teacher unions as a power bloc.' Not alone are the teachers' unions consulted by state managers in formulating policy in general (as we have argued in chapter 5) but they are also well represented in any committees or review bodies set up to develop policies in particular areas. Each of the three teachers' unions has a representative on the 16-member National Council for Curriculum and Assessment set up in 1987; the 21-member Primary Education Review Body (1988) has eight union representatives.

The formal consultative role granted to the teachers' unions by state managers shows the extent to which teachers' representatives occupy a powerful position in developing policy. Teachers' unions have been willingly incorporated into the decision-making machinery of the state. While individual teachers, or even small groups of teachers, do seek radical changes in education, in line with the interests of children from low-income families or with the needs of travellers, for example, this has not historically been the corporate project of the unions as a mediating group. They have sought modification and limited reform; in the primary sector, for example, a liberal compensatory and cultural deficit model has informed policy, not an egalitarian model based on assumptions of cultural difference (see Dowling, 1992). While their pressure for reform has no doubt been of importance in forestalling the implementation of severe cut-backs in the provision of education at different times, the full force of the corporate might of the unions has not been employed in seeking radical change.

As an occupational group, teachers also have a specific class interest in countering resistances and recycling them, when possible, into educational products.

Teachers (as we have seen in chapter 5) are very much part of the propertyless middle class, whose power and influence is contingent on maintaining traditional hierarchical distinctions between different forms of labour. If mental labour were no longer defined as superior to manual labour (and we are aware that these are spurious distinctions, as all manual labour requires mental work) then the whole basis of teachers' differentials, which distance them from manual workers, would not be legitimated. There is no reason, therefore, why teachers would try to employ pupil resistances to generate a crisis in education that might result in a redefinition of what is valuable knowledge. Even at a pragmatic level, if teachers were to do so it would very likely threaten the organisational order on which their own authority is vested in the first place. Furthermore, teachers are not very likely to be granted sufficient autonomy by school administrators to manipulate resistances for revolutionary purposes, as the Tyndale case in Britain has shown.

We are not suggesting that teachers are always indifferent to the specific inequalities that are reproduced in education, or indeed that they necessarily oppose change. Neither are we suggesting that all three teachers' unions have identical policies: clearly they have not, as the TUI has consistently been more radical in its approach to equality issues than the ASTI, for example. However, one must distinguish between the minority or secondary interests of the teaching body and the primary or majority interests of teachers as a corporate entity. As John Coolahan's analysis (1984) of the largest union for second-level teachers shows, concerted political action from the foundation of the ASTI in 1909 up to the present day has been largely confined to industrial action over pay differentials. Industrial action by all teachers in the spring and summer of 1986 was also primarily concerned with maintaining differentials between teachers and other non-manual and manual workers.

In a certain sense, therefore, teachers' counter-resistance often takes the form of compliant indifference rather than overt action. However, second-level teachers' unions, in particular the ASTI, have actively counter-resisted when changes proposed were likely to erode their own status. In the late 1930s the ASTI opposed the use of set texts, as it feared that this would facilitate unqualified teachers and thereby lower the status of secondary teachers as a whole (Coolahan, 1984, 166). For the same reason the ASTI opposed affiliation to the Irish Trades Union Congress and the INTO in the 1940s and opposed joint conciliation and arbitration with other teachers' unions in the late 1960s and early 1970s (ibid., 281–308). While the ASTI welcomed 'free education' in the late 1960s, it was less than enthusiastic about the rationalisations that might be required to implement it (ibid., 257–63). In more recent times the ASTI has consistently supported the continued state financing of the élite fee-paying secondary schools, while the TUI has demanded its abolition.

Whether teachers will it or not, their mediation of state policies in schools adds its own weight to the legitimacy of the prevailing system. Teachers are certified and registered by public organisations (colleges of education, universities, Registration Council, etc.) before they can teach in schools. Such certification creates public faith in the neutrality of their position vis-à-vis different kinds of pupils. Their professional image helps legitimate the school organisation as an impartial distributor of knowledge and expertise.

What is being suggested is that teachers' own class and power interests are bound up with recycling resistance into organisationally non-threatening forms. This is a conscious and deliberate exercise. Secondly, teachers' own credentialised status implicitly legitimates the education system with its semblance of impartiality and 'professionalism'.

THE CHURCHES AS MEDIATORS

Although a number of churches exercise control over educational services in Ireland, the Catholic Church is by far the most powerful and influential one. (Unless otherwise stated, references to the church from here on refer only to the Catholic Church.) The church-state relationship in Irish schools represents a form of trade-off. In return for its capital investment in schools and its silent collaboration in the facilitation of capitalist culture, the church is granted the right to propagate its own dogmas and rituals in all schools. The state lays down no regulations regarding religious education in schools except that religion should be taught. All churches are granted complete autonomy over religious socialisation in their respective schools, so that religious education generally means education in the doctrines and dogmas of a particular denomination. Having negotiated a zone of influence for itself within the present school sector, therefore, neither the Catholic Church nor the other churches have any immediate power interests in radically altering a system of education that grants them unprecedented power and influence. Without its current degree of access to schools, the ideological impact of the Catholic Church in Irish society would be greatly reduced.

Just as teachers are part of the professional middle classes of society, so too are the religious personnel—something that is often forgotten in social analysis. The corporate location of religious in the middle classes has meant that they have often acted in line with the interests of that particular class rather than promoting the interests of the unemployed or the working class in education.

The church has in fact been an agent of counter-resistance in a number of ways. From the foundation of the state in 1922 up to the 1960s it was evident that there were glaring class inequalities in access to second-level and third-level education. While individual religious orders and personnel showed care and concern for this situation, as a corporate entity the Catholic Church was largely indifferent. The setting up of vocational schools in the 1930s—aimed primarily at providing technical education for working-class pupils—elicited little interest from the church. It merely sought, and received, an assurance from the state that 'general education' would not take place in these schools (Coolahan, 1981, 97): they were to be strictly practical and vocational in emphasis, thereby providing no threat to the church-controlled secondary and national sectors. Consequently, for over thirty years the small-farm and working-class children who were the principal participants in vocational schools were deprived of access to the academic and intellectual subjects that their middle-class contemporaries availed of in the largely church-controlled secondary school sector.

The Council of Education report on secondary education (1962) is further proof of the corporate indifference of certain church members to the plight of working-class and small farmers' children and of counter-resistance to social equity. The council was largely composed of religious personnel. In discussing the 'nature and aim of secondary education' the council proclaimed that its primary concern was that schools should 'prepare pupils to be God-fearing responsible citizens' (1962, 88). The intellectual development of the few was seen as the other major concern of secondary education. The notion of free education for all was rejected as 'untenable' and 'utopian', the argument being that 'only a minority of pupils would be capable of profiting by secondary (grammar school) education' (1962, 252). When free secondary education did come about in 1967 it was at the initiative of the state managers, not the churches.

In more recent times the corporate interest of all churches in facilitating the perpetuation of class privilege is evident from the fact that the majority of fee-paying secondary schools are either run directly by religious personnel or are under the patronage of some religious body. While the majority of Catholic schools are non-fee-paying—and indeed one can see a growing tension within the church between those who do not support the principle of élite schools and those who do—both recent historical and contemporary evidence suggests that the Catholic Church as a corporate entity has served the educational interests of the middle classes and the bourgeoisie more effectively than those of the working class in Ireland. To say this is not to deny the important contribution of individual religious orders and bodies to promoting equality in education. As the OECD team observed in the discussion on the relationship between the church and the state,

> for one thing the Church, although playing a leading role, is not monolithic. On the contrary, there have always been tensions between the bishops and the religious orders about how secondary schools should be managed and organised, and there have always been differences of approach and style among the religious orders. Some members of the Church hold advanced and even radical educational ideals, and many of its schools and colleges are always ready to experiment and innovate. (OECD, 1991, 38–9)

The church's involvement in education may be reproducing inequality in an indirect manner, however. As Clancy (1983, 15–17) has observed, the status of religious in Irish society is high. By virtue of its high moral status the church brings an aura of moral legitimacy to bear on the educational process, thereby immunising it from attack. In addition, unlike lay teachers, religious teachers have no conspicuous class interests of their own. This is not to say, of course, that they cannot be located structurally in class terms, as we have pointed out above. However, their religious status supersedes their corporate class identity in the public eye. This further contributes to the image of impartiality that religious bring to bear on education. In effect, through the dominance of religious in education the church's own legitimating armoury is transferred to the educational scene. It becomes unthinkable that the church (as arbiter of moral goodness in society) would be a prime mover in a system of education that is daily involved in the reproduction of inequalities. The combination of the church's power interests in education and the impact of its legitimating armoury helps pre-empt the emergence of radical dissent. Given its corporate interests (i.e. its interests as a social institution concerned with organisational survival), therefore, the church's survival, like that of the teachers' unions, is contingent on recycling resistances into viable educational commodities.

THE VECs AS MEDIATORS

By virtue of their composition,[9] the vocational education committees are a highly politicised and powerful mediating force in second-level education. While the VECs are in some ways a part of the state machinery—in the local rather than the national sense—their interests are by no means synonymous with it: the conflict in 1986 between the VECs and the Minister for Education over the failure of the latter to promote VEC-controlled schools is indeed proof of this.[10] Neither are their interests synonymous with those of teachers, although the latter form a significant group within the VECs. The fact that teachers in vocational schools are in a separate trade union (the TUI) shows how they differ in their sectional interests from teachers in the secondary sector.

The VECs and their staff, therefore, are distinctive administrative and organisational entities with their own survival problems within the educational site. Indeed, because vocational schools (for a variety of historical and political reasons) exemplify some of the more negative particularistic aspects of education—low retention rates, high levels of streaming, sexist curricular provision, etc. (Hannan et al., 1983; Hannan and Boyle, 1987)—they have little to gain by encouraging resistances in their schools. Given the fact that they are in daily competition with the more prestigious and selective secondary sector, an overelaboration of the contradictions of schooling could bring about the demise of the VEC sector itself.

The class composition of the VECs would also suggest that they are more likely to be agents of counter-resistance than facilitators of resistance in education. The VECs are largely controlled by representatives of local authorities; local authorities in turn are dominated by middle-class personnel (Chubb, 1982, 91). The success of the middle classes in benefiting from the educational status quo has already been noted. Given this, it is highly unlikely that representatives of that class would want to radically alter the patterns of educational outcome reproduced in schools, whether these schools be vocational or not.

Finally, just as the religious bring an aura of moral righteousness to bear on the educational site that may reproduce inequalities by camouflaging the real outcomes of schooling, so too may the seemingly democratic representativeness of the VECs serve the same function. Being composed of elected personnel, the VEC seems to be a highly representative body serving the educational interests of a wide array of class groups. The VECs bring an aura of democratic representativeness to bear on the educational site, which immunises the education system from attack. After all, if local elected representatives do not find the education system wanting or inegalitarian, then why should radical change be necessary?

PARENT BODIES AS MEDIATORS

Parent bodies represent another powerful mediating group in education. Unlike the teachers and the churches, however, they are relatively recently organised as a mediating force, only gaining momentum in the last fifteen years; it was only in 1975 that parents in primary schools were allowed formal representation on boards of management. The two most powerful groups among parent organisations are the National Parents' Council (Primary Branch) and the National Parents' Council (Post-Primary Branch). The executive of these two bodies is selected at the annual delegate conference. The delegates at that conference are selected from the county branches of the National Parents' Council, which in turn represent the various parent representatives on individual boards.

To date, there has been no major analysis of parent bodies. We know very little about which groups (in the social class sense, for example) exercise control within them. Casual observation would suggest that parent bodies are female-dominated and predominantly middle-class. However, such observations have yet to be confirmed by research. While it is the explicit policy of the National Parents' Council to avoid 'élitism or exclusiveness', it is not at all clear from the handbook of the NPC, for example, what strategy is employed to achieve this. Encouragement is the only strategy mentioned (NPC, 1991, 14).

Research conducted in the late 1960s in Britain has indicated that middle and upper socio-economic groups have tended to dominate parents' committees and councils in schools (McGeeney, 1969, 105). If this is also the case in

Ireland, parent bodies are quite likely to operate as conservative forces in education. Middle-class children have been the primary benefactors from free education. If middle-class parents control parents' councils and other representative bodies, it is highly likely that they will pursue their own class-related agendas through these bodies; this would naturally mean protecting and expanding middle-class gains within the system. And unless the questions of social class, gender, ethnic and religious representation become issues within parent bodies themselves, it is very likely that they will be dominated by the middle classes in particular.

Such dominance would be concealed behind the cloak of democratic representativeness. By this we mean that because parent bodies are democratically elected, the fact that certain groups have not got the time, resources or confidence to seek election will be hidden. Parent bodies will carry the cloak of democratic representation even if minorities, and significant minorities at that, are not proportionately represented on them. The cloak of democracy will bring further legitimation to the education system, no matter how unrepresentative the representative body may be.

Conflict Between the Mediators

So far we have identified two factors that would support the claim that the mediators of educational services are forces of counter-resistance in education. Firstly, we saw how the class, power and status interests of mediating groups are often bound up with the educational status quo. Secondly, we showed how the legitimating armoury of the mediating groups themselves serves the ideological purpose of bolstering existing patterns of provision and consumption of education. A third factor that explains why mediators are frequently agents of counter-resistance is power conflicts between the mediating groups themselves (see table 6.1).

What is being suggested is that conflict among any, some or all of those groups mediating educational services itself acts as a stabilising force within the education system. Should the churches decide, for example, not to reproduce capitalist culture in the form required by the state, the latter could withdraw funds and expand vocational or lay control. Thus, the churches would lose their power base. Territorial conflicts between educational mediators therefore forestall the possibility that any one will exploit the contradictions of schooling to the point where they threaten their power base.

The possibility of developing 'radical pedagogies' for emancipatory purposes as prescribed by Giroux (1983, 115–16) and Aronowitz and Giroux (1985; 1991) does not seem to take the power and influence of educational mediators into account. Neither does it address the influence of unique cultural and political contexts on education.

Table 6.1

Significant educational mediators: their interests, legitimating armouries, and potential conflict paths

	The churches	*The VECs*	*The teachers*	*Parents' councils*
1. Power interests as institutions	Maintaining religious ethos: i.e. maintaining influence over consciences	Maintaining vocational ethos & jobs and career maintenance	Control of working conditions & maintaining status differentials	Accountability of other mediators & protecting the interests of existing success-ful consumers in education
2. Legitimating armoury	Moral authority	Democratic representativeness	Professional autonomy	Democratic representativeness

	Contestants (examples)*	*Possible power issues*
3. Potential conflict paths in the matrix of power groups	Church v. VEC	School expansion or survival (This takes the form of inter-school competition for pupils)
	Church v. teachers v. parents	Administrative control within schools
	Parents v. teachers	Teachers' autonomy claim conflicts with parents' accountability claim

*Any one or more of the mediating groups can, of course, form alliances with others to pursue specific interests at a given time.

CONCLUSION

Our first conclusion is one that is broadly in concurrence with Roger Dale's observation (1982, 140) that 'the capitalist mode of production does not determine the form that education state apparatuses will take' within a given society. There are both practical and organic limits to governmental control over education; the practical limits arise from the scale of the educational operation, while the organic limits are rooted in the unique histories of the education system (ibid., 139). Understanding organic limits is particularly important in the case of Irish education. While Ireland is a capitalist state in terms of its economic infrastructure, the form education takes is very different from the form it takes in other European capitalist countries in the late twentieth century. While some of these differences can be accounted for by what Archer terms the 'operational autonomy' of education systems (1982, 8)—Ireland is, for example, more like France than Denmark or England in that it has a highly centralised system of education; this in turn means that political manipulations rather than external transactions or internal initiations are likely to be employed as mechanisms for change (see Archer, 1979, 239–62, for a discussion of this point)—the organic limits arising from Ireland's unique history are perhaps more significant for understanding the dynamics of policy changes and social reproduction in education.

Ireland's most distinctive historical feature is that it is a postcolonial state of just seventy-one years' duration. Several hundred years of colonisation by a capitalist power left it bereft of profits for capital accumulation (Crotty, 1986). This pre-empted the development both of an indigenous industrial sector and the powerful bourgeoisie that went with it. Post-independence Ireland, therefore, is very similar to other recently independent postcolonial states in both its economic and social infrastructure.

Just as a number of the postcolonial states of western and south-eastern Asia did not generate the development of powerful polar classes of proletarians and bourgeoisie (Ahmad, 1985, 43–65), neither did Ireland. Rather, what emerged in the Irish Free State were powerful intermediate classes or middle classes. The independence movement was inspired and led by middle-class people, drawing support from all classes (Chubb, 1982, 264). In subsequent years politics has been dominated both at local and national level by the same intermediate classes (ibid., 91–111, 189–90). Furthermore, it is the offspring of the middle classes— in particular of the lower middle class—who have tended to be the mainstay of the civil service (ibid., 265). The strategic location of the intermediate classes within the state machinery puts them in a powerful position therefore to influence state policies—including educational policies—especially in a highly centralised system.

The absence of a powerful indigenous industrial sector has also meant that, like so many developing countries, Ireland has relied on multinational invest- ment and the state sector to provide employment. This has been especially noticeable in the post-1950s period, when the state abandoned protectionist policies and began to rely on the industrial and services sectors rather than the agricultural sector to produce wealth. Both the state and the multinationals—for very different reasons—make intensive use of educational credentials to select and allocate people to jobs. Educational credentials (credentialised cultural capital) assume an importance, therefore, in allocating people within the labour market that would not be possible in a society in which material capital played a more central role in determining one's occupational status.

Because education plays a powerful role in both the production and distri- bution of privilege, and because the politically numerous and powerful middle classes have been the most successful group in using education to consolidate their own class position, there has been limited scope for either radical teachers or students to exploit the contradictions of schooling in the manner that Giroux and others regard as desirable. This is not to say that change cannot or will not occur. Rather, it is to identify the obstacles to change and the contexts in which change is likely to occur. While one cannot deny that the mechanisms of social and cultural reproduction are frequently ineffective and are often faced 'with elements of opposition' (Giroux, 1983, 100), it is, we think, necessary to high-light the conditions under which resistances are likely to be effective and those in which they are not. Using evidence from Ireland, we would suggest that the possibilities for resistances leading to radical educational change are greatly reduced (*a*) when credentialised knowledge plays a key role in both producing and distributing privileges, as is the case in many postcolonial states, (*b*) when large and politically mobilised groups (such as the propertyless middle class in Ireland) are already highly successful in employing the education system to perpetuate their own class power and when no alternative route for the reproduction of their class power is readily open to them, and (*c*) when groups mediating educational services are sufficiently powerful—either independent of or because of their class affiliations—to become agents of counter-resistance. The strategic location of mediating groups at the centre of the educational enterprise is, we suggest, an important factor in explaining how resistances get recycled into educational products. Having access both to classrooms and to centres of administration, mediating groups can identify resistances at an early stage and redirect them into viable educational products should they think it desirable.

Should the above conditions not prevail, and in particular if education is operating in a rapidly changing political situation (as in South Africa or in the West Bank in the early 1990s), then the scope for politicising resistance and mobilising it into a force for radical change is greatly increased. When the climate is one of political stability and when the mediators, managers and class groups have investment in education in the manner set out above, then the strategy for change must be different. At the very least it must take account of the political and institutional realities outlined here, rather than pretend they do not exist.

Notes
1. The Irish Free State was established in 1922; only in 1949 did the twenty-six counties of the former Free State leave the British Commonwealth. The remaining six counties of Ireland comprise Northern Ireland, and are still under British colonial rule.
2. Emigration did not begin with the foundation of the new state. From the Famine period to independence (1848–1922 approximately) emigration had been both facilitated and encouraged by the colonial government. Emigration in the immediate post-independence period was perceived as a kind of 'natural' response to unemployment, and went largely unquestioned for years.
3. One of the factors that must be borne in mind when examining the role of education in Irish society is that Ireland did not experience the rapid expansion of the white-collar public (modern) sectors characteristic of the immediate post-independence period of postcolonial states until nearly thirty years after independence. Thus, education did not become *the* major determinant of status

and power until the early 1960s, when the public service sector expanded rapidly to direct the newly planned industrial expansion.

4. The Leaving Certificate examination is taken on completion of second-level education, which is generally of five years' duration (at approximately seventeen or eighteen years of age). The Intermediate Certificate examination was taken after three years of second-level education, and the Group Certificate after two years; from 1989 the Junior Certificate replaced both the Intermediate and Group Certificates.

5. By 'bourgeoisie' we mean here those who are owners of capital *and* employers of labour in the industrial, services and agricultural sectors—what Rottman and Hannan (1982, 24) refer to as the economic classes of large proprietors. By 'middle classes' we mean all higher and lower professional workers (including both self-employed and employee professionals and senior and junior executive and administrative employees) and intermediate and routine non-manual employees, including the junior ranks of non-manual workers in industry, commerce, and public administration, as well as qualified technicians. The classifications used are based on those by Rottman, Hannan et al. (1982, 24–5). (See chapter 7 for a fuller discussion of issues in social class classification.)

6. In 1985, 39 per cent of all males who were in employment were classified as non-manual (middle-class) workers, while a further 19.5 per cent were classified as skilled manual workers (Breen et al., 1990, 57). In all, therefore, 59 per cent of all males in employment belong to groups whose advantages vis-à-vis other groups in the labour market are highly dependent on their educational credentials.

7. As Clancy (1988, 22) and Breen et al. (1990) have shown, both the upper and lower non-manual groups are currently among the most successful consumers of educational services in Ireland. They are therefore well educated and well able to articulate their interests when the need arises.

8. A very large proportion of public service workers in Ireland are white-collar workers (Central Statistics Office, 1990, *Labour Force Survey, 1989*, table 23).

9. Of the 792 second-level schools in 1990/91, 248 (31 per cent) were vocational schools controlled and managed by the thirty-eight county-based vocational education committees. (See chapter 1.) The original remit of the vocational schools was to provide technical and continuation education at the postprimary level. Since 1966 the vocational schools have also been free to offer any or all of the academic subjects traditionally confined to secondary schools, and virtually all have availed of this opportunity. Each VEC consists of fourteen members, between five and eight of whom must be elected members of the local authority; the remainder of the committee is composed of representatives of specific interest groups, including trade unions, employers, and groups with specific educational interests. (See chapter 1.)

10. In the spring of 1986 the national organisation representing all the VECs threatened to cease co-operating in the development of new community schools unless the Minister for Education made a more concerted effort to promote and develop vocational schools.

References and Further Reading

Ahmad, A. (1985), 'Class, nation and state: intermediate classes in peripheral societies' in D. Johnson (ed.), *Middle Classes in Dependent Countries*, Beverly Hills: Sage.

Archer, M. (1979), *Social Origins of Education Systems*, London: Sage.

Archer, M. (1982), 'Introduction: theorising about the expansion of educational systems' in M. Archer (ed.), *The Sociology of Educational Expansion*, Beverly Hills: Sage.

Aronowitz, S., and Giroux, H. (1985), *Education Under Siege: the Conservative, Liberal and Radical Debate Over Schooling*, London: Routledge and Kegan Paul.

Aronowitz, S., and Giroux, H. (1991), *Postmodern Education*, Minnesota: Temple University Press.

Bourdieu, P. (1986), 'The forms of capital' in J. Richardson (ed.), *Handbook of Theory and Research for the Sociology of Education*, New York: Greenwood.

Breen, R. (1984), *Education and the Labour Market* (ESRI paper no. 119), Dublin: Economic and Social Research Institute.

Breen, R., et al. (1990), *Understanding Contemporary Ireland*, Dublin: Gill and Macmillan.

Central Statistics Office (1990), *Labour Force Survey, 1989*, Dublin: Stationery Office.

Chubb, B. (1982), *The Government and Politics of Ireland*, London: Longman.

Clancy, P. (1982), *Participation in Higher Education: a National Survey*, Dublin: Higher Education Authority.

Clancy, P. (1983), 'Religious vocation as a latent identity for school principals', *Economic and Social Review*, 15, 1–23.

Clancy, P. (1988), *Who Goes to College?: a Second National Survey of Participation in Higher Education*, Dublin: Higher Education Authority.

Coolahan, J. (1981), *Irish Education: History and Structure*, Dublin: Institute of Public Administration.

Coolahan, J. (1984), *The ASTI and Post-Primary Education in Ireland, 1909–1984*, Dublin: Cumann na Meánmhúinteoirí, Éire.

Crooks, T., and McKernan, J. (1984), *The Challenge of Change*, Dublin: Institute of Public Administration.

Crotty, R. (1986), *Ireland in Crisis: a Study in Capitalist Colonial Underdevelopment*, Dingle: Brandon.

Dale, R. (1982), 'Education and the capitalist state: contributions and contradictions' in M. Apple (ed.), *Cultural and Economic Reproduction in Education*, London: Routledge and Kegan Paul.

Department of Education (1962), *Report of the Council of Education on the Curriculum of the Secondary School*, Dublin: Stationery Office.

Department of Education (1992), *Education for a Changing World: Green Paper on Education*, Dublin: Stationery Office.

Department of Labour (1987), *Economic Status of School Leavers, 1986*, Dublin: Department of Labour.

Dowling, T. (1992), 'The teacher unions, class inequality in Irish education and the compensatory approach' (master of equality studies thesis, University College, Dublin).

Foras Aiseanna Saothair (1989), *School Leavers' Survey—Five Years Later*, Dublin: FÁS.

Giroux, H. A. (1983), *Theory and Resistance in Education: a Pedagogy of Opposition*, London: Heinemann.

Hannan, D., and Boyle, M. (1987), *Schooling Decision: the Origins and Consequences of Selection and Streaming in Irish Post-Primary Schools* (ESRI paper no. 136), Dublin: Economic and Social Research Institute.

Hannan, D., et al. (1983), *Schooling and Sex Roles: Sex Differences in Subject Provision and Student Choice in Irish Post-Primary Schools* (ESRI paper no. 113), Dublin: Economic and Social Research Institute.

Joyce, L. (1985), *Administrators or Managers?: an Exploratory Study of Public and Private Sector Decision Making*, Dublin: Institute of Public Administration.

Lynch, K. (1982), 'A sociological analysis of the functions of second-level education', *Irish Educational Studies,* vol. 2, 32–58.

McGeeney, P. (1969), *Parents Are Welcome*, London: Longman.

McRobbie, A. (1978), 'Working class girls and the culture of femininity' in Women's Studies Group, *Women Take Issue*, London: Hutchinson.

National Parents' Council (Primary Branch) (1991), *Parent Associations: Making Them Work*, Dublin: National Parents' Council.

Organisation for Economic Co-operation and Development (1991), *Review of National Policies for Education—Ireland*, Paris: OECD.

Offe, C. (1984), *Contradictions of the Welfare State*, London: Hutchinson.

Peillon, P. (1982), *Contemporary Irish Society: an Introduction*, Dublin: Gill and Macmillan.

Rottman, D., Hannan, D., et al. (1982), *The Distribution of Income in the Republic of Ireland* (ESRI paper no. 109), Dublin: Economic and Social Research Institute.

Skocpol, T. (1979), *States and Social Revolutions*, London: Cambridge University Press.

Whelan, C., and Whelan, B. (1984), *Social Mobility in the Republic of Ireland: a Comparative Perspective* (ESRI paper no. 116), Dublin: Economic and Social Research Institute.

Williams, K., and McNamara, G. (1985), *The Vocational Preparation Course*, Dublin: Cumann na Meánmhúinteoirí, Éire.

Willis, P. (1977), *Learning to Labour: How Working Class Kids Get Working Class Jobs*, Aldershot (Hampshire): Gower.

III

The Reproduction of Inequality

7

Social Class and Education

Perhaps the dominant and most enduring preoccupation in the sociology of education has been the relationship between social class and education. In North American and European sociology we can identify this as a 'tradition' even as far back as before the Second World War. Certainly in the sociological research and debates in the postwar reconstruction period in Britain, Europe and North America the relationship between social class and education emerges as a major focus. In Ireland, however, it is not until the 1960s that we see the beginnings of a widespread debate on social class and education. This may well be because before the 1960s education had been viewed as a consumer service rather than an economic investment (Coolahan, 1981, 131). Postprimary education was largely privately managed and controlled, and the minutiae of the provision of education were thought to be matters best left to the churches rather than requiring intervention by the state.

The drive for economic expansion in the 1960s led not only to greatly increased state involvement in and funding of education, especially at postprimary level, but also to a recognition of the inequalities that existed in the provision and consumption of education (*Investment in Education*, 1966). These factors, combined with a greater openness and awareness of the wider world among the community at large and among academics (many of whom were receiving their postgraduate training abroad) led to an increasing involvement with international debates and research on education and to a concern with educational inequality.

THE CONCEPT OF SOCIAL CLASS

Social class is probably the most frequently used concept in sociology. However, it is also one on which there is considerable divergence. Not all sociologists mean exactly the same thing by 'social class'. While the intricacies of this rather complex debate need not concern us here, we need to have an acquaintance with the definitions currently in use, especially in Irish sociology, to be able to evaluate the data. (For a more detailed discussion see Drudy, 1991.)

Occupation is normally used as the best, albeit somewhat inadequate, single indicator of class position. Occupation, though, is not exactly equivalent to social class position, which rests on a number of factors. Occupation is one, but also included are factors such as relations to property, the ability to command resources, educational background, income, wealth, and 'life chances'—i.e. access to factors such as good health, housing, and educational opportunities for one's children. Nevertheless, virtually all studies of education and social class use a measure based on occupation, usually that of the father. This again reflects the somewhat sexist bias in much sociology. Indeed, studies that have examined the influence of mothers' present or former occupation and, most importantly, their education have found that these factors are significantly related to the educational achievement of the children.

Occupations, when used to indicate social class, are grouped together into a number of categories, according to the exigencies of a scale of occupations. There are two principal types of occupational scale in wide use today. One type ranks occupations according to their prestige or 'social standing' within the community and their average level of remuneration. This type of scale is most compatible with a functionalist perspective. However, because this is the basis of the classifications used by Government censuses (at least in Ireland and Britain), this type of scale is also sometimes used by researchers with other perspectives. Scales of this sort usually begin with a number of 'socio-economic' groupings. These will normally range from 'employers and managers' and 'higher professionals' down to 'unskilled manual workers'. These categories may be further subdivided into 'social class' groupings, which may be ranked in descending order of prestige from 1 to 6, for example. The difficulty with these scales is that they do not take into account more complex social factors such as relationship to property or position in the production process.

The second type of scale, one that is more validly a social *class* scale in a sociological sense, is the kind based on an attempt to take some of the other factors mentioned above into account and that is based on a Weberian or Marxist theory of class. For both Weber and Marx the key to understanding the class structure of capitalist societies is the distribution of productive property or wealth. Although associated with each other, income and wealth are analytically distinct. Wealth is that which may generate income and profit. Income, on the other hand, may derive from many sources—from the ownership of wealth such as land, capital, stocks and shares, etc., from wages or salaries, or from social welfare payments. Property (wealth) and lack of property are, both for Marxists and Weberians, the basic categories of all class situations. Both see class position as a matter of the place occupied by people in the system of production. Both see shared class position as a potential basis for recognition of common interests and for collective class organisation and action in consequence.

While there are also many differences between the two perspectives in relation to the nature and operation of the class structure, occupational scales based on both perspectives show remarkable similarities (Drudy, 1991). Weber speaks of a class when a number of people have in common a specific causal component of their life chances. Property and the lack of property are, according to Weber, the basic categories of all class situations. He distinguishes three types of class: a 'property' class, primarily determined by property differences; a 'commercial' class, determined by the marketability of goods and services; and a 'social' class, which makes up the totality of these class situations. Social classes are (1) those privileged through property and education, such as employers, senior administrators and managers, and some professionals; (2) the propertyless intelligentsia and specialists; (3) the petty bourgeoisie—the self-employed, small shopkeepers, etc.; and (4) the working class. Weber also uses 'status' as an analytical concept. According to Weber, status is founded on style of life, formal education, and hereditary or occupational prestige. Although status may rest on class position, it is not solely determined by it (Weber, 1968).

Marx wrote of three principal classes: (1) the bourgeoisie—owners of the means of production, employers of wage labour; (2) the petty bourgeoisie; and (3) the proletariat or working class. Neo-Marxists add a fourth category, the 'new petty bourgeoisie', which includes the majority of white-collar, technical and professional occupations that have arisen as the result of technological change (Poulantzas, 1977).

Much Irish research into education and social class has used categories derived from the census classification of occupations, or some other form of prestige ranking. Until recently the Central Statistics Office used scales based on this concept only. However, the *Classification of Occupations* of the 1986 census (CSO, 1988) includes for the first time a social class scale that is based on sociological theories of class. This represents a considerable improvement on the former situation (theoretically at least) and should undoubtedly in time result in greater comparability between different studies of class and education.

In the past, educational researchers using the census classification have relied on the census 'socio-economic status' (SES) groupings, which are not, strictly speaking, social class categories at all. These divide the population into eleven major groupings based on an assessment of the level of skill or educational attainment required by each occupation (CSO, 1986). Researchers either use all eleven categories, as does Clancy, whose work is discussed below, or group some of them together, as does Breen, whose work is also discussed later. The SES categories are very useful and certainly allow us to observe major educational inequalities; they do not tell us anything, however, about the relationship to property of the people in the occupations concerned.

A major problem with classifications based on occupation is their inability to theorise on the relations of the unemployed to the production process.

Occupational classifications also fail to locate the contribution of unpaid (mostly female) labour to the generation of wealth. This means that in countries such as Ireland the use of these classifications fails to explain the social class position of approximately 300,000 unemployed people and about 700,000 home workers (99 per cent of whom are women). These two groups combined are equivalent to the paid work force. The problem of the unemployed, home workers and others not in the paid labour market is perhaps better dealt with by neo-Marxist scholars than by those from other perspectives. In neo-Weberian class theory, in Ireland at least, these groups are treated as a 'residual' category, on the grounds that they are not regular participants in any form of economic activity (Rottman et al., 1982, 9). However, these groups are seen as a more integral part of the class structure by neo-Marxist theorists (e.g. Braverman, 1974), who see them as a 'reserve army of labour' on which capitalist enterprise may call during times of economic expansion but that will leave the labour market, without too much social upheaval (for the capitalist), during times of economic recession.

Much valuable research into education and social class has been carried out in recent years by the Economic and Social Research Institute. Its approach to the class structure is Weberian, specifically influenced (as we suggest in chapter 2) by the work of the English neo-Weberian Giddens and his theory of 'class structuration'—i.e. the way in which classes are formed and perpetuated (Rottman et al., 1982, 16–18).

In their analysis of the relations between class and education, Rottman et al. suggest that four major cleavages in the social structure are central. There is a *bourgeoisie* (large proprietors, and farmers of over 100 acres employing labour); a *petit-bourgeoisie* (small proprietors, and farmers not employing outside labour); a *middle class* (higher and lower professionals and inter-mediate and routine non-manual workers); and a *working class* (skilled, semi-skilled, service and unskilled manual workers) (Rottman et al. 1982, 25).

It is clear that in practice, both in the census classifications and in the ESRI's own work on education, it is very difficult to get sufficient information to iden-tify the bourgeois (or substantial property-owning or employer) class as such. This is because the sort of detail that would be required on ownership and num-bers employed is normally not available in sample surveys (Goldthorpe, 1980; Drudy, 1991). Therefore, in the great majority of discussions on the relationship of education to class, what is at issue is the difference in participation and performance between working-class and middle-class children. The role of the education system in the reproduction of the bourgeois class is, by and large, the province of small-scale studies, since sample surveys either omit, undersample or misclassify this small but very powerful group, for the reasons outlined above.

EDUCATION AND SOCIAL CLASS: WHAT THE RESEARCH SHOWS

Irish educational research since the 1960s has had an enduring interest in the relationship of social class and education. The problem has generally been posed in terms of the equality of opportunity debate (in chapter 2 we have given details of the nature of this debate). As we suggested earlier, the first major inquiry into the education system was the *Investment in Education* report (1966). This report catalogued substantial social class inequalities in the rates of access and participation in postprimary schooling. The study showed that in 1963 just 69.1 per cent of boys and 74.8 per cent of girls transferred to post-primary school on completion of their primary education. There were substantial differences according to socio-economic background; for example, the percentages for group B/C (professional, employers, managers, salaried and intermediate non-manual worker categories) were 87.1 for boys and 89.6 for girls. This compared with 54.0 per cent of the sons and 54.4 per cent of the daughters of workers in group F, the semi-skilled and unskilled manual workers (*Investment in Education*, 1966).

As we have seen, with these findings and equality considerations in mind, and with the drive for economic expansion, Irish educational spending increased significantly. From a figure of almost £29.5 million in 1961/62 (*Investment in Education*, 1966) it increased to over £307.5 million by 1977, until by 1990 the figure was over £1,274 million (Department of Education, 1992, 11). Total annual expenditure on education by the state is exceeded only by expenditure on social welfare and on health (Breen et al., 1990, 130).

However, following the rapid growth in educational expenditure in the 1960s, Government expenditure on education, as a share of gross domestic product, remained roughly constant over the 1980s, at around 6 per cent, and was 6.1 per cent in 1985 (ibid.). By contrast, in the 1980s in Northern Ireland education accounted for closer to 10 per cent of GDP, and was 9.8 per cent in 1984/85 (McGill, 1987). If we compare Northern Ireland with the Republic it can be argued that the economies of both are dependent and peripheral within the EC. Both are characterised by high levels of unemployment. Yet there appear to be significant differences in their proportionate allocation of resources to education.

As we saw in chapter 1, increased expenditure was accompanied by marked increases in the numbers availing of postprimary education. The number engaged in full-time second-level education in 1965 was 134,090. By 1991 the number was 345,941. While this increase in participation obviously bene-fited all classes, not all classes benefited to the same degree. For example, in 1961 the proportion of the population aged 15 to 19 in full-time education was 24.9 per cent. By 1971 the proportion of young people aged between 14 and 19 in full-time education was 47.9 per cent (Rottman et al., 1982, 32). In 1987 the proportion of the 15–19 age cohort in full-time education was 63.1 per cent (based on figures obtained from the Department of Education).

It was clear, however, that, contrary to the expectation of increased equity, the rise in educational expenditure and in participation rates disproportionately benefited the middle classes. Report after report showed that middle-class children were better represented at all levels of the postprimary system and at entry to third-level education than their working-class counterparts (Clancy, 1982; 1988). The figures showed that, from an early stage after the introduction of 'free' postprimary education, inequalities of access by social group actually sharpened. When the rates of participation in full-time education of the children of semi-skilled and unskilled manual workers and those of the children of professionals, employers and managers were compared for 1961 and 1971, the differential between them had increased. Though the rate of increase was greater among those families with least resources, the absolute differential between the two social groups had widened slightly (Rottman et al., 1982, 52).

Similar social class differences in participation rates have been noted in other studies. Greaney and Kellaghan's longitudinal study (already referred to in chapter 2) showed marked differences in educational participation by class. Of the five hundred children they followed through the education system from primary school, some 92 per cent entered a second-level school on completion of primary education and three-quarters stayed at school to complete a junior-cycle course, while less than half (45 per cent) completed a senior-cycle course (Greaney and Kellaghan, 1984, 248).

There were considerable social class variations in these survival rates. In general, Greaney and Kellaghan's findings on socio-economic background indicated that from the end of primary schooling up to third-level education, the representation of students from the lower socio-economic groups decreased, while the representation of those from the higher groups increased. The data suggested that the higher one goes in the education system, the greater the disparity in participation by socio-economic status. They argued, though, that inequalities of opportunity, for the most part, had done their damage at the early stages of schooling. The conditions that affected a student's future educational chances, and presumably life chances, were laid down relatively early in life, and were clearly in evidence before the end of primary schooling.

For those who survived, they argued that the inequalities were reduced, though not entirely eliminated (ibid., 252–3, 262). This was disputed by Whelan and Whelan (1984, 7), who suggested that socio-economic inequalities (in probability of survival at each point of the education system) increase rather than decline as one moves up through the system. However, what made the Greaney and Kellaghan study controversial was the conclusion that, because verbal reasoning ability (VRA) played such an important role in the educational progress of the students, the 'meritocratic ideal' was being approached if not quite attained (ibid., 263). This observation was vigorously challenged; the parameters of the debate have been set out in chapter 2.

In a comparative study of the relationship between education and male social mobility, Whelan and Whelan suggest that the association between social origins and educational achievement is stronger in Ireland than in a number of other countries—France, Sweden, England, and Wales. This, they suggest, is important, as intragenerational or career mobility is particularly restricted and educational qualifications are a particularly strong determinant of class position. Occupational positions are passed from one generation to another not, as in the past, through direct inheritance but through the medium of differential access to educational qualifications. They argue furthermore that the Irish education system is confronted not simply with a minority of disadvantaged children and schools that have obvious social problems but rather with the wider problem posed by the great majority of working-class children, who achieve significantly below their potential (Whelan and Whelan, 1984).

In an assessment of changes that have occurred since the introduction of 'free' education in 1967, in the matter of class differentials in participation rates, Breen et al. argue that little headway has been made in the lessening of class disparities in educational outcomes. The expansion of the education system and the growth of credentialism have acted as intervening factors between class origins and class destinations, but do not appear to have changed them to any marked degree. In addition, they suggest that public educational expenditure is regressive, i.e. the benefits tend to accrue to pupils of better-off families (Breen et al., 1990, 133).

The 1980s have seen continued increases in participation rates in second-level schools for all social classes. Part of this may be due to high rates of unemployment, which have severely restricted the opportunities for the less well qualified (Department of Labour, 1991). Rising expectations in an increasingly competitive education system may also play a part. Although there are still significant social class differentials in participation rates and achievement at postprimary level, it is at the point of entry to higher education that these are most clearly visible.

This phenomenon is not new. It was certainly observed by the *Investment in Education* team. In 1965, at the time of this report, the share of university places taken up by the least advantaged socio-economic groups—i.e. other non-manual, skilled manual, semi-skilled and unskilled manual and other agricultural occupations—was 11 per cent. By 1986 the share of this group had increased to 14.8 per cent of university places (Clancy, 1988).

However, when we look at the position of the most advantaged groups— higher and lower professional, employers and managers, salaried employees, and intermediate non-manual workers—we see that their share of university places increased by a somewhat greater degree, from 65 per cent in 1965 (*Investment in Education*, 1966) to 69.1 per cent in 1986 (Clancy, 1988). Therefore, over the period the inequalities in university participation between the children of the most and least advantaged members of the labour force increased rather than diminished. Clancy's work shows that this disparity becomes even more pronounced when field of study is examined. The inequalities between socio-economic groups are greater the more prestigious the sector; they are greatest of all in the professional faculties (Clancy, 1988). This finding is confirmed by a more recent study of university entrants by Dowling (1991), in which students from semi-skilled and unskilled working-class backgrounds were either not represented at all or were very poorly represented in the professional faculties such as dentistry, law, medicine, and commerce. The disparities between this group and others were less marked in arts and science faculties.

The picture is perhaps somewhat better in the technological colleges and in the colleges of education. Though still underrepresented, working-class students, and the children of lower-income groups generally, are better represented in these colleges. Clancy's research shows that in 1986 in the technological sector, i.e. in the regional technical colleges and in the Dublin Institute of Technology, the number of new entrants from the five lowest-income groups already mentioned was 33.3 per cent and 29.4 per cent, respectively, while the higher-income groups formed 38.9 and 59.2 per cent (Clancy, 1988). Farmers' children also transfer to RTCs in great numbers. However, colleges of education still attract the highest proportion of farmers' children, especially their daughters. Since the 1960s, the third-level participation rate of the farming group has been close to (if somewhat lower than) its proportion in the population as a whole. In 1963 farmers comprised 25 per cent of the population, while they accounted for 20 per cent of university entrants, a figure that does not include entrants to the colleges of education (*Investment in Education,* 1966).

Clancy, in his research on third-level entry in the eighties, has calculated 'participation ratios' for each socio-economic group. Perfect representation according to the proportion of the group in the population would give a figure of 1.00. By 1980 the participation ratio of farmers was 1.04 (Clancy, 1982), and by 1986 it was 1.45 (Clancy, 1988). Farmers were the only group to have increased their share of third-level places from 1980 to 1986 (ibid.). The increased participation of farmers' children may indeed be related to the decline in the proportion of small farmers in the country, which is especially evident in recent years (CSO, 1992). Land is being consolidated in fewer 'farming hands', with inevitable consequences: it both increases the ability of farmers to place their children in higher education and places pressure on them to do so.

There are, of course, differences in the transfer rates to third-level colleges from different types of school. The schools with the highest transfer rates are secondary schools, and those with the lowest transfer rates are vocational schools (Clancy, 1988). This primarily reflects differentials in social background among the intake of these schools rather than differences in school effectiveness. Furthermore, as we point out in chapter 12, because they are private institutions, secondary schools have been in a position to select at entry, whereas public sector schools may not. However, it should be said that there is a growing awareness in the secondary sector that practices of selection at entry are undesirable (Conference of Major Religious Superiors, 1989, 22).

Nevertheless, the position remains that there are significantly lower proportions of working-class pupils (especially males) in secondary schools than in other types of school. For example, Breen (1986) indicates that at the end of the junior cycle 29 per cent of male secondary school pupils are from working-class backgrounds, while the figure is 63 per cent in vocational schools and 53 per cent in community schools. In the case of working-class girls the proportions are 45 per cent (secondary school), 70 per cent (vocational school), and 57 per cent (community school) (Breen, 1986, 15). In relation to performance in public examinations, at first glance it might appear that pupils in vocational schools perform more poorly than others. However, once intake differences are taken into account there is no evidence that vocational schools are less effective than others (ibid., 92).

Although inequalities in educational participation rates are most obvious at the point of third-level entry they are also evident at other points in the system. There is evidence that the proportion of boys and girls reaching Leaving Certificate stage declines as we move from the 'upper non-manual middle class' to 'semi-skilled manual' occupational groups (see table 7.1). The educational attainment levels of the different social classes (as measured by final examination taken) thus indicate educational inequality. For example, drawing on survey data taken from national manpower surveys of school leavers in the early 1980s, Breen's analysis shows clear differences in attainment according to the social class of the leavers.

As we have seen in chapter 1, the most vulnerable group within the labour market and those most prone to unemployment are those who leave school with no qualifications. It is clear that this group are disproportionately drawn from the working class—in particular from the semi-skilled and unskilled working class. Greaney and Kellaghan (1984) claimed that, in their study, performance in examinations was not related to socio-economic status. This would suggest that the differential examination achievements of the various social classes observable above are more a function of variations in participation rates.

On the other hand, subsequent analysis by Breen (1986, 88) of a sample of students surveyed by the ESRI found a significant relationship between social class and both Intermediate and Leaving Certificate results, even after differences in participation are taken into account. Using Leaving Certificate grade point average (GPA) as a measure, this study found that there was a significant relationship between GPA and social class, and that working-class pupils performed more poorly than others.

Table 7.1

Educational level attained according to father's occupational group, 1980–82 weighted aggregate results (percentages)

Educational level of leaver	Upper non-manual	Lower non-manual	Skilled manual	Semi-skilled/ unskilled manual	Farmer
		Father's occupational group			
Leaving Cert.	93.0	74.5	53.2	37.6	67.5
Inter Cert.	5.3	16.7	25.8	28.1	20.5
Group Cert.	1.0	4.4	11.1	16.4	6.5
None	0.7	4.4	10.0	17.9	5.5
Total	100.0	100.0	100.0	100.0	100.0
Number interviewed	794	2,036	1,656	1,771	1,433

Source: Breen (1986), 11.

A recent survey of a national sample of over a thousand adults examined the present standard of formal education of the adult population (Mac Gréil and Winston, 1990). The study compares standards with those of the adult population in a similar survey carried out by one of the authors in the early 1970s (Mac Gréil, 1974). The findings show a considerable improvement in the level of participation over the past twenty years. However, there was also evidence of substantial inequalities in educational participation. Mac Gréil and Winston's research also found a high correlation between the educational standard achieved by respondents and their subsequent occupation.

We can see, therefore, that the greatly increased educational expenditure since the 1960s has not eliminated educational inequality. Have there been any gains for the groups that were educationally most disadvantaged in the 1960s, especially the working-class groups? The answer would appear to be that there have been some gains. Rising participation rates have benefited all social categories; however, while working-class groups have improved their educational position in absolute terms, they have not gained any great advantage in relative terms compared with middle-class groups.

In the 1960s, as we have seen, substantial proportions of young people terminated their education at the end of primary school. The majority of these were the children of working-class parents or small farmers. By 1990/91 transfer to postprimary education was virtually universal, with 99 per cent of those aged between six and fifteen in full-time education (Department of Education, 1992, 2).

As we saw in chapter 1, the proportion of unqualified school leavers is approximately 12 per cent. This group face very grave labour market difficulties. We have also seen that participation rates are high overall, even up to Leaving Certificate. Almost three-quarters of school leavers have sat for the Leaving Certificate (see chapter 1). This increased participation obviously includes a large number of young people from working-class and small farm backgrounds.

However, the potential of these gains has been eroded by a number of factors. Firstly, economic recession, technological change and greatly increased levels of unemployment have meant that a large number of jobs formerly available to early (more socially and economically disadvantaged) school leavers have simply disappeared. Secondly, the existence of 'qualification inflation' (higher levels of qualification as a prerequisite for entry to any job) has caused a further deterioration in the job opportunities for the poorly qualified, and even for those in the more highly qualified categories. This has meant that qualifications generally have become a weaker currency within the labour market. Thirdly, as we have seen, it has been the higher-income middle-class groups that have gained most in increased participation rates, social mobility opportunities, and consolidation of socio-economic advantage. At a time when possession of third-level qualifications is more important than ever in obtaining employment, the advantaged position of the middle-class groupings is most apparent at transfer to third-level education. Thus, overall, the greatest beneficiaries of educational change since the 1960s have been the middle and upper middle or bourgeois classes.

Explaining Class Inequalities in Participation and Achievement

We have just documented substantial and persistent class inequalities in participation rates and achievement in Irish education. While these inequalities are more pronounced in Ireland than in a number of other European countries (Whelan and Whelan, 1984), they are far from unique. Indeed, they are to be found throughout the western world. How, then, can we explain their extent and endurance?

In the following sections we examine the research in Ireland and a number of other countries to provide an overview of the explanations that have been offered, and to evaluate these explanations. Internationally, research attempting to explain educational inequality falls under two broad headings. The first type is that which focuses on presumed deficiencies in the child's cognitive, cultural and linguistic abilities and those of her or his family and community. Much, but by no means all, of this research emanates from a functionalist frame of reference. The second type of explanation focuses on the role of knowledge systems, school organisation and educational practices in the reproduction of inequality. Finally, we ourselves would like to refocus attention on a very obvious but somewhat neglected explanation of educational inequality: poverty.

THE CHILD, THE FAMILY, AND THE COMMUNITY

In a somewhat pessimistic review of progress on the reduction of social inequalities, Heath (1989, 187) argues that in the face of the remarkable resilience of class inequalities, educational reforms seem powerless, whether for good or ill. He suggests two reasons for this: (1) the rhetoric of the reforms has often been much bolder than the reforms themselves, and (2) educationally ambitious families can adjust their children's chances under any new rules of the game. As the previous sections of this chapter have shown, 'educationally ambitious' families are predominantly middle-class. By and large, they have the economic and cultural resources to adjust their plans to new rules. But what of children from less privileged backgrounds?

Clearly, as our review of research shows, a proportion of children from all social classes (even the educationally least advantaged, i.e. the unskilled manual class and the unemployed) succeed and remain up to the highest level of the system. However, educational failure is disproportionately concentrated among the children of the semi-skilled and unskilled class and the unemployed. This has been a consistent pattern in all western societies since the end of the Second World War. The reforms introduced in the postwar period were, in most countries, initially directed at the removal of financial barriers to participation. Not surprisingly, poverty was identified as an important explanatory variable. However, researchers found that, in the variables under scrutiny, poverty did not fully explain lack of attainment (Reid, 1986, 203). As a result, research began to focus on a variety of other issues in the background of the child.

ABILITY

As we argue in chapter 11, the way we define 'intelligence' or 'ability' has a profound effect on what is defined as legitimate knowledge in schools. As one therefore might expect, the effect of measured intelligence has been examined in relation to the achievement and survival rates of the different social classes. Many of these intelligence tests have been defined in rather narrow linguistic and logical-mathematical terms. Some of the earliest use of such tests showed social class differences in ability (Floud, 1970). However, it was soon to be suggested that such variations had less to do with innate abilities than with the design of the tests. Those that relied on verbal reasoning ability (VRA) were particularly vulnerable to social class variations in knowledge of, and ability and willingness to use, language in particular ways (Reid, 1986, 199).

In Ireland, Greaney and Kellaghan used a VRA test, the Drumcondra Verbal Reasoning Test, to measure ability in their longitudinal study. They argued that of the primary school factors that were related to persistence in or withdrawal from the education system, the most important was the VRA of the student (Greaney and Kellaghan, 1984, 248). Verbal ability was again found to be important in achievement in public examinations. It correlated more highly with overall performance in the Intermediate and Leaving Certificate examinations than did any other variable. Of the variables about which information was obtained when the student was still at primary school, the student's VRA had the highest correlation with future occupation. They argued that none of the 'educationally irrelevant' variables included in the study (socio-economic class, gender, or location) played as significant a role as ability. Of the 'educationally irrelevant' variables, socio-economic status was the most important (ibid., 249–51).

It is difficult to accept, as Greaney and Kellaghan argued, that because VRA was highly correlated with achievement, meritocracy is being approached. The main difficulty with this argument is that VRA and social class are themselves closely related. Research suggests that, even where 'ability' or intelligence have been held constant, social class differences are still apparent and therefore remain to be explained (Bowles and Gintis, 1976). Furthermore, it has been argued that IQ tests have served as an instrument of oppression against the poor—dressed in the trappings of science rather than politics (Reid, 1986, 201). (We discuss social class and related problems with intelligence testing in greater detail in chapter 11.)

ATTITUDES AND VALUES

Although poverty was identified as a significant variable from the earliest research into educational underachievement, the fact that the correlation was less than perfect led researchers to explore the attitudes, values and culture of poor and working-class communities. It may also be the case that these researchers (middle-class themselves) were influenced by their own 'domain' assumptions as well as by the functionalist assumptions of the dominant paradigm of the time (Lynch and O'Neill, 1992). The importance of 'domain assumptions' has been highlighted by Gouldner (1970), who suggested that social scientists are influenced not only by the theory of their disciplines but also by their own life and cultural experiences; researchers, being predominantly middle-class (and male), were predisposed to interpret the culture of others in the light of their own values and life-styles.

In the 1960s and 1970s in particular there was a great deal of emphasis on attitudinal factors in educational underachievement, especially in the case of working-class families. This was based on the theory that working-class families have different life chances and life experiences from middle-class families, which dispose them towards different views of the world around them and of their place in it (Banks, 1976).

For example, in explaining class differences in university entrance, Ryan argued that the differences in the educational aspirations of the various social classes lay not so much in their desires but rather in the attitudes that parents and their children had that the educational goals could be attained (Ryan, 1966). Craft

(1970) argued that the reason working-class children had far lower educational and occupational aspirations than middle-class children was linked to their 'value orientations'. This was the notion that fundamental beliefs on three essential items governed all one's basic decision-making: attitudes to time; attitudes to activity; and attitudes to individualism. He suggested that the position a person, a class or a society took in relation to these major value orientations was an outcome largely of the way that individual or social group earned its living. The daily work of a business executive or a professional requires the capacity to take initiatives, to plan ahead, and above all to assume that the future can be shaped. The labourer, on the other hand, whose work situation demands little initiative and is fundamentally insecure and perhaps physically dangerous, is more likely to assume that the future will just happen (ibid., 20). Furthermore, he argued, a passive acceptance of the limitations of the environment seems an appropriate response to years on the housing list, or insecure and poorly paid employment, especially when a more 'activist' role requires either geographical or social mobility and a weakening of the traditionally close bonds with family and friends (ibid., 21).

The relationship between value orientations and educational achievement was explored by Craft in a study of children in a working-class suburb of Dublin (Craft, 1974). The study found that the value orientations of parents (especially mothers) were related to whether teenagers were early leavers or whether they intended to stay on at school past the minimum age. In particular, he found that the children of parents who were future-oriented were more likely to remain at school (ibid.).

Studies of working-class attitudes and values have suggested that the background and education of mothers had an important bearing on the attitudes of their children. For example, mothers in Britain who had married 'downwards' from a middle-class background had a better chance of a son going to college. Mothers whose occupation before marriage was 'superior' in status to that of their husbands were more likely to have children who were successful in the Eleven Plus examination. It was argued that such mothers were motivated by a strong desire to regain status. Their close association with the middle classes through their social origin, their job or their educational background provided them with the necessary knowledge and values to ensure a successful school career for their children (Banks, 1976). This form of analysis, as we can see, assumes a hierarchy of occupations, based on status, income, and education. It also implies (perhaps unintentionally, especially in the case of Banks) a deficit model of working-class life.

Some of these issues were explored in a study of a sample of 'educationally retarded' children (those whose literacy or numeracy fell below the norm for their age group) and 'educationally advanced' children (those whose literacy or numeracy was above the norm) and their mothers in a small town on the east coast of Ireland (Cullen, 1969). This study suggested that the majority of the educationally 'retarded' children came from homes where neither parent had experienced postprimary education. It found that educational aspirations of children were markedly lower in the educationally retarded group, where nearly half the mothers were satisfied with first-level education only. The study suggested that 'culturally induced educational retardation may occur where the child is deprived of a stimulating relationship with an adult during his infancy and childhood' (ibid., 128).

While the deficit model of (some) working-class family life is evident in Cullen's work, it was even more explicit in some of the studies conducted in Britain and the United States. A study by Dale and Griffeth (1970) claims that while 'defective home backgrounds' can occur in any class, 'deteriorators' (children who had been moved from an upper stream to a lower one in grammar school) tended to congregate in the skilled, semi-skilled and unskilled manual working classes. The study, which focused on streaming, argued that a good supporting home background was of crucial importance for the satisfactory academic progress of children. The authors did not, however, raise fundamental questions about the implications of streaming itself.

It would appear, in essence, that deficit models of children who are under-achieving educationally, and their families, tell us more about the perspectives of the researchers than about the children. We ourselves emphatically reject any explanation that rests on a deficit model of the children of the poor, as deficit theory is based on untenable assumptions about the superiority of one set of cultural values vis-à-vis others.

LANGUAGE AND EDUCABILITY

Perhaps one of the most controversial approaches to the problem of the educability of children from different social classes has been Bernstein's work on language and social class (Bernstein, 1971). Bernstein's work has been very influential in teacher education, and has also frequently been misinterpreted. At times his work has contributed to a deficit theory of working-class children's linguistic capacities, though he himself has rejected such interpretations (Bernstein and Brandis, 1970, 123).

According to Bernstein, language is one of the most important means of initiating, synthesising and reinforcing ways of thinking, feeling and behaviour that are functionally related to the social group. He distinguished two different forms of language: 'public' (later called 'restricted code'), which both the working class and the middle class use, and 'formal' (later called 'elaborated code'), which tends to be confined to the middle class. Public language, he contended, contains a high proportion of short commands, simple statements and questions where the symbolism is descriptive, tangible, concrete, visual, and of a low order of logical implications. Formal language, on the other hand, was described as rich in personal and individual qualifications, and its form implied sets of advanced logical operations. Non-verbal means of expression took second place (Lawton, 1968, 80).

Bernstein suggested a link between linguistic codes and authority and control structures in families. In the middle-class family a dynamic interaction is set up: the pressure to verbalise feelings in a personally qualified way socialises the child into elaborate patterns of verbal articulation. This becomes part of the socialisation process of the middle-class child, and it synchronises with what is required in school. The person-oriented middle-class family is contrasted with the position-oriented working-class family. In the latter case, Bernstein argued, roles are fixed. There is less negotiation about status boundaries, and therefore less emphasis on the individual elaboration of feeling (Bernstein, 1971).

This now provides the link with education. For the middle-class child, the school, which links the present to a distant future, does not clash with the values of the home. The ability of the child to switch from public to formal language enables him or her to communicate appropriately in a wide range of social circumstances. The working-class child, on the other hand, comes from a situation where long-term goals are less tenable than immediate gratification, because the general notion of the future is vague, dominated by chance rather than planning. The language between the mother and child is 'public', containing few personal qualifications and employing concrete symbolism. It is claimed that this tends to limit the verbal expression of feeling, and that consequently the emotional and cognitive differentiation of the working-class child is less developed.

The working-class environment is said to be in conflict with formal education in a number of ways, including an inability to communicate with the teacher on the teacher's own level and difficulty in dealing with more abstract concepts in mathematics and other subjects (Lawton, 1968, 80–2). In short, for the working-class child there is a cultural discontinuity between the home and the school, and the ability of the child is depressed (Bernstein and Brandis, 1970, 120).

Bernstein's work is conducted from a very Durkheimian, functionalist perspective, and his use of the terms 'working-class language' and 'middle-class language' refers more to the extremes of the class structure. However, there are some similarities between his analysis and that of the French neo-Marxist Bourdieu. Bourdieu and Passeron (1977, 115) suggest that at the two extremities of the scale there are two well-defined modes of speech: 'bourgeois parlance' and 'common parlance'. Bourgeois parlance, they argue, has a high proportion of lexical and syntactic borrowings from Latin. Thus the bourgeois language can be adequately handled only by those who, thanks to the school, have been able to convert their practical mastery, acquired by familiarisation within the family group, into a second-degree aptitude for the quasi-scholarly handling of language. Bourgeois language has a tendency to formalism, abstraction, and intellectualism.

Common parlance, or working-class language, is expressive and moves from particular case to particular case, from illustration to parable, and uses devices such as banter and joking. Bourdieu and Passeron argue that unequal class distribution of educationally profitable linguistic capital constitutes one of the best-hidden mediators through which the relationship between social origin and scholastic achievement is set up (ibid., 115–16).

Although there are similarities in the analysis provided by Bourdieu and Passeron and that of Bernstein, there is a shift in the French work to the notion of language as a form of linguistic or cultural capital, which the middle class have at their disposal. (We return to the theme of cultural capital below.) Also, Bourdieu is persistent and vehement in his rejection of cultural hierarchies in a way that Bernstein is not.

The work of Bernstein, whose sociolinguistic theories are perhaps better known than those of Bourdieu and Passeron, provoked a considerable debate and, in time, a good deal of criticism. Most notably this was articulated by Labov (1973; 1977). Labov suggested that the poor verbal skills that had been attributed to working-class children and those from ethnic minorities were more the result of the context in which the research was carried out than of innate deficiencies in the children. He illustrated this by demonstrating the improvement in linguistic skills that became apparent in New York children from a poor minority background when interview situations were made progressively less formal and less threatening.

It has to be said, however, that while Bernstein's work is included in his critique, Labov's main target was a body of American research, mainly by psychologists, that comes under the heading of 'cultural deprivation theory'. This theory referred to the complex of variables that it was believed were responsible for retarding the child's progress at school. The term 'cultural deprivation' became a euphemism for saying that working-class groups and ethnic minorities have cultures that are at least dissonant with, if not inferior to, the 'mainstream' culture of society. Culturally deprived children, it was argued, come from homes where mainstream values (i.e. middle-class values) do not prevail and are therefore less 'educable' than other children (Keddie, 1973, 8).

The essential fallacy of the verbal-cultural deprivation theory, Labov contended, lay in tracing the educational failure of the child to her or his personal deficiencies, and in suggesting that these deficiencies were caused by her or his home environment. Rather, Labov suggests, when failure reaches grand proportions it is necessary to look at the social and cultural obstacles to learning, and the inability of the school to adjust to the social situation (Labov, 1973, 55).

Some similar themes are raised in a more recent English study. Observations of girls in nursery school and in the home setting support the contention that the context in which speech is used has a marked effect on the language style of working-class children (Tizard et al., 1988). Working-class girls displayed a smaller range of complex language usages in talking to their teachers than to their mothers, and their talk to teachers contained a smaller proportion of these usages. There was no difference in the middle-class children's use of language at home and at school. For middle-class children there were more points of resemblance between home and school (for example in play equipment, and the teacher's accent and speech style). The middle-class mothers were more confident in their relations with the teachers (ibid.). This work suggests, then, that it is the school rather than the home that has inhibiting effects on the language usage of working-class children.

The message for teachers from the research on language and social class is that there may well be cultural discontinuities between the home or community and the school for certain categories of working-class children. However, in no sense has it been proved that there is any deficit in the linguistic skills of these children. Recent research suggests that such children have verbal skills well in excess of their performance levels in school and on standardised tests, and that the schools themselves are the inhibiting forces. The way forward may be to develop the pedagogical expertise needed to develop the language skills of children from culturally diverse backgrounds.

PARENTAL INTEREST

Perhaps the greatest educational cliché in current usage is the statement, 'The parents you really want to see never come to parent-teacher meetings.' It is consequently not surprising that educational research has focused attention on the question of 'parental interest' in the attempt to explain educational underachievement.

One of the earliest and most influential of such studies was carried out in England by Douglas (1964), who suggested that middle-class parents take more interest in their children's progress at school than manual working-class parents do, and that they become relatively more interested as their children grow older. They visit the schools more frequently to find out how their children are getting on with their work, and when they do so they are more likely to ask to see the head as well as the class teacher, whereas the manual working-class parents are usually content to see the class teacher only. The most striking difference, according to Douglas's study, was that many middle-class fathers visited the schools to discuss their children's progress, whereas manual working-class fathers seldom did (ibid., 53). Douglas found a high correlation between 'parental interest' and scores on standardised attainment tests. The Plowden Report, the major report on primary education in England in the 1960s, referred to similar findings (Central Advisory Council for Education, 1967).

However, examination of the way in which 'parental interest' is measured indicates that it is based partly on comments made by class teachers and partly on a record of the number of times each parent visited the school to discuss their children's progress (Douglas, 1964, 53). Such a measure is, therefore, more a measure of teachers' perceptions of parental interest than the level of interest itself. Another reason why it is problematic to equate parental interest with visits to the school, especially in the case of low-income or unemployed parents, relates to the educational experiences of these parents during their own time at school. As we have seen earlier in this chapter, people in low-income occupations, and those who are unemployed (see chapter 1), are more likely than others to have few or no qualifications on leaving school. We have also seen from Hannan and Shorthall's (1991) survey of young people in the labour market that those who were unqualified displayed the most alienated attitudes to the education system. Thus low-income parents in semi-skilled and unskilled working-class jobs, or those who are unemployed, are most likely to have found their own schooling to be unrewarding and alienating, and to have experienced failure. Consequently, parents who visit the school infrequently, or who miss parent-teacher meetings, are more likely to be displaying lack of confidence and lack of knowledge of the purpose of the meetings than lack of interest (M. O'Brien, 1987). They are also most likely to lack the knowledge and economic resources to make best use of the school system and to compensate for any inadequacies that it may have—for example by getting grinds for their children.

CULTURAL CAPITAL
We referred to the issue of 'linguistic capital' when we discussed language, and to the possibility that low-income parents may lack the sort of knowledge about the school system that could help their children. These issues have been drawn together by the French sociologist Bourdieu in his use of the concept of cultural capital.

This concept derives from a frame of reference that is predominantly neo-Marxist, but because of the way Bourdieu uses it, and because it 'fits' with much other research (even some of the 'cultural deficit' research), it has now become part of the common currency of educational discourse. The term has been adopted by a number of other researchers—for example by Halsey, Heath and Ridge (1980) in their study of male social mobility in Britain, and by Breen (1986) in his study of subject availability and student performance. 'Cultural capital' refers to the cultural goods transmitted by different families, the amount of which, according to Bourdieu and Passeron (1977, 30, 74), can be inferred by the father's occupation. Bourdieu (1986) claims that cultural capital can take three different forms. It exists in the *embodied state* in the form of long-lasting dispositions of mind and body (such as accent, tone, ways of holding one's body); it also exists in the *objectified state,* in the form of cultural goods such as books, films, works of art, and machines. Finally, cultural capital exists in *institutionalised form,* in the character of educational credentials.

Cultural capital is not evenly distributed throughout the population. The dominant classes (i.e. the middle and upper classes) possess much greater quantities of cultural capital, which they bring to their interactions within the education system, than do the subordinate classes (i.e. the working class and the unemployed). However, the distribution of both cultural and economic capital among the various dominant groups is not identical. Teachers and professionals, for example, possess greater quantities of cultural capital, whereas heads of industry and commerce possess greater amounts of economic capital (Bourdieu, 1973). This contributes to the relative autonomy of the academic market and education system and, he suggests, gives the appearance of a justification of meritocratic ideology, according to which academic justice provides a kind of resort for those who have no other resources than their 'intelligence' or 'merit'. This, he claims, is true only if we choose to ignore, firstly, that 'intelligence' represents but one particular form of capital that comes to be added, in most cases, to the possession of economic capital and the correlative capital of power and social relationships; and, secondly, that the holders of economic power also have more chances than those who are deprived of it to have cultural capital. In any case, those with economic capital are more easily able to do without cultural capital, since academic qualifications are a weak currency and possess all their value only within the limits of the academic market (Bourdieu, 1973).

However, we would suggest that, while academic qualifications may be a weak currency in more economically developed countries, where alternative opportunities for advancement may exist, in an economically peripheral, postcolonial society such as Ireland they have much higher value. It is through the uneven distribution of credentialised cultural capital in particular that the education system reproduces social and cultural inequalities in society. A further lacuna in Bourdieu's theory is that it does not explain why it is that certain working-class children succeed while others do not (Lynch, 1989, 24).

In his examination of performance at the senior cycle of Irish second-level schools, Breen (1986) assesses the impact of cultural capital on performance. The educational qualifications of fathers and mothers are used as an indicator of cultural capital. It is implied that this can be used as a referent for the skills, attitudes and abilities of pupils 'that derive from their home environment' (ibid., 89). In the analysis, cultural capital, thus measured, was found to have had a more significant impact on senior cycle performance than did other dimensions of class difference.

The question of cultural capital is closely linked to the issue of cultural reproduction. In the well-known ethnographic study of a small group of working-class boys in an English secondary school, Willis (1977) argues that there are direct and basic continuities between the anti-school culture of these underachieving 'lads' and the 'shop-floor' culture of their fathers and the local community. The most profound transition made by these boys, he argues, was not their physical passage from school to work but rather their entry into the distinctively non-conformist group and its culture within the school. This had occurred between the second and fifth years—around the age of thirteen or fourteen. This can be understood, Willis argued, as a kind of self-election to future class membership: that of the middle and lower working class (ibid.).

From a similar perspective, McRobbie (1978) looked at the culture of a group of working-class schoolgirls. The culture of these girls was typified by an ultimate, if not wholesale, endorsement of the traditional female role and of femininity, simply because to the girls it seemed to be 'natural'. Most of them realised that for them marriage would be an economic necessity, that the wages they would get would be insufficient to keep them, for example, in a flat. However, for a group of middle-class girls attending the same school there were possibilities of a career other than marriage alone. Middle-class girls, McRobbie argued, are directed to different kinds of jobs than working-class girls, although both are pushed in the direction of the home (ibid., 96–108).

These two studies suggest to us that schools are involved in cultural as well as social reproduction. They also suggest that there is a certain degree of self-election on the part of working-class youth to future working-class culture and occupations. Schools are among the sites where such reproduction occurs.

There are a number of strengths and shortcomings in these analyses. On the one hand they focus our attention on qualitative issues in the school, on cultural processes and on cultural resistance. On the other hand, Willis's work fails to give an adequate account of conformist working-class boys (Lynch, 1989, 19).

The 'cultural capital' thesis and theories of social and cultural reproduction seek to explain how families and education interact to reproduce and reinforce social and economic inequalities in society. Some of the key features of these mechanisms include patterns of inheritance. Inheritance continues to be one of the major ways whereby inequalities persist over time (Morgan, 1988). Another way in which advantage may be secured is in the purchase of private education. This is still an important factor in the background of top decision-makers in society. Slightly less directly, as Bourdieu argues, upper and middle-class families have a variety of forms of cultural capital that they are able to hand on to their children. These can range from 'social skills' or a 'good' accent to the ready access to an élite or middle-class culture—books, word-processors, and sporting or leisure facilities (Morgan, 1988, 50).

Knowledge Systems and School Organisation

As we have seen, when seeking to explain educational inequality much functionalist and some neo-Marxist work was directed to the home background and culture of the child. However, the publication of Young's *Knowledge and Control* at the beginning of the 1970s focused interest on the role played by knowledge and the curriculum in the perpetuation of inequality. Fundamentally,

Young's argument (which heralded the so-called 'new' sociology of education) was that, far from being beyond scrutiny, knowledge was socially constructed. The question then posed was, whose knowledge is reflected in the school curriculum? This directed attention to the class content of education and the bias in the curriculum in favour of middle-class values and the middle-class child. 'Formal education is based on the assumption that the thought systems organised in curricula are in some sense superior to the thought systems of those who are to be (or have not been) educated' (Young, 1971, 13).

The question of the bias of the curriculum has led Giroux and his associates in the United States to focus on the kinds of strategy that teachers could employ to combat this. They suggest that teachers would have to develop forms of knowledge, and classroom social practices, that validate the experiences students bring to school. This would demand acknowledging the language forms, style of presentation, dispositions, forms of reasoning and cultural forms that give meaning to student experiences. Thus the cultural capital of students from subordinate social categories must be related to the curriculum developed or taught, and to the questions raised in classes (Aronowitz and Giroux, 1985, 156).

In Ireland at present this type of approach is more likely to be found in community education than in the mainstream system. Accounts of educational programmes with working-class communities in Dublin suggest some possibilities. Such programmes are open in nature, and informal. They are flexible, they start from people's real positions, and place great emphasis on the social aspects of the programmes. Acquiring 'self-confidence' is seen as just as important as acquiring 'vocational skills' (D. O'Brien, 1987; Faughran, 1987). Working with young people who are extremely alienated from the mainstream system demands skills in the fields of group work, counselling, and developing relevant programmes (Faughnan, 1987).

Fresh approaches to the education of working-class people are required. The dilemma for working-class students who succeed in the education system, whereby they have to abandon certain features of their background 'habitus' (or system of dispositions) in a way that is not really true for other socially mobile groups, has to be addressed. In the present order of educational relations, once educated one ceases to be working-class in a way that a woman, no matter what her social position, will never cease to be a woman, a person who is black will never cease to be black, and those with a major physical disability will never be without it (Lynch and O'Neill, 1992, 14).

It may be argued that this structural isolation of the working class does not occur to the same degree for any other group because no other group's culture is defined in its totality as being structurally inferior and inadmissible in education. In the content of education it is in the arts, humanities and social sciences that one finds the most obvious exclusion of working-class culture. Working-class literature, music, art, history and social analysis are generally ignored in education (ibid.). The same could be said of the culture of such minorities as we have in Ireland, notably travellers, but also Muslims and Jews. The curriculum, therefore, is another mechanism through which social and educational inequality is perpetuated.

SCHOOL ORGANISATION

We have seen in chapter 1, and earlier in this chapter, that the second-level system in Ireland comprises three distinct sectors, which predominantly cater for different combinations of social classes. These different school types have different retention rates and different transfer rates to higher education (Clancy, 1982; 1986; 1988). While it is clear that the differential performance of the various types of school reflects differences in individual pupil characteristics at intake, it is also certain that the social class composition of schools has a significant effect on student aspiration and achievement, independent of the class background of any individual student (Clancy, 1986). There were similar findings on school composition and achievement in Breen's study of student performance at senior cycle (Breen, 1986). The institutionalisation, within a system of publicly funded education, of invidious status hierarchies between different postprimary schools serves to reproduce existing status hierarchies (Clancy, 1986).

As we point out in chapter 12, one of the reasons why there are substantial intake differences is that some schools—those in the voluntary private sector— are entitled to select at entry, whereas those in the public sector are not. Research into the second-level system (Lynch, 1989) suggests that secondary schools are perceived as being educationally advantageous, since over half the secondary schools sampled had more than one application for each place. Vocational schools, on the other hand, were rarely in a position where there were more applicants than places. Secondary schools were obviously the most likely to operate a competitive system at entry, and vocational schools the least likely to do so. This pattern was reversed at the class allocation stage. Vocational schools were the most likely to stream pupils (ibid., 83). A high proportion of second-level schools either stream or band. The practice of streaming, combined with a pattern where many schools select at entry (as we argue in chapter 12), reinforces social and economic inequalities.

Such practices become part of the hidden curriculum of the school. One of the best-known arguments on the unwritten functions of school life is presented in Bowles and Gintis's *Schooling in Capitalist America* (1976). They argue that the education system helps to integrate youth into the economic system through a structural correspondence between its social relations and those of production. The structure of social relations not only inures the student to the discipline of the work-place but also develops the types of personal demeanour, modes of presentation, self-image and social class identifications that are the crucial ingredients of job adequacy. The inheritance of wealth, family connection and other more or less direct advantages play a role also.

Bowles and Gintis argue, as do many functionalists (indeed their analysis shares many characteristics with functionalism), that the experiences of parents on the job tend to be reflected in the social relations of family life. Thus, through family socialisation, children tend to acquire orientations towards work, aspirations and self-concepts preparing them for similar educational positions themselves. The American education system works, they contend, to justify economic inequality and to produce a labour force whose capacities, credentials and consciousness are dictated in substantial measure by the requirements of profitable employment in the capitalist economy (ibid., 131–51).

Bourdieu also analyses the hidden curriculum of education, but in a somewhat less mechanistic manner than Bowles and Gintis. The social functions of education outlined by Bourdieu seem to be fourfold: to produce individuals with predispositions and attitudes (habitus) capable of adapting to social and economic structures; to allow for the controlled mobility of a limited category of individuals, carefully selected and modified by and for individual ascent; to legitimate the perpetuation of the social order and the transmission of power and privileges; and to mask the real nature of its relationship to the structure of class relations, i.e. its role in the perpetuation of inequality (Bourdieu, 1973, 71–112; Bourdieu and Passeron, 1977, 208).

Aronowitz and Giroux also address the issue of the hidden curriculum of education, drawing much on the work of Bourdieu. However, their analysis is very critical of what they see as the mechanistic notions of power and domination and the overdetermined view of human agency that characterises much of this work (Aronowitz and Giroux, 1985, 83). Their analysis of education leads them to emphasise the necessity to use the formal curriculum to develop a critical pedagogy. Such a critical pedagogy would stress forms of learning and knowledge aimed at providing a critical understanding of how social reality works, and it would take students' experiences as a starting point for developing a critical classroom pedagogy, that is, it would begin with popular experiences to make them meaningful in order to engage them critically (Aronowitz and Giroux, 1985, 217; 1991).

Thus, the research and analysis that focuses on school knowledge, school organisation and the formal and hidden curriculum suggest that it is the nature of the education system itself and its relationship with the economic system that must be challenged if inequality is to be tackled. This analysis moves away from any notions of 'deficit' in the working-class or underachieving child, although it recognises that, given the education system that we have, children enter it relatively advantaged or otherwise depending on their inheritance of particular types of cultural and/or economic capital from their social class of origin.

POVERTY

As we suggested earlier, poverty is an issue that has received less attention than might have been expected in the analysis of class inequalities in education. Part of the problem here is undoubtedly the fact that working-class people do not write about themselves and their problems in education: their problems and issues are filtered through the lens of middle-class academics, who, no matter how well-intentioned or theoretically informed they may be, have no on-going experience of the effects of poverty on educational participation. When working-class people begin to speak for themselves, as for example in O'Neill's research (1992), problems are defined differently. There is a great need for a stronger working-class voice on working-class problems in education.

While there are a number of definitions of poverty, the one that underlies our comments here is one that is very widely used and on which the study of poverty in Ireland by Callan et al. (1989) is based. A person is in poverty when, because of lack of resources, he or she is excluded from ordinary living patterns, customs and activities in their society. Callan et al. use a 'relative poverty line' method, which calculates income thresholds as proportions of average income. Using 60 per cent of average income as the threshold, Callan et al. calculate that about 30 per cent of the population are living in poverty. They suggest also that there has been a substantial increase in the numbers living in poverty since the mid-1970s. Households headed by an unemployed person face a very high risk of being in poverty and make up a significant proportion of poor households. There has also been a sharp increase since the mid-1970s in the risk of poverty for households with children, particularly for larger families. Another significant proportion of those in poverty are farm households (Nolan and Farrell, 1990).

We are not suggesting that the issue of poverty and education has never been addressed. In a study of children who terminated their education at the end of national school in the early 1970s, Rudd (1972) pointed out that for about one-fifth, financial considerations were the overriding factor. Also in the 1970s, Robinson argued that people who suffer income deprivation are more likely to experience inadequate housing, an excess of pollution, and lack of schools, hospitals, transport, and social services. Poverty is associated with under-achievement in school. The association is not perfect, and there are children from very disadvantaged backgrounds who do succeed, but generally the child born into poverty 'does not perform well on the educational track' (Robinson, 1976, 112).

Two recent studies (undertaken in two separate working-class areas in Dublin) suggest that the principal problem working-class people have in relation to education is that they lack adequate income to maximise the advantages that the system could offer. They are seriously deprived of resources relative to the middle-class people with whom they must compete for credentials. There is nothing 'wrong' with their attitudes or values, in the sense that the great majority of parents were keenly aware of the importance of education and valued it for their children (M. O'Brien, 1987; O'Neill, 1992).

Parents in these studies also experienced a sense of alienation from the school—which perhaps mirrors the sense of alienation among unqualified school leavers observed by Hannan and Shorthall (1991). In O'Neill's study, over 87 per cent of respondents felt that schoolbooks did not reflect working-class life-styles, while nearly two-thirds felt that teachers did not understand working-class people (O'Neill, 1992). O'Brien's earlier study also points to a certain level of alienation from school among working-class mothers. Over a third of the mothers said that they themselves had either hated or did not like school. Many of the parents were unaware of what precisely was taught in school, and few had any knowledge of how the school functioned organisationally (M. O'Brien, 1987, 221).

Both of these studies indicated that low income had a direct bearing on students' inability to participate fully in education. Half the women O'Brien interviewed said they spent a lot of time worrying about money. This left little time to be concerned about what happened in school. Being 'summoned' to the school to account for children's misdemeanours was named as a major source of stress in both studies; the absence of this kind of stress was interpreted as meaning that all was well.

Another insight into the relationship between income and education is provided by Dowling's study of the preparation for university experienced by a cohort of university entrants (Dowling, 1991). Students usually sit for the Leaving Certificate at the end of a five-year programme. However, there are schools that take six years to complete the course. These tend to be the more prestigious academic secondary schools, many of them fee-paying. Dowling examined the educational histories of a cohort of first-year university entrants; she found that students from social classes 1 and 2 (the higher and lower professional and managerial and large farmer categories) had considerable advantages over students from other classes. Just under half of these spent at least six years in second-level education, compared with just a quarter of students from social classes 3 to 6. But it was students from the higher professional and executive classes (social class 1) who were the most likely to have had an extended school career.

In addition, although students from all social classes obtained extra help (such as grinds) outside school hours, students from social class 1 got more help than any of the others. Dowling argues that while there is no way of establishing how much advantage this confers, the fact that tutoring is embarked on voluntarily and paid for privately suggests that those who get it believe it to be valuable. Furthermore, this group in particular were overrepresented in a number of the higher-point professional faculties, such as law, engineering, dentistry, and medicine (ibid., 24–5).

CONCLUSION

In the first part of this chapter we examined the concept of social class, and demonstrated that increased educational expenditure since the 1960s has not eliminated class inequalities in educational participation or achievement. The main beneficiaries of the expanded educational opportunities have been the middle and upper middle classes. Substantial proportions of low-income children from working-class, small farm and unemployed backgrounds are still underachieving.

In seeking to explain the persistence of inequality, we have outlined a range of approaches to the issue in the sociology of education. A number of these focused on factors in the child's background. Others have concentrated on aspects of school organisation and on the formal and the hidden curriculum. The findings of Irish studies on poverty and education suggest that while theories that emphasise cultural capital and inegalitarian practices in educational institutions have validity, income may have a stronger explanatory power than many studies have implied. The fact that the more secure and well-paid sector of the working class in Ireland (skilled manual workers) has consistently higher participation rates in third-level education than other working-class groups (Clancy, 1982, 1988) would suggest that working-class people can achieve well in the education system when they have the resources to do so and when economic conditions make education essential for participation in the labour market. What is being suggested, therefore, is that social class differences in style, language and attitude between working-class children and the institution of the school are of far less significance for understanding inequality in education in postcolonial contexts such as Ireland, where education is a highly valued commodity by almost everyone, than is poverty. If income and wealth differentials were eliminated, the problem of working-class 'failure' in education would be significantly reduced.

References and Further Reading
Aronowitz, S., and Giroux, H. (1985), *Education Under Siege: the Conservative, Liberal and Radical Debate Over Schooling*, London: Routledge and Kegan Paul.
Aronowitz, S., and Giroux, H. (1991), *Postmodern Education: Politics, Culture and Social Criticism*, Minneapolis: University of Minnesota Press.
Banks, O. (1976), *The Sociology of Education*, London: Batsford.
Bernstein, B. (1971), *Class, Codes and Control—vol. 1*, London: Routledge and Kegan Paul.
Bernstein, B., and Brandis, W. (1970), 'Social class differences in communication and control' in W. Brandis and D. Henderson, *Social Class, Language and Communication*, London: in Routledge and Kegan Paul.
Bourdieu, P. (1973), 'Cultural reproduction and social reproduction' in R. Brown (ed.), *Knowledge, Education and Cultural Change*, London: Tavistock.

Bourdieu, P. (1986), 'The forms of capital' in J. Richardson (ed.), *Handbook of Theory and Research for the Sociology of Education*, New York: Greenwood.

Bourdieu, P., and Passeron, J.-C. (1977), *Reproduction in Education, Society and Culture*, London: Sage.

Bowles, S., and Gintis, H. (1976), *Schooling in Capitalist America*, London: Routledge and Kegan Paul.

Braverman, H. (1974), *Labor and Monopoly Capitalism*, New York: Monthly Review Press.

Breen, R. (1986), *Subject Availability and Student Performance in the Senior Cycle of Irish Post-Primary Schools*, Dublin: Economic and Social Research Institute.

Breen, R., et al. (1990), *Understanding Contemporary Ireland: State, Class and Development in the Republic of Ireland*, Dublin: Gill and Macmillan.

Callan, T., et al. (1989), *Poverty, Income and Welfare in Ireland*, Dublin: Economic and Social Research Institute.

Central Advisory Council for Education (1967), *Children and their Primary Schools: Report, 1967*, London: HMSO.

Central Statistics Office (1986), *Census of Population of Ireland, 1981—vol.7: Occupations*, Dublin: CSO.

Central Statistics Office (1988), *Census of Population of Ireland, 1986—Classification of Occupations*, Dublin: CSO (unpublished).

Central Statistics Office (1992), *Labour Force Survey, 1991*, Dublin: CSO.

Clancy, P. (1982), *Participation in Higher Education: a National Survey*, Dublin: Higher Education Authority.

Clancy, P. (1986), 'Socialisation, selection and reproduction in education' in P. Clancy et al. (eds.), *Ireland: a Sociological Profile*, Dublin: Institute of Public Administration.

Clancy, P. (1988), *Who Goes to College?: a Second National Survey of Participation in Higher Education*, Dublin: Higher Education Authority.

Conference of Major Religious Superiors (1988), *Inequality in Schooling in Ireland*, Dublin: CMRS.

Conference of Major Religious Superiors (1989), *Inequality in Schooling in Ireland: the Role of Selective Entry and Placement*, Dublin: CMRS.

Coolahan, J. (1981), *Irish Education: History and Structure*, Dublin: Institute of Public Administration.

Craft, M. (1970), 'Family, class and education: changing perspectives' in M. Craft (ed.), *Family, Class and Education*, London: Longman.

Craft, M. (1974), 'Talent, family values and education in Ireland' in J. Eggleston (ed.), *Contemporary Research in the Sociology of Education*, London: Methuen.

Cullen, K. (1969), *School and Family: Social Factors in Educational Attainment*, Dublin: Gill and Macmillan.

Dale, R., and Griffeth, S. (1970), 'The influence of the home' in M. Craft (ed.), *Family, Class and Education*, London: Longman.

Department of Education (1966), *Investment in Education: Report of the Survey Team*, Dublin: Stationery Office.

Department of Education (1992), *Statistical Report, 1990/91*, Dublin: Stationery Office.

Department of Labour (1991), *Economic Status of School Leavers, 1990,* Dublin: Stationery Office.

Douglas, J. (1964), *The Home and the School,* London: McGibbon and Kee.

Dowling, T. (1991), 'Inequalities in preparation for university entrance: an examination of the educational histories of entrants to UCC', *Irish Journal of Sociology*, vol. 1, 18–30.

Drudy, S. (1991), 'The classification of social class in sociological research', *British Journal of Sociology*, vol. 42, no. 1, 21–41.

Faughnan, P. (1987), 'Evaluation of the Lourdes Youth and Community Services project' in T. Crooks and D. Stokes (eds.), *Disadvantage, Learning and Young People,* Dublin: CDVEC Curriculum Development Unit, Trinity College.

Floud, J. (1970), 'Social class factors in educational achievement' in M. Craft (ed.), *Family, Class and Education,* London: Longman.

Goldthorpe, J. (1980), *Social Mobility and Class Structure in Modern Britain,* Oxford: Clarendon Press.

Gouldner, A. (1970), *The Coming Crisis of Western Sociology,* London: Heinemann.

Greaney, V., and Kellaghan, T. (1984), *Equality of Opportunity in Irish Schools,* Dublin: Educational Company.

Halsey, A., Heath, A., and Ridge, J. (1980), *Origins and Destinations,* Oxford: Clarendon Press.

Hannan, D., and Shorthall, S. (1991), *The Quality of Their Education,* Dublin: Economic and Social Research Institute.

Heath, A. (1989), 'Class in the classroom' in B. Cosin, M. Flude, and M. Hales (eds.), *School, Work and Equality,* London: Hodder and Stoughton.

Investment in Education: Report of the Survey Team (1966), Dublin: Stationery Office.

Keddie, N. (1973), 'Introduction' in N. Keddie (ed.), *Tinker, Tailor . . . the Myth of Cultural Deprivation,* Harmondsworth (Middlesex): Penguin.

Labov, W. (1973), 'The logic of nonstandard English' in N. Keddie (ed.), *Tinker, Tailor . . . the Myth of Cultural Deprivation,* Harmondsworth (Middlesex): Penguin.

Labov, W. (1977), *Language in the Inner City: Studies in the Black English Vernacular,* Oxford: Blackwell.

Lawton, D. (1968), *Social Class, Language and Education,* London: Routledge and Kegan Paul.

Lynch, K. (1989), *The Hidden Curriculum: Reproduction in Education: a Reappraisal,* Lewes: Falmer.

Lynch, K., and O'Neill, C. (1992), 'Equality and Education: What Has Happened to the Working Class?' (paper presented at annual general meeting of American Sociological Assocation, Pittsburgh, 20–26 August 1992).

McGill, P. (1987), 'The financing of education in Northern Ireland' in R. Osborne, R. Cormack, and R. Miller (eds.), *Education and Policy in Northern Ireland,* Belfast: Queen's University (Policy Research Institute).

Mac Gréil, M. (1974), *Educational Opportunity in Dublin*, Dublin: Catholic Communications Institute of Ireland.

Mac Gréil, M., and Winston, N. (1990), *Educational Participation in Ireland*, Maigh Nuad: Coláiste Phádraig (Aonad Suirbhé agus Taighde, Roinn na Staidéar Sóisialta).

McRobbie, A. (1978), 'Working class girls and the culture of femininity' in Women's Studies Group, Centre for Contemporary Cultural Studies (eds.), *Women Take Issue*, London: Hutchinson.

Morgan, D. (1988), 'Socialisation and the family: change and diversity' in M. Woodhead and A. McGrath (eds.), *Family, School and Society*, London: Hodder and Stoughton.

Nolan, B., and Farrell, B. (1990), *Child Poverty in Ireland*, Dublin: Combat Poverty Agency.

O'Brien, D. (1987), 'Lourdes Youth and Community Services' in T. Crooks and D. Stokes (eds.), *Disadvantage, Learning and Young People*, Dublin: CDVEC Curriculum Development Unit, Trinity College.

O'Brien, M. (1987), 'Home School Relations in Inner City Dublin' (MA thesis, Education Department, University College, Dublin).

O'Neill, C. (1992), *Telling It Like It Is*, Dublin: Combat Poverty Agency.

Poulantzas, N. (1977), 'The new petty bourgeoisie' in A. Hunt (ed.), *Class and Class Structure*, London: Lawrence and Wishart.

Reid, I. (1986), *The Sociology of School and Education*, London: Fontana.

Robinson, P. (1976), *Education and Poverty*, London: Methuen.

Rottman, D., et al. (1982), *The Distribution of Income in the Republic of Ireland: a Study in Social Class and Family Cycle Inequalities*, Dublin: Economic and Social Research Institute.

Rudd, J. (1972), 'Survey of national school terminal leavers', *Social Studies*, vol. 1, no. 1, 61–72.

Ryan, L. (1966), 'University and social class in Ireland', *Christus Rex*, vol. 20, no. 2, 108–24.

Tizard, B., et al. (1988), 'Language and social class: is verbal deprivation a myth?' in M. Woodhead and A. McGrath (eds.), *Family, School and Society*, London, Hodder and Stoughton.

Weber, M. (1968), *Economy and Society—vol. 1*, New York: Bedminster.

Whelan, C., and Whelan, B. (1984), *Social Mobility in the Republic of Ireland: a Comparative Perspective*, Dublin: Economic and Social Research Institute.

Willis, P. (1977), *Learning to Labour*, London: Saxon House.

Young, M. (ed.) (1971), *Knowledge and Control*, London: Collier Macmillan.

8

Gender Differentials and Education

The position of women in Irish education is somewhat contradictory. While girls have attained higher aggregate grades than boys in major public examinations (Department of Education, 1983; Greaney and Kellaghan, 1984, 180; Clancy, 1987, 13; see also table 8.9 below) and while they are more likely to stay on to complete second-level education than their male counterparts—in 1989/90, for example, 55.2 per cent of seventeen and eighteen-year-olds in second-level education were girls (Department of Education, 1992a, table 3.2 and 3.3)—males slightly outnumber females in third-level education and greatly outnumber them in the expanding technological sectors of higher education (Clancy 1988, 17, 18).

To comprehend the contradictory position of women in education one needs to examine their position in other social institutions. This chapter begins therefore by outlining the economic and social position of women in Irish society. Following this, an analysis of gender differences in educational participation is undertaken. Gender differences in curricular choice and educational attainment are then examined in detail. Finally, we present an analysis of gender differences in school ethos and highlight the need for further research on the relationship between gender and social class.

THE ECONOMIC AND SOCIAL POSITION OF WOMEN

Under the Constitution of Ireland, a woman's place is clearly defined as being in the home. Indeed, it is implicit in article 41.2 that womanhood and motherhood are synonymous:

> 1° In particular, the State recognises that by her life within the home, *woman* gives to the State a support without which the common good cannot be achieved.
>
> 2° The State shall, therefore, endeavour to ensure that *mothers* shall not be obliged by economic necessity to engage in labour to the neglect of their duties in the home. [Emphasis added]

While no legislation has been passed giving legal force to this article, the fact remains that only 26.9 per cent of married women are in the paid labour force, compared with an average of 41.6 per cent in other EC countries; it is interesting to note, however, that 38.9 per cent of women who are separated or divorced are in paid employment (Blackwell, 1989, table 3.8; CSO, 1992, table 11).

Women's dependence on men within marriage is therefore not just a constitutional prescription: it is an economic reality. That dependence takes on an even more problematic meaning when one realises that divorce is prohibited under the Constitution. With high unemployment (at approximately 20 per cent of the population), no state-funded child care facilities (McKenna, 1988), and no divorce, most married women with children are locked into a state of economic subordination to men, whether they wish it or not.

To suggest that the position of women is one of unbridled subservience to men would, however, be far from true. Over the last twenty-five years major social and economic changes have occurred that have advantaged women in several ways. The most obvious economic development was that Ireland changed from being a predominantly rural society largely dependent on farming to being an urban-industrial society highly dependent on manufacturing and service industries. Industrial expansion led to increased job opportunities for women. Married women in particular became more active in the paid labour force, and their rates of participation are increasing rapidly. From table 8.1 one can see that women comprised a noticeably larger proportion of the paid labour force in 1991 (32.2 per cent) than they did seventeen years previously (25.7 per cent). Also, married women's participation, though still low by international standards, was much greater in 1991 than it was in 1971 or even in 1981: while married women comprised only 13.6 per cent of the female paid labour force in 1971, they constituted 44.4 per cent in 1991. With greater paid labour force participation came greater financial independence.

One should not exaggerate the significance of paid labour force gains for women, however. Women still dominate the part-time labour market: 72 per cent of all part-time workers are women (CSO, 1992, 13). Vertical segregation is also very much in evidence: a study by McCarthy of forty-six companies in 1972 and 1983 found that only 11 per cent of senior management and professional posts were held by women (1988, table 2). This represented a slight improvement from 1972, when 9.5 per cent of these posts were occupied by women. In addition, few women are employers (84.7 per cent of all employers are men); within the agricultural sector 95 per cent of the self-employed (mostly farmers) are men and 91 per cent of those who are agricultural employers are also men (CSO, 1992, table 21).

Women predominate among the unpaid workers engaged in home duties, at 99 per cent (ibid., table 11). We have seen in chapter 5 that women are also seriously underrepresented in senior management positions in schools, colleges, and universities. A similar situation obtains in allied academic institutions, such as research institutes, and in the Department of Education itself. The position of women in the civil service generally is also one of subordination. From table 8.2 we see that none of the Secretaries or Deputy Secretaries of Government departments are women, while only 1 per cent of Assistant Secretaries, 5 per cent of principal officers and about 25 per cent of assistant principal officers and administrative officers were women in 1987.

Table 8.1

Changes in women's paid labour force participation, 1971–1991

Paid labour force*	1971	1981	1991
Total†	1,125,400	1,272,000	1,333,500
Total women	289,300	370,000	429,100
Women as percentage of total	25.7	29.1	32.2
Married women‡ in paid labour force			
Total	39,200	112,000	190,700
As percentage			
of female paid labour force	13.6	30.2	44.4

*We use the term 'paid labour force' to alert readers to the fact that while most women work—at home—only a minority are in paid employment. What is currently defined as the 'labour force' does not include people on 'home duties', 99 per cent of whom are women.
†Figures are rounded.
‡Includes separated and divorced women. In 1991, 11,500 (2.7 %) of the total of 429,100 women in the paid labour force were separated or divorced.

Source: Blackwell (1989), table 3.1; CSO (1992), table 11.

The absence of women from senior posts in the civil service is paralleled in other areas of public life. In 1986 only six of the eighty-three judges (7.2 per cent) were women, while women constituted only 10.4 per cent of the members of the national executive committees of the four main political parties (Department of the Taoiseach, 1987, 52, 55, 57).

As is the case internationally, horizontal sex segregation also occurs in the labour market: 74 per cent of all clerical workers are female, while men predominate in manufacturing as producers, makers, and repairers (84 per cent) (CSO, 1992, table 21). Two occupational groups account for over half the women in paid work: 28 per cent of all women in employment are clerical workers, while 24 per cent are professional and technical workers, mostly nurses and teachers (ibid.).

Finally, as is true in many countries, women's earnings are considerably less than those of men: the average hourly earnings of women in all industry are 67.1 per cent of those of men (Blackwell, 1989, 48).

Table 8.2

**Percentage of women in civil service (general service grades),
January 1983 and October 1987**

Grade	Jan. 1983	Oct. 1987
Secretary	0	0
Assistant Secretary	1	1
Principal officer	3	5
Assistant principal officer	18	23
Administrative officer	31	26
Higher executive officer	35	34
Executive officer	40	44
Staff officer	61	67
Clerical officer	69	68
Clerical assistant	84	83

Source: Mahon (1991), 21, table 1.

While labour market gains for women have been fairly slight in recent years, there have been some legislative advances. It was, however, the EC directives of the 1970s and Ireland's accession to a UN convention that precipitated the enactment of legislative changes beneficial to women. The Anti-Discrimination (Pay) Act, 1974, the Employment Equality Act, 1977, the Unfair Dismissals Act, 1977, and the Social Welfare (No. 2) Act, 1985, were all passed in response to EC directives (Department of the Taoiseach, 1987, 25). It was Ireland's accession to the 1985 UN Convention on the Elimination of All Forms of Discrimination Against Women that precipitated the enactment of the Irish Nationality and Citizenship Act, 1986, and the Domicile and Recognition of Foreign Divorces Act, 1986, both of which gave greater rights to married women.Were it not for EC membership in particular, it is doubtful if much of this legislation would have been passed; in 1975, for example, the Government sought a derogation from the Anti-Discrimination (Pay) Act and attempted to delay its implementation. This is not to deny the important work done by the women's movement in pressing for social and political reform over the last twenty years. However, even members of the women's movement have admitted that many of their efforts to promote women's rights have met with limited success (Barry, 1988; Smyth, 1988; 1992).

One of the areas where there has been some advancement is in the establishing of structures and in the formulation of policies at Government level to promote equal opportunities. A Commission on the Status of Women (1970) paved the way for the formation of the Council for the Status of Women in 1973. This organisation functions to co-ordinate the work of women's organisations, to examine and contest discrimination, and to consider legislative proposals concerning women. The Employment Equality Agency was established in 1977 and has done much to promote the awareness and practice of equal opportunities policies in the work-place. A further encouraging development in 1982 was the appointment of a Minister of State at the Department of the Taoiseach responsible for promoting action on women's affairs, and, in 1992, the establishment of a full Department of Equality and Law Reform. The Government has formally adopted policies for promoting equal opportunities between men and women in employment, legislation, and education. The Department of Education has specific responsibility for the elimination of sexism and sex stereotyping in the education sector, and has put forward a number of proposals in the Green Paper (Department of Education, 1992b) for promoting greater equality for women and girls in education.

While several legislative changes have guaranteed women equal rights with men, these have precipitated few changes in the socio-economic status of women. Women still constitute a majority of those in the part-time labour market and of those engaged in home duties. They are far less likely to be employers than men, and those who are employees tend to earn less than their male colleagues. However, as the work of McCarthy (1988) and Blackwell (1989) shows, women have made slight gains in recent years. There are considerably more married women in paid employment than there were in the early 1970s, and women are also slightly more likely to be in senior management positions than they were previously—although it must be remembered that many married women are in part-time work: for example, 71 per cent of part-time women workers are married (Drew, 1990, 18).

The weakness of promoting equality for women (or any group) within a formal liberal equal opportunities framework is very evident in Ireland. While it is important to have the right to equal pay, working conditions, education, and so on, one cannot fully exercise those rights without 'equality of condition'. That is to say, freedom from constraints does not mean equality; only when 'violent contrasts of income and condition' are eliminated will there be real equality. Only the relatively privileged (middle-class women, for example) can gain from the formal elimination of barriers; for the majority, formal (as opposed to substantive) equality of opportunity means having the opportunity to become unequal (Tawney, 1964, 100–17).

PATTERNS OF PARTICIPATION
As noted in chapter 4, there is a strong tradition of denominational education in Ireland, and a not unrelated tradition of single-sex education. (See chapter 9.) Gender differences are also evident in patterns of educational participation. From table 8.3 we can see that while girls have a higher participation rate at second level than boys, this advantage is lost at third level, where males outnumber females.

Table 8.3

Female and male participation rates at the three major education levels

	Females		Males	
	Number	*Percentage*	*Number*	*Percentage*
First level (age 4–12 approx.)	272,592	48.6	288,278	51.4
Second level (age 12–17/18 approx.)	174,872	51.1	167,492	48.9
Third level (age 17/18+ approx.)	30,738	46.6	35,211	53.4
Total	478,202		490,981	

Source: Department of Education (1991), table 1.

Research by Clancy indicates, however, that sex differences in third-level participation rates are declining continuously. While women constituted only 27.4 per cent of full-time higher education students in 1955/56 and 29.4 per cent in 1965/66, by 1990/91 they accounted for 47.4 per cent (Clancy 1989, 1; Department of Education, 1992b, table 1). Women made up 48 per cent of higher education entrants in 1986 (Clancy, 1988, 68). Clancy suggests that if present growth rates continue, women will shortly constitute a majority of new entrants to higher education (1989, 1).

CURRICULAR OPTIONS
All pupils pursue the same curriculum at primary level: Irish, English, mathematics, social and environmental studies, arts and crafts, music, physical education, and religion. This is not to suggest that boys and girls have identical educational experiences. Although little research has yet been undertaken on pupils' experiences in primary schools (such as classroom interaction, use of textbooks, and teacher behaviour), the evidence, including that from other countries, would suggest that gender differences are likely to be common at the classroom level (Council of Europe, 1982; Marland, 1983; Stanworth, 1983; Mullin et al., 1986; Wilson, 1991; see also chapter 9).

Evidence from the *Teacher's Handbook,* containing the official guidelines given to primary teachers (Department of Education, 1971, 213), certainly indicates that sex-stereotyping is alive and well. With regard to the teaching of music, the handbook suggests that 'while a large number of songs are suited to both boys and girls, some songs are particularly suited to boys e.g. martial, gay, humorous, rhythmic airs. Others are more suited to girls e.g. lullabies, spinning songs, songs tender in content and expression.'

Evidence of sex-stereotyping is also clearly in evidence in the section dealing with physical education (p. 310). In senior primary classes the handbook suggests that 'separate training in movement may be made for boys and girls. Boys can now acquire a wide variety of skills and techniques and girls often become more aware of style and grace. Control and resiliency become more important.'

At second level, pupils pursue a core curriculum up to the completion of the Junior Certificate examination at the age of fifteen approximately. The core varies slightly with school type. Irish, English and mathematics are compulsory subjects in all types of second-level school; in addition, history and geography are compulsory in secondary schools, together with two other subjects from the prescribed list of twenty subjects. In community, comprehensive and vocational schools, pupils can take either art, commerce, mechanical drawing, or home economics, together with two other subjects from the prescribed list. For the senior cycle Leaving Certificate examination, Irish is the only compulsory subject (in terms of attendance) out of the total of thirty-one subjects. One can see, therefore, that science is not a core subject either for boys or girls, and that schools and pupils (depending on school size especially) have considerable latitude in their choice of subject.

One can also note that there are no social science subjects offered at Leaving Certificate level, no political science, and no courses in new areas of knowledge such as media studies, women's studies, or equality studies. The curriculum is traditional and is biased towards language, business subjects, science, and applied science. Little time or attention is given to certain forms of knowledge and the related abilities (which we discuss in chapter 11).

The freedom given to schools in curriculum and timetabling, especially at senior level, has resulted in very noticeable gender differences both in the availability and the take-up of particular subjects (Hannan et al., 1983). In table 8.4 we present details of the proportion of schools that offer the various subjects at Leaving Certificate level. This shows that technical subjects, such as technical drawing, engineering, and construction studies, are rarely available as options for girls, while timetabling in co-educational schools often means that girls are excluded. Boys, on the other hand, are rarely given the option of doing home economics. (In chapter 9 we discuss this issue further.) The pattern at junior level is very similar (Department of Education, 1992a, table 14.5).

In the sciences and mathematics, gender differences have been reduced considerably in recent years. As can be seen from table 8.5, 89.4 per cent of girls' schools offered higher-course mathematics at Leaving Certificate level in 1989/90, and 78.8 per cent offered physics, compared with 73.9 per cent and 34.8 per cent offering higher mathematics and physics, respectively, in 1980/81. The proportion of girls' schools offering physics has more than doubled, therefore, in six years, while the proportion offering higher mathematics and chemistry is now almost equal to that of boys' schools.

Table 8.4

Relationship between gender mix in schools and availability of Leaving Certificate subjects

Subject	Percentage of single-sex schools offering subject		Percentage of mixed schools offering subject		
			to boys only	to girls only	to both
	Boys	Girls			
1 Irish (higher)	89.5	89.9	1.6	1.4	71.5
2 Irish (lower)	90.1	89.9	0.9	0.5	82.4
3 Irish (common)	8.0	11.6	—	—	19.2
4 English (higher)	91.4	91.0	1.4	0.5	77.1
5 English (lower)	89.5	88.4	2.3	0.5	81.0
6 English (common)	9.9	14.3	—	0.2	20.6
7 Latin	14.2	7.9	0.7	0.2	1.9
8 Greek	1.9	0.5	0.2	—	—
9 Hebrew studies	—	—	—	—	0.2
10 French	95.7	99.5	0.9	3.5	89.6
11 German	22.2	55.0	0.7	2.1	19.7
12 Italian	1.2	2.1	0.5	—	0.2
13 Spanish	9.3	23.3	0.9	1.2	5.8
14 History	92.0	97.4	2.8	1.9	71.5
15 Geography	95.1	94.2	2.5	1.2	78.2
16 Mathematics (higher)	90.7	89.4	10.4	0.7	60.9
17 Mathematics (lower)	93.2	95.2	0.7	0.2	86.8
18 Mathematics (common)	5.6	5.3	—	—	15.0
19 Applied mathematics	32.1	5.3	2.5	—	8.3
20 Physics	92.6	78.8	7.9	0.2	59.5
21 Chemistry	87.0	88.9	1.9	0.7	47.5
22 Physics & chemistry	12.3	6.3	2.3	0.2	17.4
23 Agricultural science	21.0	2.6	5.6	0.2	16.2
24 Biology	87.7	97.9	1.4	3.7	88.9
25 Agricultural economics	3.7	0.5	0.7	—	2.1
26 Engineering	13.0	0.5	42.1	—	17.4
27 Technical drawing	62.3	3.2	47.0	—	37.5
28 Construction studies	29.6	—	46.8	—	17.4
29 Home economics (scientific & social)	19.1	97.4	—	26.6	60.2
30 Home economics (gen.)	1.9	33.3	—	7.9	6.5
31 Accounting	85.2	83.1	1.2	7.2	66.2
32 Business organisation	85.8	85.7	0.9	6.5	70.1
33 Economics	68.5	41.8	1.4	—	34.5
34 Economic history	2.5	1.	—	0.2	0.5
35 Art (incl. crafts)	64.8	95.8	2.1	4.4	68.8
36 Music & musicianship	13.6	57.7	0.9	4.2	12.5
37 Physical education	63.6	85.7	1.9	1.2	58.1
38 Classical studies	4.9	3.2	—	—	0.9

Source: Department of Education (1991), table 14.9. (We gratefully acknowledge the assistance of the Statistics Branch of the Department of Education in preparing this table.)

Table 8.5

Proportion of single-sex schools offering particular subjects to Leaving Certificate pupils, 1980/81 and 1989/90

Subject	Girls' schools		Boys' schools	
	1980/81	*1989/90*	*1980/81*	*1989/90*
	%	%	%	%
Mathematics (higher)	73.9	89.4	91.7	90.7
Physics	34.8	78.8	79.2	92.6
Chemistry	73.9	88.9	83.3	87.0
Biology	100.0	97.9	75.0	87.7
History	95.7	97.4	84.0	92.0
Technical drawing	0	3.2	33.3	62.3
Home economics (scientific & social)	95.7	97.4	4.2	19.1

Source: The 1980/81 figures are from Hannan et al. (1983), table 5.7. The 1989/90 figures are from Department of Education (1991).

What has been happening is a limited levelling out of gender differences in subject provision, apart from practical and technical subjects. From table 8.5 one can see, for example, that boys' schools have increased their provision of what may be called the more typically 'female' subjects—biology, home economics (scientific and social), and history—while improving their science provision at the same time, though not at the same rate as girls' schools. The increased provision of subjects such as biology and home economics (and, in the early 1990s, of German) in boys' schools shows that there has been some, albeit very slight, movement of male schools into the 'female subject world'. (Subject provision and take-up in single-sex and co-educational schools is further discussed in chapter 9.)

Changes in second-level education are not confined to the area of curricular provision. As table 8.6 shows, many changes are also occurring in the take-up of particular subjects. Overall, both boys and girls are moving out of the arts, humanities and certain languages into the sciences (with the exception of chemistry among boys) and business subjects. Boys are moving into the practical and technological subjects as well (excluding home economics), but girls are not.

The move away from the arts and humanities is especially noticeable among girls. In 1989/90 only 30 per cent of Leaving Certificate girls were studying geography and only 27.5 per cent were studying history, compared with 73.7 per cent studying geography in 1972/73 and 42.1 per cent studying history. The drop in the proportion of boys taking history and geography over the same period was from 45.3 to 27.6 per cent and from 70 to 40.6 per cent, respectively.

Table 8.6

Proportion of Leaving Certificate (lower course) cohort taking each subject, 1972/73 and 1989/90

Subject	1972/73[*]			1989/90[†]		
	Girls %	Boys %			Girls %	Boys %
Languages						
Irish	97.9	96.5	Irish (higher)[‡]		34.0	28.4
			Irish (lower)	97.4	54.7	95.9	60.2
			Irish (common)		8.7	7.3
English	99.6	97.8	English (higher)		48.8	44.4
			English (lower)	98.4	40.0	97.6	44.6
			English (common)		9.6	8.6
French	58.6	33.0			73.0	51.0
Spanish	10.7	4.4			2.4	1.2
German	3.1	1.4			9.5	4.4
Italian	0.6	0.3			0.1	0.1
Latin	27.7	42.9			0.3	1.3
Greek	0.0	0.7			<0.01	<0.01
Hebrew	0.03	0.02			<0.02	<0.01
Arts & humanities						
History	42.1	45.3			22.5	27.6
Geography	73.7	70.0			30.1	40.6
Art	29.1	14.9			22.5	13.7
Music & musicianship	3.8	0.5			3.8	1.2
Classical studies		Not offered			0.2	0.5
Practical-technological						
Home economics (gen.)	51.4	0.2			5.9	0.5
Engineering	0.0	5.1			0.4	16.4
Technical drawing	0.001	8.6			0.9	29.1
Construction studies	0.0	5.5			0.4	19.1
Sciences & applied sciences						
Mathematics	78.2	97.1	Maths (higher)		15.0	26.1
			Maths (lower)	98.4	77.1	98.1	65.3
			Maths (common)		6.3	6.7
Applied mathematics	0.05	4.4			0.4	3.5
Physics	1.9	22.3			9.6	31.0
Chemistry	7.6	30.5			13.4	18.8
Biology	28.6	21.1			60.1	35.7
Physics & chemistry	2.0	7.4			2.2	4.9
Agricultural science	0.1	4.3			1.2	7.6
Home economics (scientific & social)	3.8	0.1			49.9	5.8
Business subjects						
Accounting	21.0	17.6			28.3	26.3
Business organisation	23.0	19.1			41.7	35.0
Economics	12.3	21.9			9.0	17.5
Economic history	1.0	1.2			<0.01	0.1
Agricultural economics	0.0	0.9			0.0	0.7

*1972/73 figures are based on the number who sat the Leaving Certificate examination in 1973. They refer, therefore, to *one year's* cohort. In 1973, 13,449 girls and 11,831 boys sat the Leaving Certificate examination.
†1989/90 figures are based on the entire senior cycle student body studying for the Leaving Certificate. They refer, therefore, to the entire *two-year* Leaving Certificate cohort. In 1989/90, 59,450 girls and 54,619 boys were studying for the Leaving Certificate.
‡The distinctions between those taking higher, lower and common courses in Irish, English and mathematics for 1989/90 are presented for interest. Virtually all students sit examinations in these three subjects.

Source: Department of Education (1974; 1991).

What is also interesting to note from table 8.4, in the context of the breaking down of traditional gender-specific subject choices, is the extent to which girls' participation in most of the business subjects has kept pace with that of boys from 1972 to 1990, while their rate of involvement in the sciences has grown dramatically—albeit from a low starting base, especially in subjects like physics.

The reduction of gender differences in the provision, allocation and choice of Leaving Certificate subjects has not resulted in the elimination of gender differences in the take-up of particular sex-typed subjects. Boys still predominate in the sciences (with the exception of biology), while girls predominate in art, music, and Continental languages.

What Hannan et al. (1983, 154) observed from their major study of gender differences and education some years ago still holds true:

> Although there are differences between the sexes in provision and allocation in the subjects we analysed, these differences are . . . less than gender differences in the true rate of choice. In other words, the sex difference in pupils' own choices was greater than in either the provision or allocation of subjects to them. This finding suggests that simply increasing the provision or allocation of a subject to whichever gender . . . will not automatically lead to a substantial reduction in the sex differences in take-up.

Overcoming the cultural barriers that discourage pupils from choosing non-traditional subjects for their particular sex is still a major task for those wishing to eliminate inequalities arising from curricular choices. (In chapter 9 we return to the question of female versus male take-up in selected subjects and examine the patterns in different types of school.)

Given the pattern of subject take-up in second-level schools, it is not surprising to find that girls continue to predominate among entrants to the arts and humanities in higher education and are poorly represented in the technological fields. From table 8.7 we see that only 14.7 per cent of all entrants to the technological fields are female, while 63.9 per cent of entrants to the humanities and arts and 75 per cent of entrants to social science are female; table 8.7 also shows that while 40 per cent of men entering higher education undertake technological courses, only 8 per cent of women do. What is interesting to note from this table, however, is that women now constitute a higher proportion of entrants to the sciences (including the medical sciences) than men.

Given that the entry requirements for these faculties are not dissimilar to those required for the technological fields, namely a good mathematics and scientific background in the Leaving Certificate, it is clear that girls are eligible for many of the technological courses on offer. Few opt for these. It must be borne in mind, however, that while female participation in the technological field is still very low, it is considerably higher now than it was in the past. Nine per cent of university students in the field of technology were female in 1980, while there were no females in this area in 1950 (Clancy, 1989, table 4). In addition, 14.8 per cent of all new entrants to engineering were female in 1984/85, compared with 5.1 per cent in 1975/76 (Higher Education Authority, 1977; 1986).

It would be inappropriate to complete a section on gender differences and the curriculum without reference to the patriarchal content of knowledge itself. The subjects taught and the syllabus within the different subjects have not yet been subjected to substantive analysis from the point of view of their inclusion of women's issues and interests. However, even a cursory glance at school syllabuses shows that women's literature, art, history and scientific interests are not treated on a par with male interests and issues. The absence of research makes analysis difficult, but the problem remains: much of what is presented as knowledge in schools is knowledge as men have researched it, defined it, and written it.

Table 8.7

Distribution of all new entrants to higher education by gender, and representation of women within each field of study, 1986

	Males	*Females*	*Total*		*Representation of women*
	%	*%*	*Number of students*	*Percentage of all students*	
Humanities (incl. arts)	10.9	21.2	2,720	15.9	63.9
Art and design	2.4	5.7	683	4.0	67.9
Science	12.9	16.6	2,531	14.8	54.2
Agriculture	2.3	0.7	265	1.5	23.0
Technology	40.4	7.6	4,240	24.7	14.7
Medical sciences	3.2	4.1	626	3.7	53.8
Education	2.8	8.1	916	5.3	72.6
Law	1.4	1.8	273	1.6	53.5
Social science	1.8	5.9	639	3.7	75.0
Commerce	20.7	24.0	3,817	22.3	51.5
Hotel, catering, tourism	1.2	4.2	449	2.6	76.8
Total—per cent	100.0	100.0	—	100.0	47.8
—number	8,964	8,195	17,159	—	—

Source: Clancy (1989), table 5.

EDUCATIONAL ATTAINMENT

Two national studies of thirteen-year-olds in the fields of mathematics and science were conducted by the Educational Testing Service (United States) in conjunction with the Educational Research Centre (Dublin) in the late 1980s and early 1990s (International Association of Educational Progress, 1992a; 1992b; 1992c). These studies have a number of limitations arising from their attempts to compare curriculum and performance in completely different cultural contexts (Oldham, 1991). Bearing these limitations in mind, we find what appears to be conflicting evidence regarding girls' performance in mathematics, although not in science. In the 1989 study no significant overall difference was found between thirteen-year-old Irish girls and boys in mathematics. The 1992 study found that there was an overall significant gender difference in mathematics performance in favour of boys. The decline in the performance of girls vis-à-vis boys is, however, most probably related to the fact that in the later survey there were substantially (about 15 per cent) fewer items on number and operations (on which girls tend to do well) and correspondingly more on geometry (where girls tend to perform poorly) and on algebra (where girls' performance is uneven). The 1992 study obtained data on nine-year-olds, but this was not collected in the 1988 study; in this case girls and boys performed equally well in mathematics.

Boys performed significantly better than girls in science at age thirteen in both studies. Given that virtually no science is taught in schools before this age, what these tests suggest (although research is needed to confirm this) is boys' superior socialisation into scientific culture by early adolescence. It must be noted, however, that both these studies only assess two subjects, and that they rely heavily on the use of multiple-choice tests (unlike Irish public examinations); there is considerable evidence that the multiple-choice mode of assessment disadvantages girls (Bolger and Kellaghan, 1990; Meeder and Dekker, 1992).

Research undertaken by Carey (1990, 44–54) comparing the performance of girls and boys in mathematics in both the Intermediate and Leaving Certificate found that a higher percentage of boys than girls not only passed the mathematics examination but passed with honours (grade C or higher) each year from 1975 to 1983. Carey also found, however, that the gender gap in performance had narrowed over the years. Unfortunately, no data is available for 1983 to 1989, but figures for 1990 indicate that gender differences in mathematics are continuing to decline (Lynch, Close, and Oldham, in press).

To focus solely on science and mathematics in the discussion of attainment would present a very unbalanced picture of gender differences in performance— although this is the area that has received most attention in recent years. From table 8.8 one can see that girls' performance in languages at both Intermediate and Leaving Certificate was noticeably superior to that of boys in 1990.

Table 8.8

Gender differences in performance in selected range of languages, Intermediate and Leaving Certificate, 1990

Grade	A		B		C		D		E		F		No grade	
	F	M	F	M	F	M	F	M	F	M	F	M	F	M
Intermediate Certificate														
Irish (higher)	3.4	1.7	22.1	13.8	43.8	37.8	27.3	38.4	3.2	7.5	0.1	0.7	—	0.1
Irish (lower)	3.2	0.8	25.7	13.4	31.1	25.7	21.9	25.8	9.4	13.6	6.4	12.7	2.3	8.0
English (higher)	3.9	2.8	19.3	13.6	42.7	36.7	31.2	40.9	2.8	5.8	0.1	0.2	—	—
English (lower)	0.3	0.1	13.2	8.0	49.7	40.9	32.8	41.8	3.8	7.7	0.3	1.4	—	0.2
French	6.1	2.9	20.5	14.5	30.4	26.8	27.6	31.4	11.2	16.5	3.9	7.2	0.3	0.7
German	9.8	3.9	36.3	20.7	31.9	31.8	16.0	25.3	4.9	11.9	1.0	5.8	—	0.6
Leaving Certificate														
Irish (higher)	5.4	3.3	26.4	19.1	44.4	41.5	22.4	31.8	1.2	2.7	—	0.5	0.2	1.1
Irish (ordinary)	1.5	0.5	15.7	6.8	35.6	25.4	31.9	37.4	9.9	15.3	4.6	11.7	0.9	2.9
English (higher)	4.1	2.9	16.7	14.1	42.0	37.2	34.2	39.9	2.9	5.5	0.1	0.3	—	—
English (ordinary)	0.6	0.4	9.7	6.5	47.4	36.8	38.4	48.1	3.5	7.4	0.3	0.8	—	—
French (higher)	4.2	2.4	20.2	16.0	41.0	38.1	30.8	36.4	3.7	6.6	0.1	0.4	—	—
French (ordinary)	0.2	0.2	10.8	8.4	39.5	38.6	39.6	40.9	8.8	10.3	1.1	1.6	—	—
German (higher)	8.6	5.8	30.2	19.7	36.0	36.5	23.2	31.6	1.9	6.3	0.1	0.2	—	—
German (ordinary)	1.3	0.3	24.2	12.2	43.8	44.3	26.0	35.3	4.0	6.0	0.8	1.6	—	0.3

F: female; M: male.

Source: Department of Education (1991).

Analysis of the 1991 Leaving Certificate results shows similar gender differences (NCCA, 1992), as did an earlier analysis of Leaving Certificate results
in 1983 (Department of Education, 1983).

In aggregate performance in public examinations, research indicates that girls
tend to do better overall (Greaney and Kellaghan, 1984; Clancy, 1989; Lynch,
1991; NCCA, 1992). In his analysis of the Leaving Certificate results for 1980,
Clancy found that a higher proportion of girls obtained grade C or higher in
sixteen of the twenty-nine subjects taken by both sexes (1989). An analysis of the
Leaving Certificate results of 1983 also found that girls got higher grades in more
subjects than boys (Lynch, 1991). The findings from the 1991 Leaving Certificate results confirm these earlier trends (see table 8.9).

Table 8.9

**Gender differences in Leaving Certificate performance among
candidates taking the full Leaving Certificate for the first time, 1991**

Percentage obtaining each grade
(all examinations combined)

	A	B	C	D	E	F	NG	A+B
Higher-level papers								
Girls	5.0	21.0	39.0	29.0	5.0	1.0	0	27.0
Boys	5.0	20.0	36.0	31.0	6.0	1.0	0	26.0
Ordinary-level papers								
Girls	4.0	17.0	33.0	32.0	9.0	4.0	1.0	21.0
Boys	4.0	15.0	30.0	33.0	11.0	6.0	2.0	18.0

Source: National Council for Curriculum and Assessment (1992, tables 34, 48).

If one is to take the level of degree awarded as a measure of performance in
higher education, then women do not achieve quite as highly as their male
colleagues, although the differences are not great and appear to be declining.
In 1983, 1984 and 1985 women constituted 37.9, 38.1 and 39.6 per cent,
respectively, of those obtaining first-class, upper second-class or undifferentiated
second-class honours degrees, although they constituted 44.0, 44.1 and 44.3 per
cent, respectively, of those obtaining degrees (Clancy, 1989, table 6). Women
also constitute a minority among master's degree and doctoral graduates: only
36 per cent of master's degree graduates and 29.2 per cent of doctoral graduates
were women in 1985 (ibid.).

Overall, the pattern of performance we have observed among women in
education is an uneven one. While girls perform more highly than their male
colleagues in the Intermediate and Leaving Certificate and have higher

grades entering higher education, they do not seem to retain this advantage within higher education. In particular, they are considerably less likely than males to pursue higher degrees, despite their favourable academic record.

THE ETHOS OF SCHOOLS

One of the crucial questions that must be asked in education is, do schools contribute directly or indirectly to the promotion of gender inequality? It can be argued that because schools have a formal remit to operate according to universalistic as opposed to particularistic principles, they are more egalitarian than other social institutions. Certainly if one is to take performance in public examinations as a measure of how egalitarian schools are in gender terms, then they would appear to enhance equality for women in society. Stockard (1985, 310) has noted, for example, that in the United States, gender variations in average educational attainment are virtually non-existent, especially when compared with gender disparities in income. However, this is a very narrow way in which to measure outcomes. Also, it fails to address the issue of social class differentials among girls and young women themselves. It is middle-class women who have gained especially from women's expansion into higher education. Working-class women are the most unrepresented group in higher education; their representation is lower than that of working-class men, and lower again than that of middle-class women (Clancy, 1988, 73).

Focusing on examination results also ignores two other important ways in which schools can reinforce inequality. Firstly, it ignores the fact that much of the curriculum is patriarchal in both form and substance; the knowledge is also biased in its emphasis and consideration towards white middle-class culture. Secondly, it does not address the wider issue of school ethos or climate.

While girls, in particular middle-class girls, may be performing very well in schools, their high performance may conceal the fact that they are being socialised implicitly through the type of subjects they study, the texts they read and the syllabus they follow into an acceptance and appreciation of patriarchal values and culture (Spender, 1980; 1985; Bordo, 1986). (The focus on stereo-typed images in texts is only a tiny part of a much bigger problem. If the content of what is taught is patriarchal and class-biased, then having non-sexist images is but a small part of the solution.)

Apart from the formal curriculum, the hidden curriculum of schooling is often very different for boys and girls. And this applies in both single-sex and co-educational schools.

When we talk of the hidden curriculum we are referring to the social norms and values that are implicitly communicated to pupils in schools by the way in which school and classroom life is organised. These norms and values are not the publicly declared goals of schooling. Whether a school selects or does not select, whether it bands pupils or does not band, whether it places emphasis on examination results as a primary goal or not, what type of pupil intake (and staff) it has, whether it has a tradition of local community involvement or not, or the style of management adopted (for example hierarchical or democratic, open or closed): these are but some of the organisational practices that determine the ethos or social climate of a school and that collectively contribute to the hidden curriculum.

In a national study of the hidden curriculum of second-level schools, Lynch (1989a; 1989b) found that boys' and girls' schools differ considerably in their social climates. In the extracurricular sphere, Lynch found that the aesthetic, moral-religious and socio-personal development of pupils were higher priorities in girls' schools than in boys'. Furthermore, girls' schools placed greater emphasis on developing qualities such as caring for others, sincerity, gentleness, 'refinement' and self-control than their male counterparts.

Table 8.10 gives some quantitative evidence of the ways in which male and female schools differed in the extracurricular sphere. It shows in particular how artistic and religious-moral activities are generally more central to the agenda of girls' schools than boys'.

Lynch's data (1989a; 1989b) also showed that girls' schools give considerably more time on the daily timetable to the teaching of religion, that they allocate more time to personal development and pastoral care, and that control of dress and behaviour in girls' schools is strict compared with boys'. In their statement of aims, for example, Lynch (1989a) found that the development of self-discipline or self-control were cited as aims in all thirteen girls' schools that made their policy statements available. None of the twelve boys' schools that made theirs available made any reference to the desirability of developing self-discipline or self-control.

Boys' schools, on the other hand, were found to place a high priority on the development of physical prowess and motor skills. In their prospectuses and school magazines, boys' schools highlighted the quality of their sports facilities and their sporting achievements. A number of the school magazines and reports from boys' schools displayed pages of teams that participated or succeeded in sporting events. No such display existed in girls' schools' magazines; photographs of girls playing the harp or piano, or reading quietly in the library, replaced the male images of physical prowess on the sports field.

An important finding from Lynch's data, however, is that girls' schools did not sacrifice academic achievement for the sake of moral, religious or socio-personal goals. She found that girls' schools had a strong achievement ethos in the academic sphere—measured in the frequency and compulsoriness of assessments and the extent of prizegiving. Indeed, the achievement ethos in girls' schools was frequently stronger than in boys'. It seems, therefore, that girls' schools 'tend to present girls with two seemingly contradictory role models: on the one hand they are educated to compete and succeed within the formal educational system . . . on the other hand they are socialised to be guardians of the moral order, to be unselfish and non-assertive' (ibid., 27).

Table 8.10

Differences between boys' and girls' second-level schools in extracurricular provision in the arts and in religion-related societies and activities

	Girls' chools ($n = 21$) %	Boys' schools ($n = 20$) %	Statistical significance
Religion-related			
Temperance society	76.2	40.0	$p < 0.05$
Legion of Mary	28.4	5.0	—
St Vincent de Paul Society	19.0	25.0	—
Charitable events	33.0	15.0	—
Arts			
Debating, public speaking	100.0	75.0	$p < 0.05$
Drama	85.7	40.0	$p < 0.01$
Arts and crafts	71.4	25.0	$p < 0.01$
Dancing	14.3	0.0	—
Musical activities	100.0	55.0	$p < 0.01$
School magazine	57.1	50.0	—
Board games (esp. chess)	33.3	60.0	—
Irish club (cultural club)	23.8	10.0	—
Photography	19.0	20.0	—

Note: All the girls' schools and all but two of the boys' schools were managed by Catholic authorities. Both girls' and boys' schools were fairly similar in social class intake. The schools were part of a stratified random sample ($n = 90$) of second-level schools.
Source: Lynch (1989a), 11–31.

Boys are not presented with these dichotomous models to the same degree: entry into employment is encouraged in a much more single-minded manner among boys. To understand why women do not realise their potential as much as men at the more advanced stages of education and in the paid labour market generally, one needs to examine the hidden curriculum of schools more closely. Girls are constantly reminded that involvement in paid employment is only one of their many responsibilities in life; boys do not receive this message to the same degree.

We are not suggesting that female socialisation into dual roles happens exclusively in single-sex schools. The limited evidence available on co-educational schools certainly indicates that girls in these schools can also experience traditional sex-role socialisation (Lynch, 1989b; Hanafin, 1992). The problem seems to be that schools reflect the ethos and culture of the wider society. Both girls and boys receive anticipatory socialisation in all types of school (to varying degrees) for their future roles. Girls are generally socialised to be the bearers and the carers of the personal and socio-emotional orders of society; at the same time they are encouraged to achieve in job or career terms. The inherent conflicts between the two systems that these worlds represent (the worlds of caring and capital) are not really explored or examined in schools. It remains a private dilemma for individual women, not a public problem to be resolved. The double burden is not posed as a problematic. For boys the future expected is generally that of employment in the paid labour market. The personal and emotional needs of self, family and others are commonly presented as 'incidentals' in men's lives.

GENDER AND SOCIAL CLASS

Throughout this chapter women and men have been treated as undifferentiated social groups. However, as class inequalities are, if anything, even more conspicuous in Irish education than gender inequalities, one must advert to the relationship between social class and gender at this point.

Although no major study has yet been undertaken on the differences in educational opportunity for working-class and middle-class women *per se,* the research available on all working-class students indicates that working-class women are much more disadvantaged in education than their middle-class counterparts. Working-class pupils, including girls, are likely to leave school considerably earlier than middle-class pupils (Breen, 1984, 32). The under-representation of working-class women especially in higher education has already been noted above.

The experience of working-class girls and boys in schools is frequently very different from that of their middle-class and upper-class counterparts as well. This is particularly evident when one compares fee-paying secondary schools with publicly controlled schools. Fee-paying schools have far better extracurricular facilities, relative to their size, than public schools (Lynch, 1989b, 112–15). Girls and boys attending fee-paying schools also have access to a culture and ethos that emphasises social confidence, artistic accomplishment, and styles of behaviour that anticipate power; the same does not obtain for girls attending public schools (Lynch, 1987; 1989a). To fully comprehend the position of women and men in Irish education, further research is necessary, particularly research that examines the relationship between social class, disability ethnicity and gender in education.

CONCLUSION

Women's retention and performance rates within Irish education are generally satisfactory. However, women are still largely absent from the technological programmes, and they do not undertake higher degrees as often as men, despite their adequate undergraduate performance. Men's higher degrees give them a competitive labour market edge in a society that strongly emphasises the use of credentials in selection for all types of job. In addition, the syllabi and curricula presented in schools are often male-biased, and women are frequently socialised in schools into attitudes that facilitate their subordination, namely docility, compliance, and caring for others. While caring for others, being considerate and sensitive are undoubtedly valuable social qualities, they become social millstones for women when men are not socialised into them as well. This is surely one of the unspoken problems in Irish schools. While much has changed for girls in education in the last twenty years in participation rates, curriculum choices, and performance, it is not clear if much has changed for boys. We know very little about what changes, if any, are occurring in single-sex boys' schools especially, and there is a great need for research in this area.

References and Further Reading

Barry, U. (1988), 'Women in Ireland' in A. Smyth (ed.), *Women's Studies International Forum*, vol. 2, no. 4.

Blackwell, J. (1989), *Women in the Labour Force*, Dublin: Employment Equality Agency.

Bolger, N., and Kellaghan, T. (1990), 'Method of measurement and gender differences in scholastic achievement', *Journal of Educational Measurement*, 27.

Bordo, S. (1986), 'The Cartesian masculinization of thought', *Signs*, vol. 11, no. 3, 1–10.

Breen, R. (1984), *Education and the Labour Market* (ESRI paper no. 119), Dublin: Economic and Social Research Institute.

Brennan, M. (1986), 'Factors Affecting Attainment in the Irish Leaving Certificate Examination' (MEd thesis, University College, Dublin).

Carey, M. (1990), 'Gender differences in attitudes and achievement in mathematics: a study of first year students in Irish post-primary schools' (MEd thesis, Trinity College, Dublin).

Central Statistics Office (1992), *Labour Force Survey, 1991*, Dublin: Stationery Office.

Clancy, P. (1987), 'Does school type matter?: the unresolved questions', *Sociological Association of Ireland Bulletin*, no. 49.

Clancy, P. (1988), *Who Goes to College?: a Second National Survey of Participation in Higher Education,* Dublin: Higher Education Authority.

Clancy, P. (1989), 'Gender differences in student participation at third level' in C. Hussey (ed.), *Equal Opportunities for Women in Higher Education*, Dublin: University College.

Constitution of Ireland (1937), Dublin: Stationery Office.

Council of Europe (1982), *Sex Stereotyping in Schools*, Lisse: Swets en Zeitlinger.

Department of Education (1971), *Primary School Curriculum: Teacher's Handbook*, Dublin: Stationery Office.

Department of Education (1974), *Statistical Reports, 1972/73*, Dublin: Stationery Office.

Department of Education (1983), *Leaving Certificate Examinations Results*, Athlone: Department of Education.

Department of Education (1987), *Statistical Reports, 1985/86*, Dublin: Stationery Office.

Department of Education (1991), *Statistical Report, 1989/90*, Dublin: Stationery Office.

Department of Education (1992a), *Statistical Report, 1990/91*, Dublin: Stationery Office.

Department of Education (1992b), *Education for a Changing World: Green Paper on Education*, Dublin: Stationery Office.

Department of the Taoiseach (1987), *United Nations Convention on the Elimination of All Forms of Discrimination Against Women: First Report by Ireland*, Dublin: Stationery Office.

Drew, E. (1990), *Who Needs Flexibility?*, Dublin: Employment Equality Agency.

Greaney, V., and Kellaghan, T. (1984), *Equality of Opportunity in Irish Schools*, Dublin: Educational Company.

Hanafin, J. (1992), Submission on Co-education to the Joint Oireachtas Committee on Women's Rights, 24 September 1992.

Hannan, D., et al. (1983), *Schooling and Sex Roles* (ESRI paper no. 113), Dublin: Economic and Social Research Institute.

Higher Education Authority (1977), *Accounts and Student Statistics, 1975/76*, Dublin: Higher Education Authority.

Higher Education Authority (1986), *Accounts and Student Statistics, 1984/85*, Dublin: Higher Education Authority.

Higher Education Authority (1988), *First Destination of Award Recipients in Higher Education, 1987*, Dublin: Higher Education Authority.

International Association of Educational Progress (1992a), *Learning Mathematics*, New Jersey: Educational Testing Service.

International Association of Educational Progress (1992b), *Learning Science*, New Jersey: Educational Testing Service.

International Association of Educational Progress (1992c), *A World of Differences: an International Assessment of Mathematics and Science*, New Jersey: Educational Testing Service.

Irish National Teachers' Organisation (1988), *Central Executive Committee Report*, Dublin: INTO.

Kellaghan, T., Fontes, P., et al. (1985), *Gender Inequalities in Primary School Teaching*, Dublin: Educational Company.

Lynch, K. (1987), 'The universal and particular: gender, class and reproduction in second-level schools' (working paper no. 3) in *Women's Studies Forum, UCD.*

Lynch, K. (1989a), 'The ethos of girls' schools: an analysis of differences between male and female schools' in *Social Studies*, vol. 10, nos. 1–2, 11–31.

Lynch, K. (1989b), *The Hidden Curriculum: Reproduction in Education: a Reappraisal,* Lewes: Falmer.

Lynch, K. (1991), 'Girls and young women in education—Ireland' in M. Wilson (ed.), *Girls and Young Women in Education: a European Perspective,* Oxford: Pergamon.

Lynch, K., Close, S., and Oldham E. (1992), 'Gender differences in mathematics in the Republic of Ireland' (paper presented at the European Colloquium on Differential Performance in Assessment of Mathematics at the End of Compulsory Schooling, University of Birmingham, 15–18 May 1992).

McCarthy, E. (1988), *Transitions to Equal Opportunity at Work in Ireland: Problems and Possibilities.* Dublin: Employment Equality Agency.

McKenna, A. (1988), *Child Care and Equal Opportunities,* Dublin: Employment Equality Agency.

Mahon, E. (1991), *Motherhood, Work and Equal Opportunity: First Report of the Third Joint Oireachtas Committee on Women's Rights,* Dublin: Stationery Office.

Marland, M. (ed.) (1983), *Sex Differentiation and Schooling,* London: Heinemann.

Meeder, M., and Dekker, T. (1992), 'Differential Performance in Assessment of Mathematics at the End of Compulsory Schooling: the Netherlands' (paper presented at the European Colloquium on Differential Performance in Assessment of Mathematics at the End of Compulsory Schooling, University of Birmingham, 15–18 May 1992).

Mullin, B., Morgan, V., and Dunn, S. (1986), *Gender Differentiation in Infant Classes,* Belfast: Equal Opportunities Commission for Northern Ireland.

National Council for Curriculum and Assessment (1992), *The 1991 Leaving Certificate Examination: a Review of Results,* Dublin: NCCA.

Oldham, E. (1991), 'Second level mathematics curricula: the Republic of Ireland in international perspective', *Irish Educational Studies,* vol. 10, no. 1.

Smyth, A. (1984), *Breaking the Circle: the Position of Women Academics in Third-Level Education in Ireland,* Dublin: EC Action Programme on the Promotion of Equal Opportunities for Women.

Smyth, A. (1988), 'The contemporary women's movement in the Republic of Ireland' in A. Smyth (ed.)., *Women's Studies International Forum,* vol. 2, no. 4.

Smyth, A. (ed.) (1992), *The Abortion Papers,* Dublin: Attic.

Spender, D. (1985), *Manmade Language,* London: Routledge and Kegan Paul.

Spender, D., and Spender, E. (1980), *Learning to Lose: Sexism in Education,* London: Women's Press.

Stanworth, M. (1983), *Gender and Schooling,* London: Hutchinson.

Stockard, J. (1985), 'Education and gender equality: a critical view' in A. Kerckhoff (ed.), *Research in Sociology of Education and Socialization,* vol. 5.

Tawney, R. (1964), *Equality,* London: Allen and Unwin.

Wilson, M. (ed.) (1991), *Girls and Young Women in Education: a European Perspective,* Oxford: Pergamon.

9

The Co-Education Debate

The declining birth rates and falling pupil numbers that are bringing about rationalisation, amalgamations and new educational structures in the Irish school system are also increasing the proportion of co-educational schools each year. Until recently, this aspect of changing educational structures has received little analytical attention. The implications of the changes taking place could be far-reaching, however, for pupils and teachers alike. They certainly merit widespread consideration and debate.

In this chapter we examine the implications of co-education for gender equality and consider three broad issues: subject options, attainment, and classroom interaction and school organisation.

There is a long tradition of single-sex education in Ireland. As we saw in chapter 1, close to two-thirds of the second-level system is owned and managed by voluntary (private) bodies—mainly Catholic religious orders and diocesan authorities. Since their establishment, the great majority of schools in the voluntary sector have been single-sex. This was in line with traditional Catholic thinking, reflected, for example, in the papal encyclical *Divinis Illius Magistri* of 1929, which stated that co-education was based on a belief in naturalism, which denied original sin (Plateau, 1991, 18).

Schools in the vocational and community-comprehensive sectors have, with a very small number of exceptions, always been co-educational. In the past, however, many vocational schools were in fact co-institutional, with separate entrances and classes for girls and boys. Statistical reports from the Department of Education show that the dominance of single-sex schooling has changed significantly over the last two decades.

Table 9.1 shows that co-educational schools are now in the majority throughout the education system, in particular at primary level. The proportion of *pupils* in co-educational primary schools is markedly lower than the total proportion of such schools; this is because of the high proportion of small primary schools (which we referred to in chapter 1) and the tendency for more of these small schools to be co-educational, especially in rural areas. Girls are, however, less likely than boys to attend co-educational schools: at primary level 61.7 per cent of girls, compared with 66.7 per cent of boys, are in co-educational schools. This tendency is more pronounced at second level, where 50.4 per cent of girls are in co-educational schools, compared with 61.3 per cent of boys (Department of Education, 1992, 16, 38). Girls are also more likely than boys to attend secondary schools, which are the least technically oriented schools in their curriculum. A total of 67.0 per cent of all girls at second level are in secondary schools, compared with 57.2 per cent of boys (ibid., 38). While participation in co-educational schools is increasing, it is still much lower than in most other European countries and in North America, where co-education is the norm.

Table 9.1

Percentage of schools and pupils at primary and second levels, single-sex and co-educational, 1990/91

Type of school	Primary		Second-level	
	Schools	Pupils	Schools	Pupils
Co-educational	78.0	63.0	58.9	55.3
Single-sex	16.6	26.5	41.1	44.7
Single-sex with mixed infants	5.4	10.5	Not applicable	
Total	100.0	100.0	100.0	100.0
n	3,235	532,240	794	342,416

Source: Department of Education (1992a), 16, 38.

The Research Findings
Very little research into co-education and its implications has been undertaken in Ireland. However, since the beginning of the 1980s the topic has been the focus of a good deal of attention elsewhere (see, for example, work by Spender and Spender, 1980, Steedman, 1983, Kelly, 1986, and Mahony, 1985, in Britain; Plateau, 1991, in Belgium; and Wernersson, 1982, in Sweden.) The research findings do not provide conclusive answers with regard to the merits or otherwise of co-education; since the studies have been conducted in different contexts, using different methodologies, it is also difficult to compare their findings. They do, however, raise important questions, to which school managers and the teaching profession should give close consideration.

SUBJECT TAKE-UP
Subject take-up and curricular differentiation have been a particular focus of study in Irish schools (Hannan et al., 1983; Lynch, 1989). This research

indicates that girls and boys have very different curricular experiences in second-level schools. As we have seen in chapter 8, girls have higher participation rates at second level, especially at senior cycle. Their levels of achievement are also higher overall than those of boys, but in very different areas of the curriculum. The analysis of the Leaving Certificate results for 1991 shows that 53 per cent of the 'school regular candidates' (those doing the Leaving Certificate for the first time and attending school) were girls, while 55 per cent of the 'external candidates' (candidates not attending a recognised school) were girls. On the other hand, 56 per cent of the 'school repeat' candidates were boys (Martin and Hickey, 1992, 9).

Because of the curricular differentiation and variation in school ethos (which we referred to in chapter 8), it is difficult to discuss co-educational or single-sex schools without looking at the variations in school type. The major study in this field in the 1980s, by Hannan et al. (1983), suggested that boys' secondary schools offer a highly specialised curriculum, giving pupils little choice of subjects, with a concentration on science subjects and commerce. Girls' secondary schools presented almost the opposite picture. Although on average girls' secondary schools offered more subjects than any other type except community schools, their curriculums were markedly unspecialised and contained an above-average proportion of languages only. A wide choice of subjects was offered to pupils in girls' secondary schools, as compared with most other school types. Co-educational secondary schools seemed to fall between the two types. Vocational schools, which tended to be small, were characterised by a small curriculum, a low degree of specialisation, concentration on technical subjects, and a low concentration on science. Community schools had large unspecialised curriculums, with considerable choice offered to pupils (Hannan et al., 1983). This study highlighted differences in the take-up rates by girls and boys in a number of subjects as a particular problem, especially in the areas of higher mathematics, physics, and chemistry.

Hannan et al. (1983) argued that girls attending co-educational schools were slightly advantaged in mathematics and science as compared with girls in single-sex schools (ibid., 322). As the data in this study was collected in the early 1980s, however, it has to be interpreted with caution; since that time there has been a growing awareness that poor take-up of mathematics and science could be a problem for girls in relation to future occupational opportunities (Ó Conaill, 1991). There have also been a number of intervention programmes in second-level schools, such as the 'Futures' project, co-funded by the Department of Education and the EC (Department of Education, 1992b). As noted in chapter 8, there is evidence that provision for higher mathematics, physics and chemistry has improved considerably in single-sex schools in recent years.

Apart from the science subjects, concern has been expressed that girls either select or are directed towards the domestic crafts rather than technical or engineering subjects. On the other hand, boys' education is more restricted to the scientific and technical, with just a limited involvement in languages, social sciences, and domestic crafts (Arnot, 1984; Plateau, 1991; Wernersson, 1991). The subject at senior cycle that combines a social science element and domestic craft is home economics (scientific and social); as we have seen in chapter 8, a very small proportion of boys do this subject.

Given previous research, it is useful to examine a number of key subjects that have been found to have been very gender-differentiated in the past, to see if current provision and take-up of these subjects at Leaving Certificate level among girls and boys has changed. Table 9.2 presents this data according to type of school for 1990/91.

Table 9.2

Provision of selected subjects to girls and boys* enrolled for Leaving Certificate,† classified by co-educational and single-sex schools, 1990/91

Proportions to whom subjects are provided

	Secondary Single-sex		Secondary Co-ed.		Vocational (Co-ed. only)		Comm./comp. (Co-ed. only)	
	Girls %	Boys %	Girls %	Boys %	Girls %	Boys %	Girls %	Boys %
Physics	91.2	99.2	87.0	91.4	63.7	68.8	88.5	93.1
Chemistry	93.3	94.8	81.7	86.8	40.1	39.5	79.0	83.3
Maths (higher)	92.8	97.4	89.1	90.8	65.8	71.0	81.0	86.4
Biology	99.5	94.7	99.5	97.7	94.4	92.3	100.0	100.0
French	100.0	99.3	99.8	99.9	96.4	91.9	98.9	99.0
Home economics	99.7	24.4	93.9	61.7	91.8	70.4	98.9	88.6
Technical drawing	1.5	69.3	40.2	73.6	48.5	95.1	61.2	100.0
Total (*n*)	31,250	22,883	11,354	11,498	9,147	12,707	7,207	7,192

*In the notes on the subject tables (Department of Education, 1992a, 43) a distinction is made between a subject being 'offered' and 'provided'. These tables are based on returns showing the number of pupils taking each subject at senior cycle in the school. Hence a school that offers a subject but whose pupils do not take up that offer would not be included under that subject. A mixed school that offers a subject to both sexes but in which no boy decides to take the subject is therefore classified as a school that provides the subject to girls only.

†The totals given are of those enrolled at senior cycle in second-level schools (59,191 girls and 55,055 boys), less 775 boys in single-sex vocational and community or comprehensive schools and 233 girls in single-sex vocational schools, i.e. 58,958 girls and 54,280 boys.

Source: Department of Education (1992a), calculated from tables 18s, 18t, 18u, 18v, 18w, 18x.

In table 9.2 we present the provision of each ⌐ the subjects in terms of the proportion of girls and boys in each of the school types who are provided with the subject. Using this method of classification, it would appear that physics, chemistry and higher-course mathematics are best provided within boys' single-sex secondary schools.

For girls the best provision in these subjects is in girls' single-sex secondary schools. Provision is less favourable for girls in physics, chemistry and honours mathematics in co-educational secondary schools than in single-sex ones. Vocational schools are weakest of all in the provision of these subjects. As social class is strongly related to students' choices of mathematics and science subjects (see, for example, McEwen and Curry, 1987), the weak provision in vocational schools probably reflects their higher intake of working-class children rather than their co-educational structure. This may also be a factor in the lower provision of all sciences except biology in community and comprehensive schools.

The somewhat lower provision for girls in physics, chemistry and honours mathematics in co-educational secondary than in single-sex secondary schools may well be related to the co-educational structure of these schools, but to be certain we would need to have details of school size, location and social class composition, and this information does not accompany the subject tables.

French was provided slightly more frequently in secondary schools, both single-sex and co-educational, than in other school types. However, only in girls' single-sex schools was it provided to all pupils. The category of pupil with the lowest provision in French was the 'vocational school boys' category. Again the poor provision in vocational schools may reflect intake variables, but the higher provision for girls in these schools suggests that notions about the sex-appropriateness of the subject play a part. However, it is important to remember that over 90 per cent of all school types offered French to all pupils, male and female.

As we saw in chapter 8, the practical areas are where sex differences are most pronounced. The provision of practical subjects is very sex-divided in all school types. Curricular differences are most marked here in single-sex schools, and indicate that there has been just limited change since the early 1980s. Girls' secondary schools have the highest provision in home economics, and boys' single-sex secondary schools by far the worst. The provision of home economics for girls is lower in co-educational than in single-sex secondary schools. Apart from girls' single-sex secondary schools, the highest provision for both girls and boys in home economics is in community and comprehensive schools.

The lowest provision of technical drawing is in single-sex girls' schools. This, combined with poor provision of other technical subjects, does not augur well for the proposed introduction of technology as a compulsory subject in these schools (Department of Education, 1992c, 95), unless substantial investment is made in in-service teacher education and in facilities. Indeed, the provision of technical drawing is low in all secondary schools, whether girls' or boys' single-sex or co-educational. In the light of their tradition, it might have been expected that vocational schools would have the highest provision in this subject, but in fact the best provision is in community and comprehensive schools.

Table 9.3 presents data on the take-up of the subjects outlined in table 9.2 in the schools where they are provided, classified by type of school. This table illustrates the proportion of girls and boys in each school type who take a selection of subjects in the senior cycle of schools where these subjects are provided. In physics and chemistry the variation in the proportion of girls who take the subject when it is provided in the school is negligible. However, this has to be assessed in the light of the variations in provision that we saw in table 9.2. The take-up rate in chemistry among girls is slightly better in co-educational secondary schools than elsewhere, but chemistry is less likely to be provided in these schools than in single-sex secondary schools. The take-up rate in higher mathematics among girls is also slightly better in co-educational secondary schools than in others, but provision for girls, though better in these schools than in vocational or community and comprehensive schools, is not as good as in girls' single-sex secondary schools. Among boys, the take-up rate in physics is highest in vocational schools, while it is highest in chemistry and higher mathematics in single-sex schools. Provision in these subjects is best for boys in single-sex schools. The take-up of biology is highest for girls in all types of co-educational school, but not for boys.

In the case of French, the variation in take-up rates among girls is between those in vocational and other school types rather than between those in co-educational or single-sex schools. This is also true for boys, although a higher proportion of boys take French in single-sex than in co-educational secondary schools or community and comprehensive schools.

Provision for home economics (scientific and social), as we saw in table 9.2, was very low for boys in all school types but especially in single-sex secondary schools. However, where it is provided in boys' single-sex secondary schools the take-up rate is higher than that in other school types, although that in co-educational secondary schools is second-highest. The take-up rate for girls of this subject is highest in vocational schools.

Technical drawing presents almost the reverse of the pattern of home economics (scientific and social). Table 9.2 showed poor provision in all school types, being worst in single-sex girls' secondary schools and best in community and comprehensive schools. Table 9.3 shows that girls' take-up of this subject, even where it is provided, is still very low. However, the highest take-up rates by girls is in vocational schools. It seems likely that this is a result of the curricular tradition of these schools rather than the fact that they are co-educational, since the highest take-up for boys is also in these schools—although provision was best in community and comprehensive schools.

Overall, then, the examination of patterns of subject provision and take-up in relation to the subjects selected does not show any consistent reduction in sex-stereotypical patterns depending on whether schools are organised along co-educational or single-sex lines. Rather the patterns appear to reflect attitudes among schools and pupils concerning sex-appropriate subjects, the traditions of the three school sectors, and the social class composition of the different types of school.

Table 9.3

Girls and boys taking selected subjects as a proportion of the total female or male Leaving Certificate enrolment* in schools where subjects are provided to them, classified by co-educational and single-sex schools, 1990/91

Subject	Secondary Single-Sex		Secondary Co-ed.		Vocational (Co-ed only)[†]		Comm./comp. (Co-ed. only)[†]	
	Girls %	Boys %	Girls %	Boys %	Girls %	Boys %	Girls %	Boys %
Physics	12.0	35.0	11.7	33.4	11.6	35.3	10.1	31.9
Chemistry	14.8	25.7	16.9	23.6	14.1	17.8	15.7	14.8
Mathematics (higher)	17.6	32.7	19.0	27.9	12.0	15.7	16.6	22.4
Biology	57.2	37.0	64.3	35.7	64.4	37.8	61.6	26.6
French	77.7	61.7	74.2	56.9	59.2	35.9	67.8	43.9
Home economics	47.6	15.9	53.6	13.9	69.6	11.6	52.1	10.8
Technical drawing	1.7	21.6	3.4	29.5	7.6	60.3	3.1	34.3

*Totals vary in each category. They can be calculated from the proportion of pupils provided with each subject, presented in table 9.2.

†There was a very small number of girls and boys in single-sex vocational schools, and a very small number of boys in single-sex community or comprehensive schools, in tables 18u, 18v, and 18w (see note to table 9.2). These are excluded from the calculations.

Source: Department of Education (1992a), calculated from tables 18s, 18t, 18u, 18v, 18w, 18x.

With regard to the science subjects and higher mathematics, which have been perceived to be a particular problem for girls, the analysis shows that the best provision for physics, chemistry and higher mathematics is to be found in girls' single-sex secondary schools. The best take-up rate for girls in physics is in single-sex secondary schools, and for chemistry and higher mathematics is in co-educational secondary schools; it must be remembered, however, that differences between all school types in girls' take-up rates in these subjects are small. Moreover, it is likely that these variations would be more adequately explained in social class terms than according to whether schools are single-sex or not. As we saw in chapter 7, secondary schools have a higher proportion of middle-class pupils than other types of school. Research in Northern Ireland has shown that girls from professional and managerial backgrounds are more likely to choose mathematics and science subjects at second level than girls from manual working-class backgrounds (McEwen and Curry, 1987, 142). Furthermore, it is important to note that attitudes towards mathematics and science as a 'masculine' subject area cannot be overlooked. The attitudes of pupils and staff in schools are part of the hidden curriculum and are acquired outside the school environment and reinforced or otherwise within it (ibid.). These are problems that apply in all school types (Kelly, 1985).

The issue of girls' take-up rates and achievement in mathematics and science has engaged much attention internationally in recent years (Ó Conaill, 1991). While there is considerable evidence that girls are underrepresented in physics, chemistry, and higher mathematics (Arnot, 1984; McEwen and Curry, 1987), there is also evidence that the gender gap in attainment in the field of mathematics and science is declining, especially in countries where there has been a deliberate attempt to promote equality. In Sweden in 1989, for example, in all subjects except physics, girls in upper secondary schools were given better marks than boys (Grevholm and Nilsson, 1992, 16). In Norway there is evidence from 1980 that girls do better than boys in national tests in mathematics at the end of compulsory schooling, although boys get higher marks for class work (Berge and Varøy-Haga, 1992, 16). In Ireland there is also evidence that the gender gap in the take-up of higher mathematics and the sciences has closed somewhat and that achievement differences in mathematics have declined considerably in recent years. (See chapter 8.)

This is not to suggest that the issue of female alienation and detachment from the fields of mathematics, science and technology is resolved: clearly it is not. However, the issues at stake are not simply those of 'coaxing' girls to study the science, technology and mathematics that men have created. While lack of opportunity and encouragement, poor or indifferent teaching and negative attitudes may well have alienated girls from these subjects in the past and at present, part of the problem is undoubtedly the intrinsic nature of the knowledge and modes of thinking within the disciplines themselves (Burton, 1990; Whyte, 1986; Keller, 1985; Kelly, 1981). The problem is not simply with women but with the way these fields of knowledge have developed in almost exclusively male hands.

ATTAINMENT
As we have argued above, there is no clear evidence that either co-educational or single-sex schools encourage less stereotyping in subject options. The question of attainment is similarly problematic. There is a limited amount of research in Ireland on this matter. Furthermore, the interpretation of such data is not straightforward, as the effect of intervening variables, such as the social

class intake in the school, attitudes of teachers, grouping of pupils etc. should be taken into consideration; yet they have not been analysed in any depth.

One of the main problems arising from comparisons made between single-sex and co-educational schools is that one is not comparing like with like in terms of pupil intake. Bearing this in mind, Brennan (1986) analysed the Leaving Certificate results of girls and boys in Irish, English and mathematics in co-educational and single-sex secondary schools. The data for this study was based on a national sample of 3,950 pupils collected by the Economic and Social Research Institute for its sex roles and schooling study.

Brennan found that girls in co-educational secondary schools performed more highly than girls in single-sex secondary schools in all three subjects. The differences were greatest in Irish and mathematics. Brennan's conclusions (ibid., 185) are as follows: 'When social class is controlled for, as it is to a certain extent in comparing secondary schools only, we find co-education to have no adverse effects on girls' performance within this sector. Indeed, the opposite seems to be the case. Girls in co-educational secondary schools do better than girls in all other school types in Irish, English and mathematics.'

It is interesting that boys in single-sex secondary schools performed better than boys in co-educational schools. However, this is not surprising in view of the fact that Hannan et al. (1983) found that boys' secondary schools were more socially selective and more academically oriented in pupil culture than other secondary schools.

Brennan also compared the educational aspirations of girls in co-educational and single-sex secondary schools. Those in co-educational schools had significantly higher educational aspirations than those in all other school types (ibid., 186). Yet girls in co-educational secondary schools were the least likely of all girls to see mathematics as 'interesting', while girls in community schools were the most likely to think this way.

The question whether co-education affects examination performance was again examined by Hanafin (1992). This was a study of 1,242 pupils in sixteen secondary schools and one vocational school in Limerick city and county. Leaving Certificate and Intermediate Certificate results were obtained for all pupils. The main finding was that when social background and school effects (i.e. school selectivity and frequency of discipline problems) were taken into account, co-education had a significant negative effect on girls' examination performance, and no effect on boys' examination performance. Hanafin suggests that the poorer performance of girls in co-educational schools is explained by social-psychological differences between girls in single-sex and co-educational schools. The study also claims that girls in single-sex schools had significantly higher educational aspirations and expectations than girls in co-educational schools.

The findings of these two studies are contradictory in relation to attainment and aspirations in single-sex and co-educational secondary schools. One possible explanation is that one of the studies is based on a national sample, while the other is based on a county sample. However, as only a short synopsis of Hanafin's findings was available at the time of writing, it is not really possible to explore here the reasons for the differences in findings.

What the research data generally implies, however, is that whether girls or boys do well in a particular type of school depends on the pupils' own social class background and their ability in different subjects. It also depends on how individual schools are organised, and whether teachers are positive, encouraging, and competent in different fields. There is no clear evidence to suggest that merely organising girls or boys into pre-defined sex groups is going to help their school performance. It is interesting to note, for example, that in countries such as Germany and Sweden, where there has been a long tradition of co-education throughout the education system, there is no evidence to suggest that girls are underachieving. In fact in both countries girls tend to outperform boys at the end of compulsory schooling (Wernersson, 1991, 174; Kaiser, 1991, 192).

CLASSROOM INTERACTION AND SCHOOL ORGANISATION

In recent years it is the research into classroom interaction and school organisational variables that has caused the most concern internationally in relation to co-education. There is substantial evidence that teachers—even those well disposed to the provision of equal opportunities—interact differentially with their male and female pupils, and that this operates to the disadvantage of female pupils. Observations in classrooms have shown that boys both demand and get more teacher attention (Askew and Ross, 1988; Wilson, 1991).

This is so even in countries like Sweden that have had sex equality as an educational goal for a considerable time (Wernersson, 1991). A significant amount of the attention boys get is in the form of disciplinary interventions. Boys of all ages also receive more praise from both female and male teachers, even though teachers are adamant that they do not give more attention to boys than to girls (Kaiser, 1991, 197). Observations in German classrooms suggest that more than two-thirds of teacher-pupil interaction in primary and secondary schools is oriented towards boys, and that the greater part of this is taken up with admonishments (ibid.).

British studies have found similar patterns and have suggested that teachers often exploit rivalry between the sexes to motivate or manage pupils. Boys tend to dominate classroom talk, and there is evidence to suggest that teachers deliberately gear the content of lessons towards boys' interests in order to retain attention and control (Wilson, 1991). Girls remain largely passive and 'invisible' in class, and teachers have been found to downgrade their achievements (Stanworth, 1983).

A number of British studies have found evidence of negative stereotyping and harassment of girls in mixed schools. Studies suggest that boys talk for longer than girls and get restless or groan if girls talk too much (Stanworth, 1983). Boys occupy more space in the playground and also in the classroom (Mahony, 1985; Askew and Ross, 1988). Certain studies suggest that girls are subjected to physical molestation from boys (Jones, 1985). Furthermore, it is argued that boys often extract services from girls both inside and outside the classroom, for example in supplying pens and pencils, getting crisps or sweets from the shop, and helping with homework (Mahony, 1985). These studies suggest that such negative interactions between boys and girls affect girls' self-esteem and confidence.

Classroom interaction studies are based mainly on ethnographic research in schools. There has been much less of this type of research in Ireland than in other countries; however, there are a few studies that offer us some comparisons. An ethnographic study in an urban primary school by Buckley (1988) found some processes in teacher-pupil interaction similar to those described in other countries. Tasks in the classroom and around the school were rather stereotypical for girls and boys. There was a tendency for greater teacher interaction with male pupils than with female pupils, partly at least because of the greater demands placed on the teacher by boys. Boys, it was argued, received more specific teacher reaction and benefited from longer, more precise and intense educational interaction than did girls (ibid.). However, like teachers in Germany and other countries (Stanworth, 1983; Kaiser, 1991), teachers were not conscious of differentiating.

Ethnographic research in a primary school in Northern Ireland offers similar findings (Morgan, 1991). In this study it was quite clear that there was no intentional sex discrimination. None of the teachers treated any children less favourably than those of the other sex. But there were a number of areas where differences that had a sex dimension were detected in interactions and behaviour patterns. There were 'visible' and 'invisible' children in these classrooms; girls were more likely to be in the latter category. The levels of teacher interaction were higher with boys than with girls, both in reprimanding the boys and in giving them praise. This, it was argued, implied that boys were getting more experience of various types of interaction with teachers, and in many instances this also seems to mean that they were getting more opportunities for developing strategies to handle their relationships with teachers.

There was also evidence that in the playground boys monopolised space for games such as football, while girls played in groups around the edges of the play space. Inside, each room had certain 'high status' toys, such as construction toys or sand and water trays. Boys more often seemed to gain access to these when conflicts arose. The study suggested that there may be long-term educational implications from this. If girls are failing to get equal access to and sustained periods with educationally valuable toys, this may affect the development of manipulative and spatial skills and of extended concentration span (ibid., 4).

Work with second-level trainee teachers indicates similar tendencies. With regard to the distribution of teachers' questions, boys were asked significantly more questions than girls (Ní Chárthaigh and Harrison, 1988; Uí Chatháin and Drudy, work in progress). As a result of girls being less frequently addressed than boys, they were asked fewer high-cognitive questions and were less intellectually challenged than boys. When teachers asked questions of the group of pupils as a whole, the boys monopolised the responses, so that any imbalance in the distribution of questions by sex was most pronounced in lessons during which the teachers failed to specify the pupils they wished to answer (Ní Chárthaigh and Harrison, 1988).

It has been argued that inequalities in teacher-pupil interaction, such as those outlined above, can adversely affect girls' self-image and expectations (Morgan, 1991). The evidence from ethnographic classroom research has led some to argue for a return to single-sex schooling in Britain (Shaw, 1984). While this claim is understandable, it must be asked what type of single-sex schooling it is possible to provide and how effective it is likely to be in raising girls' self-esteem and confidence. What is often forgotten in the call for a return to single-sex education is that single-sex schools, no less than their co-educational counterparts, are set in the context of particular cultures and societies. There is no guarantee that girls' single-sex schools are, or will be, paragons of feminist virtue; indeed there is some evidence from Ireland that both girls' and boys' single-sex schools reinforce traditional sex roles through their formal (Hannan et al., 1983) and hidden curriculum (Lynch, 1989b).

The textbooks teachers use, and the way these are interpreted, can also have an effect on self-image. Although there has been a growing awareness of this in recent years, research in Britain, for example, indicates that many textbooks and other reading material for children remain highly stereotyped. Many such books present girls as passive and immobile, usually engaged in indoor activities and seldom in a leadership role. Girls and women are frequently portrayed in children's reading schemes as helpmates to boys and men, bystanders to the narrative drama of stories (Wilson, 1991).

In Ireland research has been conducted into the incidence of sexist and sex-stereotyped content in Irish-language readers. The older reading schemes, which are still in use in many schools, are extremely sex-stereotypical in their approach. In the new readers the situation has changed greatly, but as yet there are many children who have to be exposed to them. Although some of the new reading schemes have improved with regard to the number of stories about women and girls and also with regard to the types of activity in which both males and females are engaged, they still portray stereotypical images in gender, social class and racial terms (Daly, 1992; McGowan, 1992).

There have been some studies that have examined the implications of co-educational schooling in Ireland, but they have not used ethnography as part of their methodology. On a superficial reading, the results of these studies are somewhat different from the ethnographic studies, in that they focus on rather different phenomena. The findings of the ESRI study, the largest one carried out in this area (Hannan et al., 1983), are somewhat at odds with the classroom observation studies. The ESRI study administered a questionnaire to pupils but did not observe them in classrooms, and this is no doubt a reason why their findings tend to differ from those elsewhere. In the girls' responses to the questionnaire they indicated that they were significantly more likely to be asked and to answer questions in class and to be more positively rewarded for and stimulated by such classroom participation.

Seemingly contrary to the findings in other countries, in this study girls across all school types consistently reported higher levels of perceived scholastic rewards than boys. On average they found classroom interaction a more rewarding experience than did boys. And consistently, from both sexes, vocational school pupils had the highest level of perceived rewards, and secondary schools the lowest. There were no significant differences in average scores between single-sex and co-educational secondary schools: both had the lowest perceived level of reward. Girls felt significantly more rewarded in their educational work than did boys in all school types.

In some ways, however, the ESRI study does reflect the findings elsewhere. In general, boys reported more negative sanctioning in all school types. Girls had, on average, significantly higher levels of satisfaction with teacher supportiveness and with the general approachability of teachers (ibid.). With regard to pupil attitudes, the ESRI research team found that boys in single-sex secondary schools were most sexist in their beliefs in response to questions relating to education and careers for women. Boys and girls in the newer community schools had fewest sexist beliefs, while both sexes in secondary schools were the most sexist. Secondary school boys were the most sexist of all.

A comparison of two co-educational community schools in an urban area indicates the possibility of improving sex equality through positive intervention programmes. One of the schools pursued a positive action programme to encourage non-traditional subject choices among girls and boys; the other had a subject choice policy that incorporated no specific action either to encourage or discourage non-traditional subject choice (Uí Mhaonaigh, 1991). In the school with the positive action programme it was found that both girls and boys demonstrated significantly less traditional performance in and choice of subjects than pupils in the other school. For example, although girls in the school with a positive action programme were still in a minority in mechanical drawing, woodwork and metalwork classes, they were proportionately as likely as boys to consider these subjects among their best subjects—indicating a high degree of confidence in these areas (ibid.).

Intervention programmes such as the above are often accompanied by a heightening of awareness and more positive attitudes on the part of teachers. Indeed, it has been argued that intervention must concern itself with changing the attitudes, expectations and supportive behaviour of administrators, teachers, pupils, and parents (Breen and Hannan, 1987). Research into teachers' attitudes in Britain, for example, showed a majority in favour of reducing sex discrimination in schools in general and in favour of the view that every school should have an anti-sexist policy (Wilson, 1991). However, it has also been suggested that teachers are often not willing to admit that there is a problem in their own schools (ibid.).

Research carried out in Ireland with primary and second-level teachers involved in intervention projects to introduce sex equality into the curriculum indicates that while teachers tend to believe in sex equality, they have a lower level of awareness of sex discrimination in education. This research also showed that female teachers had a significantly stronger belief in equality than male teachers (Drudy, in press). The study also suggested the benefits of pre-service teacher education in raising awareness of sex discrimination in education.

CONCLUSION

As we have seen, the research outlined above, both internationally and in Ireland, is somewhat contradictory and inconclusive with regard to the impact of co-education on gender equality. This points to the conclusion that it is less a question of whether schools are organised along single-sex or co-educational lines than of examining what is done within these schools. The key issues are school policy and practices in relation to sex equality, whether they are co-educational, single-sex girls' or single-sex boys' schools.

Genuine equality of the sexes, Arnot (1983) suggests, has not yet become an educational goal. If it is now to become one, she argues, what is needed are reforms in teacher education and in-service programmes to reshape teachers' classroom practice, the redesign of curriculums, the rewriting of textbooks, and the re-education of parents and employers. In the context of such a programme of educational reform, co-educational schools may well have the resources to offer a more equal education to girls and boys (ibid., 88).

Overall, then, the research comparing single-sex and co-educational schools and their effects on pupils is somewhat inconclusive. From an equality perspective, how schools and classrooms are managed and how the curriculum is implemented is probably more important than whether the school is co-educational or single-sex.

References and Further Reading

Arnot, M. (1983), 'A cloud over co-education: an analysis of the forms and transmission of class and gender relations' in S. Walker and L. Barton (eds.), *Gender, Class and Education*, Lewes: Falmer.

Arnot, M. (1984), 'How shall we educate our sons?' in R. Deem (ed.), *Co-education Reconsidered*, Milton Keynes: Open University Press.

Askew, S., and Ross, C. (1988), *Boys Don't Cry*, Milton Keynes: Open University Press.

Berge, L., and Varøy-Haga, M. (1992), 'Assessment in Norwegian schooling' (paper presented to European Community Colloquium on Differential Performance in the Assessment of Mathematics at the End of Compulsory Schooling, Birmingham University, 15–18 May 1992).

Breen, R., and Hannan, D. (1987), 'School and gender: the education of girls in Ireland' in C. Curtin, P. Jackson, and B. O'Connor (eds.), *Gender in Irish Society*, Galway: Officina Typographica.

Brennan, M. (1986), 'Factors Affecting Attainment in the Irish Leaving Certificate Examination' (MEd thesis, University College, Dublin).

Buckley, T. (1988), 'The Reinforcement of Gender Roles in a Mixed Primary School Classroom' (MEd thesis, St Patrick's College, Maynooth).

Burton, L, (ed.) (1990), *Gender and Mathematics: an International Perspective*, London: Cassell.

Daly, M. (1992), 'Gender, Class, Race and Ethnic Bias in the English Language Programmes in Primary Schools' (master of equality studies thesis, University College, Dublin).

Department of Education (1992a), *Statistical Report, 1990/91*, Dublin: Stationery Office.

Department of Education (1992b), *Futures: Exploring Equal Opportunities: an Introduction*, Dublin: Department of Education.

Department of Education (1992c), *Education for a Changing World: Green Paper on Education*, Dublin: Stationery Office.

Drudy, S. (in press), 'Teacher attitudes and strategies for change in education' in D. Ní Chárthaigh (ed.), *Equal Opportunities and Teacher Education: Strategies for Innovation—vol. 2*, Brussels: Association for Teacher Education in Europe.

Grevholm, B., and Nilsson, M. (1992), 'Gender differences in mathematics in Swedish schools' (paper presented to European Community Colloquium on Differential Performance in the Assessment of Mathematics at the End of Compulsory Schooling, Birmingham University, 15–18 May 1992).

Hanafin, J. (1992), Submission on Co-education to Third Joint Oireachtas Committee on Women's Rights, 24 September 1992.

Hannan, D., et al. (1983), *Schooling and Sex Roles: Sex Differences in Subject Provision and Student Choice in Irish Post-Primary Schools*, Dublin: Economic and Social Research Institute.

Jones, C. (1985), 'Sexual tyranny: male violence in a mixed secondary school' in G. Weiner (ed.), *Just a Bunch of Girls*, Milton Keynes: Open University Press.

Kaiser, A. (1991), 'West Germany' in M. Wilson (ed.), *Girls and Young Women in Education: a European Perspective*, Oxford: Pergamon.

Keller, E. (1985), *Reflections on Gender and Science*, London: Yale University Press.

Kelly, A. (1981), *The Missing Half: Girls and Science Education*, Manchester: Manchester University Press.

Kelly, A. (1985), 'The Construction of Masculine Science', *British Journal of Sociology of Education*, vol. 6, no. 2.

Kelly, A. (1986), *Gender Differences in Teacher-Pupil Interaction: a Meta-Analytic Review*, Manchester: University of Manchester (Department of Sociology).

Lynch, K. (1989a), *The Hidden Curriculum: Reproductin in Education: a Reappraisal*, Lewes: Falmer.

Lynch, K. (1989b), 'The ethos of girls' schools: an analysis of differences between male and female schools', *Social Studies*, vol. 10, no. 1–2, 11–31.

McEwen, A., and Curry, C. (1987), 'Girls' access to science: single-sex versus co-educational schools' in R. Osborne, R. Cormack, and R. Miller (eds.), *Education and Policy in Northern Ireland*, Belfast: Queen's University (Policy Research Institute).

McGowan, G. (1992), 'An examination of Irish language readers used in primary schools for sexism and sex-stereotypical content', *Oideas*, vol. 38, 82–99.

Mahony, P. (1985), *Schools for the Boys*, London, Hutchinson.

Martin, M., and Hickey, B. (1992), *The 1991 Leaving Certificate Examination: a Review of the Results*, Dublin: National Council for Curriculum and Assessment.

Morgan, V. (1991), 'Gender differentiation in primary schools: a northern view', Coleraine: University of Ulster (Faculty of Education).

Ní Chárthaigh, D., and Harrison, R. (1988), 'A training instrument for use in pre-service microteaching courses designed to promote equity in the quality of teacher interaction with girls and boys' in P. Hübner (ed.), *Teacher Education and Training in Europe: Present Challenges and Future Strategies*, Berlin: Free University.

Ó Conaill, N. (1991), 'Girls and science: equality in school or society?', *Irish Educational Studies*, vol. 10, 82–95.

Plateau, N. (1991), 'French-speaking Belgium' in M. Wilson (ed.), *Girls and Young Women in Education: a European Perspective*, Oxford: Pergamon.

Shaw, J. (1984), 'The politics of single sex schools' in R. Deem (ed.), *Co-education Reconsidered*, Milton Keynes: Open University Press.

Spender, E., and Spender, D. (1980), *Learning to Lose*, London: Women's Press.

Stanworth, M. (1983), *Gender and Schooling*, London: Hutchinson.

Steedman, J. (1983), *Exam Results in Mixed and Single Sex Schools: Findings from the National Child Development Study*, London: Equal Opportunities Commission.

Uí Chatháin, M., and Drudy, S., 'Gender equality in classroom interaction', Maynooth: St Patrick's College, Education Department (work in progress).

Uí Mhaonaigh, M. (1991), 'The Effectiveness of a Positive Action Programme in Encouraging Non-Traditional Subject Choice' (MEd thesis, University of Dublin).

Wernersson, I. (1982), 'Sex differentiation and teacher-pupil interaction in the Swedish compulsory school' in Council of Europe, *Sex Stereotyping in Schools: Report of a Workshop, 5–8 May 1981*, Lisse: Swets en Zeitlinger.

Wernersson, I. (1991), 'Sweden' in M. Wilson (ed.), *Girls and Young Women in Education: a European Perspective*, Oxford: Pergamon.

Whyte, J. (1986), *Girls into Science and Technology*, London: Routledge and Kegan Paul.

Wilson, M. (1991), 'England and Wales' in M. Wilson (ed.), *Girls and Young Women in Education: a European Perspective*, Oxford: Pergamon.

IV

Curriculum Issues and the Organisation of Learning

10

Education and the Economy

In this chapter we examine the relationship between the curriculum in schools and colleges, especially at second level, and the types of job available in the paid labour market. In the absence of any longitudinal study on the relationship between education provision and the requirements of the paid labour market, all we can do here is map the relationship between the stated skill requirements of occupations with education provision at this time.

Although there is a dearth of research on the precise relationship between the skill requirements of jobs and what education offers, there is much debate. The early 1990s saw the publication of three reports that addressed this issue in varying degrees: the OECD report (1991), the Culliton Report (1992), and the Green Paper (Department of Education, 1992). Before going on to analyse the available empirical evidence we must set the debate in the context of general discussions about the nature of work and about human capital theory.

PAID LABOUR AND UNPAID LABOUR

While the focus of this chapter is on the paid labour market, it is important to make some introductory comments on the concept of labour itself. The definition of the 'labour market' currently in use is profoundly patriarchal. Because it equates paid employment with labour, it ignores the vast amount of labour that is involved both in domestic work and in caring (Lynch, 1989a). In so far as language elicits, reinforces and generalises distinct kinds of relationship in society (Bernstein, 1971), the current interpretation of the term 'labour market' reinforces the view that the only real form of work is paid work.

What has happened in essence is that classical economists and Marxists have tended to assume that the essence of our 'species being' or 'human nature' is defined in our economic relationships. Work is defined as a process involving humankind and nature as an economically productive activity (Stacey, 1981). There is, however, an increasing awareness that work is not confined to economically productive activities (Hochschild, 1989). The activity of caring is work (whether it be of children, the elderly, the sick, or between two sets of adults, such as husband and wife), and most of those who do it do not get paid for it. This is a major area of work in all societies, including Ireland. The 1991 Labour Force Survey (CSO, 1992) shows that while 44 per cent of those over the age of fifteen are 'at work' (i.e. in paid employment), a further 25 per cent— 99.6 per cent of whom are women—are engaged in 'home duties'.

As caring is a primary responsibility of those in home duties, and as most of those who are in paid employment are also carers, one can see that the work of caring is a central one indeed. Education, therefore, should not just focus on preparing people for paid employment, or what is normally labelled the 'labour market': it should also prepare people for undertaking other types of work in society, such as caring, without which the economy could not function.

To name caring as a form of labour is not to deny the other non-work-related purposes of education; it is merely to demonstrate by way of one example how important it is to recognise the multiple functions that education serves. Mindful of this, therefore, in the rest of this chapter we will address the relationship between education and the paid labour market only.

HUMAN CAPITAL THEORY AND EDUCATION

As Collins (1979) has noted, the increasing trend towards more technically oriented education is regarded by many as natural and inevitable. It is assumed that 'education prepares students in the skills necessary for work, and skills are the main determinant of occupational success. That is, the hierarchy of educational attainment is assumed to be a hierarchy of skills, and the hierarchy of jobs is assumed to be another such skill hierarchy. Hence education determines success, and all the more so as the modern economy allegedly shifts toward an increasing predominance of highly skilled positions' (ibid., 7).

The problem with this type of technical functionalism, Collins claims, is that empirical evidence does not tend to substantiate it, or at best only substantiates it in a very limited way. Drawing on research from a range of both highly developed and less developed countries (in the capitalist sense), Collins points out that there has been little study of what is actually learnt in school or (more importantly perhaps) how long it is retained. What evidence there is suggests that vocational training is derived primarily from work experience rather than from formal school training; in the professional and managerial sectors many of the skills used are also learnt on the job, 'and the lengthy courses of study required by business and professional schools exist in good part to raise the status of the profession and to form the barrier of socialisation between practitioners and laymen [*sic*]' (ibid., 17).

Collins claims that, at an aggregate level, the main contribution of education to economic productivity occurs at the level of transition to mass literacy, and not significantly beyond that (ibid., 15). On the other hand, if one examines the relationship between education and *individual* productivity, as Berg has done in the

United States, there is no evidence that better-educated employees are more productive than less-educated employees at any given level (Berg, 1970, 85–104,
143–76).

While Collins's and Berg's comments on the relationship between education
and jobs are primarily focused on the so-called developed (i.e. well-off, mostly
capitalist) countries, there has also been a considerable amount of research on
this subject in the 'developing' countries. Commenting on basic literacy, for
example, Fagerland and Saha (1983, 42–3) point out that the relationship
between literacy and development is 'a highly complex one'. In the sphere of
subsistence agriculture, for example, output can be increased through basic
innovations and technology, without literacy. A similar point is made by
Lockhead et al. (1980) in a review of research in this field; the relationship
between education and agricultural productivity was found to be much higher
under modern conditions than under non-modern conditions. Little (1984, 96)
reports a later study by Jamison and Lau (1982) in Korea, Malaysia and
Thailand also confirming this.

Outside the agricultural sector, however, there is considerable research evidence to suggest that increased educational credentials do not necessarily lead
to greater productivity or efficiency. Studies of factory workers by Fuller (1972)
in India, of a variety of tradespeople by Godfrey (1977) in Kenya, and of other
workers in Ghana, Mexico and Sri Lanka (reported by Oxenham, 1984, 60)
indicate that the relationship between level of education and productivity is not
especially strong.

While there is some evidence of a relationship or correspondence between
general education and job performance, Oxenham (1984) reports on a major
study in Liberia from 1974 to 1979 indicating that this is far from meaning that
specific technically oriented courses in schools improve job performance.
Indeed Oxenham (ibid., 60) reports on a major study undertaken by an Anglo-
American multinational corporation that was considering restricting its management in Britain to an all-graduate body. It undertook a study of its existing
graduate and non-graduate managers and found the differences in managerial
skills to be negligible, and therefore continued to recruit school leavers as well
as graduates as trainee managers.

Summing up the relationship between education and productivity, Little
(1984, 108–9) points out that education may be a necessary condition but is
certainly not a sufficient one for the achievement of increased productivity. A
variety of organisational factors seem to influence productivity, including
decision-making procedures, communication links, promotion procedures, and
in-service training; these factors have little to do with education *per se*. 'If the
unfilled promises of education over the last two decades have anything to tell us,
it is that if education is to contribute to productivity, then other factors must
also change simultaneously' (ibid., 108).

The human capital assumption, therefore—that the key to economic growth lies in developing the human capital stock through the increased technical education of individuals—has been shown to be wanting. There are many structural factors outside education at local, national and global level that influence growth, productivity, and development.

If education, in the narrow technical sense, does not increase productivity to the degree originally presumed by theorists of human capital, why has it continued to influence public policy to such a degree? Karabel and Halsey (1977, 9) and Lauglo and Lillis (1988, 1–25) claim that the answer lies in the 'comforting ideological character of its message,' both for national governments and for institutions such as the World Bank, the OECD, and the International Monetary Fund. The theory suggests, and continues to suggest—see the report *Education in Sub-Saharan Africa* (World Bank, 1988)—that so-called Third World countries are poor not because of the structure of international economic relations but because of their internal difficulties, including their lack of human capital. This is politically a very palatable theory, both to multilateral agencies such as the World Bank and to national governments, as it does not require any radical structural change in the sociopolitical or economic order. Economic changes are assumed to flow, in considerable part, from the increased educational development of individuals.

In contrast to Karabel and Halsey, economic theory suggests that increasing the skills and educational levels of a given population is one of the few strategies open to governments for promoting growth in a global market. It is also argued that the pace of technological development requires a greater capacity to adapt: improved education, it is believed, increases the adaptability and flexibility of the work force in a constantly changing environment, and this in turn improves competitive advantage. Outside the economic context, *per se,* education is also regarded as a key to the development of innovation in society. An improved innovative and critical capacity is seen as important for the general social and political development of a society (McCarthy, 1992).

Margaret Archer (1982) attributes the continued expansion of education systems to the internal dynamics of education itself. She claims that the problems of educational relevance or irrelevance stem from internal contradictions within the education system: 'as the educational system matures it begins to take on a life of its own . . . becoming increasingly independent as a social institution and decreasingly regulated by other parts of society' (ibid., 42). She suggests that as the increased size and scope of the system 'represents a parallelogram of corporate and primary pressures, the result is not something *anybody* wants' (ibid., 43).

More specifically, she goes on to point out that as the education system has become bigger and bigger it has become a major employer of its own products (e.g. teachers). Professional reproduction, therefore, has become a major task of the system. This has precipitated a considerable increase in self-determination, which has not been highly contingent on economic and political conditions (ibid., 44).

While Archer is correct in pointing to the internal dynamics generating conservatism in education systems, her analysis is limited by its lack of reference to sociopolitical structures. As Bowles and Gintis (1976) have noted, while schooling may contribute little to technical expertise, it most certainly socialises students into sets of attitudes and values that are prized in modern large-scale organisations, including punctuality, obedience, conformity, a sense of duty, and deference to authority. That employers value these qualities has been shown by Noah and Eckstein (1988) in studies of Britain, France, and Germany. On the other hand, it does not reward creativity, curiosity, independence, or cooperative group work (Jackson, 1968; Bowles and Gintis, 1976; Brook and Oxenham, 1984; Lynch, 1989b).

The kinds of social quality that schools reward, therefore, may be economically useful, but in the social rather than the technical sense. And perhaps this is what employers want? After all, research on employers internationally (in France, Indonesia, Panama, and Kenya) shows that while employers do use educational attainment as a criterion for recruitment, in all four countries education was not the decisive criterion for entry into every job category, and it was less important for internal promotion than for initial hiring (Hallak and Caillods, 1980). In addition, Oxenham (1984, 74–6) and Wilms (1988, 81–93) report that employers give preference to applicants with general rather than technical or vocational education, especially from the second-level system. While Oxenham notes that this may reflect the traditional prejudice of employers against the type of people who pursue vocational courses—that they are less able, and are more likely to come from a working-class background—it certainly indicates that vocational training in schools is not regarded by employers as being of pre-eminent importance when hiring staff.

The research evidence available—and it is rather scarce, as Lauglo and Lillis (1988, 25) point out—suggests that a more technically oriented education, especially at second level, is not one that is either favoured by employers or guarantees greater productivity. While few would deny that having a more educated paid labour force is of benefit to a given economy, there is a growing belief that a general education rather than a skills-oriented one may be of greater benefit to the economy in the long run. While it is crucial to have high levels of technological and/or industry-specific skills, such skills appear to be most effectively deployed when allied to a good general education. Certainly in countries like Germany, 'the interaction of broad vocational training with significant general educational requirements appears to be a characteristic of [their] training system' (McCarthy, 1992, 12).

THE ORIENTATION OF SECOND-LEVEL AND THIRD-LEVEL EDUCATION: CULLITON AND AFTER

'There is not enough emphasis in Irish second level education on technical and vocational training' (Culliton, 1992, 53).

Irish education has been guided for the last twenty-five years by the principles of human capital theory, informed by what might be called technological functionalism. By this we mean that Irish educational policy (in common with that of most other western European countries) has been based on the assumption that the process of acquiring skills and knowledge through education is a form of productive investment and not a form of consumption. It is assumed that investment in human capital (particularly in the technological field) not only increases individual productivity but by so doing also lays the technical base for the type of labour force necessary for rapid economic growth (Schultz, 1961).

After the publication of *Investment in Education* (Department of Education, 1966) education was increasingly defined as a mechanism for developing the technical skills in the paid labour force, which would promote rapid economic growth. A large section of the report (208–21) was devoted in particular to highlighting the need for technicians. Although the report had no brief 'to engage in any extensive analysis of curricula' (ibid., 390), it was clear from comments made about the classical grammar orientation of secondary schools, and the observation that 'nearly half of the pupil hours in secondary schools is devoted to languages' (ibid., 277), that there was a belief that the curriculum of second-level education needed substantial overhauling, and that the changes should be in the technical direction.

The publication in 1992 of both the Culliton Report—and in particular the background paper on industrial training by Roche and Tansey (1992)—and the Green Paper (Department of Education, 1992) heralded a new thrust towards technical education. The OECD report published a year earlier (OECD, 1991, 69) had also referred to the 'acute' problem created by 'the weight of the classical humanist tradition' that secondary schools had to bear. While much evidence was supplied in the *Investment in Education* report (Department of Education, 1966) to substantiate claims about the low level of technical skills provided by education for industry at that time, virtually no evidence is provided to substantiate similar claims in the reports of the 1990s. Indeed the empirical evidence available actually suggests that there is no real skills shortage. The FÁS Skills Survey (Fox, 1991) did not find any serious skilled labour shortages among the 1,000 industries and enterprises surveyed. The OECD report also showed that, comparatively, Irish businesses reported few skill shortages for the years 1973–88 (see table 10.1).

In responding to findings such as these, Roche and Tansey point out that those industrialists who claim there is no skills shortage are not sufficiently aware of the skill differential that exists between Irish workers and those in 'our com-

Table 10.1

Percentage of firms surveyed reporting shortages of labour and of skilled labour generally in business surveys, 1973–1988

	Skilled labour shortage							General labour bottleneck			
	Canada	Finland	Ireland	Norway	New Zealand*	Sweden	Britain	Australia	New Zealand	Denmark	France
1973		41.5	15.8		−50.3	41.1	36.0	33.5	45.8	50.3	
1974		47.5	16.5	13.0	−21.3	58.2	35.3	24.3	38.8	15.0	
1975		44.0	8.0	4.5	19.0	41.7	16.7	6.3	11.8	4.3	
1976	12.6	16.0	9.3	3.5	−1.3	35.8	13.1	6.5	10.8	9.0	
1977	8.6	2.5	10.5	3.0	1.3	22.0	19.4	6.3	8.3	6.8	
1978	9.8	2.8	18.9	3.3	−1.8	19.3	21.7	5.5	3.3	12.8	
1979	11.8	16.3	20.6	5.0	−24.5	37.1	21.1	6.8	7.5	24.0	5.0
1980	13.0	34.3	6.9	6.8	−6.3	45.4	8.4	9.5	2.0	6.8	5.0
1981	12.7	24.0	3.6	5.8	−18.3	20.8	2.5	12.3	6.8	2.8	2.5
1982	4.7	13.3	2.3	3.3	−10.5	13.1	3.0	4.3	5.0	0.8	4.0
1983	2.0	11.5	3.0	0.3	2.8	18.3	4.4	1.0	1.8	0.8	4.0
1984	2.8	18.0	1.3	0.8	−37.0	30.0	8.2	3.5	8.8	1.8	3.0
1985	3.4	26.8	0.3	4.3	−47.5	31.3	13.2	7.8	11.5	5.8	3.8
1986	4.8	25.5	0.3	4.8	−25.3	33.8	11.7	8.3	9.3	5.0	2.5
1987	5.7	29.5	0.4	4.8	−15.3	44.8	14.2	10.8	5.8	2.3	1.8
1988	10.0	31.0	0.6	2.0	19.0	59.0	22.0	13.0	1.3	1.7	4.3

*The skilled labour shortage series for New Zealand is a skilled labour 'tendency', for which more positive numbers represent recession conditions.

Source: OECD (1991), 19.

petitor countries'. They claim that the level of skill deficiency in industry can only be determined by comparing Irish industry with international best practice in competitor countries. They claim that there are two areas where Irish industry will face severe skill shortages in the future: 'an absence of multiskilling, both among technicians and craftspeople; and an absence of integrated technical and financial skills at management level' (Roche and Tansey, 1992, 81).

However, these do not, on the face of it, seem to be matters that can be resolved in second-level education, or even third-level education, alone. As is pointed out in the report itself, FÁS and other educational agencies would have no difficulty supplying multiskilled personnel if industry was prepared to recruit them. The problem here is one of demarcation disputes between employers and trade unions (ibid., 76). This is clearly not an educational matter. Indeed, it is interesting to note from the survey of leading industrialists by Roche and Tansey (ibid., 70) what they had to say about factory-floor workers, the majority of whom are recruited directly from second-level schools: 'In terms of basic skills, the Irish schools system was seen as the equal of its German counterpart by foreign employers. A number of respondents pointed to the improvement in the workforce over time by contrasting the well-educated recruits of today with poorly-educated older workers. Where difficulties were perceived, they related to recruits' unfamiliarity with the world of work rather than any deficiencies in formal schooling.'

This certainly implies that the large industrial employers, including foreign ones, surveyed for the Culliton and Roche-Tansey reports feel that young school leavers employed as operatives are as well prepared for the work they are required to do as their German counterparts. The largest employer of apprentices in the country also reported that they had no difficulty recruiting high-standard applicants; many applicants for apprenticeships had enough points to enter third-level education, and there were six applicants for each available apprenticeship place (ibid., 72).

This suggests that the skill deficiency projected for Irish industry is not primarily a problem arising from the nature of education *per se*. The problem is more likely to be the ability and willingness (or otherwise) of Irish industry to provide appropriate in-career training and education for its own workers. Roche and Tansey allude to this themselves. Indeed if, as the reports suggest, Irish industrialists are not aware of how deficient in skill their employees are relative to their European or other international competitors, surely then the problem first is to educate the industrialists themselves. If industrialists do not know their own business—and this is in effect what the reports imply—then Irish industry is in trouble, but this is not primarily a problem for second-level schools.

The critique of education set out in Culliton and the proposal to respond to the wishes of Culliton by making 'enterprise and technology' a compulsory subject in the junior cycle of second-level education (Department of Education, 1992) must, however, be set in context. As Hyland (1992) has pointed out, the call for greater technicalisation has been a recurrent theme in Irish education since the nineteenth century. What is significant about this call in the early 1990s is the absence of empirical evidence to substantiate the claims made about the lack of skills. This was not as conspicuously true at earlier periods of history. What would seem to be happening, however, and what is certainly a common phenomenon in other countries, is that in times of recession, education becomes the scapegoat for industrial and economic problems that are not of its making.

As the recession began to hit Britain and the United States in the 1980s, one can identify a similar trend. There were claims that schools lacked accountability, that standards were poor, that greater excellence should be sought, and that more technology was required. The context in which this was happening was one in which industries in the United States and Britain were failing to compete successfully in the free market. Schools were a convenient, visible and manageable scapegoat.

CHANGE AND DEVELOPMENT IN IRISH EDUCATION

From the late 1960s to the early 1990s the curricular changes and subject participation patterns at both second and third level indicate the degree of success achieved in the 'technicalisation' of education. The term 'technical' here is used as a synonym for technological, scientific and commercial studies (see Lynch, 1989b). Clancy's research (1989) shows that just over 65 per cent of those entering higher education in 1986 were studying technical subjects, as defined above (see table 10.2). An analysis of subject participation rates at the senior cycle of second level reveals a similar trend (see table 8.6). This shows that participation in the arts and humanities declined significantly, among both boys and girls, between 1972/73 and 1990. The languages have also languished to some degree, with the exception of French and, in the last two to three years, German. By contrast with this, participation in most of the sciences and in accountancy and business organisation has increased to a considerable degree among both sexes.

In the technological sphere *per se,* participation has increased significantly, but only among boys. This gender difference is undoubtedly influenced by the fact that most co-educational schools still offer engineering, construction studies and technical drawing to boys only, while no single-sex girls' school offers engineering, only one offers building construction, and three offer technical drawing (Department of Education, 1991, table 14.5). The supply-side 'problem' is most evident in the technical field as a girls' problem. It is interesting to note, however, that no mention is made of these gender differentials in either the Culliton Report or the Roche and Tansey study. This is an example of the gender-blindness we referred to in chapters 3 and 8.

Table 10.2

**Distribution of all new entrants to higher education by gender and
representation of women within each field of study, 1986**

	Males	Females	Total number of students	Total percentage of students	Representation of women
Humanities (including arts)	10.9	21.2	2,720	15.9	63.9
Art and design	2.4	5.7	683	4.0	67.9
Science	12.9	16.6	2,531	14.8	54.2
Agriculture	2.3	0.7	265	1.5	23.0
Technology	40.4	7.6	4,240	24.7	14.7
Medical sciences	3.2	4.1	626	3.7	53.8
Education	2.8	8.1	916	5.3	72.6
Law	1.4	1.8	273	1.6	53.5
Social sciences	1.8	5.9	639	3.7	75.0
Commerce	20.7	24.0	3,817	22.3	51.5
Hotel, catering, tourism	1.2	4.2	449	2.6	76.8
Total percentage	100.0	100.0	—	100.0	100.0
Total number	8,964	8,195	17,159	—	—

Source: Clancy (1989), table 5.

Table 10.3 outlines the ten most popular subjects taken by 'school regular' candidates (i.e. those doing the entire Leaving Certificate for the first time) in 1991. This shows that while languages still command a central place in the curriculum, five of the ten subjects are in the science (mathematics and biology), applied science (home economics, scientific and social) and business (accountancy and business organisation) areas. What the table does not show, however, is the steady downward trend in take-up rates in the arts and humanities subjects, such as history and geography, over the last twenty years. Although 37 per cent are studying geography and 24 per cent studying history now at Leaving Certificate level, 74 per cent of girls and 70 per cent of boys were studying geography in 1972/73, and 42 per cent of girls and 45 per cent of boys were studying history (see table 8.6).

The overall decline in the arts and humanities, the absence of all social-scientific,[1] psychological and philosophical studies and the rise in participation in technical studies certainly indicate that the type of intellectual consciousness being formed in second-level schools and in higher education is radically different from what it was twenty years ago. Pupils are increasingly studying subjects where the focus is on such factors as technical know-how (in the technological subjects), the pursuit and management of profit (in the business subjects), and empirical verification and experimentation with certain natural phenomena (in the natural sciences). While these studies are valuable in themselves, there is little scope in their educational agenda for the development of that socially critical consciousness that comes with philosophical and social-scientific thinking. Ireland remains unique within the EC in having no philosophical or social-scientific subjects in its second-level curriculum. Although there is a suggestion in the Green Paper that some type of social and political analysis should be included in the junior cycle curriculum and that there might be a module in political and social studies at Leaving Certificate (Department of Education, 1992), the failure to make any concrete proposal for change is a serious omission.

Table 10.3

Ten most popular Leaving Certificate subjects, 1991

	Percentage
English	99
Mathematics	99
Irish	92
French	65
Biology	48
Business organisation	41
Geography	37
Home economics	32
Accountancy	27
History	24

Source: National Council for Curriculum and Assessment (1992), 12.

Students are therefore socialised increasingly into a technical mode of consciousness without any complementary education in the social or political sciences or in philosophy. Yet these latter disciplines are crucial for the understanding of the sociopolitical and cultural order. It seems extraordinary that while few would now hire someone to fix a car, do the plumbing, build a bridge or cook a meal without checking their credentials, we are quite prepared to send all our young people out of school to rear children, make marriages, organise community life and run the sociopolitical system of the country without any rigorous education in these fields.

What is lacking in the field of curriculum planning is a clear and articulated vision of the overall purpose of education. It has been argued by a number of critics that this is particularly evident in the section of the Green Paper that deals with the curriculum. Apart from the obvious preoccupation with fostering a spirit of enterprise in schools, there is no clear analysis of what the overall purpose of education is. (See the *Irish Education Decision Maker*, no. 6, autumn 1992, for various comments on this.)

While the influence of the Culliton Report and indeed of the Education Act, 1988, in Britain is very evident in defining the context for the 'broadening of education', what requires further articulation is a clear understanding of the multiple purposes that education serves. As suggested in chapter 11, human ability takes multiple forms, and all of these have relevance for the development of the person and of society.

PATTERNS OF EMPLOYMENT AND EDUCATION
The Labour Force Survey indicates that the services sector is by far the largest of the employment sectors in Ireland (see table 10.4). In addition, the survey shows how the services and industrial sectors have expanded since 1988 while employment opportunities in agriculture have declined in that period. The services sector has been the fastest-growing one, especially in the early 1990s. Nor is this pattern confined to the 1980s. While total employment over the 1970s increased by almost 15,000 a year, the increase in employment in the services sector accounted for 80 per cent of this. In addition, within the services sector the areas that expanded most in the 1970s were the public sector and the insurance and finance area of private services (Breen et al., 1990, 135). The expansion of the services sector is not confined to Ireland: Rassekh and Vaideanu (1987, 52), reporting from a study by Sheppard and Carroll (1980), predict that this trend is likely to continue to the year 2000.

Table 10.4

Distribution of labour force (total in paid work) by sector, 1988 and 1991

	1988		1991	
	Number	Percentage	Number	Percentage
Agriculture	166,000	15.2	154,000	13.7
Industry	300,000	27.5	322,000	28.6
Services	626,000	57.3	649,000	57.7
Total	1,092,000	100.0	1,125,000	100.0

Source: CSO (1992), table 8.

When one analyses labour force statistics in more detail it becomes clear, however, that much of the employment in the services sector is not particularly skilled, in the technical sense (see table 10.5). In the banking and finance area, for example, 11,544 (94.5 per cent) of the 12,214 women employed are clerical workers; 5,483 (54.4 per cent) of the 10,079 men are also in this category (CSO, 1985, table 14). The same kind of pattern holds true in the insurance area (ibid.), although most of the men here—58 per cent—are employed as insurance agents. If one examines Government departments (other than the Department of Defence and Garda Síochána) one also finds a preponderance of clerical workers: while 3,043 (16.8 per cent) of the 18,069 men employed are professional or technical workers, 7,699 (42.6 per cent) are clerical; also, 13,759 (87 per cent) of the 15,882 women employed are clerical workers (ibid., 156–7).

Although a majority of those employed in health and education are professionals, they are predominantly teachers and nurses, not exactly new technical occupations (ibid., 158–61)

Table 10.5

Proportion of all workers who are clerical workers in banking and finance, insurance, and Government departments

	Men			Women		
	Total	Clerical		Total	Clerical	
	Number	Number	Percentage	Number	Number	Percentage
Banking & finance	10,079	5,483	54.4	12,214	11,544	94.5
Insurance	6,864	772	11.2	4,724	4,077	86.3
Government depts*	18,069	7,699	42.6	15,882	13,759	86.6

*Excluding Department of Defence and Garda Síochána
Source: Central Statistics Office (1985), table 14.

While many might argue that the impetus to make education more technically relevant to the labour market has come from the industrial rather than the services sector, an analysis of some employment patterns in selected industries certainly indicates that a large proportion of industrial workers are semi-skilled or unskilled.

First, a study by Walker and Casey (1988) shows that 47 per cent of the 34,890 employees in the electrical and mechanical engineering industries are production operatives, i.e. basically semi-skilled or unskilled workers (table 10.6). In the electrical engineering industry *per se,* 70 per cent are operatives, and 70 per cent of all women in the mechanical and electrical engineering industries are also operatives (ibid.).

These findings concur with earlier research by Wickham (1986), who found that 57.4 per cent of all workers in the electronics industry in 1981 were operatives. Research on the chemical and allied products industry by AnCO (Smyth, 1987) also found that almost half the employees (47 per cent) were operatives (see table 10.7) As was the case with the engineering industry, over a quarter (28 per cent in this case) of the remaining workers were either managers, super-visors, administrative, professional or clerical workers. In both industries it is clear that while technologically skilled people are employed, they comprise only about 25 per cent of the work force in the engineering sector and 18 per cent of those in the chemical industry.

Table 10.6

Distribution of jobs in mechanical and electrical engineering industry

Occupational group	Number	Percentage of overall employment
Manager-supervisors	4,890	14.0
Technologists*	540	1.5
Technicians	1,120	3.0
Professional/admin./clerical/sales	4,010	11.5
Production operatives	16,420	47.0
Other workers	1,220	3.5
Craftspeople	5,060	14.5
Apprentices	1,630	5.0
Total	34,890	100.0

*Engineers and scientists
Source: Walker and Casey (1988).

The studies noted above are about the labour power needs and requirements of two major industries in the 1990s, yet in neither case is there any mention of pre-work education. In fact there is a strong emphasis in both on the need to update skills on an in-service basis. Speaking of the training needs of production operatives in the mechanical and electrical engineering industries, Walker and Casey claim (1988, 3.6, 11) that 'teamwork, flexibility and initiative are becom-ing increasingly important qualifications to employers, i.e. "soft qualifications" as opposed to technical qualifications.' What this data suggests, and what we have already stated above, is that the 'skills problem' in industry, services and agriculture, in so far as it exists, appears to be one indigenous to the specific sectors. What appears to be required is more in-career training and development and not a massive restructuring of second-level education.

CONCLUSION
Education is about the holistic development of the person within the context of society. One of its purposes, but by no means its only or most important one, is to prepare young people for paid employment. In so far as education can serve the needs of the economy its function is to provide a sound general education in the compulsory phase of education. This involves giving young people access to

all forms of knowledge and understanding, including technical knowledge. The latter is no lesser or greater in its significance than other forms of knowledge.

But there are serious unemployment and economic problems in Ireland in the early 1990s, and it is tempting, and even inevitable, to have scapegoats; education is the obvious target, in Ireland as in other countries, when there is an economic crisis. However, by blaming education for our economic problems we are placing responsibility for wealth creation and job creation on a social institution that has no direct control of these areas. This is patently illogical; as Teeling (1992, 9) has pointed out, we must not 'blame education for a failure of politicians, bureaucrats and employers to create wealth and to create jobs.'

Furthermore, the available evidence, as presented in this chapter, suggests that our economic problems are not primarily due to the failure of schools and colleges to provide adequate technical education. In addition, research from abroad on the relationship between education and productivity *per se* actually suggests that, in so far as more education means more productivity, a general rather than a vocational education may be better. International research also points out that providing satisfactory technical education in schools is expensive; neither is such education particularly highly valued by employers.

If there is a lacuna in second-level education it is in the field of the social sciences and indeed philosophy. No philosophy is taught in our schools, neither is there any sociology, political science, media studies, women's studies, psychology, or social policy. Yet these are immensely relevant disciplines, not only for employment but also for people's personal and political lives.

Listening to the discussion about the nature of the curriculum of our schools and colleges, one gets the impression of isolation. There is little recognition, never mind appreciation, of the major international debates about the whole concept of 'disciplines' and about the appropriateness or inappropriateness of the 'boundaries' maintained between disciplines. Traditional disciplinary boundaries are being broken down in many fields, and pluridisciplinary and interdisciplinary approaches are increasingly employed to address social, environmental and other issues. It is important that we come to recognise the significance of these changes for the future development of the education system.

Notes

1. In the NCCA report, *The 1991 Leaving Certificate Examination: a Review of Results* (1992), history, geography, art, music and home economics (general) are all classified as 'social studies' subjects. How this classification is arrived at is not clear. Art, music, history and geography are commonly referred to as arts or humanities subjects; they are certainly not social-scientific subjects in any real sense. None of these subjects make social analysis their primary focus, and it seems misleading to classify them as 'social' studies.

Table 10.7

Occupational profile of chemical and allied products industry, by sector

Numbers/percentage employed	Plastics (health care)		Plastics (other)		Rubber		Misc. chemicals		Pharma-ceuticals		Distribution		Ceramics		Allied products		Total	
	No.	%	No.	%	No.	%	No.	%	No.	%	No.	%	No.	%	No.	%	No.	%
Managers/supervisors	460	10	802	18	345	15	1070	16	786	18	235	20	636	10	100	24	4434	14
Technologists	110	2	41	1	14	—*	237	4	256	6	4	0.5	89	1	3	1	754	2
Technicians	83	1	42	1	40	2	281	4	392	9	45	4	78	2	3	1	964	3
Prod. operatives	3057	66	2701	59	1332	57	2479	37	1617	37	188	16	2607	42	222	55	14203	47
Other workers	206	5	232	5	241	10	725	11	416	9	15	1	329	5	34	8	2198	7
Prof./admin./clerical	401	9	482	11	232	10	1152	17	671	15	668	58	576	9	33	8	4215	14
Designated craftsmen	259	6	203	4	104	5	630	9	227.	5	5	0.5	275	4	9	2	1712	6
Designated apprentices	34	1	23	1	28	1	106	2	40	1	—	-	47	1	2	1	280	1
Non-designated craftsmen	2	-	4	—	2	—	6	—	15	—	-	—	1477	24	—	-	1506	5
Non-designated apprentices	—	-	3	—	-	—	-	—	-	—	-	—	122	2	—	-	125	1
Total/percentage of total	4,612	100	4,533	100	2,338	100	6,686	100	4,420	100	1,160	100	6,236	100	406	100	30,391	100

*less than 1%

Source: Smyth (1987).

References and Further Reading

Archer, M. (1982), 'Introduction: theorising about the expansion of educational systems' in M. Archer (ed.), *The Sociology of Educational Expansion*, Beverly Hills: Sage.

Berg, I. (1970), *Education and Jobs*, New York: Praeger.

Bernstein, B (1971), *Class, Codes and Control* (vol. 1), London: Routledge and Kegan Paul.

Bowles, S., and Gintis, H. (1976), *Schooling in Capitalist America*, London: Routledge and Kegan Paul.

Breen, R., et al. (1990), *Understanding Contemporary Ireland*, Dublin: Gill and Macmillan.

Brook, N., and Oxenham, J. (1984), 'The influence of certification and selection on teaching and learning' in J. Oxenham (ed.), *Education Versus Qualifications*, London: Allen and Unwin.

Central Statistics Office (1985), *Census of Population, 1981—vol. 4*, Dublin: Stationery Office.

Central Statistics Office (1992), *Labour Force Survey, 1991*, Dublin: Stationery Office.

Clancy, P. (1989), 'Gender differences in student participation at third level' in C. Hussey (ed.), *Equal Opportunities for Women in Higher Education*, Dublin: University College.

Collins, R. (1979), *The Credential Society*, New York: Academic Press.

Culliton, J. (1992), *A Time for Change: Industrial Policy for the 1990s*, Dublin: Stationery Office.

Department of Education (1966), *Investment in Education Report*, Dublin: Stationery Office.

Department of Education (1990), *Statistical Report, 1988/89*, Dublin: Stationery Office.

Department of Education (1992), *Education for a Changing World: Green Paper on Education*, Dublin: Stationery Office.

Fagerland, I., and Saha, L. (1983), *Education and National Development*, New York: Pergamon.

Fox, Roger (1991), *The Skills Shortages Survey*, Dublin: FÁS.

Fuller, W. (1972), 'Evaluating alternative combinations of education and training for job preparation', *Nanpoon Journal*, vol. 8, part 1.

Godfrey, M. (1977), 'Education, training, productivity and income: a Kenyan case study', *Comparative Education Review*, vol. 21, no. 1.

Hallak, J., and Caillods, F. (1980), *Education, Work and Employment*, Paris: UNESCO.

Hochschild, A. (1989), *The Second Shift*, Harmondsworth (Middlesex): Penguin.

Hyland, A. (1992), presidential address to Educational Studies Association of Ireland conference, University College, Dublin, 26–28 March 1992.

Irish Education Decision Maker (1992), no. 6 (issue on the Green Paper).

Jackson, P. (1968), *Life in Classrooms*, New York: Holt, Rinehart and Winston.

Jamison, D., and Lau, L. (1982), *Farmer Education and Farm Efficiency*, Washington: World Bank.

Karabel, J., and Halsey, A. (1977), 'Educational research: a review and interpretation' in J. Karabel and A. Halsey (eds.), *Power and Ideology in Education*, London: Oxford University Press.

Lauglo, J., and Lillis, K. (1988), 'Vocationalization in international perspective' in *Vocationalizing Education*, Oxford: Pergamon.

Little, A. (1984), 'Education, earnings and productivity: the eternal triangle' in J. Oxenham (ed.), *Education versus Qualifications?*, London: Allen and Unwin.

Lockhead, M., et al. (1980), 'Farmer education and farmer efficiency: a survey' in T. King (ed.), *Education and Income* (Staff Working Paper no. 402), Washington: World Bank.

Lynch, K. (1989a), 'Solidary labour: its nature and marginalisation', *Sociological Review*, vol. 37, no. 1.

Lynch, K. (1989b), *The Hidden Curriculum: Reproduction in Education: an Appraisal*, London: Falmer.

McCarthy, D. (1992), 'Education and Economic Development', paper presented to Irish Congress of Trade Unions conference 'The Future of Education', Dublin, 5 November 1992.

National Council for Curriculum and Assessment (1992), *The 1991 Leaving Certificate Examination: a Review of Results*, Dublin: NCCA.

Noah, J. and Eckstein, M. (1988), 'Business and industry involvement with education in Britain, France and Germany' in J. Lauglo and K. Lillis (eds.), *Vocationalizing Education*, Oxford: Pergamon.

Organisation for Economic Cooperation and Development (1991), *Reviews of National Policies for Education—Ireland*, Paris: OECD.

Oxenham, J. (1984), 'Employers, jobs and qualifications' in J. Oxenham (ed.), *Education versus Qualifications*, London: Allen and Unwin.

Rassekh, S., and Vaideanu, G. (1987), *The Contents of Education*, Paris: UNESCO.

Roche, F., and Tansey, P. (1992), *Industrial Training in Ireland*, Dublin: Stationery Office.

Schultz, T. (1961), 'Investment in human capital', *American Economic Review*, vol. 51.

Sheppard, C., and Carroll, D. (1980), *Working in the 21st Century*, New York: Wiley.

Smith, S. (1987), *The Chemical and Allied Products Industry in Ireland*, Dublin: AnCO.

Stacey, M. (1981), 'The divisions of labour revisited, or Overcoming the two Adams' in P. Abrams et al., *Practice and Progress: British Sociology, 1950–1980*, London: Allen and Unwin.

Teeling, J. (1992), 'What does business want from the education system?', paper presented to Association of Principals and Vice-Principals of Community and Comprehensive Schools, 19 May 1992.

Walker, G., and Casey, T. (1988), *A Study of the Mechanical and Electrical Engineering Industry in Ireland*, Dublin: FÁS.

Whelan, C., and Whelan, B., *Social Mobility in the Republic of Ireland: a Comparative Perspective* (ESRI paper no. 116), Dublin: Economic and Social Research Institute.

Wickham, J. (1986), 'Industrialisation, work and unemployment' in P. Clancy et al. (eds.), *Ireland: a Sociological Profile,* Dublin: Institute of Public Administration.

Wilms, W. (1988), 'Captured by the American dream: vocational education in the United States' in J. Lauglo and K. Lillis (eds.), *Vocationalizing Education,* Oxford: Pergamon.

World Bank (1988), *Education in Sub-Saharan Africa,* Washington: World Bank.

11

Intelligence, the Curriculum, and Education

It may appear strange to sociologists of education to find a chapter in a book such as this on the issue of intelligence. Defining intelligence or ability is regarded as the business of psychologists rather than sociologists of education. But perhaps this is part of the problem with education, and indeed with many other disciplines, in the first place. Maintenance of boundaries between disciplines requires that you 'keep to your own patch.' But this is precisely what can stunt growth and development both within and between disciplines; by not reading about areas cognitively related to, albeit outside, one's own discipline one is confined by the insights offered in a particular field. By venturing out we can learn, create dialogue, and inform not only our own understanding of phenomena but even that of others.

The issue of intelligence is one that should concern sociologists of education even if it has not yet done so. The reason why it should concern them, and indeed all educationalists, is that what is defined as intelligence or ability has a profound effect on what is defined as legitimate knowledge in schools. If we do not define musical intelligence as being on a par with mathematical or linguistic intelligence, for example, then we will not accord it equal status with these in schools. And so the child whose primary interest or ability is in the musical area will not be given adequate scope to develop his or her musical capabilities. The same holds true for a host of other abilities: if spatial intelligence or personal intelligence are not recognised in schools, a very significant part of the human development is ignored. Furthermore, if one or two forms of ability are given precedence over others, stratification and selection (in the form of streaming and grouping within schools) will be undertaken on the basis of these. The children who do not possess the institutionally recognised abilities will be labelled as 'weak' or lacking ability; no matter how capable they may be in other areas they will become institutionally defined as 'failures'.

What is defined as intelligence or ability is socially determined. Looking at the education system from the outside, however, we see that there are some clearly defined and agreed criteria by which children are assessed and grouped. Examining education from the inside, it is clear that this is not the case. Just as sociologists of education deconstructed 'cultural deficit' and 'cultural deprivation' theories in the early 1970s, so it is necessary for them to deconstruct the absolutist images that exist in the popular, if not in the academic, mind about what constitutes the nature of human ability. Furthermore, it would seem foolhardy in analysing curriculum issues not to recognise the fact that what is included in the curriculum is strongly influenced by philosophical and psychological theories about human intelligence. If one particular form of ability is not recognised or named in psychological theory, then the knowledge related to this ability need not be included in the curriculum, as it lacks legitimacy.

In this chapter, therefore, we take a critical look at the concept of intelligence. We examine the historical background to the testing of intelligence; from there we go on to analyse some of the popular ideological assumptions regarding intelligence and ability. Finally, we briefly outline Howard Gardner's theory of intelligence and assess its significance for approaching intelligence in a more complete and holistic fashion.

IDEOLOGY, SCIENCE, AND TESTING

There are very few people who have passed through the formal education system without being classified in some way on the basis of their perceived or measured intelligence. We constantly grade, classify and treat people differently on the basis of their supposed ability. In many respects our understanding of intelligence is what determines our educational horizon: whether one is involved in education inside or outside the formal system, one's vision of what is educationally possible and desirable is strongly influenced by one's understanding of what constitutes human ability.

In our common-sense discussions about people we frequently talk about their being bright, intelligent, or able, or label them stupid, dull, 'lacking grey matter,' 'thick,' and so on. We tend to label people as either having intelligence or not having it: intelligence is defined as a singular entity, which people possess in varying quantities.

What we rarely realise when using these categories is that these codes or terms for labelling people have their origins in the nineteenth century. Mental testing began first with 'craniometrics' (attempts to measure mental ability in terms of brain size). The early craniometricians were, in a number of cases, avowed eugenicists. They saw mental testing as a tool for establishing the racial superiority of whites over other races. They also tried to show that women were less intelligent than men. They had *a priori* notions about the nature of intelligence that were essentially racist and sexist, and tried to make scientific evidence fit their preconceived prejudices. Morton (in the United States), for example, believed that intelligence varied with brain size. He estimated brain capacity and made inferences about the extent of a person's intelligence from this. Broca (in France) pursued a similar line of argument, although he claimed that the weight of the brain, not its volume, was the crucial factor in determining intelligence (Gould, 1981, 51–3).

Subsequent research has shown that intelligence is in no way related to brain size or weight. As Gould and others have shown, what craniometricians ignored is that brain size and weight are related to body size. Women's smaller heads are a function of their body size, and the same is true for various racial groups. The racist and sexist presuppositions of the craniometricians led them to make false assumptions about the nature of intelligence.

Although the science of psychometrics has moved far from craniometrics, theorists such as Jensen and Eysenck uphold many of the racist assumptions of its discredited predecessors. In recent times, for example, Jensen (1969) has made claims about the low IQ of particular national groups—including the Irish—that are based on spurious scientific evidence. Eysenck (1971; 1981) has made similar claims about social class and race. The following statements display an interesting blend of racism and classism in the work of Eysenck: 'The evidence [on the relationship between social class and IQ] . . . indicates to me that some of this IQ difference is attributable to environmental differences and some of it is attributable to genetic differences among social classes—largely as a result of differential selection of the parent generations for different patterns of ability.'

The assumption here is that low scores on IQ tests are a by-product of the inferior genetic inheritance of working-class people. Similar claims are made about Afro-Americans and the Irish: 'If, as the data suggest, Negroes in the U.S.A. show some genetic influence on their low IQs, this may well be due to the after-effects of some of the crimes committed on their ancestors—just as the Irish show a similar low IQ, probably because of the oppression they suffered for so many centuries at the hands of the English' (1971, 137).

Although it is probably true to say that the views of Jensen and Eysenck have been fundamentally undermined, by the work of Kamin especially (Kamin, 1974; Eysenck and Kamin, 1981), this does not take away from the fact that at least one generation of teachers was reared on their theories of intelligence. Furthermore, their ideas were widely popularised outside the academic world and now form part of the popular culture about intelligence. 'Even amongst relatively well-informed groups in Ireland, such as University students, there lingers the belief that it has been "scientifically" shown that the Irish have an unusually low IQ' (Benson, 1987, 10). The racist and classist connotations of Jensen's and Eysenck's work have fed popular myths about human differences in ability to the detriment of particular racial groups and social classes.

Psychometrics, like all sciences, is far from being wholly objective. As Gould observes,

> science, since people must do it, is a socially embedded activity. It progresses by hunch, vision and intuition. Much of its change through time

does not record a closer approach to absolute truth, but the alteration of cultural contexts that influence it so strongly. Facts are not pure and unsullied bits of information; culture also influences what we see and how we see it. Theories, moreover, are not inexorable inductions from facts; the source of imagination is also strongly cultural. (1983, 21–2)

What Gould is pointing to here, and what is now widely accepted among historians of science, is that scientific thought operates in a complex dialectical mode in relation to culture. On the one hand, science can be and often is a powerful agent for questioning and even overturning prevailing cultural assumptions. Yet it is also culturally embedded, so that its understanding of a particular phenomenon is frequently framed and constrained by the dominant ideologies of that culture. The research that has been undertaken on human intelligence very much reflects this classical tension within science.

That psychometricians have been influenced by powerful political and social interests in their development of measures of intelligence is without doubt. In fact tests have been developed and sought specifically for purposes of social selection. In the United States, for example, standardised tests were developed at various times to select immigrants, and to select those who would be officers during the First World War. In Britain, Cyril Burt played a central role in developing IQ tests for the Eleven Plus examination. These were used throughout Britain for over thirty years to select those who were eligible to attend the more élite grammar schools when there was a shortage of places; they are still used in Northern Ireland.

While the grosser forms of racism and sexism that were originally incorporated in tests of mental abilities have been removed, Paul Henderson (1976) has argued that the definition of intelligence or ability is still determined by the dominant groups in society, namely white middle-class men. What they have tended to do is define attributes in which they themselves excel as the measure of intelligence and ability; in this way they have maintained control over education and the definition of what is educationally relevant and valuable. Control of education has enabled them to control access to a whole array of occupations as well. For example, standardised tests and school examinations are predominantly verbal tests. This means that people who are not verbally proficient cannot be defined as intelligent in the present system. Working-class children in particular have been found to perform more poorly on IQ-type tests than their middle-class counterparts (Kellaghan and Macnamara, 1973). Similar problems have arisen in the United States with Afro-American children (Labov, 1977).

The significance of this for Ireland is that a considerable number of Irish schools use IQ tests to examine and group children, especially the DVRT, AH4, and AH2. The schools that do not use these tend to use other standardised tests, and most of these have never been standardised for Ireland. In a study of the use of standardised tests in a stratified random sample of 100 second-level schools in the Dublin area, MacNamara (1987, 104–11) found that there were 48 different tests in regular use, although 28 of these were not included on the 'approved list' of tests circulated by the Department of Education. The most popular test in use was the Differential Aptitude Test, which was used in 93 per cent of the schools surveyed. The AH4 intelligence test was next in order of popularity, being regularly used in 51 per cent of schools, while the DVRT and AH2 were used in 39 and 35 per cent, respectively. MacNamara also found that standardised tests were widely used to group pupils in first year; in all, 68 per cent of schools surveyed used such tests before allocating pupils to a particular class (ibid., 127). MacNamara's research confirms the findings of Lynch (1989, 84–5).

Although it is fairly well known what the problems with these tests are, it is no harm to summarise the difficulties here. Indeed, a number of the problems associated with IQ-type tests also arise with curriculum-related examinations.

SOME PROBLEMS WITH EXISTING TESTS OF INTELLIGENCE

A major problem with existing tests of intelligence and with examinations generally is that they assess ability in an entirely artificial situation. Tests are given (usually to groups) in a once-off examination-type setting, so there is no scope for assessing functional ability or intelligence. Such tests cannot determine how someone will perform in a real-life situation.

Secondly, the items used in intelligence tests are a set of symbols that are both restricted in range and artificial in form. As noted already, the items are frequently class-biased. Also, they try to isolate cognitive skills and measure them independently of emotional and behavioural responses. Yet such distinctions are meaningless in real-life situations, as there is no behaviour that is either totally affective or totally cognitive (Simon, 1978, 60; Piaget, 1981, 5).

Another problem with all types of examinations and tests is that pupils' performance in them is influenced by the test context: tiredness, stress and lack of interest, for example, can lead to poor performance. Yet no account is taken of these factors when grading tests. Nor is account taken of the effects of coaching, although it is widely known that coaching in an IQ test or a similar test will boost scores (Stott, 1983).

At a more technical level, Lawler (1978) has identified a number of validity problems with IQ and other tests of mental ability. He points out that, because there is no agreement on the nature of intelligence, it is impossible to construct a test to measure various features of it. In other words, it is very difficult to establish the content validity of tests.

While IQ tests are known to be good indicators of pupils' school performance, and some use this to suggest that they have good predictive validity, on closer examination it becomes clear that the predictive power of IQ tests is not really a predictive power at all. One of the reasons why tests are good predictors of school performance is that they were originally standardised with reference to teachers' assessment of pupils' performance. It is no great surprise, therefore, to find that IQ tests predict school performance when they were designed to correlate with it in the first place.

Another factor that is very likely to make tests good predictors is their tendency to create a self-fulfilling prophecy. Those who are labelled weak or unintelligent are generally placed in lower streams or bands in schools. This can have an adverse effect on their performance. The predictive validity of tests, therefore, may be nothing more than a by-product of circumstances and processes that have little to do with the test itself.

Finally, there is the problem of the concurrent validity of these tests. The normal method whereby the concurrent validity of tests is established is by proving that they make the same discriminations as other tests. Proving that a test makes similar discriminations to others raises the question of validity, as it does not explain how the validity of these tests was established in the first place.

In both technical and educational terms, therefore, tests of intelligence pose an array of problems. These problems, combined with the ideological fall-out that comes from using such tests in schools, pose many serious questions for educationalists.

More important than the tests themselves is the mentality that comes with them. A whole ideology has developed in education consequent on the development of testing. It has set serious limits to our educational vision.

POPULAR IDEOLOGICAL ASSUMPTIONS ON THE NATURE OF INTELLIGENCE

There is very little consensus internationally on what constitutes intelligence. However, because intelligence tests have focused to a large extent on measuring people's ability to engage in abstract reasoning, this ability has become equated with intelligence. In other words, intelligence has been equated with the manner in which it is measured. As abstract reasoning ability is measured most often in terms of verbal reasoning, and sometimes in terms of mathematical reasoning, what this means for education is that only two types of intelligence have been formally recognised in any complete sense: logical-mathematical and linguistic (Gardner, 1987). We doubt if anyone has ever heard of a child being labelled 'backward' or 'remedial' because of their poor performance in art or music.

As has been pointed out in chapter 3, there is evidence from the writing of Irish educationalists that many hold a narrow view of what constitutes human ability; they tend to define ability in essentialist terms. This means that intelligence is defined as a given essence that some have and others have not. It is regarded as quantifiable (in terms of an IQ score), fixed over time, and in many cases innate. It is commonly regarded therefore as an inner capacity that precedes and determines the environment: one cannot improve on the 'amount' of it one possesses. Fontes and Kellaghan (1983, 56, 65) found, for example, that Irish teachers tended to hold the view that intelligence was innate much more strongly than their American counterparts. In addition they found Irish adults in general to be less egalitarian and interventionist in their views of intelligence than American adults. There is a common-sense belief, therefore, that intelligence is a clearly defined entity on the basis of which people can be hierarchically ordered.

By defining intelligence in narrow linguistic and logical-mathematical terms, we are in effect ensuring that most children will not be defined as particularly intelligent. This is especially true for those pupils whose non-school background or 'habitus', as Bourdieu (1977) calls it (the system of dispositions due to the unique cultural context of each child), does not encourage the development of the linguistic and mathematical intelligence required in schools.

Secondly, a narrow view of intelligence seriously circumscribes one's vision of what is educationally possible. If an education system defines intelligence as being primarily verbal or mathematical, then it condemns those who do not possess these abilities to a continuous experience of negativity and failure in schools. The implications this has for their self-esteem and sense of identity, both at the time and afterwards, have never been seriously addressed, although they are likely to be profound. It also has serious implications for the curriculum, as forms of knowledge and understanding that do not fit in to the traditional modes are automatically excluded. Equally, by claiming that intelligence is a fixed, measurable entity that individuals possess to a greater or lesser degree, one is claiming that some people are 'less human' than others. In other words one is claiming that some people lack, or possess very little of, what is a defining human characteristic, namely intellectual ability. This is both insulting and demoralising.

It seems likely that the lack of self-esteem, the sense of failure or indifference that is frequently found among those whom schools have failed (Hannan and Shorthall, 1991) is directly related to the negative labelling that ensues from this kind of thinking. Schools negatively label and disqualify large groups of students each year. Those who pass at minimal levels may also experience a sense of failure and relative disqualification. It is salutary to recall at this point that while we may have very high retention rates in education, we also have many serious problems: in the Leaving Certificate examination of 1991, 20 per cent of those taking the ordinary-level subjects received grade E or lower in thirteen out of thirty-two subjects (NCCA, 1992, 17). In addition, almost a quarter (23 per cent) of those sitting the full examination for the first time took all their subjects at ordinary level, with almost half (46 per cent) taking no more than two subjects at higher level (ibid., 12). O'Neill's research (1992) also suggests that in Dublin working-class areas the retention rates are far lower than the national average. The result for our society is a high level of alienation and disaffection from education, and an enormous waste of human potential.

A related problem is that those who are labelled slow, weak, dull, stupid and so forth are socialised into a culture of failure and self-blame. Their failure is attributed to an intrinsic characteristic within themselves (lack of ability), and they feel it is the result of a personal weakness or fault on their part. They learn implicitly that the structures of society or of education are not at fault, rather it is the individual who is to blame. Failure in school is construed as a problem of individual incapacity: we blame the victim for the inadequacy of the system, and the victim in turn internalises a sense of personal failure through the continuous experience of being labelled. *NB*

The implications of our narrow essentialist definition of intelligence go beyond the individual, however. The notion of fixed ability or intelligence also provides convenient justification for practices such as streaming and banding in schools. While schools that stream or group by ability (including primary schools)[1] may never use IQ-type tests as such, the very fact that these tests exist and are respected provides an adequate ideological justification for ability grouping. They can be called into play should the need arise. The ideology of fixed intelligence therefore makes ability grouping appear natural, inevitable, and desirable (Blum, 1978).

Because the present understanding of ability is premised on the assumption that the individual is largely accountable for his or her own failure, this helps to support the wider view in society that the individual is accountable for his or her own success or failure in other walks of life as well. What this ignores is the structural fact that lack of ability is a by-product of social inequality and not an intrinsic characteristic of individuals. It also fosters a social climate in which inequalities of all kinds can be justified. After all, if one argues that some people are inherently unintelligent, this provides justification (in a meritocratic order where IQ + effort = merit) for not rewarding (or indeed not paying) them as highly as others. In effect, the essentialist, narrow interpretation of ability that pervades our thinking provides society with the ideological justification for giving people very low pay or no pay: if ability and credentials (and credentials largely represent ability in its institutionalised and legitimised form) are theoretically the determinants of one's level of income, then those with no evident 'ability' do not deserve to be rewarded.

Within education, the ideology of fixed ability also exonerates us as teachers and educators. It exonerates politicians as well, as it places the responsibility for continued working-class underachievement in schools on the pupils themselves.

WHAT IS THE ALTERNATIVE?

What is being suggested here is that the popular understanding of intelligence is based on some very questionable and limiting assumptions. We would suggest that there is now considerable evidence for the following assertions:

(1) Intelligence is not a singular entity, rather it takes multiple forms. Most forms of intelligence are not, however, given full recognition within the formal education system (Gardner, 1983).

(2) Intelligence cannot be quantified in simple numerical terms, as is implied by IQ-related tests. IQ scores and numerical scores on similar standardised tests are in fact educationally misleading, as they label and classify people in terms of a normal distribution scale that appears scientific and objective, whereas the notion that intelligence is normally distributed in the population (in the same way as height or weight, for example) is not really scientifically tenable. In the sphere of intelligence the normal distribution scale is an artefact of test construction, not an empirical statement about the population. Tests are constructed in such a way that they will give a normal distribution of scores; thus, only very small numbers will score highly and lowly on these tests, with the bulk falling in between. The only basis for the normality assumption seems to be the analogy drawn with the distribution of physical characteristics. This is, however, a dangerous proceeding, 'since the brain and the higher nervous system represent a qualitatively different organisation of matter, about whose structures and functioning extremely little is yet known' (Simon, 1978, 65).

(3) Intelligence is best seen as a quality of human behaviour—not a mental quantity. What will be defined as intelligence in a society will vary somewhat between cultures and different historical epochs. In other words, intelligence is context-specific. One may be intelligent in one sphere of activity but not in another, or in one particular cultural context and not in another (Gardner, 1983).

(4) Intelligence is the product of experience. To develop intelligence one needs to be given the opportunity to do so.

THE IMPLICATIONS OF GARDNER'S WORK

Educationalists have been strongly influenced by the work of IQ and Piagetian theorists and, more recently, by information processing theory in their approach to human intelligence. While the weaknesses of the IQ approach are fairly well known, the weaknesses of the two other approaches are less well documented. Yet all three are limited by the fact that they focus 'on a certain logical or linguistic problem solving; all ignore biology; all fail to come to grips with higher levels of creativity; and all are insensitive to the range of roles highlighted in human society' (Gardner, 1983, 24).

Gardner has noted that although much of contemporary education places a premium on logical-mathematical and linguistic intelligence, these are only two among at least seven discrete forms. What he attempts to do therefore is to present a more dynamic view of intelligence, one that is not focused on a narrow interpretation of intellectual capacity. Drawing from research in anthropology and in the biological and neurological sciences, he points out that cognitive accomplishment can occur in a range of domains, and that there are at least seven distinct intelligences: linguistic, logical-mathematical, spatial, intrapersonal, interpersonal, bodily-kinesthetic, and musical. Within each of these cognitive domains one can identify a number of skills or competences which, combined, constitute intelligence within the given sphere.

Linguistic competence is the intelligence that seems most widely shared across the human species. In the linguistic sphere, intelligence involves skills in, and sensitivity to, the semantics of the language (the precise meaning of words); it also involves sensitivity to phonology (the sounds of words and their musical interactions with one another), a mastery of syntax (the rules governing the ordering of words), and a sensitivity to the pragmatics of speech (its functions in convincing, stimulating, conveying information, etc.) (ibid., 73–9).

Musical intelligence, on the other hand, involves sensitivity to and expertise in pitch, rhythm, and timbre (the characteristic qualities of a tone) (ibid., 104). By contrast with linguistic intelligence, musical intelligence is not strongly developed in all cultures. While it is very highly prized in societies such as the Anang in Nigeria, and to a lesser degree in other countries, such as Hungary and Japan, it plays a rather peripheral role in the formal education of children in Britain and Ireland.

In contrast to musical and linguistic intelligence, *logical-mathematical intelligence* does not have its origins in the auditory-oral sphere. Instead it can be traced to a confrontation with the world of objects. For it is in confronting objects, in ordering and reordering them and in assessing their quantity, that the young child gains her or his initial and most fundamental knowledge about the logical-mathematical realm. The core operations of this form of intelligence include speed and power of abstraction and the ability to handle skilfully long chains of reasoning (ibid., 128–42).

Gardner claims that what is central to *spatial intelligence* is the capacity to perceive the visual world accurately, to perform transformations and modifications on one's initial perceptions, and to be able to re-create aspects of one's visual experience, even in the absence of relevant physical stimuli (ibid., 173). He points out that just as deaf people develop linguistic intelligence, so can those who are blind develop spatial intelligence. Spatial intelligence is a central intelligence in the arts and in occupations such as navigation, architecture, and engineering.

Bodily-kinesthetic intelligence is the fifth type of intelligence identified by Gardner. A central characteristic of this intelligence is the ability to use one's body in highly differentiated and skilled ways for expressive as well as instrumental purposes (ibid., 207). The skills required in dancing, mime, acting, athletics, typing and the use of tools are all obvious cases where such intelligence is involved. Gardner notes that psychologists have recently discerned and stressed a close link between the use of the body and the deployment of other cognitive powers. Because skilled body use has a cognitive as well as a neurophysiological basis, one must dispense with the simple western legacy that 'mental' and 'physical' skills are completely divorced from each other.

Finally, Gardner suggests that there are two personal intelligences. *Intra- personal intelligence* involves a person's examination and knowledge of his or her own feelings, motivation, and behaviour. *Interpersonal intelligence* involves an ability to read and understand the intentions and desires of others. Those who are highly skilled interpersonally can use the understanding of others to help or influence others (ibid., 240–1). Successful political leaders, skilled teachers, therapists and counsellors all have highly developed forms of interpersonal intelligence. Unlike a number of the other intelligences identified above, the personal intelligences are intimately interrelated: knowledge of one's own person is heavily dependent on one's ability to apply lessons learnt from the observation of others, while knowledge of others draws heavily on the internal discriminations the individual routinely makes (ibid.). Like bodily-kinesthetic intelligence, and perhaps to an even greater degree, the personal intelligences have largely been ignored by students of cognition. Yet these forms of knowledge are of tremendous importance in many if not all societies (ibid., 242).

What is interesting about Gardner's interpretation of intelligence is that he takes social contexts into account in defining it: an intelligence is something that is useful and important, at least in certain cultural settings. The seven intelligences identified above all centre around distinct human problems to be resolved. They represent a set of problem-solving skills within a given field.

Gardner does not claim that his list of intelligences is irrefutable or universally accepted; he admits that much remains to be learnt about the nature of intelligences. What he does show is that the seven competences identified above meet the necessary conditions for being defined as intelligence. Firstly, they all involve some kind of problem-solving. Secondly, evidence from neuropsychology shows how the mental faculties involved in each intelligence are separate and discrete. There is therefore a real material basis (in the brain) for the different intelligences. In addition, there is considerable evidence for variability in competence in the different fields of intelligence; there is evidence that each of them has a distinct developmental history and that they are susceptible to encoding in a symbol system.

The purpose of outlining Gardner's basic theoretical presuppositions about intelligence here is to highlight the lack of debate about forms of human ability outside those conventionally recognised in schools.

While it is undoubtedly true that the multiple intelligences (MI) theory is one that requires further verification through experiment, it is also true that it has drawn already from a vast survey of research in a range of independent traditions, including neurology, developmental psychology, psychometrics, anthropology, and evolutionary theory. It is based to a considerable extent on empirical research findings, albeit findings that do not emanate only from psychology.

A further criticism that could be made of MI theory is that it has yet to provide an explanation of how each intelligence works. This is a difficult task, but it is one that is currently being researched. As Walters and Gardner observe (1986, 177), the obvious difficulty in establishing ways of measuring and assessing personal intelligences 'does not excuse our ignoring these forms of knowing, a practice that has been the rule in mainstream psychology in the last several decades.'

No doubt many of those who are familiar with psychological theory would claim that MI theory ignores the great volume of psychometric literature that suggests that humans differ from each other in general intelligence. The conventional claim is that general intelligence (labelled 'g') can be reliably measured through the statistical analysis of test scores. Gardner and his colleagues do not doubt the existence of the high statistical correlations that can be found between test scores; what they point out, however, is that the evidence for 'g' is almost entirely provided by tests of linguistic and logical intelligence. These are generally pencil-and-paper tests, which tell us little about how someone will perform outside school.

> If reliable tests could be constructed for different intelligences, and these tests used the materials of the domain being measured, we believe that the correlations responsible for g would greatly diminish. Tests of musical intelligence would examine the individual's ability to analyse a work of music or to create one, not simply to compare two single tones on the basis of relative pitch. We need tests of spatial ability that involve finding one's way around, not merely giving multiple choice responses to depictions of a geometric form as depicted from different visual angles. (ibid.)

CONCLUSION

What this chapter has attempted to show is that many of our deeply held beliefs about intelligence are based on a series of limited and questionable theoretical assumptions. The implications of this for education are extremely serious. It means that our vision of what is both educationally possible and desirable has been, and continues to be, seriously circumscribed by the narrowness of our view of intelligence and human ability. Operating with a one-dimensional view of the mind, we have developed a corresponding view of school: a uniform view. This is the view that finds expression in the narrow conceptualisation of the 'core curriculum'. It is assumed that there is a fixed body of knowledge and skill that everyone should possess or experience and that there are 'subjects' that everyone must study, regardless of their disposition or interest. While one can see and understand the rationale for this in a complex society requiring a range of skills in different fields, it must be said that much of the empirical research on education shows that there is considerable dissatisfaction with education as it stands, even if it is judged by the way in which it prepares people for society (Hannan and Shorthall, 1991).

An equally valid perspective on education is one that emphasises the individuality and interest of the student. The pluralistic view of the mind that Gardner proposes would, if incorporated in the framing of educational experience, allow schools to recognise differences in cognitive strengths and contrasting cognitive styles (Gardner, 1987).

At present formal education takes place almost exclusively in schools. Within schools, especially at second level, students are assessed in most subject areas in written examinations. While some subjects (including art, construction studies, and engineering) have practical tests, and others (modern languages) now have oral and aural assessments, the primary emphasis is still on encoding knowledge through the use of linguistic symbols (history, geography, languages, etc.). When pure linguistic skill is not the medium for expressing knowledge, logical-mathematical skills predominate, as in the sciences, applied sciences, and mathematics. Only one art subject exists to assess spatial intelligence (although technical drawing also involves the use of spatial intelligence), and one music subject to assess musical competence. These subjects are not offered, however, in a wide range of second-level schools.

While certain aspects of bodily-kinesthetic intelligence are given recognition in physical education, home economics, woodwork, and metalwork, others (e.g. drama, dancing, and mime) are not addressed in any systematic or universal fashion. As is the case with spatial and musical intelligence, so it is with bodily-kinesthetic intelligence: the opportunity to develop one's intelligence in this sphere depends greatly on the type of school attended. Many schools do not offer the examinable subjects through which these skills gain recognition (Department of Education, 1991, tables 14.5, 14.9).

Scope for the development of the personal intelligences is probably what is most conspicuously lacking from our schools. While Gardner claims that schools do allow pupils to develop intrapersonal intelligence, in so far as schooling requires one to reflect on, analyse and consciously evaluate one's own progress, such incidental introspection hardly constitutes the systematic development of intrapersonal intelligence.

Certainly it is clear that schools offer no systematic forum for the development of interpersonal competence, although in many service occupations (including management, marketing, teaching, policing, social work, and banking) interpersonal intelligence can be the key to success. How to develop interpersonal intelligence is by no means a simple matter. Much research and experimentation needs to be undertaken to find our way forward. The daunting nature of the task involved, however, does not justify abandoning it.

The value of Gardner's work is that it presents education with a pluralist rather than a singular view of the mind, 'recognising many discrete facets of cognition, acknowledging that people have different cognitive strengths and contrasting cognitive styles' (Gardner, 1987, 188). It is a view that is undoubtedly at variance with the traditional western Platonic view of human ability. In this tradition, language and mathematical logic are placed on a pedestal and all other abilities are assessed according to their degree of adherence to the cognitive norms emanating from them. Gardner's work, based as it is on the analysis of extensive cross-disciplinary research, offers us a fresh and inspiring framework in which to develop educational policies. While much empirical research needs to be undertaken to move the theory from a state where it identifies and describes faculties to where the detailed structuring and functioning of the various intelligences is identified—something Gardner himself admits (Walters and Gardner, 1986)—this does not take away from either its biological validity or its educational utility.

For educationalists with an interest in equality, Gardner's theory offers a new insight into how the system persistently produces failure. It shows that in terms of curriculum and syllabus our schools are biased in favour of those schooled in the canons of mathematical logic and practised in the field of language. It challenges us, therefore, to think of new ways in which we can recognise all human intelligences and not just those that have gained legitimacy because they accord with the principles of western Platonic thought.

Because it challenges us to re-examine our approach to intelligence, this theory has obvious implications for the education of all types of children, including those who may have some form of mental disability. If we come to recognise the discrete nature of human intelligence, then clearly all-encompassing labels such as 'the mentally handicapped' are inappropriate categories for educational reference. A child may be handicapped in one field, such as in their language or communication skills, but this does not mean that that child lacks other forms of intelligence, such as musical or spatial abilities. Educationalists will have to set about identifying the unique and diverse talents of all children. In the final analysis there is no such thing as a stupid child.

Notes

1. Within-class ability grouping in primary schools is, for some reason, rarely discussed in Ireland in the context of debates about ability grouping, although there is extensive empirical research from other countries showing that it is as problematic as streaming in its adverse effects on children who, for whatever reason, end up in the lowest reading group or ability group within a given class (Eder, 1981; 1982; Hallinan and Sorenson, 1983; 1985; 1986; see also chapter 12).

References and Further Reading

Benson, C. (1987), 'Ireland's low IQ: a critique of the myth', *Irish Journal of Psychology*, vol. 8, no. 1.

Blum, J. (1978), *Pseudoscience and Mental Ability*, New York: Monthly Review Press.

Bourdieu, P., and Passeron, J. (1977), *Reproduction in Education, Society and Culture*, London: Sage.

Department of Education (1991), *Statistical Report, 1989/90*, Dublin: Stationery Office.

Eder, D. (1981), 'Ability grouping as a self-fulfilling prophecy: a microscopic analysis of teacher-student interaction', *Sociology of Education*, vol. 54, no. 3.

Eder, D. (1982), 'Differences in communicative styles across ability groups' in L. Wilkinson, *Communicating in the Classroom*, New York: Praeger.

Eysenck, H. (1971), *The IQ Argument*, Illinois: Open Court.

Eysenck, H., and Kamin, L. (1981), *Intelligence and the Battle for the Mind*, London: Macmillan.

Fontes, P., Kellaghan, T., et al. (1983), 'Opinions of the Irish public on intelligence', *Irish Journal of Education*, vol. 18, no. 2.

Gardner, H. (1983), *Frames of Mind: the Theory of Multiple Intelligences*, London: Paladin.

Gardner, H. (1987), 'Beyond IQ: education and human development', *Harvard Educational Review*, vol. 57, no. 2.

Gould, S. (1981), *The Mismeasure of Man*, Harmondsworth (Middlesex): Penguin.

Hallinan, M. (1984), 'Summary and implications' in P. Peterson et al. (eds.), *The Social Context of Instruction*, Florida: Academic Press.

Hallinan, M., and Sorenson, A. (1983), 'The formation and stability of instructional groups', *American Sociological Review*, vol. 48, no. 6.

Hallinan, M., and Sorenson, A. (1985), 'Class size, ability group size, and student achievement', *American Journal of Education*, vol. 94.

Hallinan, M., and Sorenson, A. (1986), 'Effects of ability grouping on growth in achievement', *American Education Research Journal*, vol. 23.

Hannan, D., and Shorthall, S. (1991), *The Quality of Their Education* (ESRI paper no. 153), Dublin: Economic and Social Research Institute.

Henderson, P. (1976), 'Class structure and the concept of intelligence' in R. Dale (ed.), *Schooling and Capitalism*, London: Routledge and Kegan Paul.

Jensen, A. (1969), 'How much can we boost IQ and scholastic achievement?', *Harvard Educational Review*, vol. 39.

Kamin, L. (1974), *The Science and Politics of IQ*, Potomac, Maryland: Erlbaum.

Kellaghan, L., and Macnamara, J. (1972), 'Family correlations of verbal reasoning ability', *Developmental Psychology*, vol. 7, no. 1.

Labov, W. (1977), *Language in the Inner City: Studies in the Black English Vernacular*, Oxford: Blackwell.

Lawler, J. (1978), *IQ, Heritability and Racism*, New York: International Publishers.

Lynch, K. (1987), 'Dominant ideologies in Irish educational thought: consensualism, essentialism and meritocratic individualism', *Economic and Social Review*, vol. 18, no. 2.

Lynch, K. (1989), *The Hidden Curriculum: Reproduction in Education: a Reappraisal*, London: Falmer.

MacNamara, J. (1987), 'Standardised tests in second-level education' (MA thesis, Education Department, University College, Dublin).

O'Neill, C. (1992), *Telling It Like It Is*, Dublin: Combat Poverty Agency.

Piaget, J. (1981), *Intelligence and Affectivity*, California: Annual Reviews.

Simon, B. (1978), *Intelligence, Psychology and Education* (second edition), London: Lawrence and Wishart.

Stott, D. (1983), *Issues in the Intelligence Debate*, Oxford: NFER.

Walters, J., and Gardner, H. (1986), 'The theory of multiple intelligences: some issues and answers' in R. Sternberg and R. Wagner (eds.), *Practical Intelligence*, Cambridge: Cambridge University Press.

12

Ability Grouping in Schools: Patterns and Implications

In recent times there has been increasing debate about the effectiveness and implications of different forms of ability grouping in Irish schools. This interest has been sharpened as a result of the changes that have taken place in the postprimary system over the last decade and those that are expected in the 1990s. As we have indicated in chapter 1, increasing participation rates and the pressure to acquire points for third-level entrance have meant that many schools now have to deal with pupils of a more diverse ability range than ever before, especially at senior cycle. At junior cycle a falling population and declining enrolments have resulted in some schools drawing on sections of the pupil population from which they have not drawn in the past. As a result many schools are now re-evaluating their internal structure and organisation as well as their relationship with other schools in their localities.

It is useful, therefore, to give some detailed consideration to the different methods used to group children in schools. In this chapter we examine the principal types of grouping to be found in Irish schools. Since the debates both in Ireland and elsewhere have focused on streaming, we pay particular attention to the incidence and implications of this form of organisation. We also examine the impact of teachers' attitudes. The research and its implications are discussed in relation to primary as well as to second-level schools.

Different Forms of Ability Grouping: Second-Level Education
There are four principal forms of ability grouping commonly in use in second-level schools. These are streaming, banding, setting, and mixed-ability, although some schools may use a combination of methods. We now look at each of these in turn.

STREAMING
This involves classifying children of the same or similar age into two or more groups on the basis of some measure of ability, normally involving one or more of the following: performance on a school-based attainment test;

performance on an external intelligence and/or attainment test; and the teacher's personal and professional assessment (Reid, 1986, 152). These groups are then used as the teaching unit for all or most subjects, the rate of progress and the curriculum often being varied according to the ability of the group or class. A system of this kind, especially in a school with a selected intake, is often very homogeneous.

BANDING

Some large schools, mainly community and comprehensive schools with six to seven class intakes in first year, divide pupils into very broad bands of ability range—for example above average, average, and below average. This can result in a number of classes composed of students from each band. This is in effect a loose form of streaming. Alternatively, this type of division can be the basis for mixed-ability groupings, with each class containing pupils from each band.

SETTING

This is the system of grouping pupils by ability for individual subjects, and it is usually combined with a heterogeneous form of grouping such as mixed-ability. The most commonly 'set' subjects are mathematics, English, and other languages; children are then in mixed-ability groupings for all other subjects. This is, in theory at least, a very flexible system, and it is possible for a child to be, for example, in the bottom set for English and the top set for mathematics, according to aptitude. However, setting is sometimes combined with streaming—especially for subjects such as languages and mathematics. Most postprimary schools 'set' their students at senior cycle, even though the system is not usually called 'setting': it is simply called dividing pupils into honours and pass classes.

MIXED-ABILITY

This is a heterogeneous form of grouping. It can be achieved in two ways: (*a*) indirectly or at random, i.e. by placing children into random groupings, perhaps alphabetically or in some other arbitrary way, and (*b*) directly, i.e. by forming parallel groups through first ascertaining the ability or attainment of the age group and then ensuring that each class has representative numbers across the range (ibid). Children are then taught in these heterogeneous class groupings for all subjects.

How Widespread is Streaming?

There has been one major study of ability grouping in postprimary schools in the 1980s, carried out by Hannan and Boyle (1987). Practice and procedures in relation to ability grouping were also examined by Lynch (1989). Hannan and

Boyle's study indicated that of the total number of postprimary schools only about one-fifth had mixed-ability classes at junior cycle; the great majority streamed or banded their intake. The rigidity of the streaming varied, however. Similar findings emerge from Lynch's study, which puts the figure for streaming or banding at 75 per cent; this means that streaming or banding existed for some but not all classes in three-quarters of all schools.

Both studies are agreed that around 40 per cent of second-level schools had relatively rigid streaming at Intermediate (now Junior) Certificate level. Almost 40 per cent of schools allocated children to honours and pass levels. Very rigid streaming was almost universally associated with rigid subject distinctions and with little subject choice or teacher involvement in that choice. Many schools restricted the availability of subjects to pupils in the lower streams or bands (Hannan and Boyle, 1987, 103–5).

At the time that Hannan and Boyle's study and Lynch's study were undertaken (both in the early 1980s), boys' secondary schools and schools with large cohorts of working-class or lower middle-class pupils were far more likely than others to stream and differentiate the curriculum. Vocational schools also had a strong tradition of streaming at that time. Most community and comprehensive schools—largely by explicit policy—do not stream as such but almost universally band their wider ability intake when large enough. It is boys' secondary schools, especially those that cater for a lower middle-class, small farmer or upper working-class clientele and that select or sponsor a proportion of their more able pupils for upward social mobility, that have the most rigid streaming. At the other extreme, upper middle-class secondary schools, especially girls' secondary schools, are least likely to stream (Hannan and Boyle, 1987, 169; Lynch, 1988). These studies argue that the cultural consolidation of the advantages of an upper middle-class background is being achieved by a highly individualised schooling in which a great deal of autonomy is allowed or developed at the level of the individual pupil.

Much of the discussion in this chapter will relate to the question of streaming. The reason we focus on this is that one of the key debates relating to ability grouping centres on whether classes should be homogeneous (streamed) or heterogeneous (mixed-ability). The fact that streaming is still widely practised in second-level schools also makes it imperative to discuss the issue. Although there is very little research on banding (and no major study in Ireland) many of the issues that arise in relation to streaming also arise in relation to banding. Some would argue, indeed, that banding is the streaming system used in large schools.

Why Do Schools Stream and Band?
It is usually asserted that schools stream because they believe strongly that it is in the interests of the students to do so. For example, it may be argued that the less able pupils would suffer in mixed-ability classes because of constant compar-

isons with higher-performing pupils; at the same time, high-ability students would be held back by being grouped with slow learners. Overall, then, it has been argued by its supporters that streaming leads to better outcomes for most students, particularly those at the extremes (Hannan and Boyle, 1987). Another factor relates to pupil intake. This is affected by whether schools can select at entry or not. In Lynch's study it was found that 41 per cent of secondary schools engaged in some form of selection at entry (though a minority of these made use of academic-type procedures). Public sector (i.e. vocational, community and comprehensive) schools could not select. It was found that the secondary schools that selected at entry were the least likely of all school types to have rigid streaming. It appears, therefore, that when some schools are allowed to select while others are not, those that cannot select are under much greater pressure to stream or band (Lynch, 1988).

However, it must be noted that there is a policy issue at stake here. Boys' secondary schools engage in more streaming than girls' secondary schools, yet both are equally entitled to select at entry. Indeed, given the fact that a larger cohort of the female population attends girls' secondary than attends boys' secondary schools, girls' schools are, if anything, more heterogeneous in their intake. Yet they do not stream to the same extent as boys' schools. This implies that those who administer girls' schools have adopted a different policy on streaming, independent of the nature of their intake. Another possible, and related, explanation for the differences is that girls' schools do not see their role as that of 'social mobility agent' for the selection of a female élite, whereas there is a strong tradition of this in boys' schools.

The reasoning used by supporters of streaming is based on the concept that the child's ability is measurable and remains constant over time. This in turn can be associated with two simple beliefs: (*a*) that since children vary in their ability (however this is defined), they learn best in classes of children with similar ability, and (*b*) that classes are more easily or better taught when they are homogeneous (Reid, 1986, 154).

These concepts and beliefs have been the subject of considerable debate and controversy, both in Ireland and elsewhere. In chapter 11 we have examined issues arising from debates on intelligence. We will now examine issues arising from homogeneous grouping (i.e. streaming).

The Implications of Streaming

Much of the research on streaming summarised here has been carried out in Britain, as streaming has been commonly practised there and was a controversial issue for some time. The research is of relevance to the Irish situation, however, since streaming is, as we have seen, a common form of organisation at second level, especially in junior cycle. We shall also draw on the Irish research by Hannan and Boyle and by Lynch.

Studies in Britain have been carried out at both primary and second levels, as until relatively recently between-class streaming as well as within-class grouping was common at both primary and second level. In fact what is probably the most comprehensive study of streaming was done at primary level: Barker Lunn's *Streaming in the Primary School* (1970), a study of over five thousand children in more than seventy schools, half streamed, half unstreamed. At second level the classic studies include Hargreaves's *Social Relations in a Secondary School* (1967) and Lacey's *Hightown Grammar* (1970). We also draw on more recent research in Britain and elsewhere. We will examine the implications of streaming under a number of headings: the composition of different streams, the effects of streaming, and the attitudes of teachers.

The Composition of Different Streams
Given the rationale of streaming, one would expect different streams to be differentiated in terms of ability. Douglas (1964), in his longitudinal study of primary children, showed that pupils in the upper streams of two-stream primary schools had higher average scores on standardised attainment tests than children in lower streams (55 as opposed to 44). Not surprising, it might be said; however, there was considerable overlap in individual scores between the two groups. Similarly, Barker Lunn (1970) found that 15 per cent of the children in her sample were in the wrong streams on the basis of their attainment scores. Hallinan (1987) also found that, once assigned to ability groups, children tended to remain in them.

These findings could mean either that the measurement of ability was not particularly accurate, or that factors other than ability were being taken into account—or perhaps a combination of both. Indeed, psychologists claim only 90 per cent accuracy in even the best test (Reid, 1986); further, the averaging out of ability by use of IQ or VRQ tests to produce lists of children in ability order may disguise or enhance pupils' weaknesses on abilities.

Social class also plays a part. Douglas (1964), for example, found 11 per cent more middle-class children in upper streams and 26 per cent fewer in lower streams than would be expected from their distribution in the population. The findings of other studies also mirror this. Barker Lunn (1970) found a tendency for A streams to comprise an undue proportion of middle-class and upper working-class children. Lower streams, by contrast, had an undue percentage of children from lower socio-economic backgrounds. Middle-class pupils have also been found to be overrepresented at second level in the upper streams—by Hargreaves (1967) in secondary modern schools, by Lacey (1970) in grammar schools, and more recently by Ball (1981) in comprehensive schools. Thus, research shows that while teachers believe the system of allocation to be fair, working-class and minority pupils are overrepresented in lower streams (Troyna, 1978; Oakes, 1985; Hallinan, 1987).

There is no national study in Ireland of the class composition of different streams. What the Hannan and Boyle (1987) study does show is that working-class children (especially boys) are more likely to be attending schools that are highly streamed. One small case study undertaken in a large community school, however, confirms the findings elsewhere. O'Kelly (1986) found that pupils from unskilled manual and semi-skilled manual working-class backgrounds were significantly more likely to be found in the lowest streams and, conversely, that those from professional backgrounds were significantly more likely to be in the top stream. He also found, as with the research cited above, that there was very little mobility between streams. Organisational difficulties (e.g. class sizes), curriculum choices (students in low streams may not have taken the same courses in a subject, or the same subjects, as top streams) and friendship patterns are among the known factors foreclosing the possibility of movement upwards between streams.

The research, therefore, indicates that ability grouping involves social as well as academic differentiation. There is evidence to suggest that teachers, consciously or unconsciously, discriminate among pupils according to social criteria. However, there is also evidence that differentiation continues even where schools are in principle organised along mixed-ability lines; Ball (1981), for example, found this in his study of 'Beachside Comprehensive School', where he suggests that mixed-ability groupings appear to condense and reproduce the stratification previously found in banded classes. Similar processes have been found in other studies of primary (Sharp and Green, 1975) and postprimary classrooms (see, for example, Keddie, 1971).

The Effects of Streaming
Broadly speaking, we can divide the effects of streaming into two types: (*a*) learning or academic effects, and (*b*) social and emotional effects.

LEARNING EFFECTS
In terms of cognitive development or achievement gains, there is no consistent evidence that streaming (or 'tracking', as it is generally called in North America), combined with differential instructional processes, has an overall advantage for pupils (Hannan and Boyle, 1987). There is a good deal of evidence to show that ability grouping is a self-fulfilling prophecy: that pupils tend to perform at the expected level for their ability group when streamed. Douglas (1964), in his longitudinal study of primary school children, showed that children in upper streams improved their attainment test scores between the ages of eight and eleven, the less able improving most. Between the same ages, the scores of children in lower streams deteriorated, those of the most able among them deteriorating most, the net result being a larger difference between the two streams at the end than the beginning.

Similar findings are documented by Kerckhoff (1986), who points out that pupils in low-ability groups lose ground and pupils in high-ability groups increase their average performance level beyond that exhibited by comparable students in ungrouped settings.

Barker Lunn's study (1970) comparing streamed and non-streamed schools showed no difference in the average academic performance of boys and girls of comparable ability and social class. Nevertheless, she points out that approximately 15 per cent of the children were in the wrong stream. Furthermore, three-quarters of these remained in the wrong stream, although in principle movement between streams was possible. Lynch's study of Irish postprimary schools (1989) revealed a similar lack of mobility between streams. Children remaining in too high a stream tended to improve and those in too low a stream to deteriorate in academic performance (Barker Lunn, 1970). These studies also, then, appear to support the notion of the self-fulfilling prophecy.

In their study of streaming in the Irish postprimary system, Hannan and Boyle (1987, xv, 159) report that increasing levels of rigidity and differentiation in the schooling process have no discernible positive effects on average attainment levels, as judged from the experiences of the total entry cohort (i.e. the group of students who enter a school at the same time). The evidence indeed suggests a slight negative effect. This negative effect is evident in three areas: (*a*) increased drop-out rates, (*b*) a lowering of the average attainment levels of the total entry cohort, and (*c*) a reduction in the proportion going on to university.

These negative effects are not statistically significant; increasing differentiation, however, does have a very pronounced polarisation effect on pupils' attainment levels. It appears that increased attainments by children in highly placed streams are being bought at the cost of lower attainments by children in lower streams or bands in most streamed or highly 'banded' schools. On average, therefore, the overall effect is negative (ibid.).

While Hannan and Boyle argue that, in general, high achievements for a small élite were 'paid for' by the very poor attainments of the low achievers, they also suggest that what schools actually do with, or how well they use, streaming or curricular differentiation practices is almost as important as the choice of one form of streaming or mixed ability rather than another. The goals and objectives actively pursued by schools and the organisational ethos and management effectiveness of schools are also important 'choices'. They cite the example of one of their sample schools where streaming was chosen to maximise the achievement of the lower-ability group. Maximum teaching effort was directed to these pupils in the form of a much better teacher-pupil ratio than other classes; the most effective teachers were allocated to them; they received extra remedial attention; and appropriate pedagogies were developed, as were fresh approaches to parents and home-school liaison. The result over five years was that drop-out and failure rates diminished, and the whole ethos and effectiveness of the school improved (ibid., 173–4).

Nevertheless, in many cases the practices of streaming and curricular differentiation transmit and even amplify social class and related inequalities from generation to generation, without school decision-makers appearing to see or be concerned about these consequences (ibid., 161). In Lynch's study (1989, 107), for example, 27 per cent of the principals interviewed admitted allocating what they perceived to be the best teachers to the top ability groups or streams.

SOCIAL AND EMOTIONAL EFFECTS

In terms of social and emotional effects, the findings seem to be clear-cut. We can further subdivide these effects into those on the emotional level, friendship patterns, and the emergence of anti-school culture and behaviour.

Both Lacey (1970) and Hargreaves (1967) in their studies of grammar schools and secondary modern schools in Britain argue that those pupils who are allocated to low streams suffer a degradation of self: their sense of self-worth is undermined. In as much as the dominant official values in the school reinforce and reward academic achievement, allocation to a low stream is allocation to a position of inferior status; it is a label of failure.

O'Kelly's (1986) research on an Irish community school reports similar findings. Those in the lowest streams had very low self-images, both educationally and personally.

The negative socialising effect of being placed in a low stream is especially clear in Lacey's (1970) study of 'Hightown Grammar School'. All the children in this study came to grammar school on the basis of success in the Eleven Plus examination, and had thus had the experience of being among the best pupils in their primary schools. Yet within a short time in the highly competitive atmosphere of the grammar school some found themselves for the first time labelled as failures. Symptoms that occurred in the first year included bursting into tears when reprimanded by a teacher; refusal to go to school or to particular lessons, accompanied by hysterical crying and screaming; sleeplessness; bed-wetting; playing truant from school or from certain lessons; constantly feeling sick before certain lessons; consistent failure to do homework; high absence record; and aggravation of mild epilepsy.

These were the instances of major disturbance, but, as Lacey points out, a large number of minor ones probably never became known to the school.

Friendship patterns are also affected by streaming, as is pointed out by Lacey (1970) and Hargreaves (1967), and also by Irish research (O'Kelly, 1986). In 'Hightown Grammar School' (Lacey, 1970), although sifting, sorting and labelling went on in the first year, boys were not actually allocated to streams until the second year. Lacey noted that this affected friendship patterns: children allocated to different streams discontinued friendships, while those allocated to the same streams continued them. There were few friendships across the ability ranges—obviously, streaming results in limited interaction with pupils in other classes. O'Kelly's account (1986) of experiences of ability grouping in an Irish school gives evidence that children in high and low streams not only do not mix very much but develop some very negative stereotypes about each other.

We pointed out earlier that research indicates that very little movement between ability groups or streams occurs once children are allocated to them. Friendship patterns also play a part here. Murphy and Hallinger (1989) point to the strength of friendship groups as an inhibiting factor in pupils' movements between groups. Where friendship bonds are strong there will be little motivation for children in the lower groups to work hard and thus risk being moved to a different group that may be more suited to their achievement level. Conversely, children within the high-ability group will continue to be motivated in an effort to remain with established friends (Devine, 1991).

Studies of streaming also reveal that as one descends streams, commitment to school declines and distinctive 'anti-school' informal cultures become more apparent (Reid, 1986). In Lacey's school, for example, in the mixed-ability first year all boys displayed a high commitment to the norms of the school. In the second year they were streamed and differentiated, and progressively they became polarised into pro-school and anti-school subcultures. The experience of failure, both as a result of the streaming system itself and of the reinforcement of this in the negative perceptions held by the teachers in their daily work with low-stream pupils, led these pupils to search for alternative bases for their self-esteem. The most readily available alternatives lay in the inversion of the school's values. The low-stream anti-school cultures thus derived their initial coherence from being opposed to the values to which the teachers gave importance (Lacey, 1970).

Ball's study of 'Beachside Comprehensive School' (1981) suggests similar findings to Lacey's. When this school was banded, the adjustment of pupils to their low status was to produce an anti-school culture that made their classes difficult, sometimes impossible, to teach. However, when mixed-ability grouping was introduced pupils were no longer faced with the problem of failure due to allocation to low bands. Social classes were mixed and classroom experiences shared. Despite these changes, however, the data also suggests that academic differentiation was still taking place and that, as a result, some features of the banding system were reproduced in mixed-ability classes. Over time the relations between social class and academic performance became increasingly obvious, success roles in the classroom being dominated by middle-class pupils (Ball, 1981).

Attitudes of Teachers

The issue that arises from Ball's research, therefore, is that there is no simple solution to the problem of stratification in classrooms. This leads us to examine the attitudes of teachers. Even in mixed-ability situations, stratification and differential treatment can occur.

As Barker Lunn (1970) noted over twenty years ago, teachers' attitudes are highly significant. She identified two types of teacher, based on their attitudes and teaching methods. One type may be referred to as 'streamers'—they believed in streaming, were less interested in the slow learner, were not permissive, had low tolerance of noise and talking, favoured physical punishment, and used traditional lessons more frequently than progressive ones. The 'non-streamers' had opposing beliefs and practices. There were 72 schools in her sample—36 streamed and 36 non-streamed schools. Overall, however, she found a majority (two-thirds) of the teachers were streamers and almost half (48 per cent) of those in non-streamed schools were also streamers.

What Barker Lunn found overall was that if teachers believe in streaming—although they teach in mixed-ability situations—their ability-differentiated mentality will affect the classroom climate. Furthermore, given the fact that schools are agencies for social selection, in a highly stratified society such as Ireland it is almost inevitable that differentiated class and gender expectations will affect teachers and pupils. The main problem with streaming and with within-class ability grouping is that they formalise and reinforce differentiations in a structured setting (Rosenholtz and Simpson, 1984; Oakes, 1985).

Another interesting finding from Barker Lunn's study was that the social, emotional and attitudinal development of average and below-average pupils was affected by teacher type. These children, taught by non-streamer teachers in non-streamed schools, had better relationships with their teachers and held higher academic self-images than other children. The poorest attitudes were found among children taught by streamer teachers in non-streamed schools (Barker Lunn, 1970). Therefore, the attitudes of teachers are a crucial variable in our assessment of the implications of streaming or other forms of ability grouping.

Let us now consider what affects teachers' attitudes. Firstly, in a highly streamed system teachers themselves are most likely to be products of streamed schools and to have been allocated to the highest or higher streams during their own time in school. They have thus a conditioned acceptance of streaming. However, other factors also play a part. A British study (Reid et al., 1981) shows that teachers whose initial training contained elements concerned with mixed-ability teaching were more likely to see advantages in it than others. Attendance at in-service courses did not appear to be related to attitudes, although the amount of contact a teacher had had with mixed-ability classes during his or her teaching experience was a factor. The more mixed-ability classes the teacher had experience with, the more likely she or he was to see advantages in them.

Not all the teachers involved with mixed-ability classes, of course, thought them advantageous. Some reported them as enjoyable and challenging and bringing about an increased satisfaction with their work. However, they also said there was increased preparation and marking time and difficulties in secur-ing and developing the necessary resources and in meeting pupils' learning needs. The most commonly cited advantages were social ones, such as pupils' personal development, improved classroom atmosphere, increased co-operation between pupils and teachers, and a decrease in disruptive behaviour. The most commonly cited disadvantage of mixed-ability classes was that they led to a reduction in the motivation and achievement of the more able. Certain subjects too, such as humanities, religion, and English, were seen as more appropriate to mixed-ability classes; mathematics, science and languages were seen as less appropriate (Reid et al., 1981).

Finally, the manner in which the change to non-streaming is initiated is also important. In over two-thirds of the schools studied in one of the British projects the initiative came from the principal (Reid et al., 1981). Yet it certainly appears that to be successful, mixed-ability teaching requires far-reaching changes not only in teaching approach but also in the role of the teacher in the classroom and in the ways he or she relates to colleagues. It would seem unlikely that such changes can be effected without extensive consultation, discussion, and support. Indeed, Hannan and Boyle suggest that to change to a different form of school organisation demands that the school as a 'teacher-learner community' needs to undergo substantial change in attitudes and behaviour before a successful transition can be managed. This will demand not only willingness to change but teacher commitment and management effectiveness in the process (Hannan and Boyle, 1987, 174).

Ability Grouping at Primary Level

Although the focus of the ability grouping debate in Ireland has concentrated on grouping at second level, grouping by ability also occurs at primary level, albeit within rather than between classes. This is an issue that has received no research attention at national level in Ireland but that has serious educational implications. Indeed, as we have seen above, some of the major research studies in other countries have been focused on the primary school. Research by Hallinan and Sorensen (1985; 1986) and Eder (1981) shows that grouping children in primary classes on the basis of reading ability (the most commonly used criterion) has serious negative implications for those placed in the 'low' reading groups.

While there has been no national study of ability grouping at primary level, there have been a couple of smaller-scale studies. A study conducted among teachers and pupils in the north-west of Ireland (Carr, 1988) found that a very high proportion (almost 84 per cent) of teachers grouped pupils by ability. Of those who did, the great majority did so mainly for English reading (90 per cent) and mathematics (80 per cent).

Allocation to ability groups was mostly on the basis of the teacher's judg-ment rather than standardised tests. There was a good deal of overlap between the top and bottom groups in the two curricular areas. Carr found that the groups, once children were allocated to them, tended to remain static for the year. There appeared to be no relationship between class size and the size of groups formed: in general two to three groups were formed, irrespective of class size. This study did find, however, that the more experienced teachers were more likely to form flexible groups. Over half of the teachers indicated that they spent more time with the weak groups than with other groups (ibid.).

Carr also found that better-behaved children tended to be overrepresented in the top ability groups. There were also indications that the children of professional and managerial classes were to be found more frequently in the top-ability groups, while the children of unskilled workers were to be found more frequently in the bottom groups. Parental interest in education was also important: results suggested that pupils from families where there was a positive interest in their educational progress were more frequently found in the top-ability groups, and vice versa (ibid. 197–8).

This study concentrated on just one part of the country, and obviously further research is needed. However, if such practices are widespread in the system (and practices at second level suggest they may well be), then there is cause for concern. Research in the United States indicates that ability grouping that allocates children, especially those who may already have educational disadvantages, to lower streams or groupings removes them from a climate of success, which is necessary for educational achievement (Hallinan, 1987, 51–52). This is particularly the case for working-class children. It has been argued that, rather than making up for the initial disadvantage many children have on entering school, practices such as within-class ability grouping may further compound the disadvantage (Eder and Felmlee, 1984).

A case study of two primary schools in an urban area in Ireland examined children's own attitudes towards and experiences of within-class ability grouping (Devine, 1991). Two samples of children were compared—one grouped, one non-grouped. Differences were identified between the two groups in the quality of the instruction received. Children of weak ability were most frustrated in the grouped sample in their access to reading materials. Teachers within the grouped setting were perceived as giving children of very good ability the most challenging levels of work while setting less demanding and challenging work for children of weak ability (ibid., 215–17). Again, further research is needed here, but if this pattern is more widespread it perhaps reflects the kind of curricular differentiation to be found among different streams at second level.

The impact of teachers' expectations of different categories of children is also evident here. There is a considerable literature that suggests that teachers' expectations play an important role in what and how well children learn (see, for example, Rosenthal and Jacobson, 1968; Eder, 1981; Oakes, 1985). The findings on children's perceptions of teachers' expectations in Devine's study show that children are highly aware of differences in expectations, and that these become internalised in children's self-beliefs and academic self-images: a substantially higher proportion of children in the very good groups than in the weak groups recorded high ability concept scores.

This study, like a number of studies mentioned earlier, also showed very little movement between groups. The experiences of the children in ability groups, associated as they were with reduced confidence in the academic and social sphere for the weaker ones, give rise to increased inequalities among students, leading to differential achievement and ultimately differential positions in the social and economic hierarchy (Devine, 220–4).

CONCLUSIONS

In this chapter the form of grouping we have concentrated on is streaming, as that is the most widespread one in second-level schools. We have also discussed within-class grouping by ability in primary schools. Research suggests that both of these forms of grouping involve social as well as academic differentiation, with the children of professional and white-collar workers dominating the top groups and the children of the least-advantaged social groups more highly represented in the bottom groups.

The principal learning effect of streaming in Ireland has been a polarisation effect on attainment. It has been suggested that increased attainment in higher streams and ability groups has been bought at the expense of low attainment by weaker groups. With regard to personal and social effects, these revolve mainly around the findings on the negative self-image of those in weaker groups, the increase in disruption and anti-school behaviour in weaker groups, and the weak friendship patterns across groups or streams. Research also points to the importance of teachers' attitudes in the classroom climate of both mixed-ability and streamed groups. We have argued, in sum, that organisational and curricular differentiation in schools reinforces social and economic inequalities.

This chapter has also highlighted the lack of any Irish research at the national level on the implications of within-class ability grouping in primary schools. In line with research elsewhere, the small-scale studies that have been undertaken indicate that grouping has several disadvantages for those allocated to the 'weak' or 'low' reading and mathematics groups.

References and Further Reading

Ball, S. (1981), *Beachside Comprehensive*, Cambridge: Cambridge University Press.

Barker Lunn, J. (1970), *Streaming in the Primary School*, Slough: NFER.

Carr, M. (1988), 'The Practice of Within-Class Ability Grouping: a Study of Teachers and Pupils in the Stranorlar INTO Branch, Co. Donegal' (MEd thesis, University College, Dublin).

Devine, D. (1991), 'A Study of Reading Ability Groups: Primary School Children's Experiences and Views' (MEd thesis, University College, Dublin).

Douglas, J. (1964), *The Home and the School*, London: McGibbon and Kee.

Eder, D. (1981), 'Ability grouping as a self-fulfilling prophecy: a micro-analysis of teacher-student interaction', *Sociology of Education*, vol. 54, no. 3.

Eder, D., and Felmlee, D. (1984), 'The development of attention norms in ability groups' in P. Peterson et al. (eds.), *The Social Context of Instruction: Group Organisation and Group Processes*, Orlando: Academic Press.

Hallinan, M. (ed.) (1987), *The Social Organisation of Schools*, New York: Plenum.

Hallinan, M., and Sorensen, A. (1985), 'Class size, ability group size and student achievement', *American Journal of Education*, vol. 94.

Hallinan, M., and Sorensen, A. (1986), 'Effects of ability grouping on growth in academic achievement', *American Education Research Journal*, vol. 23.

Hannan, D., and Boyle, M. (1987), *Schooling Decisions: the Origins and Consequences of Selection and Streaming in Irish Post-Primary Schools*, Dublin: Economic and Social Research Institute.

Hargreaves, D. (1967), *Social Relations in a Secondary School*, London: Routledge and Kegan Paul.

Keddie, N. (1971), 'Classroom knowledge' in M. Young (ed.), *Knowledge and Control*, London: Collier Macmillan.

Kerckhoff, A. (1986), 'Effects of ability grouping in British secondary schools', *American Sociological Review*, vol. 51, no. 6.

Lacey, C. (1970), *Hightown Grammar: the School as a Social System*, London: Manchester University Press.

Lynch, K. (1988), 'Streaming and banding in schools: context and implications', *Journal of the Institute of Guidance Counsellors*, vol. 14.

Lynch, K. (1989), *The Hidden Curriculum*, Lewes: Falmer.

Murphy, J., and Hallinger, P. (1989), 'Equity as access to learning: curricular and instructional treatment differences', *Journal of Curriculum Studies*, vol. 21, no. 2.

Oakes, J. (1985), *Keeping Track: How Schools Structure Inequality*, London: Yale University Press.

O'Kelly, A. (1986), 'A Case Study in a Community School: an Analysis of Streaming and its Effects' (MEd thesis, University College, Dublin).

Reid, I. (1986), *The Sociology of School and Education*, London: Fontana.

Reid, M., et al. (1981), 'Mixed ability teaching: problems and possibilities', *Educational Research*, vol. 24.

Rosenholtz, S., and Simpson, C. (1984), 'The formation of ability concepts: developmental trend or social construction?', *Review of Educational Research*, vol. 54.

Rosenthal, B., and Jacobson, L. (1968), *Pygmalion in the Classroom*, New York: Holt, Rinehart and Winston.

Sharp, R., and Green, A. (1975), *Education and Social Control: a Study of Progressive Primary Education*, London: Routledge and Kegan Paul.

Troyna, B. (1978), 'Race and streaming', *Educational Review*, vol. 30.

V

A Second Chance?

13

Adult Education: a Second Chance?

Throughout this book we have tried to discuss different aspects and issues in education in the light of contemporary research; in particular we have tried to draw on Irish data and to discuss issues in the context of academic debate in Ireland. Because of the dearth of research material in particular areas, our analysis is at times not as comprehensive as we would like it to be; and there is probably no area of education where the difficulties encountered by lack of research material are more evident than in the field of adult education. While there is a certain amount of research and analysis undertaken (for example by Aontas, 1986, 1987; Carey and Slowey, 1986; Inglis, 1991; Inglis and Bassett, 1988; Mac Gréil, 1990; O'Sullivan, 1980; 1982; 1988; 1989; and Slowey, 1979) the range of research undertaken is limited by the absence of adequate resources. The fact that so little money is available for research, that there are so few third-level colleges with adult education departments and that there is no professorial post in the field of adult education in any of the universities or research institutes means that it tends to be something that is regarded as an optional extra.

Part of the problem stems from the way in which adult education developed, both in Ireland and internationally. Adult education tends to have its origins in social movements of different kinds, especially in labour, religious and agricultural movements, and more recently in the women's movement (Slowey, 1989, 88). Because it has been associated with different social projects, the emphasis has been on the realisation of the project and on the delivery of the service rather than on the analysis of the goals and achievements of adult education itself. Even when it has been undertaken by universities, adult education studies and research have not generally been a part of its agenda (Ó Murchú, 1989, 36). This has undoubtedly impoverished the development of adult education.

Participation Patterns

The report of the Commission on Adult Education (1983) remains the major source of information on patterns of participation in adult education at the national level, although Mac Gréil (1990) has also collected some data on national participation rates. The commission reported that 11 per cent of adults and young people over the age of sixteen who had left school participated in some adult education course during 1982; this contrasted with a participation rate of 16 per cent in the United States and 13 per cent in England and Wales during the same period (Commission on Adult Education, 1983, 87–8). Sixteen per cent reported participating in adult education courses over the three years before the study while a further 11 per cent reported participating at some time earlier. Almost three-quarters (74 per cent) of adults, however, had not participated in any form of education following their initial and uninterrupted full-time education; the comparable non-participation figure for England and Wales (for 1980) was 52 per cent (ibid., 88–90).

It is not especially surprising, perhaps, that those who were most likely to avail of adult education were those who had a positive view of their own schooling. The problem that arises, however, is that adult education may well be reinforcing rather than eliminating inequalities: the commission found that the more a person had availed of full-time education already, the more likely he or she was to participate in adult education. This meant that middle-class people and those who were better educated were overrepresented in adult education courses (ibid., 91–3).

This is not, however, an issue that is confined to Ireland: in all OECD countries, surveys of adults show that the typical participant is likely to be well qualified compared with the population as a whole (CERI-OECD, 1987). Such evidence challenges the claim that adult education gives working-class people or poorly educated minorities a second chance. While part of the problem here is the existence of negative attitudes on the part of those marginalised from education in their youth, other external factors play a more important role.

A number of external barriers to participation were identified in the study of the Commission on Adult Education, including lack of accurate information on the adult education options available; financial barriers; barriers arising from domestic situations, especially the lack of child care support services; and difficulties encountered with entry requirements. Research by Aontas (1986) and Inglis and Bassett (1988) has confirmed these findings in more recent years.

The common perception, therefore, that adult education provides some alternative tier of education, where those who did not succeed at previous levels can have a second chance, needs to be questioned. If anything, inequalities arising from social class, sex or disability are more evident in inhibiting access to adult education than they are in other sectors of education. There is no entitlement to adult education, in the way that one is entitled to attend primary or second-level school or, if one meets the necessary conditions, in the way that one is entitled to a grant for third level. There are virtually no student support services for adults, and what grants are available are very limited in scope.

The lack of entitlement and support is felt most strongly by those who lack financial resources. Not surprisingly, therefore, one of the groups most disadvantaged in adult education is working-class women (O'Sullivan, 1988). The lack of money available to working-class and low-income people generally is compounded in women's case by the lack of child care support services that would give them the necessary independence to enter adult education.

In 1983 the Commission on Adult Education reported (p. 94) that 'compared to their proportion in the total population under review the following groups appear to have higher proportionate representation among participants in adult education: females, the 25–44 age group, city people . . . the full-time employed and those who have taken the Leaving Certificate Examination.'

Although women are among the groups that are overrepresented in adult education programmes, it would appear likely (although there is need for more research on this) that it is middle-class rather than working-class or low-income women who are overrepresented.

The only current data available on participation rates in adult education is on courses run under the auspices of the VECs and in community and comprehensive schools. However, there is no detailed breakdown of the types of course people take or of the social class background of those who take them. What we do know is that there are 114,194 people attending part-time adult education courses in vocational, community and comprehensive schools and colleges; the majority (70 per cent) of these are women (Department of Education, 1991, 148).

But this is not the whole picture. While these schools are the principal providers of adult education, there is a variety of other agencies also involved in the provision of adult education, and a number of these are voluntary bodies. Unfortunately no data is provided in the annual statistical report of the Department of Education on participation rates in these other sectors. There is also no reliable data available on the incidence of illiteracy in Ireland, so that one cannot even estimate the needs and demand from this adult education sector. The Green Paper (Department of Education, 1992, 212) has proposed a national survey to assess the needs in this area.

As to the nature of the courses people undertake, the only national data here dates back to the early 1980s; the evidence available suggests that course take-up varies greatly across social class, gender, and region. The majority (60 per cent) of those who pursue adult education courses appear to do so for work-related reasons (Commission on Adult Education, 1983, 97). As is true in higher education (Clancy, 1988), the highest level of take-up is in the sciences and technical and business subjects, with 42 per cent taking their most recent courses in one of these areas. Sports and pastimes, arts and domestic subjects were named as the next most popular options, with 14, 11 and 11 per cent, respectively, having taken their last course in one of these areas (ibid., 96–7). No analysis of the precise relationship between social class, gender and subject options is presented in the Commission on Adult Education report, although it does show that women tend to be overrepresented in domestic, community and social subjects compared with men, while having equal representation with men in business and commercial subjects and being significantly underrepresented in the sciences and technical areas. These gender differentials are similar to those found in other areas of education, as we have already shown.

What we will try to do in the remainder of this chapter is to set the question of adult education in the context of debates about equality in education generally. One of the reasons that adult education is often not discussed in the context of general debates about educational issues is that it is seen as something separate and apart: it is not seen as part of the formal system of education. Also, the bulk of adult education provision is poorly resourced and frequently quasi-voluntary. With the exception of a small number of professionally paid workers, such as adult education organisers, it is staffed by part-time and temporary contract workers. In resource terms, the 'adult education aura', so to speak, is one of penury and voluntarism. This is not to take away from the fact that the spirit that inspires adult educationalists is one of social commitment and public service (O'Sullivan, 1989).

By locating the debate about adult education within the context of general debates about equality in education, we hope to show that adult education is neither peripheral nor secondary to other sectors of education.

Equality and Adult Education

Chapter 2 of the Green Paper (Department of Education, 1992) deals with the issue of equality in education; adult education is examined in a separate chapter. While the separation of the two is fitting, in that the adult education sector is a separate sector in its own right, it is surprising that there is almost no discussion in the paper about the equality issues that arise in relation to adult education.

The report of the Commission on Adult Education (1983, 9) defined adult education as including 'all systematic learning by adults which contributes to their development as individuals and as members of the community and of society apart from full-time instruction received by persons as part of their uninterrupted initial education and training. It may be formal education which takes place in institutions e.g. training centres, schools, colleges, institutes and universities; or non-formal education, which is any other systematic form of learning, including self-directed learning.'

Given the all-encompassing nature of this definition, it is clear that adult education refers to any form of education that takes place after an adult has completed his or her uninterrupted full-time education. As numerous research reports over the last ten years have shown, those who are most likely to terminate their full-time education at an early age are the children of unemployed, working-class or small-farmer parents (Clancy, 1982, 1988; Breen, 1984;

Whelan and Whelan, 1984). In conjunction with this, Greaney and Kellaghan's (1984) and Clancy's (1982; 1988) research shows that while girls may outperform boys at the Intermediate and Leaving Certificate levels, they are less likely than boys to enter higher education, and when they do they are less likely to go on to pursue prestigious postgraduate courses (Clancy, 1989). Those who benefit most from the formal education system, therefore, are the middle classes (especially those whose parents are professionals, large proprietors, or well-paid salaried employees).

Furthermore, when one examines the structure of opportunity in the paid labour market it becomes clear that it is the male members of the middle classes who ultimately become the main beneficiaries of formal education at third level; they occupy the most lucrative and influential positions in the paid sectors of the economy (Blackwell, 1989).

What are the implications of all these factors for adult education? Firstly, it means that a major target audience for adult education is those whom the formal education sector has failed to serve. It means, in effect, that the issue of adult education cannot be separated from that of equality in social class and gender terms. Adult education is, for many, second-chance education. This is not to deny that there are many people who pursue adult education courses on the basis of a purely personal or professional interest; they are not trying to 'catch up' with what they have missed in full-time education.

In its report on priority areas in adult education, Aontas (1986) has already identified some of the groups that are in need of a 'second chance'. These include those who lack basic skills such as reading and writing; those who are unemployed and unwaged; women; and those living in rural areas (1986, 29). When we look at this list a little more closely we can see that it contains overlaps, and perhaps categorisations that are too global. A very large proportion of those who are unwaged are also women (99 per cent of those on home duties are women). In addition it is obvious that not all those who are women wish to avail of adult education. Neither is it true that all rural dwellers want to avail of adult education services; privilege and income differentials are as evident in rural areas as they are elsewhere.

Bearing these considerations in mind, one can take a closer look at those who are most in need of another chance in education. In doing this one is not suggesting that many middle-class and indeed upper middle-class men and women might not benefit greatly from further education. There is little doubt that they would. However, because of their greater access to financial resources they can, to a large extent, gain access to whatever education they need. They may need education, but they do not need second-chance education in the same way that certain other groups do.

When one examines adult education from this point of view it is evident that there are at least three groups that are in need of a second chance in education. Their need arises from a combination of social class, gender and minority considerations. Because each group experiences distinct forms of inequality, their interest in and requirements for adult education are bound to be quite different.

SOCIAL CLASS INEQUALITIES AND ADULT EDUCATION

Mac Gréil (1990, 10–11), in a national study of participation rates in different sectors of education, reports that there was a positive link between educational standards and participation in adult education; in other words, there was some evidence that those who were least educated (in the formal sense) had the lowest rates of participation in adult education. This finding concurs with those of the Commission on Adult Education (1983) and O'Sullivan (1988). Although Mac Gréil admits that his research evidence on adult education does not offer a complete picture, he reiterates a point that has been made by many others for the last twenty years: that a 'much more positive approach, "pro-active" policies and resources would seem necessary to serve those most educationally deprived . . .' (ibid., 30).

What research by Mac Gréil, Aontas and others implies, therefore, is that there are a number of interrelated inequalities that low-income groups experience in relation to adult education, namely lack of adequate information, lack of guidance, lack of consultation with target groups about their needs, and inadequate financial and support (child care) services for those who wish to return to education. These difficulties are compounded by inflexibilities in the standard institutions of education regarding access procedures for those with non-standard educational backgrounds. While schemes such as the Vocational Training Opportunities Scheme (VTOS) and Youthreach, and the grants for mature students at third level, are welcome developments, they cater for a very small proportion of those currently availing of adult education. Also, they are schemes only available to very specific groups, so they do not touch the majority of those who might need or want a second chance.

Those who do look to adult education to overcome the inequalities they have experienced because of their social class include, among others, a very large proportion of those who are unemployed (there is ample evidence from the annual surveys of school leavers by the Department of Labour that there is a close correlation between employment status and level of education, which in turn is linked closely to social class) and many of those who lack basic literacy and numeracy skills. It is obvious, therefore, that those whose need for adult education may arise from class inequalities are by no means identical in their requirements. This being said, it is also true that the adult education needs of those who were so-called 'educational failures', or who left the education system before they received a credential or were awarded a low-grade credential, do bear some resemblance to each other: they have all been deprived of that educational currency that is required for both entry to and mobility within the paid labour market.

Irish society is one in which educational credentials are a precondition for occupational success; this is true for everyone, with the exception of that small minority who inherit sufficient material capital to survive. Many of those who are without educational credentials see adult education as a mechanism for acquiring them. That is why those who are unemployed, in particular, may see little point in attending a course that has no obvious labour market currency at the end of it. When we bear in mind that 77 per cent of those who are unemployed are men (CSO, 1992) we begin to realise that male detachment from adult education may have its roots not in some kind of inherent 'male' indifference to education but rather in the irrelevance of many adult education options (including those offered by FÁS) to people who are basically looking for a credential that has real labour market currency. To offset social class inequalities in education, therefore, we must begin by offering working-class and unemployed people a realistic chance to obtain valued education credentials.

THE EQUALITY PROBLEM AND SOCIAL CLOSURE

In equality terms, the problems in adult education are not radically different from those in other sectors of education. As we have noted elsewhere in this book, Irish educational policies, including those in adult education, have been informed by the liberal equality-of-opportunity model. This model has been interpreted in a formal rather than a substantive sense (O'Neill, 1989); that is to say, it has been concerned with equalising access in meritocratic terms, not with equalising outcomes among all social groups. (See chapter 3 for further discussion on the limits of meritocratic thinking.)

From an adult education perspective, a formal equal-opportunities model has several limitations. Most significantly, it does not address the question of equality of social condition (Tawney, 1964). It fails to address the way in which one's ability to gain access to and participate in education is a direct function of one's economic and personal circumstances. Without adequate resources, guidance and support services (for example for women and men with dependent children) there is no real choice about access or participation. Liberal equal-opportunities policies actually perpetuate inequality by fostering the myth that those who want education can avail of it once the service is formally available, when in fact the opposite is the case. Liberal equal-opportunities policies create the image that the reason people do not participate in education is that they are not interested; lack of participation is defined as an individual problem rather than a structural one, with all the implications this has for public policy. There can be no real equality of opportunity in education without equality in people's economic, political and personal circumstances, otherwise there are simply too many barriers for those without resources to pass through.

In the area of adult education the limitations of liberal equal-opportunities policies are very evident: no serious account is taken of the financial needs of low-income adults who wish to return to education; there is no tax relief, no comprehensive grants system, and no support service. By ignoring the conditions necessary for successful participation and achievement, public policy makes second-chance education an illusion rather than a realistic option for those without adequate financial resources and support services. Also, the scheduling of courses by the educational institutions themselves frequently ignores the reality of adult lives.

For those who get into the system and who succeed within it, other problems emerge, and the first and most obvious one is that of accreditation. Adult education courses are not generally formally credentialised by recognised educational bodies. Another related issue has been that, even if courses are credentialised, there has been no formal procedure for accumulating credits from these courses so that one could eventually be granted an award such as an 'Adult Education Leaving Certificate', for example. What adult students experience here is the practice of social closure, 'the process by which social collectivities seek to maximise rewards by restricting access to resources and opportunities to a limited circle of eligibles' (Parkin, 1982, 175). Those without the recognised educational credentials acquired in second-level education, for example, are effectively closed off from access to higher education and the labour market privileges to which it gives access. The exclusion of particular groups from the educational process at different stages has the inevitable effect of easing access for more privileged groups.

The reluctance of established educational institutions such as universities and other third-level colleges to recognise adult education experience is part of the practice by which the élites maintain their privileged positions in society:

> In modern capitalist society the two main exclusionary devices by which the bourgeoisie constructs and maintains itself as a class are, first, those surrounding the institutions of property; and, second, academic or professional qualifications and credentials. Each represents a set of legal arrangements for restricting access to rewards and privileges: property ownership is a form of social closure designed to prevent general access to the means of production and its fruits; credentialism is a form of closure designed to control and monitor entry to key positions in the division of labour. (ibid., 78)

Those who rely on second-chance adult education courses to improve their chances on the job market, therefore, often face insurmountable obstacles in the present system. On the one hand, access is made conditional on having the financial and personal resources to participate, itself an insurmountable obstacle for the majority; on the other hand, those who do participate find that they are offered no credentials, or credentials that are not recognised by the established accrediting bodies.

The view of adult education presented here may appear very far from the traditional liberal view of 'education for its own sake'. There is no reason to make an apology for this, as there is insufficient recognition in educational circles of the simple labour market reality that educational credentials are real forms of capital: they represent forms of credentialised cultural capital (Bourdieu, 1986), and without them one is seriously handicapped in life opportunities. While this is not true in all societies, it is certainly true in Irish society, where the limited indigenous industrial and agricultural capital available has failed to generate much wealth, and education is a major determinant of life chances.

'Education for its own sake' therefore is a real option only for those who control sufficient cultural or economic capital to have the means to a comfortable existence. In planning for adult education, then, one must provide access to recognised credentials for those who need them. Offering people certificates, diplomas, and the like, often based on short courses that are not formally recognised by established accrediting bodies (indeed often not recognised by the very authorities that provide them) seems to be an insult to the people who take the courses, and a waste of limited resources.

GENDER INEQUALITIES AND ADULT EDUCATION

As pointed out above, women make up over 70 per cent of those in adult education courses organised by the VECs and the community and comprehensive schools. Slowey's (1989) claim therefore that the women's movement has inspired an adult education movement of its own is tenable. Women are 'coming out' and making demands on the education system in a way that has not happened previously. Because of this, the unique difficulties women experience in education have to be addressed.

While we have no national data on the social class breakdown of women attending adult education classes, what is clear is that not all women are of the one social class. Working-class women inevitably experience very similar adult education needs to their male working-class colleagues. However, apart from this they will have their own educational needs, both as women and as working-class women. Middle-class women also have adult education needs that are both specific to their social class and apart from it. Overall, however, women seem to come to adult education with three types of motivation.

Firstly, there are some who come to improve their skills as parent-educators: these are people who may lack the literacy and numeracy skills they need to help their children with their homework, or they may be people who simply want to be better informed about what their children are doing in school. A second and very important motivation for women is the one identified by Inglis and Bassett (1988, 36–8): many of the women in their study were returning to 'school' because they felt trapped and alone at home and without public respect; they were returning to education to establish an identity of their own, apart from husbands and children. They wanted to be publicly respected and appreciated, and they looked to adult education to achieve this. A third motive among women is one also identified in the Inglis and Bassett study: this is the need of women to return to adult education as a means of establishing, or returning to, paid employment. These are women who have passed the 'confidence barrier' that seems to be built up among women who have been full-time home workers for years. They are the ones who are not afraid to seek paid employment even though they know the odds are stacked against them.

Women's approach to adult education is therefore just as instrumentalist as that of men, although it takes different forms at times. Most of them see it as a mechanism for gaining power and control over their own lives; and for many that means, in the long if not the short term, getting access to paid employment.

We are not suggesting that work at home, in particular caring work, is not valuable or not deserving of good payment. Quite the contrary: we regard it as essential to society and that it should therefore be highly paid. However, as long as it is unpaid the women and men who engage in it will tend to devalue it, as they can see that it is not rewarded in any substantive way in society at large. This means that when they are free to leave it, very often they will; and adult education in its various forms will be seen by many as a route out of unpaid housework and caring into a paid job.

There are a number of 'inequalities of condition' that women face when trying to participate in adult education, and these are particularly acute for low-income women. The most conspicuous problem is child care. Unless provision for adult education is made within a context where supplementary child care help is freely available, in effect women with dependent children have no choice at all about returning to education. The same holds true for all those, men and women, who are the primary carers for other dependent people, be these adults or children.

A second issue is that of financial support. Participation in education, even if it is nominally free, costs money: books, materials, transport and other essentials all involve considerable cost. The reality is that there are almost 700,000 women 'engaged in home duties' in Ireland. They constitute the largest block of workers in the country. However, most of them have no independent means of income. Grants for women returning to education would seem to be a *sine qua non*, therefore, for making equality of opportunity a reality. Also, there is the opportunity cost of attending: if one is involved in education one is often not free to undertake part-time work to supplement one's income. Financial support is needed for those women who have to forgo vital earnings in order to return to education.

MINORITIES AND INEQUALITY IN EDUCATION

Apart from those who experience educational inequality arising out of their social class or gender, there are also those who are alienated from the system because their minority status is either ignored or insufficiently addressed.

Two obvious groups that are affected in this way are people with disabilities and travelling people. Very little account is taken of those who have major disabilities in the mainstream system. The attitude generally is that they must fit into the system as it is: the system does not have to adapt for them. Once again this is a typical example of a liberal laissez-faire type of approach to equality of opportunity: the formal availability of the service is assumed to be all that is necessary to achieve equality. Practices as diverse as failing to adapt buildings to take account of those with physical disabilities, inadequate or absent support services, lack of pre-service and in-service education for all teachers on the needs of students with different disabilities and the reluctance to use the sign language of the deaf as a medium of communication with those for whom it is their first language are all examples of the weaknesses of the liberal approach to public policy.

For travelling people the problem is one of failing to recognise their unique culture and nomadic life-style; the result is that virtually none of their stories, their images or history appear as subject matter in schools. They are expected to adapt to the curriculum of schooling even though it excludes them.

In what is written about adult education in Ireland, little reference is made to the interests of minorities. Consequently, it is very difficult to establish what their adult education needs are. Because minorities include groups that are both strongly stratified within themselves (as people with disabilities and others, such as the elderly, clearly are) and that are very different from each other, meeting their educational needs is by no means simple. If adult education is there to promote equality by giving a 'second chance', however, it must examine the needs of minorities whose special needs may not be adequately addressed in the mainstream system.

CONCLUSION

Much of what has been written here may seem to imply that adult education is for fitting people out with educational credentials. Clearly it is not. Adult education is also for empowerment and emancipation, especially for those who have been disempowered by education at a previous time in their lives. The empowerment of oppressed groups, however, is not something that is 'done by adult educators to those who are oppressed' (Zacharakis-Jutz, 1988, 41–7). Rather it is a more subtle, and indeed a slower, process whereby people come to an awareness of their own oppression and develop the ability to do something about it.

The role adult education plays in this very specific kind of empowerment will vary considerably depending on the background and experience of those who participate in it. As Stanage (1986) points out, however, the realisation of empowerment is conditional on having an appropriate political context for it to happen in. Many oppressed people may benefit from empowerment at a personal level, but they may not be in any position to act on that empowerment in any broader political sense. All that any education process can do is give people the opportunity to develop a critical capacity that generates empowerment. Educationalists cannot control the use people go on to make of this capacity (O'Sullivan, 1982).

It is sometimes suggested that empowerment and the development of a critical capacity are impossible to achieve in formal systems of education, especially when credentials are being offered. While there is little doubt that this is frequently the case, this is not to say that the giving of credentials precludes the development of critical thought. The willingness and ability to develop and encourage critical thought is not the prerogative of any level or type of education. It can occur in second-level schools, in universities, regional technical colleges, or in adult education programmes, or it may not. Also, it may occur in any subject area, or it may not. As Freire (1972) clearly states, the difference between 'education for domestication' and 'education for freedom' is one of approach rather than of subject matter. The pedagogical approach adopted in any subject or at any level can be one that encourages reflection and critical thought, or it can be simply one of banking. As there are many different forms of human intelligence, so there are many different forms of knowledge and understanding (Gardner, 1983). A critical orientation is not, however, the prerogative of any one of these in particular.

While there is no necessary conflict between the development of a critical capacity and the empowerment of people on the one hand and the giving of credentials on the other, this is not to deny that when powerful interest groups control the content or subject matter of formal education, the scope for the development of critical thought in certain fields of education can be seriously limited (Lynch, 1989, 118–37). This is a problem arising out of the nature of control in education: it is not a function of the subjects in themselves, and it can happen whether education is under state control or not. As Cathcart (1989) points out, adult education is as likely to be subject to political influences and biases as other levels of education. He shows how Alfred O'Rahilly and Canon John Hayes, for example, regarded adult education as a mechanism for implementing Catholic social teaching: Muintir na Tíre, one of the better-known adult education movements, was not established to develop critical thought in rural communities but

> to unite the rural communities of Ireland on the Leo XIII principle that there must exist friendly relations between master and man; that it is a mistake to assume that class is naturally hostile to class, and that the well-to-do and

working men are intended by nature to live in mutual conflict. This new rural organisation we are launching, in the name of God, intends to unite in one body the rural workers of the country, not for the purpose of attacking any one section of the community, but to give agricultural workers in Ireland their due and proper place. (Hayes, cited by Cathcart, 1989, 123–4)

Muintir na Tíre was an essential part of the Catholic plan to develop a vocational order in rural Ireland and thereby to foreclose the development of class conflict; this, in turn, was seen as a way of warding off the perceived threat of communism (ibid.). No more than any other educational development, rural adult education was not politically neutral.

While much of the academic debate in adult education centres around issues of empowerment and emancipation at the present time (Mezirow, 1990; Bookman, 1988; Inglis, 1992), the fact is that many of those who avail of adult education see it in traditional meritocratic terms: it is a tool for individual social mobility and not a mechanism for developing critical capacities and skills that the individual will then use to help other oppressed people. For all those who participate in adult education, but especially for those who define adult education in terms of individual mobility, there is a need to develop an alternative system of credentialisation. Possibilities would include a Leaving Certificate programme that took account of adults' existing knowledge and expertise; and for those who are interested in what higher education has to offer there could be a series of College Certificates that were modular in form (so that they could be done on a part-time basis over a few years if desired) and would qualify people for degrees and diplomas of a variety of types and levels. Whatever system of accreditation is devised, it is important that clear procedures of transfer from one level of education to the next be established. The system must be flexible and imaginative, and recognised by all the established authorities, such as universities, otherwise it will become yet another barrier to equality.

Much of what is involved here is an act of will as much as an economic investment. On the will side what is needed is a more open and flexible approach by the Department of Education and the institutions of higher education. On the financial side what is required is substantial state investment in all types of adult education, including alternative adult education for those who wish to be reintegrated into the mainstream system. Indeed, investment in this kind of education is quite likely to bring significant economic and social returns, if this is the measure of things. While we do not hold the view that economic benefits should be the determinant of education policy, it does seem strange that so little money is invested in the education of adults whose futures are so likely to be in Ireland.

References and Further Reading

Aontas (1986), *Priority Areas in Adult Education*, Dublin: Aontas.

Aontas (1987), *Adult Education in the Gaeltacht*, Dublin: Aontas.

Blackwell, J. (1989), *Women in the Labour Force*, Dublin: Employment Equality Agency.

Bookman, A. (1988), *Women and the Politics of Empowerment*, Philadelphia: Temple University Press.

Bourdieu, P. (1986), 'The forms of capital' in J. Richardson (ed.), *Handbook of Theory and Research for the Sociology of Education*, New York: Greenwood.

Breen, R. (1984), *Education and the Labour Market* (ESRI paper no. 119), Dublin: Economic and Social Research Institute.

Carey, L., and Slowey, M. (1986), *Participation by Adults in Higher Education: an Overview of Institutional Policies*, Maynooth: St Patrick's College (Centre for Adult and Community Education).

Cathcart, H. (1989), 'Adult education, values and Irish society' in D. O'Sullivan (ed.), *Social Commitment and Adult Education*, Cork: Cork University Press.

Central Statistics Office (1992), *Labour Force Survey, 1991*, Dublin: Stationery Office.

CERI-OECD (1987), *Adults in Higher Education*, Paris: Organisation for Economic Co-operation and Development.

Clancy, P. (1982), *Participation in Higher Education: a National Survey*, Dublin: Higher Education Authority.

Clancy, P. (1988), *Who Goes to College?*, Dublin: Higher Education Authority.

Clancy, P. (1989), 'Gender differences in student participation at third level' in C. Hussey (ed.), *Equal Opportunities for Women in Higher Education*, Dublin: University College.

Commission on Adult Education (1983), *Lifelong Learning: Report of the Commission on Adult Education*, Dublin: Stationery Office.

Department of Education (1991), *Statistical Report, 1989/90*, Dublin: Stationery Office.

Department of Education (1992), *Education for a Changing World: Green Paper on Education*, Dublin: Stationery Office.

Freire, P. (1972), *Pedagogy of the Oppressed*, New York: Penguin.

Gardner, H. (1983), *Frames of Mind: the Theory of Multiple Intelligences*, New York: Paladin.

Greaney, V., and Kellaghan, T. (1984), *Equality of Opportunity in Irish Schools*, Dublin: Educational Company.

Inglis, T. (1992), 'Learning about power, empowerment and emancipation' (paper presented at a symposium, Sociology Department, University College, Dublin, May 1992).

Inglis, T., and Bassett, M. (1988), *Live and Learn : Day-Time Adult Education in Coolock*, Dublin: Aontas.

Lynch, K. (1989), *The Hidden Curriculum: Reproduction in Education: an Appraisal*, London: Falmer.

Mac Gréil, M. (1990), *Educational Participation in Ireland*, Maynooth: St Patrick's College (Sociology Department).

Mezirow, J., et al. (1990), *Fostering Critical Reflection in Adulthood: a Guide to Transformative and Emancipatory Learning*, San Francisco: Jossey-Bass.

Ó Murchú, M. (1989), 'Alfred O'Rahilly and the provision of adult education at University College, Cork' in D. O'Sullivan (ed.), *Social Commitment and Adult Education*, Cork: Cork University Press.

O'Neill, O. (1977), 'How do we know when opportunities are equal?' in M. Vetterling-Braggin et al. (eds.), *Feminism and Philosophy*, New Jersey: Littlefield.

O'Sullivan, D. (1980), 'Socialisation, social change and ideology in adult education', *Adult Education*, vol. 52.

O'Sullivan, D. (1982), 'Adult education, social change and the interpretive model', *Aontas Review*, vol. 3, no. 1.

O'Sullivan, D. (1988), 'An Irish extra-mural programme: clientele, student adaptation and class participation', *International Journal of University Education*, vol. 27.

O'Sullivan, D. (1989), *Social Commitment and Adult Education*, Cork: Cork University Press.

Parkin, F. (1982), 'Social closure and class formation' in A. Giddens and D. Held (eds.), *Classes, Power and Conflict*, London: Macmillan.

Slowey, M. (1979), 'Aspects of women's participation in adult education', *Aontas Review*, vol. 1, no. 2.

Slowey, M. (1989), 'Women in continuing education and training' in D. O'Sullivan (ed.), *Social Commitment and Adult Education*, Cork: Cork University Press.

Stanage, S. (1986), 'Unrestraining liberty: adult education and the empowerment of persons', *Adult Education Quarterly*, vol. 36.

Tawney, R. (1964), *Equality*, London: Allen and Unwin.

Whelan, C., and Whelan, B., *Social Mobility in the Republic of Ireland: a Comparative Perspective* (ESRI paper no. 116), Dublin: Economic and Social Research Institute.

Zacharakis-Jutz, J. (1988), 'Post-Freirean adult education: a question of empowerment and power', *Adult Education Quarterly*, vol. 39, no. 1.

Index

ability grouping, 244–56. *see also*
    streaming
Acker, J., 31, 42
adult education, 22, 261–73
    accreditation, 268–9, 273
    church influence, 82–3
    and equality, 264–9
    gender inequalities, 269–70
    for minorities, 271
    participation patterns, 261–4
    and social class, 266–7
Ahmad, A., 129
AIDS education programme, 79, 83
Akenson, D., 73
Althusser, L., 36, 75
Alvey, D., 77
AnCO, 221
Anti-Discrimination (Pay) Act, 1974,
    170
Aontas, 83, 261, 262, 265, 266
Apple, M., 91, 108–9
Ár nDaltaí Uile: All Our Children, 61
Archer, Margaret, 39, 128, 212–13
Arensberg, C. and Kimball, T., 65
Arnot, M., 196, 202
Aronowitz, S. and Giroux, H., 109, 127,
    158, 160
Askew, S. and Ross, C., 198, 199
Association for Comprehensive and
    Community Schools, 13, 14, 15
Association of Secondary Teachers,
    Ireland (ASTI), 7, 81, 106, 108,
    122
    position of women in, 107

Baker, J., 34, 62
Ball, S., 248, 249, 252
banding, 86, 235, 245, 252. *see also*
    streaming
    reasons for, 246–7
    spread of, 246
Banks, O., 149, 150
Barrett, M., 66
Barry, U., 170
Bell, D.L., 59
Benson, C., 230
Berg, I., 210–11
Berge, L. and Varøy-Haga, M., 196
Bernstein, B., 151–3, 209
Bernstein, B. and Brandis, W., 151, 152
Bidwell, C.E., 55
birth rate, 17
Blackledge, D. and Hunt, B., 39
Blackwell, J., 168, 169, 171
Blum, J., 235
boards of management, 7, 98
    in Green Paper, 15–16
    national schools, 77
    second-level schools, 13, 14, 81–2
    VECs, 12
Boards of Management of Catholic
    Secondary Schools Manual, 81
Bolger, N. and Kellaghan, T., 179
Bookman, A., 273
Bordo, S., 182
Bourdieu, P., 50, 55, 116, 157, 234, 269
    cultural capital, 155–6
    hidden curriculum, 160
    on teachers, 91

Bourdieu, P. and Boltanski, L., 36
Bourdieu, P. and Passeron, J.-C., 36, 40, 152–3, 155, 160
Bowles, S. and Gintis, H., 28, 36, 60, 149, 159–60, 213
Breen, R., 5, 12, 145, 156, 264
   senior cycle performance, 159
   social class, 139
Breen, R. and Hannan, D., 202
Breen, R. and Whelan, B., 4
Breen, R. et al., 27, 39, 54, 61–2, 119, 141, 220
Brennan, M., 197
Britain, 21, 30, 126, 137, 138, 143, 213, 217, 237
   adult education, 262
   classroom interaction, 198–9
   co-education, 200, 202
   cultural capital, 156–7
   curriculum development, 102–3
   interactionism, 40–41
   IQ tests, 231
   language and educability, 153–4
   social class, 150, 151, 154
   streaming, 247–9, 251–4
   teachers, 94
Broca, P., 230
Brook, N. and Oxenham, J., 213
Buckley, T., 199
Burgess, R., 94
Burke, A., 90, 106, 108
Burt, Cyril, 59, 231
Burton, L., 196
business studies, 173, 217

Callan, T. et al., 161
Canada, 21
capitation grants, 11
Carey, L. and Slowey, M., 261
Carey, M., 179
Carr, M., 254
catechetics, 76, 82
Cathcart, H., 272–3
Catholic Church
   and adult education, 272–3
   and co-education, 189
   differences within, 73–4, 79–80, 84–5, 124

influence of, 63–4, 65, 80–82, 115
   as mediator, 121, 123–5
   ownership and management, 7, 11, 13, 14–16
   and primary education, 76–8
   and second-level education, 80–82
   sociological influence of, 73–4
census categories, 138
Central Advisory Council for Education, 154
Central Statistics Office (CSO), 114, 139, 144, 168, 169, 210, 267
Chafetz, J., 41
child care, 263, 266, 270
Chubb, B., 115, 118, 126, 129
Church of Ireland, 77
Church of Ireland College of Education, Rathmines, 20
churches, 28, 115, 117. *see also* religious personnel
   consultative role of, 79–80
   as mediators, 121, 123–5
   ownership and management, 6, 11,13, 14–16, 74–87
   relationship with state, 74–8
   significance of church influence, 83–7
   as sociological force in education, 73–87
Cicourel, A. and Kitsuse, J., 40
City of Dublin VEC, 12
civil service, 115–16, 118, 129, 221
   women in, 169–70
Clancy, P., 139
   gender differentials, 167, 172, 182, 265
   higher education survey, 12, 32, 42, 54, 62, 94, 119, 143–4, 178, 263, 264–5
   Leaving Cert. results, 181, 217
   on principals, 104
   religious in schools, 75, 125
   selection at entry, 159
Clancy, P. and Benson, C., 62
Clancy, P. and Brannick, T., 42
Clancy, P. et al., 27, 29, 83
classes
   ethnography, 38
   internal dynamics, 40–41, 198–202
   size of, 17–18

classroom interaction, 198–202
co-education, 17, 173, 185, 189–202
    attainment, 196–8
    classroom interaction, 198–202
    intervention programmes, 201–2
    school organisation, 198–202
    subject take-up, 190–96
    technological studies, 217
colleges of education, 18, 19–20, 22, 57,
        64, 84, 123
    church influence, 79, 82–3
    patriarchal, 65–6
    statistics, 96–7
    study of entrants, 94, 144
    women on staff, 100–101
Collins, R., 39, 210, 211
Commission on Adult Education, 83,
        261–4, 266
community colleges, 6, 12
    church influence, 80, 81
    ownership and management, 11, 12–13
community education, 158
community schools, 6, 12, 17, 106, 247, 269
    adult education, 263
    banding, 245, 249
    church influence, 80–81, 84
    co-educational, 189, 191
    curriculum, 193, 194
    deeds of trust, 14, 92
    description of, 7, 14
    part-time courses, 22
    promotional posts, 97–9
    sexism, 201
    social class, 145
    teachers, 93
comprehensive schools, 6, 12, 106, 247, 269
    adult education, 263
    banding, 245
    church influence, 80–81, 84
    co-educational, 189
    curriculum, 193, 194
    description of, 13–14
    part-time courses, 22
    promotional posts, 97–9
    teachers, 93
Confederation of Irish Industry (CII), 28
Conference of Major Religious Superiors,
    145

consensualism, 49
    among academics, 53–5
    implications of, 55
    in official reports, 50–53
    social context of, 63–4
Constitution of Ireland, 1937, 78, 167–8
contraception, 85
Coolahan, J., 4, 12, 14, 19, 20, 63, 107,
        124, 137
    on ASTI, 106, 122
    church in education, 73, 74
    curriculum, 6
    study of education, 48, 92
Cooney, M., 105
Council for the Status of Women, 170–71
Council of Education, 56, 124
Council of Europe, 172
Craft, M., 31, 149–50
craniometrics, 229–30
credentialism, 143
critical pedagogy, 160
Crooks, T. and McKernan, J., 54
Crotty, R., 114, 129
Cullen, M., 150–51
Culliton Report, 209, 214–20
cultural capital, 153, 155–7
    role of education, 116–19
    social closure, 269–70
cultural deprivation theory, 53, 153
cultural discontinuity, 152
curriculum, 73, 79, 107, 200. *see also*
        hidden curriculum
    challenging religious values, 85–7
    change and development in, 28, 217–20
    church influence, 82, 83
    co-educational, 190–96
    'core curriculum', 239–40
    counter-resistance changes, 120
    deficiencies in, 173, 219, 223
    and gender, 172–8
    and increased participation, 4–5
    and intelligence, 228–41
    need for in-service education, 103
    patriarchal, 178, 182
    perpetuation of inequality, 157–9
    teachers and change, 102–3, 109
    technology in, 214–20
Curriculum and Examinations Board, 28

Curriculum Awareness Action Group, 4
Curriculum Development Units, 12

Dale, R., 74, 117, 128
Dale, R. and Griffeth, S., 151
Daly, M., 16, 200
Davis, K. and Moore, W., 31
deeds of trust, 14, 92
deficit theory, 150–51, 160
Delamont, S., 40, 101–2
Denmark, 21, 128
Denscombe, M., 40, 102
Denzin, N., 40
Devine, D., 252, 255–6
Dewey, J., 29
Diggins, P., 92, 105
disabilities, students with, 116, 271
discovery techniques, 104
Divinis Illius Magistri, 79, 189
domain assumptions, 65, 86, 95, 149
Domicile and Recognition of Foreign
    Divorces Act, 1986, 170
Douglas, J., 154–5, 248, 249
Dowling, Teresa, 144, 162
Dowling, Tom, 52, 121
Drew, E., 171
Drudy, P., 202
Drudy, S., x, 3, 30, 38, 40, 41, 48, 54, 103,
    137, 139
Drumcondra Verbal Reasoning Test, 58,
    60, 148–9
Dublin City University (DCU), 18–19
Dublin Institute of Technology Act, 1992, 19
Dublin Institute of Technology (DIT), 12,
    19, 144
Durkheim, Émile, 29, 38, 152

Economic and Social Research Institute
    (ESRI), 39, 140, 145, 197, 201
Economic and Social Review, 33
economy, the
    and education, 209–23
Eder, D., 254, 255
Eder, D. and Felmlee, D., 255
education. *see also* funding; participation
    change and development in, 217–20
    context of, 114–16
    as distributor of privilege, 116–19

dominant ideologies, 49–66
dynamics of control and resistance,
    113–30
and the economy, 209–23
and empowerment, 271–3
gender differentials, 167–86
human capital theory, 210–13
and intelligence, 228–41
overview of, 3–23
ownership and management, 6–16
paradigms and perspectives in, 48–66
retention rates, 114
role of, 26–9, 116–19
role of churches in, 73–87
and social class, 137–63, 141–7
and society, 26–44
sociology of, 29–41
Education, Department of, ix, 4, 5, 74, 114,
    141, 146, 167. *see also* Green Paper,
    1992
and adult education, 263, 273
and churches, 79
control of, 118
Futures project, 191
gender equality, 171
inspectorate, 100
IQ tests, 232
rationalisation of schools, 16–17
reports by, 56–7, 61
second-level education, 6, 7–13
statistics, 92, 93, 172, 173–7, 189, 190,
    193, 217, 240
teacher appointments, 77
teacher statistics, 91, 92
and teachers' unions, 106–7, 108
third-level education, 18–21
and VECs, 125
women in, 100, 169
Education Act, 1944 (Britain), 32
Education Act, 1988 (Britain), 220
education policy, 61
Educational Research Centre, 57, 179
Educational Testing Service, 179
educationalists, 64, 272
    analysis of, 48–66
    multiple intelligences theory, 241
emigration, 4, 17, 114
employment. *see* labour market

Employment Equality Act, 1977, 170
Employment Equality Agency, 171
English language, 197
enterprise culture, 52
Equality and Law Reform, Department of,
    171
equality of opportunity, 31–5, 43, 61–3,
    137, 146–7
  adult education, 264–9
  attitudes and values, 149–51
  and churches, 123–5
  cultural capital, 116–19, 153, 155–7,
    269–70
  explaining inequalities, 147–57
  language and educability, 151–4
  parental interest, 154–5
  poverty, 161–2
  reproduction of inequalities, 36–7
  research results, 141–7
  and teacher's social class, 95
essentialism, 49, 55–6, 233–5
  and academics, 57–60
  implications of, 62–3
  in official reports, 56–7
  persistence of, 65–6
ethnography, 38, 41, 156–7
  classroom interaction, 199–201
European Community (EC), 170, 191, 219
Eysenck, H., 230
Eysenck, H. and Kamin, L., 230

Fagerland, I. and Saha, L., 211
farmers, 144, 161
FÁS, 52, 115, 216, 267
  Skills Survey, 214–15
Faughnan, P., 158
fee-paying schools, 122, 124, 162, 185
feminist theory, 41–2
Floud, J., 148
Floud, J., Halsey, A. and Martin, F., 31, 32
Flude, M. and Ahier, J., 53
Fontes, P. and Kellaghan, T., 234
Fontes, P. et al., 59
Fox, R., 214
France, 40, 114, 128, 143, 213, 230
  cultural capital, 155–6
  linguistic capital, 152–3
free scheme, 7, 11, 92, 120, 122, 124, 143

Freire, P., 29, 272
friendships
  and streaming, 249, 251–2
Froebel College of Education, Blackrock, 20
Fullan, M., x
Fullan, M. and Hargreaves, A., ix, 18, 102,
    103
Fuller, W., 211
functionalism, 29–35, 37, 40
  explaining inequality, 147, 149, 152, 157
  hidden curriculum, 160
  human capital theory, 31, 210
  occupational scale, 138
funding, 74–5, 141
  in Green Paper, 16
  regressive, 143
  second-level education, 7, 11, 15, 16
  universities, 18–19
  vocational schools, 13
Futures project, 191

Gardner, Howard, 59, 229, 233, 236–9,
    240–41, 272
gender, 34, 108, 167–71. *see also*
    co-education
  and adult education, 264–5, 269–70
  and attainment levels, 179–82
  curricular options, 172–8
  negative stereotyping, 198–9
  and participation in education, 171–2
  and school ethos, 182–5
  and social class, 185
  and teachers, 97–101, 109
  of teachers, 92–3
  and technological studies, 217
  in trade unions, 107
gender equality, 41–2
geography, 173–7, 218
German school, 7
Germany, 21, 198, 199, 213, 216
Ghana, 211
Giddens, A., 39, 140
Gilmore, B., 107
Giroux, H., 29, 127, 129–30, 158
Glass, G. et al., 17
Godfrey, M., 211
Gould, S.J., 60, 65, 230–31
Gouldner, A.V., 65, 86, 95, 149

governing bodies, 19
Greaney, V. and Kellaghan, T., 31, 32, 33,
	142, 145, 167, 181, 265
	analysis of work, 54, 59, 62
	on education policies, 61
	on intelligence, 58, 148–9
Greaney, V., Burke, A. and McCann, J., 94
Green Paper, 1992, ix, 15–16, 209
	adult education, 263
	consensual, 52
	curriculum, 120, 219–20
	equality of opportunity, 34
	gender equality, 171
	management, 77, 78, 81–2, 98
	political/social studies, 219
	social control, 28
	teachers' responses, 107
	technology, 214, 216–17
	third-level education, 21
Grevholm, B. and Nilsson, M., 196
grinds, 155, 162
Group Certificate, 5, 115

Hall, S., 62
Hallak, J. an : Caillods, F., 213
Hallinan, M., 248, 255
Hallinan, M. and Sorensen, A., 254
Halsey, A., Floud, J. and Anderson, C., 30
Halsey, A., Heath, A. and Ridge, J., 41, 155
Hanafin, J., 185, 197–8
Hannan, D. and Boyle, M., 86, 125
	streaming, 245–7, 249–51, 254
Hannan, D. and Katsiaouni, L., 65
Hannan, D. and Shorthall, S., 5, 6, 155,
	162, 234, 240
Hannan, D. et al., 42, 54, 62, 125, 173, 175,
	177, 190, 191, 200, 201
Hargreaves, D., 248, 251
Hayes, Canon John, 272–3
health education, 120
Heath, A., 148
Henderson, Paul, 231
Herron, D., 104–5
Heywood, J., McGuinness, S. and Murphy,
	D., 57
hidden curriculum, 26, 28, 200
	challenging religious values, 85, 86–7
	and gender, 182–5

and inequality, 159–60
	and teachers, 102–3
hierarchy, 65–6
higher diploma in education (HDE), 22, 96
higher education. *see* third-level education
Higher Education Authority Act, 1971,
	20, 21
Higher Education Authority (HEA), 19,
	20–21, 22, 93, 178
history, 173–7, 218
Hochschild, A., 209
home economics, 173, 192, 193, 194
human capital theory, 31, 210–13, 214
Hungary, 237
Hyland, A., 78, 217

ideologies
	consensualism, 49, 50–55, 63–4
	essentialism, 49, 56–60, 62–3, 65–6
	influence of churches, 75
	meritocratic individualism, 49, 60–63,
		65–6
illiteracy, 263, 265, 266–7
in-service education, 103, 105–6, 107, 108
income distribution, 27
India, 211
Indonesia, 213
industrial development, 3, 30, 114, 129, 168
industrial schools, 41
inequalities. *see* equality of opportunity
Inglis, T., 73, 74, 75, 85, 261, 273
Inglis, T. and Bassett, M., 261, 262,
	269–70
inheritance, 157
inspectorate, 100
Institute of Adult Education, 83
intelligence, 55
	alternative understanding of, 235–6
	and educational curriculum, 228–41
	Gardner's work on, 236–9
	genetics, 230
	ideological assumptions, 233–5
	IQ theory, 63
	measurements of, 148–9
	problems with tests, 232–3
	sources of, 56–60
	streaming, 248
	testing and ideology, 229–32

intelligence *continued*
  testing for, 57, 58–60, 149
  types of, 237–8, 240
Intermediate Certificate, 5, 115, 120, 145,
    149, 197
  Council of Education report, 56
  gender differentials, 179–81
  streaming, 246
*Intermediate Certificate Examination
    Report*, 57, 61
International Association of Educational
    Progress, 179
International Monetary Fund (IMF), 212
Investment in Education, 31, 32, 33, 51, 61,
    137, 214
  second-level education, 141
  third-level education, 143, 144
IQ. *see* intelligence
Irish Business and Employers'
    Confederation (IBEC), 28
Irish Congress of Trade Unions (ICTU), 28
Irish Journal of Education, 59
Irish language, 120, 197
Irish National Teachers' Organisation
    (INTO), 100, 103, 104–5, 106, 122
  church control of appointments, 79
  position of women in, 107
  and women as principals, 108
Irish Nationality and Citizenship Act, 1986,
    170
Irish Trades Union Congress (ITUC), 122
Irish Universities Act, 1908, 19
Irish Vocational Education Association
    (IVEA), 11–13

Jackson, P., 55, 213
Jamison, D. and Lau, L., 211
Japan, 237
Jensen, A., 230
Jewish culture, 7, 159
Johnson, T., 90–91
Jones, C., 199
Joyce, L., 118
Junior Certificate, 7, 12, 57, 102–3, 107,
    108, 173, 246
  school-based assessment, 108

Kaiser, A., 198, 199
Kamin, L., 230

Karabel, J. and Halsey, A., 54, 212
Keddie, N., 153, 249
Kellaghan, T. and Macnamara, J., 231
Kellaghan, T. and Newman, E., 58
Kellaghan, T. et al., 93, 100
Keller, E., 196
Kelly, A., 190, 196
Kelly, S., 93–4, 103
Kenya, 211, 213
Kerckhoff, A., 250
Kleinig, J., 57
knowledge systems, 157–9
Konrad, G. and Szelenyi, I., 66
Korea, 211
Kuhn, T., 42

Labour, Department of, 4, 5, 63, 115, 143,
    266
Labour Force Surveys, 210, 220
labour market, 62–3
  and adult education, 267, 270
  importance of qualifications, 5–6, 28,
      115, 145, 146–7, 209–23
  in-career training, 216, 222
  occupational classifications, 139–40
  paid/unpaid labour, 209–10
  patterns of employment, 220–22, 224(t)
  women in, 168
Labov, W., 153, 231
Lacey, C., 248, 251–2
languages, 120, 173–7, 179–80, 193, 194,
    217
Lauglo, J. and Lillis, K., 212, 213
Lawler, J., 60, 232
Lawton, D., 152
Leaving Certificate, 7, 12, 32, 57, 149
  academic bias, 119, 120
  attainment levels, 197
  curriculum, 4–5, 173–7, 218, 219
  failure rates, 234
  gender differentials, 173–7, 179–81,
      192–4
  gender proportions, 191
  and labour market, 115
  participation rates, 4, 147
  six-year cycle, 162
  social class, 145
Lewis, J., 39

Liberia, 211
life skills programme, 79, 83
linguistic capital, 151–4
Lipset, S. and Bendix, R., 31
literacy, 210–11
Little, A., 211
local authorities, 126
Lockhead, M. et al., 211
Lortie, D., 95–6
love labour, 59, 209
Lunn, Barker, 248, 250, 253
Lynch, K., 34, 95, 106, 156, 157, 159, 217, 272
  curricular differentiation, 183, 190
  girls' schools, 40
  on Greaney and Kellaghan, 33, 54
  ideologies, 48, 49
  IQ testing, 232
  labour market, 31
  love labour, 59, 209
  neo-Marxist, 54–5
  role of churches, 73, 75, 82
  role of education, 3, 213
  schools' social climates, 183–5
  streaming, 86, 245–6, 247, 250, 251
  women and education, 42, 181
Lynch, K. and O'Neill, C., 149, 158
Lynch, K., Close, S. and Oldham, E., 179

McCarthy, E., 171, 212, 213
McCluskey, D., 62
McEwen, A. and Curry, C., 193, 196
McGeeney, P., 126
McGill, P., 141
McGowan, G., 200
Mac Gréil, M., 62, 146, 261, 262, 266
Mac Gréil, M. and Winston, N., 146
McKeown, K., 106
McKernan, J., 73
McMenamin, P., Fogarty, C. et al., 108
McNamara, G. and Williams, K., 5
MacNamara, J., 232
McRobbie, A., 157
Madaus, G. and Macnamara, J., 56–7, 61
Mahon, E., 42
Mahony, P., 190, 199
Malaysia, 211
Marland, M., 172

Marshall, T., 31
Martin, M. and Hickey, B., 4, 5, 191
Marx, Karl, 138–9
Marxism, 209. *see also* neo-Marxism
Mary Immaculate College of Education, Limerick, 20
Mater Dei Institute of Education, Dublin, 20
mathematics, 173–7, 179, 191–4, 195–6, 197, 218
  and ability grouping, 254–5
mechanical drawing, 201
mediators of education, 117–18
  churches as, 123–5
  conflict between, 127–8
  interests of, 113
  parent bodies as, 126–7
  and state managers, 121–7
  teachers' unions as, 121–3
  VECs as, 125–6
Meeder, M. and Dekker, T., 179
mental handicap, 241
Meredith, D., 16
meritocracy, 33, 37, 55, 142
  adult education, 273
  cultural capital, 156
  VRA tests, 149
meritocratic individualism, 49, 60
  and academics, 61–2
  implications of, 62–3
  in official reports, 61
  persistence of, 65–6
methodological empiricism, 54
Mexico, 211
Mezirow, J., 273
middle classes. *see* social class
Miliband, R., 36
Ministers and Secretaries Act, 1924, 118
minority cultures, 159, 271
mixed-ability grouping, 245
modernisation, 30
Morgan, V., 200
Morton, S., 229–30
mothers, attitude of, 150–51, 162
Muintir na Tíre, 272–3
Mulcahy, D.G., 53–4
Mullin, B. et al., 172
multidenominational schools, 75, 76–7
multinationals, 129

multiple-choice tests, 179
multiple intelligences (MI) theory, 236–9
Murphy, J. and Hallinger, P., 252
Murray, B., 42
Muslim culture, 159

National College of Art and Design, Dublin
    (NCAD), 120
National College of Industrial Relations, 83
National Council for Curriculum and
    Assessment (NCCA), 12, 28, 79,
    106, 109, 121, 181, 234
National Council for Educational Awards
    (NCEA), 19, 20
National Institutes for Higher Education
    (NIHEs), 18
National Parents' Council, 74, 126
national schools, 77–8
National University of Ireland (NUI),
    18–19, 20, 83
nationalism, 63
natural law, 65
neo-Marxism, 35–8, 40, 41
neo-Marxist perspective, 35–8, 40–41, 43,
    54, 66, 139, 140, 157
    cultural capital, 155–7
    language, 152–3
neo-Weberian perspective, 35, 38–40, 43,
    54, 140
Nettl, J.P., 49
'New Curriculum', 83
Ní Chárthaigh, D. and Harrison, R., 200
Nigeria, 237
Noah, J. and Eckstein, M., 213
Nolan, B. and Farrell, B., 161
Northern Ireland, 4, 106, 141, 196, 199
    IQ tests, 231
Norway, 196
Nuffield science, 102

Oakes, J., 248, 253, 255
O'Brien, D., 158
O'Brien, M., 155, 162
Ó Buachalla, S., 11, 73, 79–80
Ó Catháin, S., 56
occupational classifications, 139–40
Ó Conaill, N., 191, 196
O'Dowd, Liam, 50, 63–4

Offe, C., 75, 116, 119
O'Flaherty, L., 7, 11, 12, 14, 15
O'Kelly, A., 251–2
Oldham, E., 179
Ó Murchú, M., 261
O'Neill, C., 161, 162, 234
O'Neill, O., 62, 267
O'Rahilly, Alfred, 272
Organisation for Economic Co–operation
    and Development (OECD), 212, 262
    report, ix, 17–18, 28, 52, 98, 105–6,
    121, 124, 209, 214
Ó Síoráin, P., 102
Ó Súilleabháin, S., 29
O'Sullivan, D., 41, 58, 272
    adult education, 261–7
    educational policy, 48, 55
    teachers, 94, 95, 104
Our Lady of Mercy, Blackrock, 20
Oxenham, J., 211, 213
Ozga, J. and Lawn, M., 90, 91

Panama, 213
paradigm shift, 42
parents
    and ability grouping, 255
    parent bodies, 115, 117, 121, 126–7
    parental interest, 154–5
    role of, 104
Parkin, F., 268
Parsons, T., 30
participation, 3–6, 32, 34
    in adult education, 261–4
    gender patterns, 171–2
    increased rates of, 244
    numbers, 141
    and social class, 54, 140, 142, 146
*Partners in Education: Serving Community
    Needs*, 51, 52
pastoral care, 120
patriarchy, 107, 178, 182, 209–10
Peillon, M., 64, 73, 74, 86, 119
philosophy, 219, 223
physical education, 172–3
Piaget, J., 232
Plateau, N., 189, 190
Plowden Report, 154
positive action programme, 201

positivism, 64
Poulantzas, N., 37, 91, 139
poverty
    and inequality, 147, 149, 161–2
pre-employment courses (PECs), 120
primary education, 52, 106, 107, 121
    church influence, 124
    church ownership and management, 75,
        76–9
    class size, 17
    classroom organisation, 104
    evidence of inequality, 142
    participation in, 5
    role of principal, 104–5
    school size, 16
    sex-stereotyping, 172–3
    streaming, 235, 248, 249, 254–6
    teachers, 93, 97, 98, 103
    teachers' handbook, 51
    women as principals, 99–100
Primary Education Review Body, 20, 52,
        79, 106, 121
principals
    religious as, 97, 99, 105
    role of, 104–5
    women as, 108
private education, 74, 157
professionalism, concept of, 90–91
professions, entry to, 162
Programme for Economic Progress (PESP),
        106
Protestant schools, 7, 11, 14, 76–8
    management, 13
psychometrics, 230–31
public examinations, 5, 56, 115, 120, 145,
        149, 197, 246. *see also*
        Leaving Certificate
    girls v boys, 167, 179–81
    and VRA, 148–9
*Public Examinations Evaluation Project,
    The*, 57, 61
Public Examinations report, 56–7, 61
pupil-teacher ratio (PTR), 17–18
pupils. *see also* gender
    age of, 3–4
    'disadvantaged', 52–3, 116
    and family background, 148–57
    gender differentials, 157, 167–86

grading of, 86
individual potential of, 56–60
negative labelling of, 234–5
proportion in co-education, 189–90
school leaver surveys, 115
sense of alienation, 162
social class, 95, 120

qualification inflation, 147

radical pedagogies, 127
Raftery, A. and Hout, M., 33, 54, 59
Rassekh, S. and Vaideanu, G., 220
reading ability, 254
Regional Technical Colleges Act, 1992, 19
regional technical colleges (RTCs), 12, 19,
        22, 106, 144
Registration Council, 123
Reid, I., 148, 149, 247, 248, 252
Reid, M. et al., 253–4
religious education, 76, 78, 82, 85
religious personnel
    middle class, 123
    as principals, 97, 99, 105
    as teachers, 92, 97–8
resistance in education, 113, 129–30
    counter-resistance, 119, 123–4
Revenue Commissioners, 118
Review Body on Primary School
        Curriculum, 52, 78, 79, 106
Riordan, E., 107
Robinson, P., 161
Roche, F. and Tansey, P., 214, 216, 217
Rosenholtz, S. and Simpson, C., 253
Rosenthal, B. and Jacobson, L., 255
Rottman, D. et al., 32, 39, 54, 62, 140, 142
Royal College of Surgeons, 18
Ruane, W., 107
Rudd, J., 161
'Rules for National Schools', 77, 78
rural society, 63, 64, 65
Rutland Street Project, 58
Ryan, L., 41, 149

St Angela's College, Sligo, 20
St Catherine's College, Blackrock, 20
St Mary's College of Education, Marino, 20
St Patrick's College, Maynooth, 18, 83

St Patrick's College of Education,
    Drumcondra, 19–20
school-based assessment, 108
school inspectorate, 100
school leaving age, 4, 41, 120
schools
    adjusting to social class, 153–4
    collaborative cultures, 103
    'disadvantaged', 34
    dynamics within, 38, 40–41, 43
    ethos of, 82, 182–5
    organisation of, 159–60
    ownership and management, 6, 16
    perpetuation of inequality, 157–9
    size of, 16–18
Schultz, T., 214
science, 82, 85, 173–7, 179, 191–6, 217
second-level education
    ability grouping, 244–6
    counter-resistance, 120
    curriculum, 119, 173–7, 214–20
    drop-out level, 5–6
    experience of girls v boys, 173–7, 191–6
    free scheme, 7, 11, 92, 120, 122, 124, 143
    ownership and control, 8–10(t), 75,
        80–82
    participation in, 4
    proportion of co-education, 190
    proportion of girls, 167
    role of principal, 105
    school size, 16–18
    school types, 6, 16
    and social inequalities, 159–60
    study of performance, 156
    teachers, 97–100
    transfer to, 146
Secondary Education Committee, 11
secondary schools, 12, 106, 125
    attainment, 197
    church influence, 81–2, 124
    classroom interaction, 201
    denominational, 11
    description of, 6–7
    entry selection, 247
    free scheme, 7, 11
    number of pupils, 14
    promotional posts, 97–9
    selection at entry, 145, 159, 245, 247

    sexist, 201
    social class, 145
    staff of, 15, 92, 93
    streaming, 246–7
    subject take-up, 195–6
    third-level transfer rates, 144
    transfers to third level, 144–5
secondary tops, 23n
Secretariat of Secondary Schools, 7
selection at entry, 16, 145, 159, 245, 247
setting, 245
Sexton, J., Whelan, B. and Williams, J., 5
sexual harassment, 198–9
Shannon Comprehensive School, 12
Sharp, R. and Green, A., 249
Shaw, J., 200
Sheehan, J., 22
Sheppard, C. and Carroll, D., 220
Silver, H., 31, 32
Simon, B., 232
skills shortage, 52, 214–16
Skocpol, T., 115
slogans, 48
Slowey, M., 261, 269
Smith, S., 221, 224
Smyth, A., 170, 221
social class, 27, 35–8, 51, 123, 129, 148, 265
    and adult education, 262–3, 266–7, 269
    and attainment, 198
    attitude of Catholic Church, 123–4
    attitudes and values, 149–51
    concept of, 137–40
    control and resistance, 113
    cultural capital, 155–7
    'deficit model', 95
    'disadvantage', 52–3
    and education, 137–63
    and gender, 185
    inequality of opportunity, 143, 147–57,
        161–2
    influence of schools, 53–4
    and intelligence testing, 60, 231
    and language, 151–4
    language and educability, 152–4
    middle class interests, 116–19
    negative labelling, 234–5
    parent bodies, 126–7
    and parental interest, 154–5

and participation, 140
participation rates, 54, 140, 142
and school organisation, 159–60
and state managers, 118–21
and streaming, 248–9, 252, 255
structural isolation, 158–9
subject take-up, 193, 196–7
and teachers, 95, 107
of teachers, 93–5, 122
and teaching methods, 104
and VECs, 126
women and education, 182, 185
working-class underachievement, 53
social closure, 268–9
social mobility, 26–7, 31, 37, 61–2, 143,
        247, 273
social networks, 76
social relations, 27–8, 36
social science, 173, 219, 223
Social Welfare (No. 2) Act, 1985, 170
socialisation, 26, 53–4, 213
sociology of education, 48–9, 90–91
    Catholic sociology, 83
    feminist theory, 41–2, 43
    functionalism, 29–35, 37–8, 40, 43
    and intelligence, 59, 228–9
    neo-Marxism, 35–8, 40, 43
    neo-Weberian, 35, 38–40, 43
    symbolic interactionism, 40–41, 43
special schools, 41
Spender, D., 182
Spender, D. and Spender, E., 190
Sri Lanka, 211
Stacey, M., 209
Stanage, S., 272
Stanworth, M., 172, 198, 199
state, the, 39
    education and the economy, 209–23
    role in education, 115–18
state managers, 115–16
    and mediators, 121–7
    relations with social classes, 118–21
Steedman, J., 190
Stott, D., 232
streaming, 86, 151, 159, 235, 244–5
    composition of streams, 248–9
    effects of, 249–52
    implications of, 247–8

little mobility, 249, 250, 252, 256
    reasons for, 246–7
    spread of, 245–6
structuralism, 37
subsidiarity, principle of, 79
Swan, T.D., 58
Sweden, 21, 143, 196, 198
Sweeny, S., 28
Switzerland, 21, 42
Sydie, R., 41
symbolic interactionism, 40–41, 43

Taoiseach, Department of the, 169, 170, 171
Tawney, R., 171, 267
teachers, 15, 16, 90–109, 117. *see also*
        teachers' unions
    appointments of, 76, 77, 79, 81
    classroom interaction, 198–202
    description of, 91–5
    and educational change, 107–9
    gender of, 92–3
    and intelligence assessment, 59–60
    and management structure, 97–101
    numbers of, 91
    part-time, 91, 93, 96
    payment of salaries, 7, 11, 15
    roles of, 101–3
    social background of, 93–5
    and streaming, 252–6
    teaching as career, 95–101
    training of, 19–20, 84
    view of their roles, 103–6
Teacher's Handbook, 51, 56, 77–8
    sex-stereotyping, 172–3
Teachers' Union of Ireland (TUI), 106,
        108, 122, 125
teachers' unions, 52, 106–7, 109
    influence of, 18
    as mediators, 121–3
technical drawing, 173, 193–4, 217
technological colleges, 18, 19, 21–2, 144
    women on staff, 100–101
technological education, 52, 82
technological functionalism, 214
technology, 85, 119
    and gender, 167, 177–8, 186
    increased participation, 218–19
    post–Culliton, 214–20

Teeling, J., 52, 223
textbooks, 79, 122, 182, 200
Thailand, 211
third-level education, 4, 244
    adult education, 268
    church influence, 82–3, 84
    gender and achievement, 186
    gender and performance, 181–2
    gender and subject choice, 177–8
    gender distribution, 217(t)
    mature students, 266
    participation of women, 172
    participation rates, 21–2, 163
    post-Culliton orientation, 214–20
    social class, 142
    structures of, 18–21
    teachers, 93
    technical orientation, 119
    transfers to, 7, 12, 144–5, 147, 159
    women on staff, 100–101
Thomond College, Limerick, 20
Tizard, B. et al., 153–4
Tong, R., 42
tracking. *see* streaming
transition year, 7, 120
travelling people, 116, 159, 271
Trinity College, Dublin, 18–19, 20
Troyna, B., 248
Tumin, M., 62
Tussing, A., 32
Tyndale case, 122

Uí Chatháin, M. and Drudy, S., 200
Uí Mhaonaigh, M., 201
unemployment, 143, 145, 266–7
Unfair Dismissals Act, 1977, 170
unions. *see* teachers' unions
United States of America, 21, 30, 40, 59,
        137, 158
    ability grouping, 255
    adult education, 262
    co-education, 190
    deficit theory, 151, 153
    Educational Testing Service, 179
    educationalists in, 64, 65
    and gender, 182
    hidden curriculum, 159–60
    human capital theory, 210–11

intelligence testing, 229–30, 231, 234
    teachers, 95–6
    technology, 217
universities, 18–19, 21–2, 64, 123
    inequalities, 143–4
    patriarchal, 65–6
    study of entrants, 94, 162
    unequal transfer, 149
    women on staff, 100–101
University College, Cork (UCC), 18–19
University College, Dublin (UCD), 18–19
University College, Galway (UCG), 18–19
University of Dublin, 18–19
University of Limerick (UL), 18, 20

verbal reasoning ability (VRA), 58, 142,
        148–9
verbal reasoning tests (VRT), 58
vocational education, 223
Vocational Education Act, 1930, 11, 12, 92
vocational education committees (VECs),
        83, 117
    adult education, 263, 269
    church influence, 80
    as mediators, 121, 125–6
    third-level education, 19
vocational preparation and training (VPT),
        7, 12, 120
vocational schools, 6, 18, 106, 123–4, 247
    classroom interaction, 201
    co-educational, 189, 191
    curriculum, 193, 194
    non-denominational, 80
    number of pupils, 14
    ownership and management, 11–13
    part-time courses, 22
    promotional posts, 98, 99
    school size, 17
    social class, 145
    staff of, 15, 92, 93
    streaming, 246
    third-level transfer rates, 144
Vocational Training Opportunities Scheme
        (VTOS), 266
vocations, decline in, 75, 92

Walker, G. and Casey, T., 221, 222
Wallace, R., 41

Walters, J. and Gardner, H., 239, 241
Weber, Max, 29, 38–40, 138–9
welfare state, 114
Wernersson, I., 190, 198
Westergaard, J. and Resler, H., 40
Whelan, C. and Whelan, B., 27, 33, 41, 54,
    59, 61–2, 114, 142–3, 147, 265
Whyte, J., 28, 74, 196
Wickham, A., 54
Wickham, J., 221
Willis, P., 29, 156–7
Wilms, W., 213

Wilson, M., 172, 198, 200, 202
women. *see also* gender
    adult education, 22
    and adult education, 269–70
    economic and social position, 167–71
    underrepresented, 168–9
Woods, P., 40
working classes. *see* social class
World Bank, 212

Young, M., 33, 157–8
Youthreach, 266